HUMAN RESOURCE MANAGEMENT
Theory and Practice

HUMAN RESOURCE MANAGEMENT
Theory and Practice

John Bratton
and
Jeffrey Gold

MACMILLAN

First published 1994 by
THE MACMILLAN PRESS LTD
Houndmills, Basingstoke, Hampshire RG21 2XS
and London
Companies and representatives
throughout the world

ISBN 0–333–58876–2 hardcover
ISBN 0–333–58877–0 paperback

A catalogue record for this book is available
from the British Library.

Copy-edited and typeset by Povey–Edmondson
Okehampton and Rochdale, England

Printed and bound in Great Britain by
Mackays of Chatham PLC, Chatham, Kent

To Amy, Andrew and Jennie

'People developed and upgraded on a continuous basis will be your edge towards 2000. The competition can copy your technology, but they cannot copy the creativity, knowledge, judgement and skills of your committed workforce.'

The authors

Contents

List of Tables

List of Figures

List of Abbreviations

ACAS	Advisory, Conciliation and Arbitration Service
APEX	Association of Professional, Executive, Clerical and Computer Staff
AEU	Amalgamated Engineering Union
AEEU	Amalgamated Engineering and Electrical Union
AUEW	Amalgamated Union of Engineering Workers
ASTMS	Association of Scientific, Technical and Managerial Staffs
CBI	Confederation of British Industry
CNC	Computer numerically controlled (machine tools)
COHSE	Confederation of Health Service Employees
EEF	Engineering Employers' Federation
EETPU	Electrical, Electronic, Telecommunication and Plumbing Union
EOC	Equal Opportunities Commission
GMB	General, Municipal Boilermakers' Union
HRD	Human resource development
HRM	Human resource management
HRP	Human resource planning
JCC	Joint Consultative/Consultation Committee
JIT	Just-in-time
MSF	Manufacturing, Science and Finance Union
NUPE	National Union of Public Employees
TASS	Technical, Administrative and Supervisory Staffs
TGWU	Transport and General Workers' Union
TQC	Total quality control
TQM	Total quality management
TUC	Trades Union Congress
WIRS	Workplace Industrial Relations Survey (UK)

Preface

In the 1990s human resource management has become one of the most dynamic and challenging areas of European business. The turbulent business climate in Britain today, brought by changing markets and increased global competitiveness, changing technologies, changing employment legislation, and changing work force composition is challenging managers to utilize their human resources more effectively to gain competitive advantage. The changes in the nature of employment toward more knowledge-based, self-paced work in both the manufacturing and service sectors will demand greater skill and 'empowerment' of workers than was required in the past. Managers must understand the importance of creating work structures and human resource processes that enable people to work more effectively within organizations. In academia, human resource management has been the area of fastest growing teaching and research interest within the broad subject area of business studies. Since the early 1980s, new courses in human resource management (HRM), at undergraduate and graduate levels, have been created in higher education institutions in the United States, Britain and Canada. Research on HRM has focused on constructing new theoretical frameworks or models to study HRM. In addition, empirical-based data has been gathered, analyzed and published on the extensiveness of HRM practices in North American and British industry.

The field of HRM is in a state of rapid transition. HRM scholars are adopting new perspectives and theoretical frameworks and placing more emphasis on strategic considerations. The purpose of *Human Resource Management: Theory and Practice* is to provide our readers with a comprehensive knowledge and understanding of the latest relevant theories, practices, and functional activities of human resource management. For some time there has been a tendency of textbooks on personnel management to be much more prescriptive and practical than analytical. *Human Resource Management: Theory and Practice* is intended as a rigorous, but readable, coverage of contemporary theories and concepts in key human resources activities such as recruitment and selection, appraisal, training and development and rewards management. This book was written to meet the needs of undergraduate Business Studies students. We have based the structure and contents on our own teaching, consultancy and research experience in HRM, and on current research findings and literature in the field. This book has been written specifically for the British audience, but it draws examples and literature on HRM from North America. This helps readers to compare international developments in HRM and to develop a broader understanding of HRM beyond the UK issues and practices.

■ Pedagogical features

Human Resource Management: Theory and Practice includes a number of features that help the learning process:

- **Chapter Outline and Learning Objectives**. Each chapter opens with a topic outline and a set of learning objectives to guide the reader through the material that follows.
- **'HRM in Practice' Boxes**. These are strategically placed in the chapter to help illustrate current developments or practices in HRM.
- **Diagrams and Tables**. Some of the conceptual material is presented by graphic diagrams. The aim is to help the reader to visualize the key elements of the theory being discussed. Data are presented to facilitate interpretation of key trends in HRM.
- **Theory and Practice**. This book bridges the gap between those books that are primarily theoretical and the textbooks that discuss what the personnel manager does, or should be doing (the prescriptive approach). This book is both theoretical and prescriptive. It reviews and discusses relevant HRM concepts and includes up-to-date references to support the theory and research. It also has a practical orientation – the 'how to' activities of HRM. For example, it discusses how to recruit and select and how to design training programmes.
- **Chapter Summary and Discussion Questions**. All chapters end with a summary, a list of key concepts, a set of discussion questions to test readers' understanding of core concepts and to facilitate classroom or group discussion.
- **Further Reading**. All chapters end with references for further reading to provide elaboration of topics discussed in the text.
- **Chapter Case**. Each chapter includes a case to facilitate application of the theoretical material in the text and to help the reader appreciate the challenges of managing people at work.
- **Glossary**. A glossary is provided at the end of this book to help the reader review and define the key terms used in the text.
- **Bibliography**. A bibliography provides the student with a comprehensive list of sources/works cited in the text.
- **Index**. At the end of the book an index is included to help the reader search for relevant information and make this book a valuable resource for completing assignments or projects.

We are confident that these features will make *Human Resource Management: Theory and Practice* a valuable learning resource. We are also confident that this book will encourage the reader to question, to doubt, to investigate, to be sceptical and to seek multi-causality when analyzing the problems and challenges of HRM in Britain.

■ The plan of this book

This book is divided into four major parts. These parts are, of course, interconnected but, at the same time, they reflect different focuses of study.

Part 1 introduces the role of HRM and addresses some of the controversial theoretical issues surrounding the field of HRM. The external contexts that affect human resource management policies and actions inside the organization, changes in job design, and occupational health and safety are also examined in this section. This discussion provides the context of HRM and prepares the groundwork for Parts 2 to 4.

Parts 2 and 3 examine the key components that comprise the HRM cycle illustrated in Figure 1.7: selection, appraisal, human resource development, and rewards. Several writers have reported how each of these four areas is back in vogue. The use of the assessment centre and psychological tests measuring personality appears to be on the increase (see Chapter 6). Performance appraisal methods, both among non-manual and manual workers, is growing in organizations on both sides of the Atlantic (see Chapter 7). In the area of reward or compensation management, employers in the 1980s have been moving towards a more individualist approach to the wage–effort bargain: merit pay, for instance, is increasingly replacing the traditional practice of the rate for the job (see Chapter 8). Human resource development is seen by theorists as a vital component, if not the pivotal component, of the human resource management cycle (see Chapter 9).

In Part 4 we address some of the developments in communications and industrial relations. There is evidence that organizations are devoting more resources to employee communication programmes and introducing employee involvement arrangements (see Chapter 10). In the area of industrial relations, the traditional 'pluralist' or 'Donovan' model is undergoing change (see Chapter 11).

Acknowledgements

This textbook was inspired by, and to a large extent draws upon, teaching and research in which we were involved at Leeds Business School, at Leeds Metropolitan University and the University College of the Cariboo.

In writing the book a number of acknowledgements are due. We would like to thank all the students we have taught in human resource management and industrial relations modules who provided us with many insights and lessons about how, and what, to teach – ideas that we have attempted to incorporate into the text. We would like to thank Carolyn Bratton and Maureen Smith at the University College of the Cariboo for reading the manuscript in draft and applying their critical eye, thereby reducing the number of errors in the book and improving the style. We would also like to thank Catrina Crowe, at the University of the Cariboo, for typing some of the chapters. We are also grateful for the enthusiasm for the project shown by our publisher, Stephen Rutt. We would also like to thank the reviewers for their reasoned comments on the manuscript. A special thanks also to Amy, Andrew and Jennie Bratton, who have endured John Bratton's absence whilst working on this book.

The authors and publishers are grateful to John Enman, University College of the Cariboo Public Relations and Publications Department, for permission to reproduce the photograph which appears on the part-title pages as well as the cover of this book. They are also grateful to the following for permission to reproduce copyright material:

ACAS, for Table 10.4, from J. Bratton and L. Sinclair, *New Patterns of Management* (1987).

Dartmouth Press, for Tables 1.1, 2.1, 2.3, 4.1, 10.1–10.3, 11.2 and 11.4, from *Workplace Industrial Relations in Transition* (1992).

Department of Employment Gazette, for Table 11.1 data.

Employment Department, for Tables 1.2, 1.4, 2.7, 4.2, 5.1, 5.4, 5.5, 5.8, 7.3 from *Workforce Industrial Relations in Transition* (1992).

IPM, for Table 7.1, from P. Long, *Performance Appraisal Revisited* (1986).

John Wiley, for Figure 5.5, from R. Loveridge, 'Labour market segmentation and the firm?' in J. Edwards *et al.*, *Manpower Planning: Strategy and Techniques in an Organisational Context* (1983).

MCB University Press, for 'Federal Express employers appraise their managers' (1992) and 'Rover learning business' (1993), from *Executive Development*, in HRM in Practice, sections 7.2 and 9.1, and for Bramley's effectiveness model in Figure 9.3, from P. Bramley, 'Effective training', *Journal of European Industrial Training* (1989).

Nationwide Building Society, for the extract in HRM in Practice, section 7.1.

Personnel Management, for the Guest model in Figure 1.5 (1989) and the Atkinson model in Figure 5.3 (1989).

Personnel Management Plus, for the cartoon in Figure 7.7, and for the extracts in HRM in Practice, sections 1.1, 3.1, 3.2, 4.2, 6.3, 8.3, 8.4, 10.3, 11.1, 11.3.

Personnel Today, for Figure 11.1, the extracts in HRM in Practice, sections 2.2, 4.1, 4.3, 5.1, 5.2, 5.3, 6.1, 6.2, 8.1, 9.2, 10.1 and 10.2, and the case study in Chapter 10, adapted from 'Working as a team member' (1991).

Philip Allan, for Figure 3.5, from A. Warde, 'The future of work', *Social Studies Review*, Vol. 5, No. 1, pp. 11–15.

The Economist, for 'What a way to make a living', in HRM in Practice, section 2.1.

TUC, for Table 11.1 and 11.3 data, from *TUC Congress Reports* and TUC Bulletins.

Every effort has been made to trace all the copyright-holders, but if any have been inadvertently overlooked the publishers will be pleased to make the necessary arrangements at the first opportunity.

PART 1

THE CONTEXT OF HUMAN RESOURCE MANAGEMENT

CHAPTER 1

Human Resource Management in Transition

Successful corporate leaders recognize that their competitive edge in today's market place is their people. They also acknowledge that few organizations know how to manage human resources effectively, primarily because traditional management models are inappropriate in our dynamic work environment.[1]

Industry does not need specialists: production managers and workers can do it themselves.[2]

If anybody had to be the last person here, I would have bet on the Personnel Manager.[3]

■ Chapter outline

Introduction
The field of human resource management
The history of human resource management
Human resource management: a new orthodoxy?
Summary

Chapter objectives

After studying this chapter, you should be able to:

1. Explain the role of human resource management in organizations and the concepts underpinning the term 'strategic human resource management'.
2. Describe the history of human resource management.
3. Summarize the major activities associated with human resource management.
4. Explain the theoretical debate surrounding the HRM model.

■ Introduction

This book is concerned with the management of people at work. The quotations opening the chapter provide insights of how the field of personnel or human resource management is viewed by business executives, practitioners and academics in the 1990s. They also suggest that the ways in which organizations choose to manage their employees is in a state of transition. In the eighties, personnel management was replaced by the term 'human resource management'. To managers and to some academics, HRM appears to offer an attractive alternative to the orthodox personnel management model with its focus on employment administration, industrial relations, legal expertise and welfare (Watson, 1977; Legge, 1989; Guest, 1990). In contrast, it is argued that the new HRM model is a more proactive approach to the management of people in which the human resource specialist is an 'architect' and an intellectual partner on the management team (Tyson and Fell, 1986).

While there is some *prima facie* evidence that the more qualified and entrepreneurial human resource specialist has been elevated to the higher echelon of management, the movement has not all been in one direction. The drive to improve performance and to pursue 'excellence' has, in many companies, produced leaner 'flatter' structures. Such experimentation in organizational design has placed greater emphasis on the role of the line manager, with non-specialists devoting more of their time to personnel and related activities (Millward *et al.*, 1992). The enthusiasm for a new approach to managing people is not a British phenomenon. The paradigm shift to the HRM model from the orthodox personnel management model, and the ensuing debates among academic observers, have taken place on both sides of the Atlantic. Support for a new approach to managing human resources is, in part, a product of the political and economic climate of the 1980s: Conservative governments headed by Margaret Thatcher in Britain and Ronald Reagan in the USA. Indeed, the 1980s are seen by many observers as a watershed in human resource management. The result, amongst other things, has been to change the core values accepted by UK and US managements in their dealings with employees and their unions.

Human resource management has been good for many academics. In the UK, Business Schools renamed their departments and courses and established new university chairs in human resource management. A spate of articles has also advocated or contested the concept, philosophy and significance of human resource management. For these people, it represents a distinctive approach to the management of the employment relationship. However, as with other changes, the HRM style has its detractors. For some HRM is a manipulative form of management control and represents a renaissance of a unitary (non-union) style of management. In recent times the HRM model, amongst both its advocates and its detractors, has come 'to represent one of the most controversial signifiers in managerial debate' (Storey, 1989, p. 4). This chapter explains the role of HRM in a modern organization and its key concepts. It goes on to describe the history of HRM and reviews some of the literature on HRM regarding its analytical framework. To help students understand this field of management, we develop a model of human resource management.

■ The field of human resource management

Although the notion of HRM has been subject to considerable debate, there is no accepted definition of human resource management. As Storey (1989) notes, the term HRM is shrouded in managerial hype and its underlying philosophy and character are not easily defined. But we obviously need a definition of the subject matter if we are to analyse and understand HRM policies and practices. We will define the subject as:

> That part of the management process that specializes in the management of people in work organizations. HRM emphasizes that employees are the primary resource for gaining sustainable competitive advantage, that human resources activities need to be integrated with the corporate strategy, and that human resource specialists help organizational controllers to meet both efficiency and equity objectives.

Naturally, our broad definition of human resource management would be incomplete without further explaining what we mean by such terms as 'human resources' and 'management'. First and foremost, people in work organizations endowed with a range of abilities, talents and attitudes influence productivity, quality and profitability. People set overall strategies and goals, design work systems, produce goods and services, monitor quality, allocate financial resources, and market the products and services. Individuals, therefore, become 'human resources' by virtue of the roles they assume in the work organization. Employment roles are defined and described in a manner designed to maximize particular employees' contributions to achieving organizational objectives.

In theory, the management of people is not different from the management of other resources of organizations. In practice, what makes it different is the nature of the resource, people. One set of perspectives views the human being as potentially a creative and complex resource whose behaviour is influenced by many diverse factors originating from either the individual or the surrounding environment. Organizational behaviour theorists, for example, suggest that the behaviour and performance of the 'human resource' is a function of at least four variables: ability, motivation, role perception and situational contingencies (McShane, 1992). Another set of perspectives emphasizes that management faces two interrelated problems with regard to employees: the dual problems of 'control' and 'commitment' (Watson, 1986). The human resource differs from other resources the employer uses, partly because individuals are endowed with varying levels of ability (including aptitudes, skills and knowledge), with personality traits, gender, role perception and differences in experience, and partly as a result of differences in motivation and commitment. In other words, employees differ from other resources because of their ability to evaluate and to question management's actions, and their commitment and cooperation always has to be won. In addition, employees have the capacity to form groups and trade unions to defend or further their economic interest.

The term 'management' may be applied to either a social group or a process. The term 'management', when applied to a process, conjures up in the mind a variety of images of managerial work. Management may be seen as a science or as an art. The image of management as a science is based on the view that experts have accumulated a distinct body of knowledge about management which, if studied and applied, can enhance organizational effectiveness. This view assumes that people can be trained to be effective managers. Classical management theorists set out to develop a 'science of management' in which management is defined in terms of planning, organizing, commanding, coordinating and controlling'. In this classical conception, management is regarded as primarily concerned with internal affairs. Another set of perspectives on the role of management emphasizes that an organization is a purposive miniature society and as such, power and politics are pervasive in all work organizations. By power we mean the capacity of an individual to influence others who are in a state of dependence. Organizational *politics* refers to those activities that are not required as part of a manager's formal role, but that influence, or attempt to influence, the distribution of resources for the purpose of promoting personal objectives. Robbins asserts that 'those who fail to acknowledge political behaviour ignore the reality that organizations are political systems' (1989, p. 354). There is no doubt that much managerial energy and activity is linked to the political arena in which individuals both compete and cooperate in cabals and alliances (Mintzberg, 1983).

An alternative image of managerial activity is to view management as art. This implies that managerial ability and success depends upon traits such as intelligence, charisma, decisiveness, enthusiasm, integrity, dominance and self-confidence. The practical implications of this are quite different from the 'management as science' approach. If management is equated with specific traits associated with successful styles of leadership, it would provide a basis for selecting the 'right' individual for managerial positions in the organization. Managerial skills can be developed but cannot be acquired by attending business schools! In other words, if management is an art, managers are born. The science-versus-art discourse is not an arid academic debate, given public and private expenditure on management education and training.

The theme of control in organizations provides yet another alternative perspective on the role of management. From this perspective, managerial control is the central focus of management activity. According to this perspective managers seek to control the labour process by deskilling workers using scientific management techniques and new technology. This approach to management has come to be associated with the seminal work of Harry Braverman (1974) and the labour process school to which his work has given rise. This perspective, which builds upon Marx's analysis of industrial capitalism, views work organizations as hierarchical in structure, where human beings are exploited and where managerial practices and technology are designed to control people: 'organizations are structures of inequality and control', asserts Litter and Salaman (1984). Not surprisingly this approach has attracted much criticism (for example, see Kelly,

1985). Perhaps the most sensible way to approach the debate of what management is, is by recognizing that management is indeed both an art and a science and that, at the same time, it is involved in both political behaviour and control. Drawing on the work of Watson (1986), these four different perspectives on management are summarized in Figure 1.1.

Taken together, these four distinct images suggest that those who attempt to define and describe the management process should find ambiguities (and conflicts) of meaning. In essence, management is that group of individuals responsible for running the organization in order to achieve specified objectives. Collectively, managers are differentiated horizontally by their function activities and vertically by the level in which they are located in their organizational hierarchy.

In recent years, the term 'human resources' has been adopted as an alternative to 'personnel' management. We would suggest there are at least three reasons for this. First, the vocabulary of management, like language as a whole, is not immune to fashion. With a growing awareness amongst practitioners and scholars of using gender-neutral language, human resource has been adopted by some to avoid gender-bias phrases such as 'manpower administration' and 'manpower planning'. Second, as the term becomes more fashionable it is increasingly being adopted by practitioners to describe that component of the management process concerned with the employment relationship. For example, many companies advertise for human resource management officers and managers when until recently these positions would have been titled 'personnel'. Many educational institutions and academics have changed the curriculum

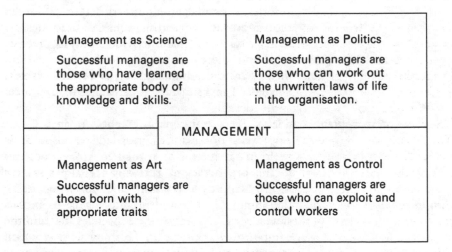

Figure 1.1   Management as science, art, politics and control

Source: Adapted from Watson, 1986.

and book titles to reflect the trend towards redefining this management activity. The Institute of Personnel Management (IPM), in the 1980s, debated at conference changing the title of the house journal from 'Personnel Management' to 'Human Resource Management'. The IPM has also sponsored a new university chair, notably in 'human resource', not in 'personnel' management. Third, the term may be used because, for both practitioners and academics, it has come to denote a fundamentally different approach to the management of people in work organizations. Personnel management is to be directed mainly at the organization's employees, recruiting, training and rewarding them, and is portrayed as a 'caring' activity. It is concerned with satisfying employees' work-related needs and dealing with their problems (Torrington and Hall, 1987). In contrast, HRM is portrayed as a central business concern which is more proactive and integrated into corporate management. There is also less emphasis on formal and collective modes of management–employee relations, and a tendency to shift to a more informal individualistic orientation (Storey, 1989, 1992). We have chosen to adopt 'human resource management' principally for the first two reasons, although we also recognize that, at least in theory, there are conceptual differences between the two terms and the meaning of HRM is contested by some academics.

■ Human resource management activities

In the 1990s, HRM in Britain covers the following five functional areas:

Staffing:	the obtaining of people with appropriate skills, abilities, knowledge and experience to fill jobs in the organization. Pertinent HRM activities are human resource planning, job analysis, recruitment and selection.
Rewards:	the design and administration of reward systems. The HRM tasks include job evaluation, appraisal, and benefits.
Employee development:	analysing training requirements to ensure that employees possess the knowledge and skills to perform satisfactorily in their jobs or to advance in the organization. Performance appraisal can identify employee key skills and 'competencies'.
Employee maintenance:	the administration and monitoring of workplace safety, health and welfare policies to retain a competent workforce and comply with statutory standards and regulations.
Employee/industrial relations:	the negotiations between management and union over decisions affecting employment. Under this heading may be a range of employee involvement/ participation schemes.

The activities HRM managers undertake vary from one workplace to another and might be affected by such factors as the size and structure of the organization (for example, single or multi-establishment organization), the presence or not of trade unions, and senior management's philosophy and strategy. Larger workplaces are more likely to employ at least one HRM or personnel specialist. Large organizations might divide HRM activities among several managers: one specialist for HR development, one for recruitment and selection and another for negotiating collective agreements and reward management. There is growing evidence of non-HRM specialists taking on responsibility for key HRM functions. In 1990, 82 per cent of non-HRM managers reported having responsibility for training and employee development (Millward *et al.*, 1992, p. 32). Table 1.1 depicts the ranking of activities, based on amounts of time spent on particular matters, undertaken by designated HRM managers and non-specialist managers. The most substantial preoccupation of designated HRM managers was recruitment, while for the non-specialist training was a significant preoccupation.

Human resource management activities are highly interrelated. Suppose, for example, senior management decides to redesign an assembly line by combining tasks and giving production workers additional responsibilities. As Chapter 3 will show, such changes in job design will impact on selection, rewards and training activities. A company that changes its manufacturing strategy by introducing 'cellular' or 'self-managed' teams will have different recruitment and selection priorities than a company that uses traditional assembly-line production employing unskilled operators. Significant changes in job design will

TABLE 1.1   Ranking of HRM activities of general managers and HRM specialists, 1990 (percentages)

	All managers	Designated HRM managers	Other managers spending 25% or more of their time on HRM matters
Staffing/HR planning	41	20	46
Recruitment	39	55	41
Training	38	24	45
Negotiating contract	27	44	20
Job evaluation	12	8	14
Reward management	10	7	6
Industrial relations procedures	8	18	8
Discipline cases	4	9	3

Source: Adapted from Millward *et al.*, 1992. Used with permission.

also require some form of systematic training. In addition, if the company chooses to combine tasks and instill greater employee autonomy, an alternative reward system may have to be designed to encourage employee cooperation and commitment. These sets of human resource activities are designed to match individuals to organizational tasks, to motivate the workforce, and to deal with conflicts and tensions at work. Human resource activities, therefore, aim to achieve two sets of objectives: improve employee performance and enhance organizational effectiveness.

To appreciate the full significance of these HRM activities it is important to recognize that HRM functions within the organization at two levels (Watson, 1986). At the first level, HRM activities are concerned with recruiting, motivating and developing competent employees. Hence, selection procedures are designed to supply the organization with employees with knowledge, abilities, and skills pertinent to their role within the organization. HRM activities then motivate the workforce by providing employees with satisfactory pay, benefits and working conditions. HRM professionals also develop individuals to ensure that they possess the knowledge and skills necessary to be effective employees.

Most academic observers of work organizations recognize that conflict is inevitable. Stephen Robbins (1989) distinguishes between functional and dys-functional conflict. The former supports the goals of the work group and improves its performance. Richard Hyman (1989) identifies two types of workplace conflict: organized and unorganized. When a group of employees engage in planned action (for example, a strike) to change the source of discontent, it is referred to as organized conflict. When employees respond to discontent or a repressive situation by individual absenteeism or individual acts of sabotage, it is referred to as an unorganized conflict. It is estimated that managers spend more than 20 per cent of every working day in some form of conflict-management activity. This brings us to the second level: HRM has responsibility for conflict management. HRM specialists are involved in a range of interventionist activities designed to alter the level and form of conflict which inevitably arise in work organizations. Ensuring that conflict does not hinder organizational performance is a central HRM role.

The role of the HRM specialist contains several types of ambiguity or paradox similar to orthodox personnel management (Watson, 1977, 1986; Legge, 1989). There is ambiguity with regard to whether the main role of the human resource specialist is a 'caring' or a 'controlling' one (Watson, 1986). A second ambiguity relates to the various HRM activities which are designed to bring order and stability to organizational life but which can also develop into sources of disorder or instability. Watson refers to this as the 'paradox of consequences' (1986, p. 183). The notion of the paradox of consequences refers to the fact that people's actions often have unintended consequences. Thus, for example, a new reward payment by results system may increase individual performance around the wage–effect bargain. But, as one of the authors found in his research, it will also create conflict as well as hindering flexibility and cooperation, which can be an obstacle to introducing flexible self-managed teams (Bratton, 1992). The 'paradox of consequences' suggests that there is no such thing as the *right* human resource procedure, system or technique and that, whatever systems are adopted, they will have to be regularly modified or replaced as their internal contradictions appear.

A third area of ambiguity exists over the nature of the human resource practitioner's authority. There is often ambiguity as to whether recommendations from HR departments are in fact recommendations or are instructions disguised as professional advice (Watson, 1986). A fourth area of ambiguity is that related to the nature and focus of human resource responsibility. In essence, HRM practitioners are considered 'staff' rather than 'line' employees since they provide specialized, legal and professional advice to operations or production 'line' managers. The human resource specialist is meant to give an HR perspective to senior and line managers, whilst managing people is not the exclusive concern of the specialist. Human resource management inheres in any managerial role. If, on the one hand, the HR manager over-emphasises the specialist function and her/his expertise, the other managers may abdicate their HRM responsibilities and, in turn, lose touch with their subordinates and become less effective leaders. If, on the other hand, they underplay or marginalize their own specialized service, they may be ignored by the rest of the management team or see their responsibilities taken over completely by other managers. The conflict, tensions and ambiguity of much HRM activity can put considerable demands on the HR profession and can be a source of both satisfaction and dissatisfaction. They certainly present constant challenges.

So far we have focused on the conceptual meaning of HRM and on what contribution it makes to the functioning of the modern organization. To make sense, however, of the HRM discourse and determine whether the advent of the HRM style actually heralds a new theoretical model or merely a repackaging of old ideas, it is important to examine the history of personnel management.

■ The history of human resource management

The foundation of modern HRM emerged from several interrelated sources. These include conflict management associated with the tensions and contradictions which are inherent in the employment relationship; the increased specialization of labour related to the growth in the scale of work organizations; the scientific approach to management to the human relation prospective to managing people; the 'empire building' activities of the specialists; and the employment-related law of the last three decades.

■ The genesis of personnel management

The history of human resource management has reflected prevailing beliefs and attitudes held in society about employees, the response of employers to public policy (for example, health and safety and employment standards legislation) and reactions to trade union growth. In the early stages of the industrial revolution in Britain, the extraordinary codes of discipline and fines imposed by factory owners was, in part, a response to the serious problem of imposing standards of discipline and regularity on an untrained workforce (Mathias, 1969). In the 1840s common humanity and political pressure began to combine with enlightened self interest amongst a few of the larger employers to make them aware of managing their workforce in terms of anything other than coercion, sanctions, or monetary reward.

In Britain and North America an increasing number of employers were accepting responsibility for the general welfare of their workers in the 1890s. In Britain, a number of philanthropic employers began to develop a paternalistic care and concern for their employees. They tended to be strongly nonconformist in belief. From the 1890s Quaker employers, for example, Cadbury and Rowntree, began to emphasize welfare by appointing 'industrial welfare' workers and building model factory villages. It was estimated that by 1914 there were probably between 60 and 70 welfare workers in Britain (Farnham, 1990, p. 20). Paternalistic employer policies were more evident in North America and Germany. In the USA, Henry Ford's autoplant, for example, established a 'Sociological Department' to administer personnel policies which were a concomitant of the '$5 a day' remuneration package. In 1900, large German companies like Krupp and Seimens were highly paternalistic (Littler, 1982). Over time, industrial welfare workers became precursors of the modern personnel/ human resource management specialist.

World War 1 (1914–18) gave an added impetus to industrial welfare activities. To deal with this haemorrhage of skilled labour from industry, many women were induced to enter industry for the first time. One outcome of this shift in employment was greater concern for workers' welfare in industrial work. By 1918 about 1000 women supervisors had been appointed to observe and regulate the conditions of work and, based upon experiments during World War 1, the relationship between welfare and efficiency was established (Pollard, 1969). In a 'tight' labour market and when employee cooperation is at a premium, the main role of the industrial welfare worker can be characterized as a 'caring' one. The expansion of capacity during the war was achieved largely by longer hours of labour and more intensive work, better equipment, better management and better workshop organization (Pollard, 1969). Changes in workshop design were often associated with the spread of premium bonus systems (PBS) and were the first stirring of systematic management. The development of complex new payment systems meant that large organizations had to create a centralized wages department which further boosted the role of personnel management (Littler, 1982). World War I also saw the emergence of the industrial relations function, in its modern sense, in Britain. In 1919 two organizations, the Welfare Workers Association and the North Western Area Industrial Association, amalgamated to form a new body, the Welfare Workers Institute (WWI), with a membership of 700 (Farnham, 1990).

The inter-war period is traditionally characterised as years of economic depression, with high levels of unemployment and severe hardship to large sections of the community. This traditional view has its origins in the highly visible 'hunger marches' and in some of the literature of the period itself: Greenwood's novel, *Love on the Dole* (1933), Orwell's *The Road to Wigan Pier* (1937), and Lewis Jones' two books, *Cwmardy* (1937) and *We Live* (1939). In the early 1970s a new thesis recognized there were periods of cyclical depression *and* recovery in the inter-war period. In the 1920s and 1930s, three developments began to influence the internal practices of organizations and the way employers view their human resources: rationalization, Taylorism, and the human relations movement. In the inter-war years, rationalization in Britain had a limited meaning: it referred to large-scale horizontal mergers of companies, plus the application of scientific methods of management and control. The shift towards corporate capitalism provides a rationale for a separate and specialist personnel department to take responsibility for effective management of people. Both scientific management and a derivative, the Bedaux system (see Littler, 1982), increased the importance of the 'controlling' personnel function. Another important development was the human relations movement. The Hawthorne experiments, pioneered by the American Elton Mayo and other researchers, were the driving force behind the movement. Advocates of this perspective on people in organizations were highly critical of Taylorists' 'economic rationality', and they advised managers to integrate employees into the organization. These developments help explain the rise in membership of the Welfare Workers Institute (renamed the Institute of Industrial Welfare Workers in 1924) from 420 in 1927, to 759 members in 1939 (Farnham, 1990).

World War II (1939–45), like World War I, immediately precipitated an increased demand for materials and labour. Britain mobilized between 1939 and 1943 no fewer than 8.5 million insured individuals (18 per cent of the total population) for the armed forces, auxiliary forces, and the munitions industries. The war fostered an increased demand for human resource specialists as the human-relations approach was embraced by many organizations anxious to maximize labour productivity and foster industrial peace. Farnham (1990) explains that personnel officers, as they were increasingly called, were seconded to munitions factories to establish personnel departments and to educate institutions to provide training programmes. In 1943 there were nearly 5500 personnel officers in factories employing over 250 employees, or three times as many as in 1939. The pattern of personnel management activities and industrial relations bequeathed by the extraordinary arrangements of war-time mobilization therefore contained the beginnings of the personnel management orthodoxy. Moreover, unlike welfare activity at the end of World War I, personnel management continued to grow in importance in the post-war period.

■ Personnel management: an established orthodoxy

After the war the personnel profession emerged stronger than ever and its members, and academics who study the field, began to establish a new orthodoxy. In 1946 the Institute of Labour Management changed its name to the Institute of Personnel Management (IPM). In addition, personnel management and industrial relations became mandatory courses for most business students (Pitfield, 1984). The development of the personnel management function after World War II must be seen against the backcloth of public policy and the pressure for workplace collective bargaining.

The post-war Labour government was committed to greater intervention in the economy; 'to combine a free democracy with a planned economy' (Coates, 1975, p. 46). The Labour government's commitment to full employment led to a growth of collective bargaining, and government agencies began to take a more active interest in the functioning of the labour market. The change of government after 1951 did not change the general pattern emerging in the British economy. The Conservative cabinet was anxious to prevent widespread industrial conflict and to encourage industrial peace through conciliation, mediation and arbitration (Crouch, 1982). Since 1960, public policy on issues affecting personnel management has not followed a steady trend. There have been vast fluctuations as one government has succeeded another, or as a government has revised its approach to regulating the employment relationship halfway through its term of office. There is no doubt, however, that government intervention encouraged the rise of a substantial corps of personnel management and industrial relations specialists.

In the 1960s and 1970s laws were passed that affected personnel management activities: the Contract of Employment Act (1963), the Redundancy Payments Act (1965) and the Industry Training Act (1964). In the 1970s, the Equal Pay Act (1970), the Sex Discrimination Act (1975), the Employment Protection Act (1975) and Employment (Consolidation) Act (1978) were the main pieces of legislation relating to the promotion of sexual equality and standards in employment. Further, in the area of compensation management, successive Conservative and Labour governments blew 'hot and cold' toward voluntary or statutory income policy. Similar developments can also be observed in North America.

In the sixties British industrial relations was the focus of intense political controversy over the allegedly intolerable level of strikes. These developments were investigated by the Donovan Commission (1965–8). A central argument of the Donovan Commission was the conflict between the formal system of industry-level bargaining and the informal system of workplace or organizational bargaining: 'Britain has two systems of industrial relations', reported the Commission (1968, p. 12). The Commission also argued that the growth in the size of organizations had brought specialization in management: 'From a tiny band of women factory welfare officers in 1914, personnel managers have multiplied to well over ten thousand today, most of them men; and the scope of the job has greatly increased' (1968, p. 25). The Commission's recommendation that management should develop joint procedures for the speedy and equitable settlement of grievances is associated with a rise in professionalism among personnel managers.

It is outside the scope of this chapter to analyse why the profession became dominated by men. But in explaining the development and importance of personnel management, Clegg makes a revealing comment on the relationship between the rise of workplace bargaining and the personnel management function: 'productivity bargaining . . . was widely welcomed by personnel managers because it extended their function into the fabric of the business – the improvement of profitability (Clegg, 1979, p. 100).

Changes in public policy mark an important phase in the development of British personnel management; a shift towards a more legalistic control of employment relations. Further, the new legislation had an impact on the personnel manager's job. New collective and individual employment provisions greatly amplified the status and power of the personnel management function in organizations because the personnel specialist was expected to give expert advice and take on new executive responsibilities (Clegg, 1979). The growth of the personnel management function within British work organizations was reflected in the increased number of personnel specialists. The quantitative growth in the professional personnel function is provided by IPM membership data and workplace industrial-relations survey data. Farnham shows that between 1956 and 1989, IPM membership rose from 3979 to 35,548 (1990, p. 24). A decade after the Donovan Report, Brown (1981) and his colleagues found that 46 per cent of the manufacturing establishments sampled had personnel offices with some responsibility for 'dealing with trade unions'; the comparable 1966 figure was 38 per cent. The status and the importance an organization attaches to personnel management can be gauged by whether or not that function is represented on the board of dire-ctors. One survey (Millward and Stevens, 1986) found that slighty more personnel management specialists were represented on the board between 1980 and 1984.

To summarize, personnel management takes place within a context of change. Its evolution has been significantly influenced by the dual pressure of public policy and the rise of workplace trade unionism and collective bargaining. It was during the 1980s, however, that the term *human resource management* emerged in Britain. As we discuss in the next section, the change to human resource management from personnel management is not just a matter of semantics. Moreover, the change did not happen in a political and economic vacuum; it reflected an ascendency of a new political ideology and the changed conditions of national and global capitalism. Figure 1.2 charts the evolution from welfare management to human resource management.

Human resource management: a new orthodoxy?

As we discussed earlier in this chapter, the notion of an HRM model is controversial. The debate centres on two fundamental questions: first, what is

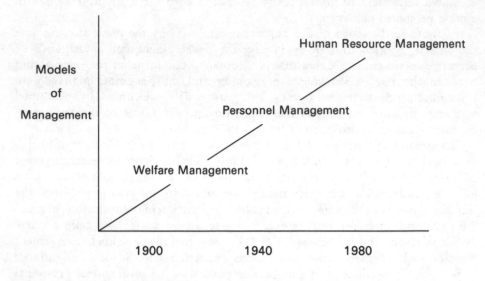

Figure 1.2   The evolution of human resource management

the nature and extent of change in HR practices which give expression to the core concepts of HRM? Early studies suggest that the extensiveness of HRM is limited in both the USA and the UK (Storey, 1989; Guest 1991). However, the most recent studies provide *prima facie* evidence of 'a remarkable take-up' of HRM-type practices by large British businesses (Storey, 1992a). The second vital question is what is meant by the term, human resource management? For some, HRM is not simply a new form of jargon to describe personnel management; it represents a new model of management with a different value system. For others, HRM remains an elusive concept, elastic and ambiguous (Storey, 1989). Furthermore, how should this model be viewed? How does it differ from the traditional personnel model? Is 'strategic' HRM a rupture from the prescriptive personnel management literature and the beginnings of a new theoretical sophistication (Boxall, 1992)? Many of the key elements of the HRM model are drawn from organizational behaviour theories, such as leadership and team building. If there is nothing particularly distinctive about the HRM model, or if it simply gives a greater prominence to organizational behaviour concepts, then HRM is just a change in style of presentation, or 'old wine in a new bottle.' Clearly, the meaning of the term is elastic and the literature reveals 'hard' and 'soft' versions of HRM (Legge, 1989).

The picture emerging from case studies and surveys in the USA and the UK is one of considerable innovation in the use of techniques to increase productivity and employee involvement in operational-level decision-making. Hitherto, however, HRM practices have not been adopted widely across organizations in the USA and the UK. A particularly judicious assessment of the diffusion of HRM in the USA is offered by Guest (1990): 'there appears to be agreement that some companies are trying to innovate in the field of HRM, but there is no evidence to support the view that this is a general trend in American industry' (1990, p. 387). Guest's assessment is significant because he argues that in the USA the central themes underlying HRM are taken very seriously and, moreover, human resource management is a contemporary manifestation of the 'American Dream'. The rhetoric and its popularity among American managers must be understood in this context.

The appeal of HRM lies in the specification of a particular way, based on organizational behaviour theory, of achieving high performance by enlisting individual employees' inherent skills and workplace wisdom. The desire for a new approach to managing employees is best expressed by such writers as Peters and Waterman (1982) and Abernathy *et al.* (1983). For example, Abernathy argues that 'Building a truly competitive organization . . . requires active enlistment of the best efforts of workers . . . Their skills, commitment and enthusiasm are the means by which strategic goals get translated into practice' (1983, p. 125).

The underlying idea here is to exploit employee wisdom in order to gain a competitive advantage. Another strand of the HRM model was its reinforcement of the importance of values, culture and leadership. If the HRM model seemed to rediscover the importance of the individual, it also reflected an explicitly anti-union perspective akin to what is referred to as radical conservatism.

The HRM model suited the ideological stance of Reagan and Thatcher (Legge, 1989). Furthermore, the new integrative HRM model appealed because of national sentiment; it was 'Made in America'. Its theoretical roots can be traced back to American writers such as Mayo, Maslow and McGregor. The US HRM model differs from the Japanese model (for example, life-time employment and enterprise unions do not feature) and the European models of co-determination. Thus, according to Guest, 'It [HRM] is American, optimistic, apparently humanistic and also superficially simple. In short, it has rediscovered elements of the American Dream. Fitting in with the political values of the Reagan years, this was a powerful message' (1990, p. 379). Judging from the plethora of articles and books (including this one) on HRM it would be easy to conclude that contemporary US and British industry is practising HRM. But, what systematic evidence exists to confirm that the HRM model has been, or at least is about to be, the new and preferred approach by US and British managers? Guest (1990) evaluates the empirical evidence from case studies and surveys to assess the diffusion of the practice of HRM in US industry.

Case studies can represent an in-depth analysis of practising HRM. But the evidence from cases on the extent to which HRM is practised seems to be limited. The number of detailed cases cited to claim that US industry is moving towards HRM (what Guest refers to as 'the regular core') is only 15. A second set of cases described by Peters and Waterman (1982) involved a sample of 62 companies. Foulkes' (1980) study of non-union firms consisted of 26 organizations. Another study of greenfield sites by Lawler (1986) covered just 20 plants. The important point is that the total number of case studies (ignoring the possibility of double-counting) claiming to be practising and moving towards HRM is only 123. Based on the limited data on the total number of US manufacturers provided by Pappas and Hirschey (1990), the number of companies practising HRM is just 0.93 per cent. There is a real possibility that the over-exposure of a relatively small number of cases gives the impression that more change is taking place than is really the case. There is some hard evidence of a significant number of important UK organizations which have adopted HRM practices (see for example HRM IN PRACTICE 1.1). A recent major UK study found 'extensive take-up of HRM-style approaches in . . . mainstream organizations' (Storey, 1992a, p. 30). And, among high technology companies, another study provides evidence of some take-up of HRM-style practices defined in terms of an emphasis on individual modes of job regulation and of high degrees of strategic integration (McLoughlin and Gourlay, 1992).

Postal surveys can provide a useful 'snapshot' of management practices and evidence of the extensiveness and influence of HRM. The large-scale survey, however, can only measure restricted dimensions of management practice and therefore the derived data tends to produce results that underscore continuity in management practice. A 1986 survey found that between 1981 and 1986, 38 per cent of the US organizations surveyed had changed the departmental title. Of these changes 81 per cent had been to the human resource title. Also, the change often led to an increase in status reflected in the change in title of the head of the function from director to vice-president and from manager to director (Guest, 1990). Freedman's (1985) evidence presented a rather different picture of the status and influence of the HRM function. Running parallel with the decline in union membership and perceived bargaining power, she found a decline in the influence of traditional personnel and industrial relations managers.

Regarding the evidence indicating the growing popularity of the HRM title, Guest makes the point that the change may simply be 'a symbolic gesture' and the policies will continue much the same. In many cases the title change may be a possible statement of intent (Guest, 1990). An interesting finding from the Millward et al. large-scale survey, which is relevant to the point, is that in 1990 the vast majority of specialists had 'personnel' in their titles, less than 1 per cent of specialist managers being called 'human resource' managers (1992, p. 29). Furthermore, Bratton's (1992) study raises questions about whether personnel managers really are the new corporate heroes. At Oil Tool Engineering and Flowpak Engineering the personnel managers became redundant, and the line managers were given responsibility for personnel functions and became closely associated with innovations in HR management. These two cases are reinforced by Millward *et al.* (1992) survey evidence. In Britain, this trend owes something to the business climate of the 1980s, when many companies switched from 'empire-building' to 'empire-demolition'. Companies were seeking to limit their full-time employees to a minimum core of people directly required to produce and market the firm's products or services. Other activities considered peripheral to this core

HRM IN PRACTICE 1.1

Shell UK pulls responsibility back to centre

by Jane Pickard

SHELL UK has had to rethink its approach to decentralisation after finding it led to worsening performance.

It discovered that pushing decision-making down to small groups and individuals in line with "fashionable human resource management ideas" in the late '80s diluted the traditional corporate culture which had proved successful in the past.

Communications suffered as business units, given more independence, became too cut off from each other and from the expertise at the centre.

Shell's response over the past year has been to improve the lines of communication between business units, making them more accountable to each other and more guided by a central company culture, while keeping the basic decentralised structure.

Speaking at an Economist conference, John Wybrew Shell's public affairs and planning director, said a conflict had emerged between professionals, such as accountants and engineers, and generalist executives who were concerned with fast decision-making and "getting things done".

In a small team, it was too easy for the professionals, who represented the "Shell way" of doing things, to find themselves losing influence.

Wybrew said that Shell started to experience overruns on some major projects and deteriorating operational reliability.

"When we tried to get a deeper understanding of this, we begin to realise that to some extent, while we had adopted new ideas with the best of intentions, it was working against some of the fundamental principles on which our business success is based. There was a need to reassert professionalism and integrity."

In advertising, for instance, the message had become "fragmented" and different parts of the organisation were presenting its image in a different way.

Shell had now built a team from the different parts of the organisation who would commission advertising and see it as part of a whole. However, responsibility for advertising in each part of the business was still devolved.

Wybrew added: "In adopting fashionable personnel management ideas, for which there are very good reasons, you have to be careful how you integrate them into the business.

"We are now working to reinforce professional standards and values shared across the organisation."

Source: Personnel Management Plus, April, 1992. Used with permission.

---

activity, such as the HRM function of training and development, are being subcontracted to consultancy firms. These alternative findings should remind us that by focusing only on HRM writers run the risk of obscuring the extent and significance of other ways of enhancing productivity through redundancies and sub-contracting.

As further evidence of the extensiveness of HRM, a number of studies have examined the introduction of management initiatives associated with HRM-type practices: employee participation, a focus on the *individual* employee, and self-managed teams. To increase employee commitment an increasing number of British managers have introduced some sort of employee involvement programme between 1984 and 1990. Also, there appears to be incontrovertible evidence of a renaissance of 'individualism' and a fall in the importance attached to 'collectivism' in the management of the employment relationship (Millward *et al.*, 1992). Sisson argues that some key concepts and practices associated with HRM are taking root in UK workplaces (1993, pp. 203–5). Case study analysis in the UK also shows extensive use of innovative techniques, such as self-managed teams and Total Quality Management (TQM) or Total Quality Control (TQC). Many of these techniques, however, could exist within either an HRM or a traditional personnel management model, depending upon both circumstances and strategic choice (Keenoy, 1990; Bratton, 1992).

One type of evidence that could support the diffusion and importance of human resource management is increased integration of HRM planning into strategic planning. The evidence of three studies strongly suggests that 'a coherent human resource strategy, including an early strategic input on human resource issues, is found in only a small minority of those organizations that may be making some use of human resource management techniques' (Guest, 1990, p. 387). The picture presented by the US reports is reinforced by Brewster and Smith (1990) who examined key trends in strategic HRM practices throughout the European Community. They found that 'in many organizations human resource strategies follow on *behind* [our emphasis] corporate strategy rather than making a positive contribution to it' (1990, p. 37). They also found that in the UK only 50 per cent of respondents claimed that the individual responsible for HR personnel is involved in the development of the corporate strategy from the outset. Little evidence of the strategic integration of HRM policies with corporate plans was found by Storey (1992).

To summarise the first area of debate, the *extensiveness* of HRM, there are two popular conflicting interpretations. The first suggests that apart from a relatively small number of cases, the hype surrounding HRM is well ahead of the actual practice in US and British industry. Guest (1990), for example, when discussing the evidence of HRM in the States, talks of the rhetoric being ahead of reality: 'there is no evidence to support the view that this [HRM] is a general trend in American industry' (p. 387). In the UK, where the values underlying HRM have never been taken very seriously, he argues, managers have been less willing to embrace HRM (Guest, 1991). The second, conversely, suggests that employment practices have radically changed as some key HRM dimensions are taken-up by managers in British mainstream companies (Millward *et al.*, 1992; Storey, 1992a). Time and further studies will show whether this take-up in large UK organizations has passed its peak or whether the practices spill over to workplaces across the board and so see a new orthodoxy establish itself.

Turning to the second area for debate, the conceptual, it is evident from reviewing the literature that the meaning and theoretical significance of HRM is contested. The 'soft' version of HRM emphasizes the importance of high motivation, high commitment, communications and enlightened leadership. Most normative HRM models, whether US or British, assert that the organization's 'human resources' are valued assets, not a variable cost, and emphasize the commitment of employees as a source of competitive advantage (Legge, 1989). Assumptions about the nature of human potential and the ability to tap that potential are based on organizational behaviour theories posited by such writers as Maslow (1954) and Herzberg (1966). The notion that commitment and performance can be enhanced by leadership style is based on the high trust assumptions of McGregor's Theory Y (1960). By contrast, the 'hard' version of HRM emphasizes the calculative, quantitative and strategic management aspects of managing the workforce in a 'rational' way (Storey, 1989). A number of writers on HRM develop a particular HRM model to demonstrate analytically the qualitative differences between conventional personnel management and HRM (see, for example, Beer *et al.*, 1984; Devanne *et al.*, 1984; Guest, 1987; and Storey, 1992).

The analytical framework of the 'Harvard model' offered by Beer et al. consists of six basic components: (1) situational factors; (2) stakeholder interests; (3) human resource management policy choices; (4) HR outcomes; (5) long-term consequences; and (6) a feedback loop through which the outputs flow directly into the organization and to the stakeholders. The Harvard analytical model for HRM is shown in Figure 1.3.

The *situational factors* influence management's choice of HR strategy. This normative model incorporates workforce characteristics, management philosophy, labour market regulations, societal values and patterns of unionization, and suggests a meshing of both 'product market' *and* 'socio-cultural logics' (Evans and Lorange, 1989). Analytically, both HRM scholars and practitioners will be more comfortable with contextual variables included in the model because it conforms to the reality of what they know: 'the employment relationship entails a blending of business and societal expectations' (Boxall, 1992, p. 72).

The *stakeholder interests* recognize the importance of 'trade-offs', either explicitly or implicitly, between the interests of owners and those of employees and their organizations, the unions. Although the model is still vulnerable to the charge of 'unitarism', it is a much more pluralist frame of reference than that found in later models. *Human resource management policy choices* emphasize that management's decisions and actions in HR management can be appreciated fully only if it is recognized that they result from an interaction between constraints and choices. The model depicts management as a real actor, capable of making at least some degree of unique contribution within environmental and organizational parameters and of influencing those parameters itself over time (Beer *et al.*, 1984).

The *HR outcomes* are high employee commitment to organizational goals and high individual performance leading to cost effective products or services. The

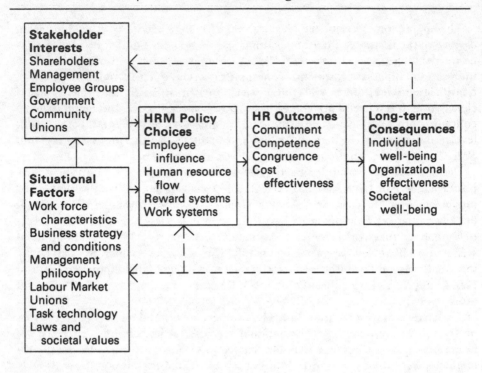

Figure 1.3   The Harvard analytical model of HRM

Source: Beer *et al.*, 1984.

underlying assumption here is that employees have talents which are rarely fully utilized at work, and they show a desire to experience growth through work. Thus, the HRM model takes the view that organizations should be designed on the basis of the assumptions inherent in McGregor's Theory Y (Guest, 1990). The *long-term consequences* distinguish between three levels: individual, organizational and societal. At the individual employee level the long-term outputs comprise the psychological rewards workers receive in exchange for effort. At the organizational level increased effectiveness ensures the survival of the organization. In turn, at the societal level, as a result of fully utilizing people at work some of society's goals (for example, employment and growth) are attained. Guest (1990) argues that the central themes of HRM are contemporary manifestations of the so-called 'American Dream': 'a king of rugged entrepreneurial individualism reflected in and reinforced by a strong organizational culture' (1990, p. 391). An important feature of the Harvard Model is its recognition of outcomes and issues at the societal level creating the basis for a critique of *comparative* human resource management (Boxall, 1992).

The sixth component of the Harvard model is the *feedback loop*. As we have discussed, the situational factors influence HRM policy and choices. Conversely, however, long-term outputs can influence the situational factors, stakeholder interests and HRM policies. The feedback loop in Figure 1.3 reflects this two-way relationship. There is no doubting the attractiveness of the Harvard model. It clearly provides a useful analytical basis for the study of HRM. The model also contains both analytical (i.e. situational factors, stakeholders, strategic choice levels) and prescriptive (i.e. notions of commitment, competence, etc.) (Boxall, 1992).

David Guest has developed an alternative theoretical framework to show how HRM is different from orthodox personnel management. Before we discuss the model, we need to identify the major assumptions or stereotypes underpinning personnel and HRM (see Figure 1.4).

Human resource management, according to the stereotypes shown in Figure 1.4, is distinctively different from orthodox personnel management because it integrates human resources into strategic management, it seeks behavioural commitment to organizational goals, the perspective is unitary with a focus on the individual, it works better in organizations that have an 'organic' structure, and the emphasis is on a full and positive utilization of human resources. Implicit in the contrasting stereotypes is an assumption that HRM is 'better'. However, as Guest correctly states, 'this fails to take account of variations in context which might limit its effectiveness . . . human resource management can most sensibly be viewed as an approach to managing the workforce' (1987, p. 508).

	PM compliance	HRM commitment
Psychological contract	Fair day's work for a fair day's pay	Reciprocal commitment
Locus of control	External	Internal
Employee relations	Pluralist Collective Low trust	Unitarist Individual High trust
Organising principles	Mechanistic Formal/defined roles Top-down Centralised	Organic Flexible roles Bottom-up Decentralised
Policy goals	Administrative efficiency Standard performance Cost minimisation	Adaptive work-force Improving performance Maximum utilisation

Figure 1.4 **Stereotypes of personnel management and human resource management**

Source: Guest, 1987.

The 'Guest model' has four main components: (1) a set of human resource management outcomes; (2) a set of human resource management policies; (3) a number of organizational outcomes; and (4) the 'cement' that binds the system. The model is summarized in Figure 1.5. The *HRM outcomes* of this normative model are strategic integration, commitment, flexibility and quality. Strategic integration is concerned to ensure that HRM is fully integrated into strategic planning. Like Beer *et al.*, Guest saw commitment as a vital outcome, concerned with the goals of binding employees to the organization and obtaining behaviour commitment to high performance. Flexibility is concerned with ensuring that workers are receptive to innovation and, using Atkinson's (1984) terminology, have function flexibility. Quality is concerned to ensure the high quality of products and services. Again, as Guest (1989) emphasises, these human resource management policy goals are a 'package' and each is necessary to ensure favourable organizational outcomes depicted on the right side of the model. Furthermore, he argues that: 'Only when a coherent strategy, directed towards these four policy goals, fully integrated into business strategy and fully sponsored by line management at all levels is applied will the high productivity and related outcomes sought by industry be achieved' (1990, p. 378).

Conventional personnel management policies and functions need to be employed to achieve the HRM policy goals. Individual HRM functions are listed on the left hand side of the model. According to Guest, HRM policies are

HRM policies	HRM outcomes	Organisational outcomes
Organisation/ job design		**High** Job performance
Management of change	Strategic integration	**High** Problem-solving Change Innovation
Recruitment, selection, socialisation	Commitment	
Appraisal, training, development	Flexibility/ adaptability	**High** Cost-effectiveness
Reward systems		
Communication	Quality	**Low** Turnover Absence Grievances

Leadership/culture/strategy

Figure 1.5   The Guest model of HRM

Source: Guest, 1989a. Used with permission.

concerned with more than 'good' selection or training: 'they are intended to achieve the human resource management policy goals' (1989, p. 49). Hence, the selection criteria should take cognizance of the potential for both the attitudinal commitment and high quality and, similarly, training should contribute to flexibility and high quality. The *organizational outcomes* shown on the right side of Guest's model are those most frequently associated with the HRM policies and HRM policy goals. The fourth component, the *cement*, is essential to ensure the success of this HRM model: 'the cement is . . . supportive leadership from the top, reflected in the organization's culture and backed by an explicit strategy to utilize human resources' (1990, p. 378).

Two conceptual issues associated with the model are recognized by Guest (1989). The first issue is that the values underpinning this HRM model are predominantly employee-oriented and unitarist. With the emphasis on long-term *individual* and corporate growth and pay related to *individual* performance, the role of trade unions within HRM has been questioned. Bramham (1989), for example, claims that there is a contradiction between the HRM organization culture and traditional trade unionism. He argues that collectivist culture, which has been the central tenet of trade unionism, poses a considerable problem for a firm pursuing a human resource management strategy. He goes on to posit, 'The HR company holds its employees in such high regard that exploitation would be *inconceivable* [our emphasis]' (p. 114). Guest (1987) recognizes that implicit in the HRM model is marginalization of trade unions; 'There is no recognition of any broader concept of pluralism within society giving rise to solidaristic collective orientation' (p. 519).

The second conceptual issue in the Guest model concerns the status of some of the concepts. The notion of 'commitment' is, argues Guest, 'a rather messy, ill-defined concept, but more importantly the empirical evidence has stubbornly failed to show the expected link between high commitment and high performance' (1989, p. 50). A central feature in the HRM model is 'strategic integration'. But this raises the problem of organizational fit. Briefly, what is the starting point of 'fit' or integration? Certainly, it seems valid to start with business strategy (Guest, 1990). Miller (1987) has also highlighted the important point that strategic HRM, for it to contribute to competitive advantage, must be linked to the organization's product market situation (p. 360).

How useful is the Guest normative model? In our view, the model is a valuable analytical framework for studying HRM. Guest focuses on the prescriptive side of the Harvard model and defines HRM as a particular style of employee relations in which management pursues goals of strategic integration, commitment, flexibility and quality. The strength of Guest's normative model is that it takes the implicit Harvard model and expresses it as a clearer, more carefully constructed set of theoretical propositions which can be empirically tested (Boxall, 1992). Its weakness is that it may simply be an 'ideal-type' towards which Western organizations can move, thus positing 'somewhat unrealistic conditions for the practice of human resource management' which must subsequently be relaxed (Keenoy, 1990, p. 367). It may also make the error of criticising general managers and HR practitioners for not conforming to an image academics have constructed for them (Boxall, 1992). Further, it presents the HRM model as inconsistent with collective approaches to managing the employment relationship (Legge, 1989). HRM could be consistent with either individual or collective approaches, although a strong corporate culture can conceal the use of collective controls by presenting the employment relationship in individualized terms (McLoughlin and Gourlay, 1992).

The 'Storey model' is derived from the speculative accounts of what the HRM paradigm might consist of and from the literature on the 'standard moderns' (see Chapter 11). The model demonstrates the differences between what Storey termed the 'personnel and industrials' and the HRM paradigm. His model also has four parts: (1) beliefs and assumptions; (2) strategic aspects; (3) line management; and (4) key levers (see Figure 1.6). The prevailing *beliefs and assumptions* of HRM, as pointed out by Guest (1987), are unitarist. According to the stereotypes depicted in Figure 1.6, HRM attempts to increase trust and employee commitment and aims to go 'beyond the contract'. The *strategic aspects* of Storey's model shows HRM central to corporate planning. The third component, *line management*, gives HRM specialists a 'transformational leadership' role in the organization. Evidence from 'core' companies suggests that general managers and line managers have emerged in almost all cases as the key players on HR issues. The *key levers* are shown on the lower portion of Storey's model and are issues and techniques strongly featured, explicitly or implicitly, in discussions of HRM. Storey found considerable unevenness in the adoption of these key levers (performance related pay, harmonization of conditions and the learning company). The model was used to devise a checklist of 25 key HRM variables to quantify the degree of movement from one approach to the other in fifteen 'core' organizations (Storey, 1992a).

Another theoretical model which emphasises the interrelatedness and the coherence of human resource management and is presented by Devanna *et al.* (1984). The human resource management cycle consists in their scheme of four key constituent components of selection, appraisal, development and rewards (Figure 1.7). These four human resource activities aim to increase individual performance. The Devanna *et al.* approach appears to be essentially prescriptive, focusing on four key HRM activities. The strength of the model, however, is that it expresses the coherence of internal HRM policies. The HRM cycle is also a simple model that serves as a framework for understanding the nature and significance of key HR activities and the interactions among the factors making up the complex fields of human resource management. As we progress through the book, we will refer to the HRM cycle to explain the relationship of each individual HRM function to other HRM activities. The weakness of this approach is that it ignores different stakeholder interests, situational factors and the notion of management's strategic choice.

The foregoing analysis has presented HRM as a more holistic orientation to organizational management and as a particular style of managing the employment relationship. It follows from this that in seeking to gain competitive advantage

PIR and HRM: the differences

Dimension	Personnel and IR	HRM
Beliefs and assumptions		
Contract	Careful delineation of written contracts	Aim to go 'beyond contract'
Rules	Importance of devising clear rules/mutuality	'Can do' outlook; impatience with 'rule'
Guide to management action	Procedures/consistency control	'Business need'/flexibility/commitment
Behaviour referent	Norms/custom and practice	Values/mission
Managerial task vis-a-vis labour	Monitoring	Nurturing
Nature of relations	Pluralist	Unitarist
Conflict	Institutionalised	De-emphasised
Standardisation	High (eg 'parity' an issue)	Low (eg 'parity' not seen as relevant)
Strategic aspects		
Key relations	Labour-management	Business-customer
Initiatives	Piecemeal	Integrated
Corporate plan	Marginal to	Central to
Speed of decision	Slow	Fast
Line management		
Management role	Transactional	Transformational leadership
Key managers	Personnel/IR specialists	General/business/line managers
Prized management skills	Negotiation	Facilitation
Key levers		
Foci of attention for interventions	Personnel procedures	Wide-ranging cultural structural and personnel strategies
Selection	Separate, marginal task	Integrated, key task
Pay	Job evaluation; multiple fixed grades	Performance-related; few if any grades
Conditions	Separately negotiated	Harmonisation
Labour-management	Collective bargaining contracts	Towards individual contracts
Thrust of relations with stewards	Regularised through facilities and training	Marginalised (with exception of some bargaining for change models)
Communication	Restricted flow/indirect	Increased flow/direct
Job design	Division of labour	Teamwork
Conflict handling	Reach temporary truces	Manage climate and culture
Training and development	Controlled access to courses	Learning companies

Figure 1.6 The Storey model of HRM

Source: Storey, 1992.

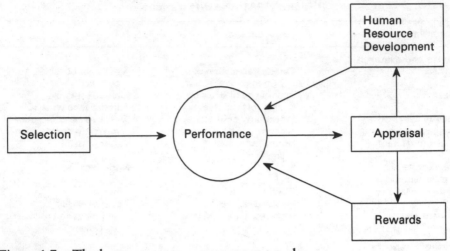

Figure 1.7   The human resource management cycle

Source: Adapted from Devanna *et al.*, 1984. Reprinted by premission of John Wiley & Sons Ltd.

there are *alternative* strategies to the management of the workforce. The notion of strategy is problematic, but an HR strategy can be defined as 'The pattern that emerges from a stream of important decisions about the management of human resources, especially those decisions that indicate management's major goals and the means that are (or will be) used to pursue them' (Dyer, 1984, p. 159).

There is no simple typology of HR strategies, one with mutually exclusive categories. However, Guest (1990) identifies four different HR strategies:

1. *Traditional/Conservative* – this approach believes in maintaining the status quo and carrying on as before, with personnel policies centring around administrative efficiency and cost minimization.
2. *Radical/Conservative* – this response recognizes that fundamental restructuring is needed to gain competitive advantage. This will often include plant closures, particularly unionized plants. It is very clearly based on a belief in management's right to manage in a context where workers are viewed as disposable.
3. *Pluralist/Innovative* – this approach recognizes that managerial prerogative has been diminished by the growth of workplace trade unionism. It seeks a more collaborative relationship between management and labour to improve productivity.
4. *Unitarist/Innovative* – such an approach is unitarist in focus. It assumes that management and workers share common goals. Guest subdivides this category:

(i) *Behavioural Taylorism* – where organizations make sophisticated use of the techniques of behavioural science alongside elements of Taylorism to promote high performance (e.g. McDonald's).

(ii) *Human Resource Management* – where organizations manage the workforce based on values and policies designed to utilize the talents of all the employees.

There is prime-facie evidence in the UK of a third sub-theme within the unitarist/innovative typology, 'Japanization' (Turnbull, 1986; Oliver and Wilkinson, 1988; Bratton, 1992). The relationships between the Harvard model and the strategic choice framework are illustrated in Figure 1.8.

The implications of Figure 1.8 are three-fold: first, it incorporates recognition of a range of different stakeholder interests and situational factors which offer management both choices and constraints; second, in seeking to improve HR and organizational effectiveness, HRM is not the only possible response – HRM is a sub-theme of the unitarist/innovative strategy; third, it is possible for a company to follow a pure strategic type or to combine the stereotypes of two or more strategies to suit its own unique conditions and meet its own objectives. For example, a company may adopt a Japanese-style manufacturing strategy (just-in-time, total quality control and cellular work-groups, see Chapter 3), but retain a traditional/conservative HR strategy. The key words here are variety and change. Management can choose from a variety of HR strategies and, given the different conditions facing each organization, each company's HR strategy is unique to its situation and is also likely to change overtime if or when economic and political circumstances and trade union power change.

This review of HRM models suggests, then, that while it is obvious that similarities exist between the normative models of HRM, whether US (Beer *et al.*) or British (for example, Guest) and those of personnel management, there are qualitative differences between HRM and conventional personnel management. First, HRM assumes a non-union or a unitary frame of reference: thus 'there will be no place in a company's HR strategy for those who threaten the continuity of the organization by attacking its basic aims', as Bramham (1989, p. 118) asserts. In a nutshell the normative HRM model represents a renaissance of unitarism. In this book we take a neutral position; the HRM policies and activities discussed may be applied, for the most part, in a non-union or unionized environment, depending upon circumstances and strategic choices. The second difference is that HRM, in theory, is integrated into strategic planning. The third difference is the importance given to cultural leadership in the organization. The purpose of culture is to provide employees with a commitment to beliefs and values that are 'larger than ourselves' (Daft, 1992). In most HRM models top management is given prime responsibility for cultural leadership. The fourth difference is that the role of line management is given a different emphasis in HRM: much greater stress is placed on the line managers' responsibility of coordinating and directing *all* resources to generate commitment and enthuse subordinates to innovate. To put it another way, HRM is too important for corporate success to be left to HR

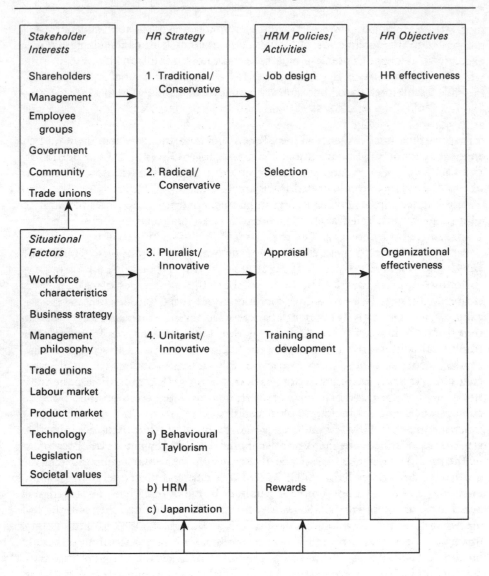

Figure 1.8 Situational factors, stakeholder interests and HR strategies: a combined model

specialists. Finally, HRM emphasizes, in theory, the importance of individual human growth and developing the management 'team'.

These five differences in emphasis suggest that HRM is a proactive central strategic management activity which is different from conventional personnel management with its implied passive connotations. However, what may be of more significance is not the message, but the messenger: that 'human resource management represents the discovery of personnel management by chief executives' as Legge (1989) has said. This accords with Storey's argument that what is different about the normative HRM model 'is not so much that the message itself has changed but that it is being received more seriously' (1989, p. 5). Over the last decade, HRM has taken on an increasing theoretical significance as it has become part of the wider sociological debate concerned with new management paradigms such as post-Fordism, Toyotism and Japanization. The core argument of this chapter is that it is legitimate to define HRM as a particular approach to the management of the employment relationship with a distinctive set of HR policies and practices designed to produce specific outcomes: to secure the greater commitment of employees and promote synergy in order to increase organizational effectiveness.

■ Summary

In this chapter we have provided an overview of the dynamic field of human resource management. We have examined its history, from so-called welfare management to human resource management. The major concern of this chapter is with theories and perspectives. The emphasis has been on understanding competing normative HRM models rather than on HRM practice itself. We have discussed some of the major contributions of management theory to consider whether human resource management now represents a new orthodoxy. Certainly the language is different. However, most of the theories underpinning the HRM model and the techniques of HRM can be found in either organizational behaviour or personnel management textbooks of a decade ago. On balance, we consider that HRM, in theory, does represent a new theoretical orthodoxy which, in North America and Britain at least, is a reflection of the hegemonic position of the new 'Radical Right'. Whether the model of human resource management becomes the norm in *practice* will depend upon, amongst other things, its perceived success in increasing organizational effectiveness and the economic and political climate. Given the different conditions facing each company, 'diversity and pragmatism' is likely to remain the norm (Sisson, 1989). Furthermore, challenges to the new orthodoxy come from within its own theoretical ambiguity and the growing influence of European rather than American management values (Guest, 1991). By considering some of these theoretical issues we have had the opportunity to discover how contesting perspectives complement and negate each other, and to gain insights into the discourse currently surrounding the field of human resource management.

■ Key concepts

- Welfare management
- Personnel management
- Human resource management
- Unitary perspective

- Management
- Scientific management
- Human relations school
- Japanization

Discussion questions

1. What is HRM? To what extent is it different from conventional personnel management or is it simply 'old wine in new bottles'?
2. Explain the development of HRM.
3. Explain the importance and purposes of HRM.
4. What are 'effectiveness', 'efficiency' and 'competitive advantage', and how are they related to HRM?

■ Further reading

Beer, M. *et al.* (1984), *Managing Human Assets*, New York: Free Press.

Guest, D. (1990), 'Human Resource Management and the American Dream', *British Journal of Industrial Relations*, Vol. 27, No. 4.

Guest, D. (1991), 'Personnel Management: The End of Orthodoxy?' *British Journal of Industrial Relations*, Vol. 29, No. 2.

Storey, J. (ed.) (1989), *New Perspectives on Human Resource Management*, London: Routledge.

Storey, J. (1992) *Developments in the Management of Human Resources*, Oxford: Blackwell.

Storey, J. (1992a) 'HRM in action: the truth is out at last', *Personnel Management*, Vol. 24, No. 4.

Sisson, K. (1993) 'In search of HRM', *British Journal of Industrial Relations*, Vol. 31, No. 2.

Watson, T.J. (1986), *Management Organizations and Employment Strategy*, London: RKP.

■ Chapter case study   A new HRM philosophy at Servo Engineering

Servo Engineering was founded in 1897 to manufacture an improved miner's safety lamp. Over the last fifty years the company has developed as a leading manufacturer of commercial vehicle components. In 1965 Servo Engineering became a subsidiary of Zipton Holding Ltd, which merged in 1977 with American Ensign. This multinational company has manufacturing plants in the UK, USA and Germany. In 1990 the UK group had four sites in Great Britain.

Between 1984 and 1988 the company replaced over half its conventional and Numerical Control machines with Computer Numerical Control. In 1985 the firm organized production into six 'cells'. The cells were product-centred: for example, one cell would manufacture a whole component such as vacuum pumps or air compressors. Each cell operated as a miniature factory within the larger factory. Each cell had sufficient machinery to complete the majority of the manufacturing stages. Processes outside the scope of the cell were sub-contracted out, either to another cell, or to an external contractor. The number of workers in each cell varied between 12 and 50. The cells operated a three-shift system: 6 am to 2 pm; 2 pm to 10 pm; and 10 pm to 6 am. The division of labour within the cells is shown below. The 'cell supervisor' had overall responsibility for the cell. The product-coordinator's job was to ensure the supply of raw materials and parts to meet cell production targets. The 'charge-hand' acted as progress-chaser. Below the supervisory grades was a hierarchy of manual grades reflecting different levels of training, experience and pay. For example, the 'setter' was apprentice-trained and was paid a skilled rate to set-up the machines for the semi-skilled operators. Semi-skilled workers received little training. In total the firm employed 442 people. Three unions were recognized by the firm for collective-bargaining purposes: AEU, MSF and APEX. The AEU was the largest union at the factory: it had 200 members out of a total of 351 manual workers, a union density of 56.9 per cent.

The personnel manager at the factory was George Wyke, who had worked for the company for 25 years. Prior to becoming the personnel manager, he was an AUEW shop steward and convener at another plant within the group. He had no formal personnel management qualifications.

The company gave cell leaders considerable discretion for employee relations. To quote George Wyke:

> What the cellular system has done as far as man-management is concerned, it has pushed that responsibility further down the chain, into the cells. So where somebody

Supervisory Grades:

Cell supervisor

Product Coordinator   Charge-hand

Manual Grades:
Setter
Setter Operator
Operator
Labour

wants disciplining, they don't say to the personnel manager: 'I want to sack this bastard. What can I do to get rid of him?' They know what they have got to do. The only time they will come to me is to seek advice on whether they are doing it right or wrong.

Although levels of unemployment were high in the area, the company had difficulty recruiting 'good' people at its factory in Yorkshire. Also, absenteeism and turnover were high, as shown here.

Absenteeism	1990	Turnover Rates
5.3	January	34.4
5.7	February	20.4
8.0	March	27.5

The apparent low level of commitment among manual employees can be explained in two ways. First, shop stewards and workers expressed considerable discontent over the bonus scheme: the standard time allowed to complete a particular task was not considered adequate to earn a 'decent' bonus. Second, the way the cells were designed resulted in operatives performing narrow, repetitive tasks, closely supervised.

The personnel manager, George Wyke, is due to retire this Christmas. The plant manager, Elizabeth Bell, has been concerned for some time over employee relations in the factory and the management style of George Wyke and some of the cell leaders. Elizabeth Bell has decided to seek an external candidate to replace the incumbent personnel manager. Gleaning through the ads in newspapers and journals she also decided to drop the term 'personnel' and advertise for a 'Human Resource' Manager.

(*Source:* Adapted from 'The Motor Components Company: Japanization in Large-batch Production', in Bratton, J. (1992) *Japanization at Work*, London: Macmillan).

Questions

---

1. Describe the main features of George Wyke's approach to HR management. How does Wyke's approach differ from the stereotype HRM approach?
2. Discuss the contribution an HRM professional could make to the company.

■ References

1. Antony, P. and Norton, L. (1991), 'Link HR to Corporate Strategy', *Personnel Journal*, April, p. 75.
2. Schonberger, R. (1982), *Japanese Manufacturing Techniques: Nine Hidden Lessons in Simplicity*, London: Collier Macmillan, p. 198.
3. Joe Greenwood, AEU Convener, quoted in Bratton, 1992, p. 139.

CHAPTER 2

Global Capitalism and Competitive Advantage

A last-ditch effort is being made to prevent Chrysler, America's third-largest car firm, from going to the wall . . . It has now laid off nearly 43,000 production workers indefinitely.[1]

About 25m people will be out of work in the 24 OECD countries this Christmas. The main reason for the grim tidings is simple: the capitalist world is still growing painfully slowly, and the United States may now be in a full-blooded slump.[2]

Recruitment is the biggest single challenge facing personnel managers in the 1990s. Current skill shortages and forecasts of a huge drop in the number of young people available for work in the coming decade point to rapidly deteriorating recruitment prospects. Certainly the situation looks bleak for those employers who fail to change their ways and are slow to look to non-traditional sources and methods of recruitment, as well as more innovative forms of employment.[3]

■ Chapter outline

Economic context
Technological context
Political context
Social context

Chapter objectives

After studying this chapter, you should be able to:

1. Identify the external contexts that affect human resource management policies and actions.
2. Understand the implications of these external contexts for the human resource management function.

■ Introduction

The prevailing economic climate has a significant influence on specific human resource management policies and activities. What happens in the national and global economy, for example, impacts on output, aggregate demand and the demand for labour. Apart from the economic context, the wider political, social and technological contexts influence and impinge upon human resource management decisions. Graeme Salaman (1979) is one of a number of organization theorists who have argued the importance of understanding the relationship between organizational activity and social stability or instability. To understand the nature and scope of human resource management it is necessary to understand the various external contexts which affect the organization.

The context of British and North American human resource management changed substantially during the 1980s. At the global level, in the advanced capitalist world, the previous dominance of the USA began to give way to a three way rivalry between North America, the European Community and the Pacific rim countries dominated by Japan and the 'four tigers' of Hong Kong, South Korea, Singapore and Taiwan. At national level, in Britain, contextual changes included: high levels of unemployment, the wide diffusion and acceptance of microprocessor-based technologies, a reassertion of a political ideology based on the pre-eminence of the individual and the free market, major pieces of government legislation affecting the employment relationship, and changes in demographics and values. In the United States the difficult environment of the 1980s has resulted in changes that have led to what some writers have called the 'transformation of American industrial relations'. Although the transformation thesis is not universally accepted, US employers have, with government indulgence, persuaded or compelled trade unions to accept significant changes in collective agreements (see, for example, Kochan *et al.*, 1986).

The aim of this chapter is not to provide a comprehensive analysis of the interrelated development of North American and UK economies, but to sketch the economic, political and social contexts affecting human resource management. This is important, because in various ways the conditions external to the organization present particular opportunities and constraints in the management of human resources. In the 1960s, changing public policies covering productivity and employment law extended the personnel management function (Clegg, 1979; Sisson, 1989). Farnham (1990) also argues that personnel management practices arose as the result of changes in the political economy. He states: 'As British industrial capitalism has developed, largely in response to changes in its market, technological and politico-economic contexts, so too have personnel management practices (1990, p. 25). Kelly (1985), for example, provides a carefully considered assessment of managerial control and job design. He argues that the origins of job design initiatives are explained in the development of product markets. In the 1980s, the context of British human resource management has been profoundly influenced by the political environment: four consecutive Conservative governments and the emergence of the European Community as a political force on the employment front (Millward *et al.*, 1992). It would, however, be too simple to regard the influence of context as a one-way flow only. Senior management tries to change the external context or environment. For example, a company might transfer its operations where there is little competition or few, if any, health and safety regulations. In addition, managements seek to influence government legislation and regulation by lobbying members of parliament. To understand fully the HRM function requires an appreciation of the external influences. The contexts of HRM are shown in Figure 2.1.

■ The economic context

Human resource management practices and the relative standing of HRM generally is strongly influenced by the prevailing economic climate. In broad terms, looking back over the 1980s, they started off with a severe recession, particularly in the manufacturing sector in the Midlands and the north of Britain; then, between 1985 and 1987, there was a period of continuous growth, until 1990 when another recession began which affected businesses and communities in the north and south of Britain. Real Gross Domestic Product (GDP) increased by 5 per cent and real manufacturing output fell by 2 per cent between 1980 and 1984. The GDP upward path remained erratic and concealed the disappearance of large tracts of industrial landscape. Nonetheless, overall, real GDP increased by 23 per cent and manufacturing output rose by 25 per cent in the period 1984–90. High unemployment, and for millions of people falling living standards, marked the 1980s.

In 1984, unemployment was 13 per cent and although many of the UK's competitors were also experiencing historically high levels of unemployment,

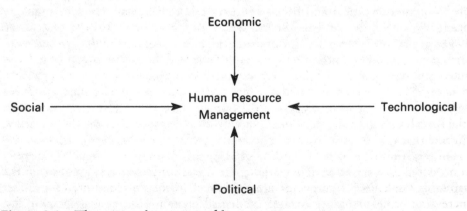

Figure 2.1 The external contexts of human resource management

only Belgium and the Netherlands surpassed the UK's unemployment rate. Real income per head of the UK population was lower in the mid-1980s than in eleven other advanced capitalist countries. Moreover, there were significant shifts between different parts of the UK economy. The percentage of output (Gross Domestic Product) accounted for by service industries had increased, while the proportion attributable to manufacturing had decreased. In 1950, manufacturing was 30 per cent of the UK's GDP, by 1984 it had fallen to 25 per cent. The UK's problems, as regards its competitiveness performance, is measured in terms of its overseas and domestic market shares. The UK's share of world exports of manufactures fell from approximately 17 per cent in 1960 to about 8 per cent in 1986. Whilst the volume of international exports of manufactures increased by almost 42 per cent between 1978 and 1987, the volume of UK exports of manufactures increased by only 23 per cent (Griffiths and Wall, 1989). In manufacturing, which is the crucial sector in terms of global competition, particularly for Britain as North Sea oil output declines, UK output increased by 6 per cent in the period 1979 to 1991, compared with the OECD average (excluding the UK) of 35 per cent. The UK was 20th out of 21 OECD economies. The UK's share of total OECD manufacturing output declined from 6.5 per cent in 1979 to 5.2 per cent in 1991; for the period 1979–92, the UK is situated at the *bottom* of the league (Michie, 1992). The shift to service industries has been substantial in terms of jobs: 35 per cent of the total in civil employment were employed in manufacturing in 1950; this had fallen to 26 per cent in mid-1984 and to 23 per cent in 1990 (Millward *et al.*, 1992, p. 17). During the same period, 1950–90, employment in the service sector increased from 47 per cent to 60 per cent of total employment.

The structural change in the UK economy has been encapsulated in the term 'deindustrialization'. Although some observers question the wisdom of using the term, the discourse on deindustrialization forms part of a wider debate on the relative performance of the UK economy in the 1980s (Blackaby, 1979; Massey, 1988). Some observers argue that the UK economy in the 1980s was at some kind of a 'crossroads', and the dimensions of structural change are embedded in broader global processes of internationalization and multilateralism (Harris, 1988). Moreover, it is argued that we cannot explain or understand the structural changes in the UK economy without understanding the global forces that have acted upon it and which UK capitalism has itself helped to shape. Major structural economic change and a wider degree of exposure to the rest of the capitalist economies were features of the 1980s. In the words of Francis Green: 'the British economy in the 1980s is but a small unsheltered inlet on the edge of a turbulent sea' (Green, 1989, p. 3).

On the transformation of the British economy, Lash and Urry (1987) offer a contrasting interpretation. They argue that Britain and the USA, amongst other capitalist societies, are moving into an era of 'disorganized capitalism'. The increasing scale of industrial and financial corporations, combined with the growth of a global market, means that national markets have become less regulated by nationally based corporations, and individual nation-states have less

What a way to make a living

Does making things really matter? There was a widespread feeling in Britain during the 1980s that it did not. Pundits pointed to the shifting nature of the economy _ from one based predominantly on large enterprises to one relying more on small firms; from heavy dependence on manufacturing to greater reliance on services. The boom in financial and information services was going to usher in a post-industrial world.

That Future has been indefinitely postponed. The warning went out even before Big Bang encouraged the City's new stock-broking conglomerates to entice 24-year-old bond salesmen with Porsches. As far as exports were concerned, a committee of the House of Lords reported in 1985 that there was nothing in the cupboard to compensate for any further decline in manufacturing.

Certainly not services, least of all financial ones. Manufacturing provides over 60% of Britain's export earnings. For every 1% fall in exports of manufactured goods, the export of services generally would have to rise by 3%. Alternatively, the export of financial services or tourism would have to increase by 10% for every 1% reduction in the sale of manufactured goods abroad. There was simply no way for them to grow that fast. Besides, the whole of the service sector was already in hock to manufacturing for a sizeable chunk of its business. "Services, as important as they are," their lordships concluded, "are no substitute for manufacturing because they are heavily dependent upon it and only 20 are tradable overseas."

The Thatcher government bequeathed one rich legacy to British manufacturers. By curbing the trade unions, lowering taxes and cutting out wasteful subsidies and government meddling, it handed them back the authority to manage their own businesses.

The freedom to manage efficiently showed up most dramatically in terms of productivity. For the first time since the early 1970s, output per employee in Britain began rising faster than practically anywhere else. In manufacturing, productivity grew by an average of 4.7% a year throughout the 1980s compared with an annual 0.9% during 1975–80. Of the leading industrial countries, only Japan did better.

The productivity miracle

That was the easy part. The improvements in value-added per employee, dramatic as they are, have come largely from having fewer employees. More than 2m jobs were shed by British manufactures during the 1980s, 30% of their total workforce. As brutal as it was, the cut was long overdue – and a necessary answer to the thicket of restrictive practices that had flourished for too long. Today, British manufacturers have never been leaner, meaner and readier to go. Some 171,000 manufacturing firms are currently registered at Companies House compared with 144,000 in 1980. But there are just 4.5m people employed in manufacturing now compared with 6.8m in 1980.

Coming along nicely

Real manufacturing value-added per person, average annual % change

	1960–68	1968–73	1973–79	1979–90
Belgium	4.9	8.2	5.0	4.7
Japan	9.0	10.4	5.0	4.6
Britain	3.4	3.9	0.6	4.1*
United States	3.2	3.5	0.9	3.3*
France	6.8	5.8	3.9	2.4
Italy	7.2	5.6	2.9	1.6
Western Germany	4.7	4.5	3.1	1.1

Source: OECD *1979–86

Ironically, the government's anti-union legislation had less of an impact than is generally supposed. Union-bashing may have worked in a handful of cases that dominated the headlines – especially at the state-owned car company, British Leyland, and in the nationalised shipyards and coal mines. Elsewhere, however, improvements in productivity stemmed from more flexible attitudes among workers and managers alike. David Metcalf of the London School of Economics compared the performance of unionised factories with non-unionised ones, only to find that both had basically similar gains in productivity during the 1980s.

Apart from having fewer workers, the surge in productivity seems to have been prodded along by the "catchup effect", as Britain app-

lied some of the improvements in manufacturing technology that America, West Germany and Japan had introduced a decade before. Another factor was the more flexible way people started doing their jobs – prompted undoubtedly by the fear of losing them.

All told, productivity increased during the 1980s by nearly a third – faster than in any G7 country except Japan. In absolute terms, however, Britain's labour productivity is still low. The value added per worker in Britain ($24,000 in 1985 money) remains little more than half that in America ($46,000) and three-quarters that in Japan ($31,000). But at least the trend is now sharply up (see table).

Source: © *The Economist*, October 1992. Used with permission.

---

direct control and regulation over large transnational companies. As part of the transformation embodied in 'disorganized capitalism' there is a huge divergence in the experience between manufacturing and service sectors. In manufacturing there is a fall in the absolute and relative numbers employed in manufacturing industry and in the significance of this sector for the modern capitalist society. Massey (1988, 1989) have similarly identified the extreme divergence in experience between UK manufacturing and services.

Whatever the academic merits of the debate, to the men and women who have lived in the UK in the 1980s the term deindustrialization has real meaning. In concrete terms it means that people experienced redundancy, long-term unemployment, immense upheaval and dislocation, poverty and despair. Unemployment levels varied markedly over the 1980s, rising from 1980 to 1986 and falling to a low point in early 1990. One problem for researchers, however, is how unemployment statistics are compiled. The number of times the method of compilation has altered since 1979 is a subject of political controversy. The Department of Employment states that there have been seven changes since 1979 which has reduced the number of 'unemployed' in the monthly count. Other commentators, more critical of the government policies, argue that there have been at least twenty changes in the way in which the unemployment series is calculated over the period 1979–90. As one observer said: 'The definition of unemployment is a question more of semantics than of economics' (Johnson, 1988, p. 82). Changing levels of unemployment had considerable implications for the industrial relations system. High levels of unemployment and structural changes shifted the balance of power in industrial relations: workers and their representatives became more tractable in order to preserve jobs, and managers found that they were more able to introduce unilateral changes in working practices.

The data collected by Millward and his colleagues provide an alternative source of information on important aspects of the changing nature of the British economic context. The findings, covering the period 1984 to 1990, show some identifiable changes in the nature of product markets and the degree of competition, as seen by their management respondents (see Table 2.1).

Overall, the markets served by the team's national sample of workplaces, both industrial and commercial, remained substantially unchanged. First, manufacturing plants continued to supply products mainly to national or international markets, with a small movement from the latter. Surprisingly, there was no noticeable shift towards international markets. A second finding that accords with mainstream economic analysis is the increased competition facing business organizations: 'more establishments faced highly competitive markets in 1990 than did so in 1984' (Millward *et al.*, 1992, p. 12). This was particularly the case in the service sector: the proportion whose sole or main product market had more than five competitors increased from 56 to 64 per cent. But in the manufacturing sector there was a smaller increase, from 49 to 54 per cent. Another indicator of competitive pressure, the sensitivity of demand to price increases, moved in the opposite direction according to the survey data.

Another major change in the British economy is the marked shift away from public ownership, largely through privatization but also through the subcontracting out of services by public organizations. Findings from the 1990 survey

TABLE 2.1   **The economic context of trading organizations, 1984 and 1990**

	Manufacturing		Services	
	1984	*1990*	*1984*	*1990*
Market for main product			*Column percentages*	
Local	6	10	45	54
Regional	18	10	18	19
National	47	53	26	20
International	29	27	12	7
Number of competitors			*Column percentages*	
None	5	6	14	10
1–5	46	41	30	26
More than 5	49	54	56	64
Price sensitivity			*Column percentages*	
Insensitive	39	43	57	61
Moderate	12	5	9	6
Sensitive	49	53	34	34

Source: Millward *et al.*, 1992. Used with permission.

show that employment in state-owned corporations fell by 38 per cent, from 1.3 million to 0.8 million, between 1984 and 1990 (Millward *et al.*, 1992, p. 17).

Corporate investment across west and east European borders and corporate restructuring are new developments in European capitalism. Between 1983 and 1990 such investment grew four times faster than global output and three times faster than global trade. Whereas in the 1970s the multinational enterprise was seen as the embodiment of almost anything negative about industrial capitalism, in the 1990s it is argued that multinational corporations (MNCs) can be viewed in a more positive light. The global corporation is back in fashion as the embodiment of modernity: high technology, rich in capital, replete with skilled jobs. Moreover, some economic theorists suggest that economic activity will be controlled by fewer and fewer companies. The United Nations estimates there are, at the time of writing, at least 35 000 multinationals, controlling some 170 000 foreign affiliates. In addition, that economic power is concentrated: the largest 100 multinationals, excluding those in banking and finance, account for $3.1 trillion of global assets in 1990, of which $1.2 trillion was outside firms' respective home countries. Table 2.2 shows the top 25 companies.

Further economic challenges face European and North America capitalism, reflecting wider economic changes in the global economy. Along with Japan, the 'Asian Tigers' are some of the most rapidly growing economies. Towards the end of 1991 the Japanese economy had slowed down, which affected Japanese business confidence. Nonetheless, Japan remains a formidable competitor as indicated by its trade surplus of over $105 billion for the 12 months between March 1991 and 1992. It is also argued that with the rapid growth of the Pacific Rim countries, Mexico, and the more prominent economies in Latin America, such as Brazil, comes increased import penetration of North American markets. Mexico, for example, has gone from exporting almost nothing except oil in the late 1970s, to a position where, in 1986, non-oil exports constituted a majority of foreign exchange earnings for Mexico. In North America, the Canada–US Free Trade Agreement (FTA), which introduced tariff reductions on commodities in stages over ten years, poses additional economic challenges to current working and HRM practices. Thus, European and North American trade policies and wider economic changes in east Europe and the Pacific Rim economies will put pressures on British companies to gain competitive advantage. The challenge to increase productivity and improve quality means that European and North American organizations will have to devote more attention to managing their human assets.

■ The technology context

Over the last ten years microprocessor-based technology has radically transformed the world of work for both blue-collar and white-collar employees. At the end of the 1970s, observers were predicting 'a new industrial revolution' based not on steam, but microelectronics (see, for example, Jenkins and Sherman,

TABLE 2.2   The top 25 multinationals (non-financial, ranked by foreign assets)

Rank	Industry	Country	Foreign assets $bn	Total assets $bn	Foreign sales $bn	% of total sales
1 Royal Dutch/Shell	Oil	Britain/Holland	n.a.	106.3	56.0	49
2 Ford Motor	Cars and trucks	United States	55.2	173.7	47.3	48
3 General Motors	Cars and trucks	United States	52.6	180.2	37.3	31
4 Exxon	Oil	United States	51.6	87.7	90.5	86
5 IBM	Computers	United States	45.7	87.6	41.9	61
6 British Petroleum	Oil	Britain	39.7	59.3	46.6	79
7 Nestlé	Food	Switzerland	n.a.	27.9	33.0	98
8 Unilever	Food	Britain/Holland	n.a.	24.8	16.7	42
9 Asea Brown Boveri	Electrical	Switzerland/Sweden	n.a.	30.2	22.7	85
10 Philips Electronics	Electronics	Holland	n.a.	30.6	28.6	93
11 Alcatel Alsthom	Telecoms	France	n.a.	38.2	17.7	67
12 Mobil	Oil	United States	22.3	41.7	44.3	77
13 Fiat	Cars and trucks	Italy	19.5	66.3	15.8	33
14 Siemens	Electrical	Germany	n.a.	50.1	15.1	40
15 Hanson	Diversified	Britain	n.a.	27.7	5.6	46
16 Volkswagen	Cars and trucks	Germany	n.a.	41.9	27.5	65
17 Elf Aquitaine	Oil	France	17.0	42.6	12.2	38
18 Mitsubishi	Trading	Japan	16.7	73.8	41.2	32
19 General Electric	Diversified	United States	16.5	153.9	8.3	14
20 Mitsui	Trading	Japan	15.0	60.8	43.6	32
21 Matsushita Electric Industrial	Electronics	Japan	n.a.	59.1	16.6	40
22 News Corp.	Publishing	Australia	14.6	20.7	5.3	78
23 Ferruzzi/Montedison	Diversified	Italy	13.5	30.8	9.1	59
24 Bayer	Chemicals	Germany	n.a.	25.4	21.8	84
25 Roche Holding	Drugs	Switzerland	n.a.	17.9	6.8	96

Source: © *The Economist*, March 1993.

1979). It was judgements of this kind, together with intense media coverage that prompted governments, industrialists and trade unions to wake up to the significance of microprocessor-based technology. Much of the debate on technological change has been conducted at the 'macro' or the societal level. Optimists describe the potential benefits of new technology in a 'leisure society', where the monotony and hazards of work are removed. Pessimists, on the other hand, point to mass unemployment, the degradation of work and new health hazards. Macro studies have examined the impact of microelectronics in particular sectors of British industry (for example Daniel, 1987). The Workplace Industrial Relations Study (WIRS) 1990 provides invaluable data on the use and introduction of what was then the still-relatively-new microelectronics technology. In Millward and Stevens' 1984 survey, the researchers analyzed three different forms of technical change:

1. *Advanced technical change*: new plant, machinery or equipment that includes microelectronic technology (for example, Computer Aided Design).
2. *Conventional technical change*: new plant, machinery or equipment not incorporating microelectronic technology (for example, containerization).
3. *Organizational change*: substantial changes in work organization or job design not involving new plant, machinery or equipment (for example, self-managed teams).

The data demonstrates just how far change has become a feature of British workplaces across all sectors of employment in the early 1980s and accords with the predictions. Each of the three types of change was common and workplaces often experienced a combination of all three. Findings from the 1990 WIRS survey confirm that the overall rate of change was maintained between 1984 and 1990. Table 2.3 summarizes the results for manual and non-manual employees

TABLE 2.3   Technical change, 1984 and 1990 (%)

	Manual employees 1984	1990	Non-manual employees 1984	1990
Proportion of workplaces experiencing in the previous three years:				
Technical change	37	40	57	55
Technical change involving micro-electronics	22	23	49	52
Organizational change	23	29	20	41
Technical or organizational change	47	53	63	67

Source: Millward *et al.*, 1992, p. 15. Used with permission.

from the 1984 and 1990 surveys. In each case the figures refer to technical or organizational changes that occurred in the previous three years. The technical changes involving microelectronics were considerably more prevalent in relation to non-manual than to manual employees in 1984 and this difference did not alter in 1990: 'Traditionally technical change was conceived of as a phenomenon that principally affected manual workers. Now it more frequently affects non-manual workers' (WIRS, 1992, p. 49). Taking all types of computing facilities together, 75 per cent of the sample had on-site computing facilities compared with only 47 per cent of workplaces in 1984 (WIRS, 1992, p. 13).

Research efforts have also been undertaken at the 'micro' or organizational level. Much of this work has been concerned with describing and interpreting the complex interplay of technical innovation, job characteristics, skills, patterns of work organization and social relations, and the differential levels of worker and trade union support for technical change (Batstone, et al, 1987; McLoughlin and Clark, 1988; Bratton, 1992; Clark, 1993; Hogarth, 1993). The analysis of technical change is not limited to Britain either. In Sweden (see, for example, Bansler, 1989; Lowstedt, 1988; Hammarstrom and Lansbury, 1991; Bengtsson, 1992), Finland (Penn, Lilja and Scattergood, 1992) and Denmark (Clausen and Lorentzen, 1993) there have been relatively recent European studies on work organization, the changing nature of employee skills, and the influence of trade unions in the process of technical change. In the early 1980s, much of this research was stimulated by Braverman's publication *Labor and Monopoly Capital* (1974), and the upsurge of interest in the labour process debate that followed in its wake (Thompson, 1983).

Running parallel with the diffusion of microelectronic technology, however, is organizational change. Between 1984 and 1990, the proportion of workplaces experiencing substantial changes in work organization or working practices affecting manual employees increased from 23 per cent in 1984 to 29 per cent in 1990. For non-manual the increase was significantly greater, up from 20 per cent to 41 per cent (Millward *et al.*, 1992, p. 15). Of particular relevance here is the influence of Japanese management concepts. The Japanese manufacturing paradigm is noted for its 'lean production' and uses flexible cellular manufacturing, just-in-time (JIT) and total quality control (TQC) systems of production. Lean production is characterized by organizational and work structures that facilitate flexible working arrangements and employee–management collaboration. Lean production is further characterized by just-in-time inventory, or 'kanban', which eliminates the need for storing large numbers of parts. JIT production has important strategic implications because it enhances the bargaining power of the nodal firm in the supplier network, as well as having HR impacts. Total quality control is the third key element of lean production. The basic concept of TQC is 'production responsibility', which means assigning the primary responsibility for quality to the people at the 'sharp end' of production. When quality control is at the point of production 'fast feedback on defects is natural', and there are also savings on human resources and raw materials (Schonberger, 1982). By the second half of the 1980s the term

'Japanization' was being used by academics to encapsulate some of the organizational changes at a number of British companies (Turnbull, 1986; Oliver and Wilkinson, 1988; Bratton, 1992). Similar arguments underlying the technological debates can be found in the current discourse on Japanization, such as the interplay of flexible cellular work structures, skill levels and autonomy, and changes in the demand for labour.

It is apparent from the various surveys and case studies that technological change is widespread. It is also clear that the process of technological change presents formidable challenges to both line managers and HRM specialists alike. Technical and organizational changes present opportunities for cooperation between managers and workers; any change has also the potential for conflict. Organizational change, in particular, generates most challenges and resistance from workers (Daniel, 1987; Hogarth, 1993). Interestingly, where HRM specialists were involved in technical changes in the workplace, their involvement had a positive impact: 'their involvement was associated with a stronger level of workers' support for the change' (Daniel and Millward, 1993, p. 69).

■ The political context

The political context of human resource management altered radically. The political context is most complex and the most difficult to analyze, both because of its power to shape the nature of the employment relationship and because of its affects on the other contexts. Governmental decisions impinge on most human resource management functions, including selection, training, and rewards. Equally, the government can intervene in the economy to support the level of aggregate demand and thereby change labour market trends. Through the 1980s we have witnessed a fundamental shift in the role played by central government, via general economic management, labour law reform, and in its conception of 'good' human resource and industrial relations management.

In Britain, the Conservative government led by Margaret Thatcher systematically eroded, using a 'step-by-step approach', both the rights of employees and the collective rights of trade unions. The individual employment legislation, or 'floor of rights', established in the 1970s was increasingly viewed by the government as a constraint on enterprise and an obstacle to efficiency and job creation. The Employment Acts of 1980, 1982 and 1988, and the Trade Union Act of 1984, aimed on the one hand to 'deregulate' aspects of individual employment protection and support for collective bargaining. On the other hand, their purpose was to increase the legal regulation of industrial action and trade union government (Lewis, 1986).

In terms of individual employment rights, amendments to the Employment Protection (Consolidation) Act, 1978, reduced unfair dismissal provision. The numbers eligible to apply to the industrial tribunals were reduced by extending the service qualification needed to make an unfair dismissal claim from six months to two years. By the end of the 1980s the changes in legislative intervention were being reflected in legal statistics. The extension of the qualifying period for unfair dismissal was represented by a fall in tribunal applications: in 1987–88 there were only 34 233 applications compared with 41 244 in 1979 (McIlroy, 1991, p. 192). A critical study of the law of unfair dismissal indicates that of those unfair dismissal applications, few were successful at an industrial tribunal; that those who were successful were rarely offered re-instatement or re-engagement; and that the levels of compensation were low (Denham, 1990). In 1986–7, for example, 10 067 cases were heard at tribunals; of these there were only 103 cases of re-instatement or re-engagement, and the median compensation was £1805 (34.6 per cent of the awards did not exceed £999). Denham argues that unfair dismissal law as it stands has given employees a very limited degree of protection and employers can often obtain the dismissals they want. For those workers who are in good health, not pregnant, and in a secure job, the changes in individual employment rights might seem to be of little consequence. However, for those workers in the enlarged peripheral labour market, primarily female, curtailment of employment protection is not inconsequential and has implications for social security (Szyszczak, 1986).

The Government's industrial relations legislation sought to regulate industrial action by, amongst other things, narrowing the definition of a trade dispute in which industrial action is lawful. The phrase 'in contemplation or furtherance of a trade dispute' no longer fulfils the same function as it did prior to the 1982 Employment Act, and as argued: 'It now denies legitimacy to many disputes which are clearly about industrial relations issues' (Simpson, 1986, p. 192). The policy objective of the statutes was designed to deter strikes and to limit their scale, and to regulate the membership, discipline and recruitment policies of unions. According to one industrial relations academic, the legislation has marked 'a radical shift from the consensus underlying "public policy" on industrial relations during most of the past century' (Hyman, 1987, p. 93).

According to the Secretary of State for Employment, the Employment Act 1988 seeks to give 'new rights to trade union members', notably protection from 'unjustified' discipline by union members and officials. The Government justified the statute in the belief that in recent years some British trade unions have meted out harsh treatment to non-striking union members (Gennard *et al.*, 1989). The purpose of the Employment Act 1988 is further to discourage industrial action and reduce the likelihood of 'militant' union leadership (McKendrick, 1988).

The Employment Act 1990 deals with the rights to union membership, the closed shop, unofficial industrial action, dismissal of strikers, and limits of secondary action. Briefly, the Conservative government legislated against the pre-entry closed shop – the workplace where existing union membership was a prerequisite for employment. The 1990 Act gives those refused employment on the grounds that they were not, or refused to become, a member of a union, a right to take the union to an industrial tribunal. Furthermore, the Act removes immunity from all forms of secondary industrial action. Thus, the complicated provisions of Section 17 of the Employment Act 1980, which made some form of secondary action lawful, was removed. As one labour lawyer observed: 'As the 1990s

HRM IN PRACTICE 2.2

Ministers under fire over lax safety laws

by Mary Williams

Union chiefs are preparing to take the Government to court claiming it has failed to fully implement European safety directives.

General union the GMB will lodge a formal complaint with the European Commission next month over the Government's interpretation of health and safety rules due for implementation next year.

If the commission accepts the complaint the Government must change its laws immediately or face the European Court of Justice.

The GMB, which has sought legal advice, believes at least three out of six new laws fail to enforce the requirements of corresponding EC directives adequately.

"These regulations confirm our worst fears. The problem is the attitude in the HSE. They should see themselves as enforcers not compromisers," said GMB general secretary John Edmonds.

"We will be following every legal avenue to change this," he added.

Senior officials at the commission's health and safety unit in Luxembourg agree the Government has failed to implement some aspects of the directives correctly.

The six include a law covering management of health and safety at work, manual handling, computer use, workplace safety, protective clothing, and equipment.

The union cites manual handling regulations as an example of poor implementation. The Government says employers must only prevent risk where it is reasonably practicable.

The GMB claims under European rules risk must be prevented at all costs. It also believes new rules on computer use are inadequate.

The Government says they only apply to employees who use computers regularly but the GMB argues all workstations should reach certain standards.

The union also argues that the EC's health and safety framework directive has not been properly implemented in Britain.

Source: Personnel Today, December 1992. Used with permission.

---

dawned it was clear that on the legislative front at least, the Conservatives had won and the unions had lost' (McIlroy, 1991, p. 190).

For many years Britain was one of a number of advanced capitalist countries most active in promoting the concept of international standards. During the 1980s, however, it is argued that the UK has largely played a negative role in relation to the improvement of international labour standards (O' Higgins, 1986). The continuous period of Conservative government from 1979, first led by Margaret Thatcher and later by John Major, has provided a period of political continuity. The Conservative government's political doctrines and policies have not gone unchallenged, however. The European Community has emerged as an effective political opposition on matters affecting HRM.

The 1991 EC Protocol states that eleven Member States 'wish to continue along the path laid down in the 1989 Social Charter [and] have adopted among themselves an Agreement to this end'. These EC initiatives have important implications for employment law and hence HRM. The European Council of Ministers is authorized, by Article 2, paragraphs 1 and 2, to proceed by qualified majority vote to 'adopt, by means of directives, minimum requirements for gradual implementation' in the following three HRM areas of activity:

- improvement in the working environment to protect workers' health and safety;
- communications and employee participation;
- employment equity (see, for example, Bercusson, 1992).

The UK's rejection of the Maastricht Accord of December 1991 is evidence of the largely negative role played by the UK government on the employment and HRM fronts. The government's refusal to accept the Maastricht Accord was, insists Towers (1992), the product of opportunism and belief that the Social Charter provisions would impose higher labour costs, leading to bankruptcies and job losses. However, UK employers may eventually be forced to accept legislative initiatives on the social dimension which will have important implications for HRM.

■ The social context

Changes in the age, the proportion of the population participating in the labour market, and the demographics of the labour force determine the size and composition of the workforce. The individuals who enter the organization bring with them different attitudes and values about work, parenthood, leisure, notions of 'fairness' and organizational loyalty. It is these external social forces which make up the social context of human resource management.

Demographic changes provide a starting point for analyzing the social context. According to the Office of Population Censuses and Surveys, the population of Britons is estimated to become 56.8 million in 1996. During the 1980s, the general pattern to emerge is that of an ageing population. Since 1951, the number of Britains of pensionable age has risen by over 40 per cent, from 5.5 million to approximately 9 million in 1989, or from just under 14 per cent to nearly 18 per cent of the population. The number of students under the age of 16 has decreased by around 12 per cent since 1971. An ageing population has important implications for HRM functions such as recruitment and selection, training and rewards management.

Changes in the labour force – the number of people in the civilian working population – not only derive from changes in the size and age distribution of the population, but also from the variations in the labour force participation rates. The participation rate represents the labour force expressed as a percentage of the working age population that actually participates in the labour force. In 1987, 50.5 per cent of women aged 16–59 were economically active: among non-married women it was 44.3 per cent, while among married women it was 54.3 per cent.

In both North America and Britain a central issue in debates is the concept of occupational segregation, that is, the gap between the kinds of jobs performed by men and those performed by women. Where men and women perform work 'of the same or broadly similar nature', equal pay for equal work legislation does afford women protection from pay discrimination. But men and women do not generally perform the same or substantially 'like work'; women are concentrated primarily in clerical, semi-skilled factory work and semi-skilled domestic work. For example, women in Britain constituted 77 per cent of clerical, 76 per cent of catering and cleaning, and 67 per cent of the professional and related (education, health and welfare) posts in 1983. Unlike equal pay for the same or like work, the concept of 'equal pay for work of equal value' recognizes that occupational segregation persists and that the concomitant undervaluation of 'women's' work is responsible for a large part of the earning gap (Conway, 1987).

The structure of employment in Britain has also been changing fundamentally since the early 1970s. In Britain, part-time working is the most pervasive form of non-standard employment and in 1988 accounted for almost 20 per cent of total employment and 40 per cent of women's employment. In the 1980s, there was a growth in part-time employment: the proportion of part-time employees went up from 14 to 18 per cent (Millward *et al.*, 1992, p. 18). The rise in part-time contracts is associated with the increased use of part-time employees in the public, newly privatized and private services sectors. Theoretical analysis of the role of the organization in structuring employment, and of the interrelationships between patriarchy and society as a whole is helping to explain the dynamics of labour markets, gender segregation, and inequalities (see, for example, Dex, 1988).

The empirical evidence on the diffusion and significance of labour flexibility, it is argued, further suggests that organizations are not passive agents simply responding to external social forces, but significantly influence the structure of employment itself. The flexible utilization of people dominated much of management thinking in the 1980s, and a European study found a considerable degree of 'convergence' between countries. Functional flexibility has become necessary on economic and technical grounds, and as a result 'all companies have moved in this direction' (Mueller, 1992, p. 202). A whole new vocabulary sprang up around an influential flexibility model developed by Atkinson (1984, 1985), with terms such as 'functional flexibility', 'numerical flexibility' and 'core' and 'peripheral' workers. The reduction of traditional craft demarcation lines with multi-skilled craftsmen, prepared to be deployed on different work stations as production requirements dictate, such as machine operators undertaking routine maintenance jobs or assembly work, is the feature of functional or task flexibility. Those workers on temporary or part-time employment contracts, sub-contracted workers and the self-employed constitute the numerical flexibility.

These arrangements facilitate 'a looser contractual relationship between manager and worker' (Atkinson, 1985, p. 17) or, to put it more bluntly, employers can hire and fire workers as circumstances change. Atkinson's 'flexible firm' model is a variant of the dual labour market approach by making a distinction between 'core' (primary) and 'peripheral' (secondary) groups of workers. The core group are the permanent workers, who will be managers, technicians and skilled manual workers, who receive favourable conditions of employment in return for flexibility and loyalty. The peripheral groups are the workers on 'looser' employment contracts, doing semi-skilled or unskilled jobs which can be easily filled from the external local labour markets. Sub-contracting, self-employment, homeworking, job-sharing and temporary employment have increased substantially (Brown, 1986, p. 161). But part-time employment constitutes the largest element of the flexible workforce, growing from 16 per cent of all jobs in 1971 to 23 per cent of the working population in 1987 (Hakim, 1987, p. 555).

A number of studies have also documented the substantial growth in subcontracting. For example, O'Reilly (1992), drawing on data from Britain and France, provides evidence of how certain 'low grade' permanent jobs in the banking sector are increasingly being threatened by, amongst other practices, the use of subcontracting. Part-time employment and subcontracting has figured prominently in discussions of flexibility in British workplaces. The flexible firm model is controversial. Critics of the model have argued that the notion of core and periphery is confused, circular and value laden, and it fails to mention that the dynamics of the 1980s is undermining the bargaining strength of all workers, including the so-called core (Pollert, 1988). Guest (1991) also argues that, along with employee commitment, the survey data reveals that there is little evidence that companies have embraced flexibility with any enthusiasm.

Culture is a concept that can mean all things to all people. Abercrombie and Warde (1988) use the term 'culture' to delineate the symbolic aspects of human society which include beliefs, customs, conventions, and values. Britain and North America are culturally diverse. Within their borders are many cultures and subcultures formed out of divisions like social class, ethnicity, and gender. In turn, these cultures and subcultures are all locally differentiated. Changing cultural values have an impact on human resource management functions. For example, as the percentage of older workers increases, work values may change: work may not be as central to the lifes of the older employee. Also, changes in traditional gender roles may change participation rates. In the industrial relations arena, the 'consumer culture' promoting individualism may erode working-class customs and solidarity, which would undermine the collectivist culture of trade unions. In addition, it has been argued that while the 1980s saw the politicisation of 'green' issues, one challenge facing organizations in the 1990s will be the reassertion of underlying value systems. Chapman asserts, 'This implies that organizations will need to develop and communicate corporate cultures with which their staff can identify and to which they are willing to ally themselves' (1990, p. 29). Changes in demographics and social values all, to varying degrees, confront the HRM specialist.

■ Summary

The external contexts have considerable implications for HRM policy and practice. The environmental domain influences the structure and functioning of an organization, and in turn, organization decision-makers influence the wider society. Thus, changes in the way an organization's human resources are managed are often a direct response to external pressures. Guest (1987) argues that interest in HRM in North America and in Britain arose as a result of the search for competitive advantage, the decline in trade union power, and changes in the workforce and the nature of work.

The global economy has become more integrated. For HR practitioners, the continuing restructuring of industry in Britain will have a profound effect on competition, and thereby on such HR activities as HR planning, recruitment and selection. Technologically sophisticated processes and equipment, and Japanese-style 'lean' production methods, must not only be seen as a threat, but also as an opportunity to harness new technology and enhance employee empowerment and job satisfaction. The linkage between the external contexts and the search for competitive advantage through employee performance and HRM activities is illustrated by the Devanna *et al.* HRM model, Figure 1.7 (see p. 28).

As far as UK and EC employment law is concerned, the initiatives associated with the Social Charter are likely to encourage senior management to have more regard for HRM. Pay equity laws, for example, have a profound effect on the HRM practitioner in terms of policies and activities. Job evaluation constitutes the foundation of pay equity, and it is critical that HRM professionals ensure that their job evaluation scheme is designed and applied without gender bias (see Chapter 8). The general indication is that the changing social context of HRM is placing more pressure on organizations to pay more attention to their social responsibilities – in particular to be more sensitive to the issues and challenges related to female employees, ethnic minorities and the disabled (Farnham, 1990).

■ Key concepts

- Competitive advantage
- Technological change
- Demographics
- Culture

- Economic context
- Political context
- Occupational segregation
- Organizational change

Discussion questions

1. Describe the major economic challenges facing human resource managers.
2. How have the political developments of the 1980s affected human resource management?
3. Explain the term 'occupational segregation' and its relevance to understanding the labour market.
4. Compare and contrast the impact of government legislation on human resource management in Britain and Canada.

■ Further reading

Curran, J. (1990), 'Re-thinking the Economic Structure: Exploring the Role of the Small Firm and Self-employment in the British Economy', in *Work, Employment and Society in The 1980s: A Decade of Change?*, Special Issue, BSA Publication, May.

Jessop, B., Nielsen, K., Kastendiek, H., Pedersen, O. K. (eds) (1991), *The Politics of Flexibility: Restructuring State and Industry in Britain, Germany and Scandinavia*, Aldershot: Edward Elgar.

Lane, C. (1991) 'Industrial Reorganization in Europe: Patterns of Convergence and Divergence in Germany, France and Britain', *Work, Employment and Society*, Vol. 5, No. 4.

Michie, J. (1992) 'Unlucky 13 for the Economy', *The Observer Sunday*, 5 April, p. 35.

McIlroy, J. (1991), *The Permanent Revolution? Conservative Law and the Trade Unions*, Nottingham: Spokesman.

Overbeck, H. (1990), *Global Capitalism and National Decline*, London: Unwin Hyman.

Urry, J. and Lash, S. (1987), *The End of Organized Capitalism*, Cambridge: Polity Press.

Chapter case study   Oil Tool Engineering faces a changing environment

Oil Tool Engineering was established in West Yorkshire in 1950, and four years later became part of Oil Tool Incorporated, an American multinational company engaged in the design, manufacture, and marketing of machinery used at the well-head in drilling for the production of oil and gas, both onshore and offshore. The company, whose corporate headquarters are in Houston, Texas, USA, has other manufacturing establishments in Scotland, Germany, France, and Mexico, and employs 4500 people throughout the world.

Oil Tool Engineering dominated the oil extraction industry for nearly forty years. After growth and continual profits things started to go wrong in 1985. Low productivity, rising production costs, a decline in oil-field exploration, and new competitors entering the industry, culminated in a £6 million loss for the West Yorkshire plant. At this point the senior management decided to bring in an outside consultancy firm, Mercury Engineers Inc.

Bill Dorfman, the plant manager, called a meeting with his senior management team and the consultants. Dorfman started the discussion: 'We all know that we have considerable autonomy from the corporate management in Texas. That means we have the task of turning this plant around. If we fail the plant will close. This is the company's biggest manufacturing operation in the world. But, it would only be a question of months before another operation could be bigger. Headquarters have moth-balled several of our operations and the French and German plants could be 'geared-up' to our size within twelve months. What has gone wrong and how do we turn this plant around?', he asked.

Yvonne Turner, the marketing manager, began: 'Our sales have fallen in the Middle East because our customers want equipment that is lighter and more mobile. The design and the materials of our block-tree valve haven't changed for ten years.' She went on: 'The Japanese are engineering equipment that is made with alloy metals and is lighter, stronger and has a microprocessor-based control system.'

Doug Meyer, the manufacturing manager, jumped in: 'Don't blame us. If the market is changing out there, it's marketing's job to tell us and keep us informed. It's not just our manufacturing practices, we all know our prices are higher because of sterling's high exchange rate. And besides,' he said angrily, 'we lost that last Middle East order because the government refused to give us an export license. Whether there is a war or not, if we don't sell them the machinery, you can be damn sure, somebody else will. We ought to get the local MP to have a word with the bureaucrats in the Board of Trade.'

At this point, Wendy Seely, the human resource manager, intervened in the discussion: 'Well, I don't know whether we can blame everything on the government in London. I do know, however, that EC Directives on pay equity and recent court decisions on retirement and pensions will push our labour costs up. We must find ways to reduce labour costs and improve quality standards,' she said.

'We can't achieve high quality standards,' retorted Doug Miller, 'because your department stopped training apprentices and we can't find the quality we need using sub-contractors.'

Feeling defensive, Wendy Seely argued, 'We ended the training programme for apprentices because the local college closed the first year apprentice course, as part of its own cost-saving measures. You can't blame my department for that.'

Bill Dorfman decided to bring the meeting to a close: 'Would each department address the issues discussed this morning? We shall meet in seven days and see whether there is a consensus on the way forward. Remember we have to be competitive to survive. We have to quit whining and save this plant,' he said.

(*Source*: Adapted from 'The Drilling Machine Company: Japanization in Small-batch Production', in Bratton, J. (1992), *Japanization at Work*, London: Macmillan.

Question

Assume you are a member of the consultancy team. Prepare a report outlining the contextual changes affecting Oil Tool Engineering. What factors from the chapter can help explain what happened to this company? How can HRM help solve some of the problems?

■ References

1. *The Economist* (1980), 'Chrysler's up against the wall – and the shooting's started', 26 April, p. 53.
2. *The Economist* (1981), 'The industrial world's workers get the sack for Christmas', 12 December, p. 75.
3. Barry Curnow (1989), 'Recruit, retrain, retain: personnel management and the three Rs', *Personnel management*, November, p. 40.

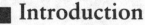

CHAPTER 3

Restructuring Work: Fordism and Post-Fordism

The one man [*sic*], one machine principle has gone completely out of the door.[1]

Workers in each cell see the manufacture of whatever they are making . . . from the assembly of components stage to completion. They are expected to be far more flexible, with some workers operating five or six machines rather than perhaps two under the old system. They are also expected to take on more responsibility.[2]

Unlike workers in many North American plants, they're also expected to think.[3]

■ Chapter outline

Introduction
The nature of work
Job design
Scientific management
Human relations movement
Job redesign movement
Japanese management
Summary

Chapter objectives
After studying this chapter, you should be able to: 1. Explain the meaning of the term 'work'.   2. Define job design and describe specific job design strategies.   3. Understand the theoretical arguments underpinning current job design practices.

■ Introduction

Since the early 1980s significant numbers of European and North American workers have experienced profound modifications in the way their paid work activities are organized. This reflects the fact that capitalist societies are dynamic and ever-changing in response to innovation and to external market pressures. Central to the debate about the changes in work practices is the perceived need amongst managers, trade unionists, politicians, journalists and academics for advanced capitalist economies to gain a competitive advantage in the face of developments in technology, materials, production processes, and the globalization of markets.

Running parallel with these changes in work structures has been a renaissance of interest amongst academics in the field of technological change and job design. But when academic observers refer to a 'degradation of work' or the 'enrichment of work', what theoretical perspectives are the authors employing? Work can be studied from two broad academic perspectives: psychological and sociological. A sociological perspective of work is concerned with the broader contextual and structural factors affecting peoples' experience of work. An important theme for sociologists is that of the *division of labour*, which refers to the way in which people in society can specialize in doing particular types of work. At the level of the organization, the internal division of labour is a basis of efficiency and control of workers. At society level, the division of labour has produced occupational structure: professional, management, clerical, skilled and unskilled manual occupations. Another important topic within the sociology of work is that of *work-based inequalities* and, within this, the social division of labour that reflects that contemporary society allocates particular work to men and to women (Littler and Salaman, 1984; Thompson, 1989).

A psychological study of people at work attempts to understand *individual* behaviour, and there is a large body of literature covering the academic field of 'Organizational Behaviour', concerned with managerial problems of motivation, job satisfaction, work stress, job design, and any other factor relevant to working conditions that could impede efficient work performance. An early theory of individual work behaviour attempted to explain the nature of motivation in terms of the types of needs that people experience (Maslow, 1954). Subsequent theoretical contributions from behavioural scientists, such as McGregor's Theory X and Y (1960), Herzberg's motivation–hygiene theory (1966), and Vroom's expectancy motivation theory (1964), have practical implications for the way organization controllers design work structures and rewards. More recently, a model has been put forward that links core characteristics of work and the critical psychological processes acting on individuals and their immediate work groups (Hackman and Oldham, 1976).

This chapter is largely an explanation of job design strategies, as seen by sociologists and industrial psychologists researching the links between motivation, job satisfaction and work design. The chapter examines the meaning of work in contemporary western society. The broader context of work should be seen as providing essential background knowledge for human resource practitioners concerned with current job-design techniques. The chapter then proceeds to discuss the links between the design of work and the HRM cycle before critically evaluating alternative job design strategies including Taylorism, post-Fordism, flexible specialization, and Japanization of work.

■ The nature of work

When we refer to the term 'work', what do we mean? Filling in the forms for a student grant is not seen as work, but filling in forms is part of a clerical worker's job. Similarly, when a mature student looks after her or his own child that is not seen as work, but if she or he employs a child minder to look after the child, that is paid work. We can begin to get a sense of what this question is about and how society views work by exploring the following definition of work:

> Work refers to physical and mental activity that is carried out at a particular place and time, according to instructions, in return for money.

This definition draws attention to some central features of work. First, the notion of 'physical and mental' obviously suggests that the activities of a construction worker or a computer systems analyst are deemed to be work. Secondly, the tendency for the activity to be away from our home and at set time periods of the day or night, 'place and time', locates work within a social context. Thirdly, the social context also includes the social relations under which the activity is performed. When a mother or father cooks the dinner for the family, the actual content of the activity is similar to that performed by a cook employed by a hospital to prepare meals for patients. But the social relations in which the activity occurs are quite distinct. The hospital cook has more in common with the factory worker or office workers because their activities are governed by rules and regulations – 'instructions' from the employer or the employer's agent. Clearly then, it is not the nature of the activity that determines whether it is considered 'work', but rather the social relations in which the activity is embedded (Pahl, 1988). Fourthly, in return for physical effort and/or mental application, fatigue, and loss of personal autonomy, the worker receives a mix of rewards, including 'money', status, and intrinsic satisfaction. Watson (1986) refers to this mix of inputs (physical and mental activities etc.) and outputs (rewards) as the 'implicit contract' between the employer and the employee.

Although this definition helps us to identify key features of the employment relationship, it is too narrow and restrictive. First, there are all the activities, both physical and mental, that do not bring in money. Such activities can be exhilarating or exhausting; they may involve voluntary work for the Citizen's Advice Bureau or may involve the most demanding work outside paid employment, child care. Again, the same activities – advising people on their legal rights and being paid for it or being employed in a nursery – would all count as 'work' because of the social relations and the monetary reward. Secondly, it is clear that the rewards, satisfaction and hazards of work are distributed highly unequally. Contemporary society rewards employees according to the kind of people they are and the kind of work they do. Men receive more money than women. For instance, the historical gap between the income of men and women has resulted in women manual workers in Britain earning 62 per cent as much as men in similar work. Between 1979 and 1990 average earnings for all full-time workers increased by 185 per cent. However, different occupations saw significantly different increases in earnings. Accountants, for example, saw their earnings increase by 237 per cent, while bus and coach drivers received a 134 per cent increase.[4] Work can also be dangerous and unhealthy, but the hazards are not distributed evenly. Despite the publicity surrounding managerial stress, the realities of the distribution of work-related hazards show that they are most prevalent among manual workers. In 1988–9, Health and Safety Executive (HSE) figures show that 514 fatal injuries and 18 933 major injuries to workers were reported.[5] Furthermore, it has been argued that this unequal distribution of work-related accidents represents the systematic outcome of values and economic pressures (Littler and Salaman, 1984).

Evidently paid work is affected by global competition, technology, managerial theories and practices, and much else besides. The nature of work affects human resource management activities. For example, the pay an employee receives is related to social attitudes and traditions rather than the actual content of the activity; pay determination requires an understanding of the social division of labour, and gender divisions of labour in particular (Pahl, 1988). Management decides how the tasks are divided into various jobs, and how they relate to other tasks and other jobs, contingent upon different modes of production and technology. Decisions are also made about control systems, the ratio of supervisors to supervised, the training of workers, and the nature of the reward system. Thus HRM is both affected by and profoundly affects an individual's experience of work. Clearly, the way work is designed impacts both on the effectiveness of the organization and the experience and motivation of the individual and work group. It is this process of job design which we now consider.

■ Job design

The need to harness human resources in innovatory ways to give organizations a competitive advantage has focused attention on the question of job design. It is defined as:

> The process of combining tasks and responsibilities to form complete jobs and the relationships of jobs in the organization.

■ Job design and the HRM cycle

Job design is related very closely to key elements of the HRM cycle: selection, development, and rewards. Job design is basic to the **selection** function. Clearly, a company that produces small-batch, high value-added products using skilled manual labour will have different recruitment and selection priorities than an organization that specializes in large-batch production using dedicated machines operated by unskilled operators. Job design also affects the **HR development**. Specifically, any change to work patterns will require some form of systematic training. If an organization chooses either to fragment or combine tasks, alternative **reward systems** may have to be designed. For example, a pay-for-output system may be an obstacle to labour flexibility.

■ Early developments

Innovations in the way work is designed have interested academics and managers for centuries. Adam Smith (1723–90), for example, the founder of modern economics, studied the newly emerging industrial division of labour in eighteenth-century England. For Smith, the separation of manual tasks was central to his theory of economic growth. Smith argued that the division of labour leads to an improvement of economic growth in three ways: output per worker increases because of enhanced dexterity; work preparation and changeover time is reduced; specialization stimulates the invention of new machinery. In his book, *The Wealth of Nations*, Smith describes the manufacture of pins and gives an early example of job design:

> Man draws out the wire; another straights it; a third cuts it; a fourth points it; a fifth grinds it at the top for receiving the head . . . the important business of making a pin is, in this manner, divided into eighteen distinct operations. (*The Wealth of Nations* (1776), Penguin, 1982, p. 109)

In the nineteenth century, Charles Babbage also pointed out that the division of labour gave the employer a further advantage: by simplifying tasks and allocating the fragmented tasks to unskilled workers, the employer may pay a lower wage: 'in a society based upon the purchase and sale of labour power, dividing the craft cheapens its individual parts' (Braverman, 1974, p. 80).

The emergence of industrial division of labour gave rise to more radical studies of job design. Karl Marx (1818–83) argued that the new work patterns constituted a form of systematic exploitation, and that workers are alienated from the product of their labour because of capitalist employment relations and the loss of autonomy at work: 'factory work does away with the many-sided play of the muscles, and confiscates every atom of freedom, both in bodily and intellectual activity' (quoted in T. Nichols (ed.), *Capital and Labour*, Fontana, 1980, p. 69).

Since the beginning of the twentieth century, interest in job design has intensified because of the writings of Frederick Taylor (1856–1915) on 'scientific management'. Between 1908 and 1929, Henry Ford developed the principles of Taylorism, but went further and developed new work structures based on the flow-line principle of assembly work. The Human Relations Movement emerged in the 1920s and drew attention to the effect of work groups on output. In the late 1960s, concern about declining productivity and the disadvantages of scientific management techniques led to the Job Redesign Movement. Current interest and discourse on job design centres around Japanese management. This deals with more than job design it emphasises management style, skill and values and aims to incorporate job design into the organization's employment strategy.

■ Scientific management

The scientific management movement was pioneered by the American, Frederick W. Taylor. This approach to job design, referred to as Taylorism, was also influenced by Henry L. Gantt (1861–1919) and Frank B. Gilbreth (1868–1924). Taylor developed his ideas on employee motivation and job design techniques at the Midvale Steel Company in Pennsylvania, where he rose to the position of shop superintendent. Littler has argued that 'Taylorism was both a system of ideological assertions and a set of management practices' (1982, p. 51). Taylor was appalled by what he regarded as inefficient working practices and the tendency of workers not to put in a full day's work – what Taylor called 'natural soldering'. He saw workers who do manual work to be motivated by money, the 'greedy robot', and to be too stupid to develop the 'one best way' of doing a task. The role of management was to analyse scientifically all the tasks to be done and then to design jobs to eliminate time and motion waste.

Taylor's approach to job design was based on five main principles:

1. Maximum job fragmentation
2. The divorce of planning and doing
3. The divorce of 'direct' and 'indirect' labour
4. Minimization of skill requirements and job-learning time
5. The reduction of material handling to a minimum.

The centrepiece of scientific management was the separation of tasks into their simplest constituent elements (first principle). Most manual workers were sinful and stupid, and therefore all decision-making functions had to be removed from their hands (second principle). All preparation and servicing tasks should be taken away from the skilled worker, and performed by unskilled and cheaper labour (third principle). According to Littler this is the Taylorist equivalent of the Babbage Principle and is an essential element of more work intensification (1982, p. 51). Minimizing skill requirements to perform a task reduces labour's control over the labour process (fourth principle). Management should ensure that the configuration of machines minimizes the movement of people and materials to eliminate time (fifth principle). Taylor's approach to job design, argues Littler, embodies 'a dynamic of deskilling' and offers to organizations 'new structures of control' (1982, p. 52).

Some writers argue that Taylorism was a relatively short-lived phenomenon which died in the economic depression in the 1930s. Rose argues that scientific management did not appeal to most employers: 'Some Taylorians invested a great effort to gain its acceptance among American employers but largely failed' (1988, p. 56). This view underestimates the diffusion and influence of Taylor's principles on job designers. In contrast to Rose, Braverman argues that: 'the popular notion that Taylorism has been "superseded" by later schools of "human relations", that it "failed" . . . represents a woeful misreading of the actual dynamics of the development of management' (1974, pp. 86–7). Similarly, Littler and Salaman have argued that: 'In general the direct and indirect influence of Taylorism on factory jobs has been extensive, so that in Britain job design and technology design have become imbued with neo-Taylorism' (1984, p. 73).

■ Fordism

Henry Ford applied the major principles of Taylorism but also installed specialised machines and perfected the flow-line principle of assembly work. This kind of job design has come to be called, not surprisingly, Fordism. The classical assembly line principle should be examined as a technology of control of employees, and as a job design to increase labour productivity: both job fragmentation and short task-cycle times are accelerated. Fordism is also characterized by two other essential features: the introduction of an interlinking system of conveyor lines that feed components to different work stations to be worked on, and second, the standardization of commodities to gain economies of scale. Fordism established the long-term principle of mass production of standardized commodities at a reduced cost (Coriat, 1980).

The speed of work on the assembly line is determined through the technology itself, not through a series of instructions. Management control of the work process was enhanced also by detailed time and motion study inaugurated by Taylor. Work study engineers attempted to discover the shortest possible task-cycle time. Henry Ford's concept of people management was simple: 'The idea is that man . . . must have every second necessary but not a single unnecessary second' (Ford, 1922, quoted in Huw Beynon, *Working for Ford*, Pelican, 1984, p. 33). Recording job-times meant that managers could monitor more closely subordinate effort-levels and performance. Task measurement, therefore, acted as the basis of a new structure of control (Littler, 1982, p. 88).

Ford's production system was not without its problems however. Workers found the repetitive work boring and unchallenging. Job dissatisfaction was expressed in high rates of absenteeism and turnover. For example, in 1913 Ford required about 13 500 workers to operate his factories at any one time, and in that year alone the turnover was more than 50 000 workers (Beynon, 1984, p. 33). The management techniques developed by Ford in response to these human resource problems serve further to differentiate Fordism from Taylorism ((Littler and Salaman, 1984). Ford introduced the Five Dollar Day – double the pay and shorter hours for those who qualified. Benefits depended on a factory worker's lifestyle being deemed satisfactory and this included abstaining from alcohol. Ford's style of paternalism attempted to inculcate new social habits, as well as new labour habits, which would facilitate job performance. Taylorism and Fordism became the predominant approach to job design in vehicle and electrical engineering – the large-batch production industries – in USA, Canada, and Britain.

As a job design and labour management strategy, scientific management and Fordist principles had limitations even when they were accepted by the work-force. First, work simplification led to boredom and dissatisfaction and tended to encourage an adversarial industrial relations climate. Secondly, Taylor-style job design techniques carry control and co-ordination costs. With extended specialization, indirect labour costs increase as the organization employs increasing numbers of production planners, controllers, supervisors and inspectors. The economies of extended division of labour tend to be offset by the dis-economies of management control structures. Thirdly, there are what might be called co-operation costs. Taylorism increases management's control over the quantity and quality of workers' performance; however, as a result, there are increased frustration and dissatisfaction leading to a withdrawal of commitment on the part of the worker. Quality control can become a major problem for management. The relationship between controller and controlled can so deteriorate as to result in a further increase in organizational control. The principles of Taylorism and Fordism reveal a basic paradox 'that the tighter the control of labour power, the more control is needed' (Littler and Salaman, 1984, pp. 36–7; see also Huczynski and Buchanan, 1991, p. 307).

The adverse reactions to extreme division of labour led to the development of new approaches to job design which attempted to address these problems. The human relations movement began to shift managers' attention to the perceived needs of workers.

■ Human relations movement

The human relations movement emphasized the fact that job design had to consider the psychological and social aspects of work. The movement grew out of the Hawthorn experiments conducted by Elto Mayo in the 1920s. Mayo set up an experiment in the relay assembly room at the Hawthorn Works in Chicago that was designed to test the effects on productivity of variations in working conditions (lighting, temperature, ventilation).

The Hawthorn research team found no clear relationship between any of these factors and productivity. The researchers then developed, *ex post facto*, concepts which might explain the factors affecting worker motivation. They concluded that workers are motivated by more than just economic incentives and the work environment: recognition and social cohesion are important too. The message for management was also quite clear: rather than depending on management controls and financial incentives, it needed to influence the work group by cultivating a climate which met the social needs of workers.

The human relations movement advocated various techniques such as worker participation and non-authoritarian first line supervisors, which, it was thought, would promote a climate of good human relations in which the quantity and quality needs of management could be met.

Criticism of the human relations approach to job design were made by numerous writers. They charged managerial bias and that the human relations movement tended to play down the basic economic conflict of interest between the employer and employee. Critics also pointed out that when the techniques were tested, it became apparent that workers did not inevitably respond as predicted. Finally, the human relations approach is criticised because it neglects wider socio-economic factors (Thompson, 1989). Despite the criticisms, the human relations approach to job design began to have some impact on management practices in the post-Second World War environment of full employment. Running parallel with the human relations school of thought came newer ideas about work which led to the emergence of a job redesign movement.

■ Job redesign movement

During the 1960s and early 1970s, job design was guided by what Rose (1985, p. 200) refers to as the neo-human relations school (Maslow, 1954; McGregor, 1960; Herzberg, 1966) and the wider-based Quality of Working Life (QWL) Movement. The neo-human relations approach to job design emphasized the fulfilment of social needs by recomposing fragmented jobs. The Quality of Working Life Movement can be traced back to the publication of two reports: the 'Work in America' report (1973) and the British report 'on the Quality of Working life' (Wilson, 1973).

Littler and Salaman (1984) put forward five principles of 'good' job design which typify the QWL movement's challenge to the principles of scientific management. First, there is the principle of closure, whereby the scope of the job is such that it includes all the tasks to complete a product or process, thus satisfying the social need of achievement. Second, there is the incorporation of control and monitoring tasks, whereby the individual or group assume responsibility for quality control. Third, there is task variety whereby the worker acquires a range of different skills so that job flexibility is possible. Fourth, there is self regulation of the speed of work. Fifth, there is a job structure that permits some social interaction and a degree of cooperation among workers. In the late 1970s, competitive pressures compelled an increasing number of Western companies to re-assess their job design strategies. Although several writers (for example Kelly, 1985) have pointed out that the recent developments in job design cannot all be grouped together, it is possible to identify three broad types: job enrichment, reorganization of assembly lines, and Japanese-style job design. The following sections consider each of these in turn.

■ Job enrichment

The term 'job enrichment' refers to a number of different processes of rotating, enlarging, and aggregating tasks. An early example of this process was the use of job rotation. This involves the periodic shifting of a worker from one work-simplified task to another (Figure 3.1). The advantage of job rotation, it was argued, is that it reduces the boredom and monotony of doing one simplified task, through diversifying the worker's activities (Robbins, 1989).

An alternative approach to job redesign was the horizontal expansion of tasks, referred to as job enlargement (Figure 3.2). For instance, instead of only grilling hamburgers, a griller's job could be enlarged to include mixing the meat for the burger or preparing a side salad to accompany the order. With a larger number of tasks per worker, the time cycle of work increases, thus reducing repetition and monotony.

A later and more sophisticated effort to address the limits of Taylorism and Fordism was the vertical expansion of jobs, often referred to in Organizational Behaviour textbooks as job enrichment. This approach takes some of the authority from supervisors and adds it to the job (Figure 3.3). Increased vertical scope gives the worker additional responsibilities, including planning and quality control. For instance, the fast-food worker from our previous example might be expected not only to grill the burgers and prepare the salad, but also to order the produce from the wholesaler and inspect the food on delivery for quality. The Hackman and Oldham (1976) model of job enrichment is an influential approach to job design. This model suggests that five core job characteristics result in the worker experiencing three favourable psychological

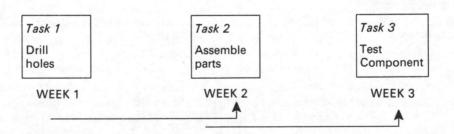

Figure 3.1   Example of job rotation

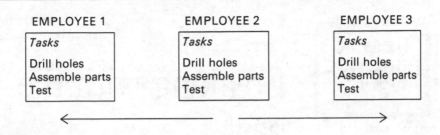

Figure 3.2   Example of job enlargement

states; these, in turn, lead to positive outcomes. The five core job character-istics are defined as:

1. *Skill variety:* the degree to which the job requires a variety of different activities in carrying out the work, requiring the use a number of the worker's skills and talents.
2. *Task identity:* the degree to which the job requires completion of a 'whole' and identifiable piece of work.
3. *Task significance:* the degree to which the job has a substantial impact on the lives or work of other people.
4. *Autonomy:* the degree to which the job provides substantial freedom, independence, and discretion to the worker in scheduling the work and in determining the procedures to be used in carrying it out.
5. *Feedback:* the degree to which the worker possesses information of the actual results of her or his performance.

For example, a chef/manager of a small restaurant would have a job high on skill variety (requiring all the skills of cooking, plus business skills of keeping

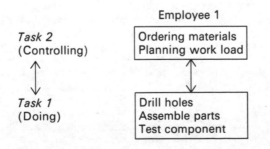

Figure 3.3   Example of job enrichment

HRM IN PRACTICE 3.1

Breaking with the past

The motor industry is not what it used to be. Inter-union rivalry and rigid demarcation lines and a readiness to resort to strike action are giving way to single-union agreements and more flexible working practices.

Typifying the industry's changing face is a new company making body panels for Jaguar cars. Venture Pressings.

The new company prides itself on being at the leading edge of technological innovation.

It is the first press shop in the UK to install Comau inter-press robots.

In its approach to personnel management, the company claims to be equally innovative. "Human resource management is seen as the key to creating the conditions that will make Venture Pressing a success," says human resource manager Tony O'Leary.

One innovation was to sign a single-union agreement with the general workers' union, GMB.

The collective agreement is heavily influenced – even in its wording – by the 1985 agreement between Nissan and the Amalgamated Engineering Union. It gives sole recognition to the GMB and provides for a company to be set up as a forum for discussion and consultation on company business.

Other key clauses in the agreement commit employees to complete flexibility and mobility.

However, in seeking to ensure industrial peace. Venture Pressings is not relying solely on its agreement with the GMB. The company's selection procedures are also directed to the same ends.

"We do everything we possibly can to ensure that the people we employ are committed to the same aims and objectives as we are," says O'Leary.

An ambitious training programme, supported by an unusually large training budget amounting this year to around 5 per cent of the payroll, also plays a part in strengthening workers commitment to the company's aims, as well as developing their skills.

New employees are given the opportunity to acquire new skills and are rewarded for doing so. Progression through 10 incremental points in each of four salary bands is determined by skill acquisition, and individuals' performance on a modular training programme is monitored by way of development plans that are discussed twice a year with their team leaders.

Multi-skilling and flexible working practices have allowed the company to recruit a workforce significantly smaller than that envisaged by the original project team.

Closely tied to flexibility is Venture Pressings' emphasis on teamwork. Production staff are divided into teams or 'cells' consisting of around 40 employees and headed by a team leader. Although cell members have specialist skills, they also have broader responsibilities and are expected to turn their hands to a range of tasks, even when this involves skilled craftsmen taking on unskilled or semi-skilled work.

Where a particular area of expertise found in one cell is needed by another, team leaders negotiate ways of sharing this expertise.

Effective communication is crucial to the success of the cellular system, and as well as taking part in weekly meetings to discuss their own work, the cell's and that of the company generally, workers also come in about 10 minutes before the start of each working day for further discussions.

All in all, Venture Pressings looks set to succeed in its avowed aim of breaking with the past. If it does, the odds are that other companies in which Ford of Europe has a stake will adopt similar personnel policies.

Source: Personnel Management Plus, November 1990. Used with permission.

accounts, etc.), high on task identity (starting with raw ingredients and ending with appetizing meals), high on task significance (feeling that the meals brought pleasure to the customers), high on autonomy (decides the suppliers and the menus), and high on feedback (visits the customers after they have finished their meals). In contrast, a person working for a fast-food chain grilling hamburgers would probably have a job low on skill variety (doing nothing but grilling hamburgers throughout the shift), low on task identity (simply grilling burgers, seldom preparing other food), low on task significance (not feeling that the cooking makes much of a difference when the burger is to be covered in tomato ketchup), low on autonomy (grills the burgers according to a routine, highly specified procedure), and low on feedback (receives few comments from either co-workers or customers).

The model suggests the more that a job possesses the five core job characteristics, the greater the motivating potential of the job. The existence of 'moderators' – knowledge and skills, growth need strength, context satisfactions – explains why jobs theoretically high in motivating potential will not automatically generate high levels of motivation and satisfaction for all workers. This means that employees with a low growth need are less likely to experience a positive outcome when their job is enriched (Figure 3.4). The job characteristics model has been tested by theorists and, according to Robbins, 'most of the evidence supports the theory' (1989, p. 210).

A more critical and ideological evaluation of job enrichment has been offered by some theorists. Bosquet, for example, argues that modern management is being forced by labour problems to question the wisdom of extreme division of labour and factory 'despotism'. Job enrichment 'spells the end of authority and despotic power for bosses great and small'; in turn, this should lead workers liberated from boring jobs to demand total emancipation (Bosquet, 1980, p. 378). An influential study by Friedman (1977) argues that although job enrichment techniques may increase job satisfaction and commitment, the key focus remains managerial control. He maintains that job design strategies such as job enrichment result in individual or groups of workers being given a wider measure of discretion over their work with a minimum of supervision, and this 'responsible autonomy' strategy is a means of maintaining and augmenting managerial authority over workers (Friedman, 1977, p. 265) or a 'tool of self-discipline' (Coriat, 1980, p. 40) over workers. One of the most penetrating critiques of job redesign techniques is offered by Thompson (1989). Drawing upon the contributions from various theorists and empirical evidence, he argues that many job enrichment schemes 'offer little or nothing that is new, and are often disguised forms of intensified [managerial] control' (1989, p. 141). By the early 1970s, over 200 factories in the USA and Europe had applied job enrichment schemes, reports Bosquet (1980).

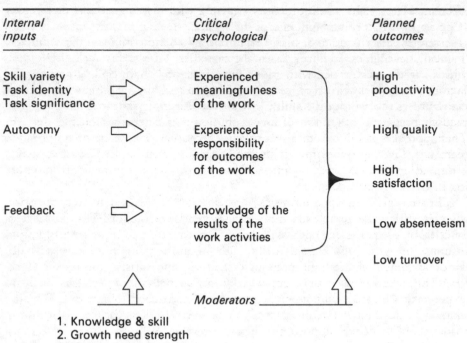

Internal inputs	Critical psychological	Planned outcomes

Skill variety
Task identity
Task significance ⇨ Experienced
meaningfulness
of the work

Autonomy ⇨ Experienced
responsibility
for outcomes
of the work

Feedback ⇨ Knowledge of the
results of the
work activities

High
productivity

High quality

High
satisfaction

Low absenteeism

Low turnover

⇧ _____ *Moderators* _____ ⇧

1. Knowledge & skill
2. Growth need strength
3. 'Context' satisfactions

Figure 3.4   The job characteristics model

Source: Adapted from J. R Hackman and G. R. Oldham, *Work Redesign*, Addison-Wesley
Publishers, 1980.

■ The reorganization of assembly lines

This type of job design change has been associated with increased product
differentiation in highly competitive consumer industries and unstable labour
relations (Coriot, 1980). The Fordist model of production is product-specific,
involving specialized machinery and labour which is not easily transferable. In
contrast, new assembly line arrangements were introduced to increase labour
productivity (Coriot, 1980) and to create more flexible work structures in order
to accommodate more rapid product changes. These redesigned assembly lines
consist of buffer inventories between distinct work stations and grouping all
automatic operations together so that small groups of workers are de-coupled
from the machine pace by the buffer. Compared to the one worker, one job, one
assembly line model, this procedure allows for increased capacity utilization
because of greater flexibility , the elimination of some jobs and the reduction of

indirect labour – the abolition of relief people and 'quality control' inspectors (Coriat, 1980; Littler and Salaman, 1982, p. 82).

Assembly lines were redesigned by the introduction of group technology. Typically, machines and workers are grouped to form a logical 'whole task' which can be performed with minimum interference. Machine tools on the factory floor or desks in an office are reorganized so that they are grouped not on the basis of their doing similar work (for example, drilling or purchase requisition), but on the basis of a contribution to a certain product or service. This approach to job design also explicitly recognizes the value of cooperative team work, group problem-solving, and peer or 'clan' control. In the 1970s, group technology was tried in large-batch industries, such as vehicle manufacturing in Germany and Sweden.

More recently, cheaper information technology based on microprocessors, together with more flexible machine tools, has encouraged the diffusion of group or cellular technology in both large-batch and small-batch manufacturing. For instance, one study reported that some 300 companies in the USA and Canada have experimented with autonomous or self-managed work teams. 'HRM IN PRACTICE 3.2' (p. 72) is an example of self-managed teams in a British company.

Volvo introduced group technology and self-managed work teams at a new plant in Uddevalla, Sweden, in 1987. Management avoided the classic problems associated with work cycles of only one or two minutes on conventional assembly lines by employing teams of seven to ten manual workers. Each team works in one area and assembles four cars per shift. Group members are trained to be flexible so they carry out job-enlarged tasks, working an average of three hours before repeating the same task.

The new work arrangements at Volvo were introduced to improve productivity and quality. The president of Volvo Car Corp., Roger Holtback, is reported as saying the company did not adopt such job design philosophy to make workers happy or because 'we are nice guys; the new plant produces cars with fewer hours of labour and better quality than its three other Swedish plants' (Kapstein and Hoerr, *Business Week*, August, 1989).

Various terms are used to describe these new developments in job design – 'flexible specialization', 'neo-Fordism', and 'post-Fordism'. All imply slightly different scenarios, but each identifies a transition away from traditional Taylorist and Fordist job design principles to a more flexible and less dehumanizing way of working. The ideal-typical characteristics of the two approaches to job design are listed in Figure 3.5. In recent years, there has been a surge of interest in job design techniques developed by Japanese managers.

■ Japanese-style job design

The Japanese approach to production and people management, and the apparent diffusion of such practices outside Japan, has attracted considerable attention from academics, students and managers. This interest in Japanese management

Toyota's Derby novices on the Kentucky track

The big difference between the British and Japanese, according to Toyota UK's head of human resources, Bryan Jackson, is that employees here ask five times as many questions. But the culture gap has had little influence on the company's new operation near Derby, where the first Carena E car rolled off the line in December.

The Toyota Production System has been transplanted from Japan with only a few adaptations, along with job structure and team-working approach. Among changes, the plant lay-out has been improved, and there is a slightly different version of 'just-in-time' to take account of a more widely dispersed supplier base.

The Derby approach has also been influenced by Toyota's plant in Kentucky.

But the Japanese approach does not mean the Burnaston factory was established by thoughtlessly following a set of rules laid down in Tokyo. In order to successfully make the transplant, the UK management team had to decide what type of person it wanted to employ, how to find them and how it would equip those people to work in the Japanese style.

Jackson devised a recruitment and training system which has gone beyond what Toyota has done in the past.

Assessment centre

So far nearly 1,400 people have been taken on, and another 600 will start this year. Each potential employee is subjected to more than 10 hours of tests and interviews, including a four-hour assessment centre and, once taken on, at least six weeks' training in each task.

The recruitment policy was rooted in an almost obsessive search after objectivity because of a desire to hire the type of personality with the set of attitudes that would fit into the Toyota way of working.

Everything is geared to continuous improvement – what the Japanese call *Kaizen*.

Employees – known as 'members' – are divided into groups of about 25, headed by group leaders and sub-divided into teams of around four of five with team leaders. Each group normally meets two or three times a day: first thing in the morning, mid-morning and mid-afternoon, each time for five or 10 minutes, to discuss problems and ideas. Anyone can pull a cord or push a button to call over their team leader if there is a problem, and the line will stop if it cannot be resolved in seconds.

The workforce is consulted over virtually every decision and problems are tackled at team and group level – in 1991 there were 40 suggestions from each Toyota employee in Japan and 90 per cent of them were adopted. "We don't have people say they can't do it, in the sense of 'won't do it'; only in order to ask for help because they haven't got the skill."

It follows that Toyota are looking for people who enjoyed working in teams, who were "capable of and desiring to use their minds, able and willing to learn and who felt they wanted to be associated with a new way of doing things". They were not looking for skills or qualifications.

This resulted in a highly disparate workforce, many of whom had never even seen the inside of a car factory. "We've got nurses, supermarket check-out operators, unemployed miners, you name it," says Jackson. Hence the need for even more extensive training than usual.

A by-product of this approach has been an opening-up of recruitment and promotion chances for women and ethnic minority and disabled employees, putting Toyota in the first division in the field of equal opportunities, even if it has yet to win the cup.

Twelve per cent of employees are women – about the proportion of women in the workforce locally – and, more surprisingly, 7 to 8 per cent of production workers are female. This is extraordinary high for a car company. Some of the women are team leaders and group leaders with men reporting to them – another unusual feature in the sector.

So far, registered disabled people make up 1 per cent of the workforce.

For its efforts, Toyota has won one of two awards by the Derbyshire Committee for the Employment of People with Disabilities this month.

Training

UK and DDI, which is used during the testing and orientation session alongside more traditional tests for numerical ability and a job-fit inventory. The aim of using video was to overcome some of the barriers to equality thrown up by pencil-and-paper tests.

"We wanted to minimise discrimination: observation is easier than reading a foreign language," commented Jackson.

Toyota has put the same thoroughness into training as it has into recruitment. It spent £7.2 million and 100 'man years' on off-the-job training before production started.

It uses a cascade approach. The company took 350 group and team leaders on a five-week round trip to Japan, Kentucky and a third plant in Canada to absorb the Toyota philosophy and production techniques and learn the firm's approach to training. It then trained team members.

Maintenance workers were sent on specially commissioned courses at local colleges. They then trained on computer-controlled rigs specially commissioned by Toyota UK, which simulated production machinery. This was rounded off by on-the-job training.

"We made sure everyone was brought up to a certain standard, whatever their previous skill level," says Jackson.

He believes their efforts were vindicated when a Toyota quality engineer from group headquarters approved the first cars off the line as being up to Japanese standards.

Source: Personnel Management Plus, March 1993. Used with permission.

---

raises two important questions. The first question has to do with the concept: what are the major characteristics of the Japanese model of management and are these characteristics so unique as to constitute the basis for a new phase in job design? The second question has to do with the impacts of Japanese-style work organization: what are the implications of such management practices for HRM? This section presents answers to these questions and subsequently reviews some of the literature on Japanese management.

■ Concepts and models

In 1986, a British industrial relations theorist, Peter Turnbull, described a new production system at Lucas Electrical (UK) which management had introduced to shift labour productivity on to a higher growth path and improve product quality.[6] According to Turnbull, the introduction of a 'module' production system led to a new breed of 'super-craftsmen', who were proficient in a wide range of skills. Turnbull used the term 'Japanization' to describe the organizational changes at Lucas Electrical (UK), because they were based on production methods used by many large Japanese corporations.

	Fordist	*Post-Fordist*
1 Technology	• fixed, dedicated machines • vertically integrated operation • mass production	• micro-electronically controlled multi-purpose machines • sub-contracting • batch production
2 Products	• for a mass consumer market • relatively cheap	• diverse production • high quality
3 Labour process	• fragmented • few tasks • little discretion • hierarchical authority and technical control	• many tasks for versatile workers • some autonomy • group control
4 Contracts	• collectively negotiated rate for the job • relatively secure	• payment by individual performance • dual market: secure core, highly insecure periphery

Figure 3.5   Ideal types of Fordist and post-Fordist production systems

Source: A. Warde, 'The Future of Work', in James Anderson and Marilyn Ricci (eds) *Society and Social Science*, Open University Press, 1990. Used with permission.

The stereotyped model of Japanese production has three elements: flexibility, quality control, and minimum waste. Flexibility is attained using module or cellular manufacturing. The system achieves flexibility in two ways: by arranging machinery in a group or 'cell' and by using a flexible multi-skilled workforce. Machines are arranged into a 'U-shaped' configuration to enable the workers to complete a whole component, similar to the group technology principle. The job design underpinning a cellular work structure is the opposite to 'Taylorism'. The specialized machinist operating one machine in one particular work station is substituted by a generalized, skilled machinist with flexible job boundaries.

Quality control is the second component of the Japanese production system. The management philosophy of Total Quality Control (TQC) attempts to build quality standards into the manufacturing process by making quality every operator's concern and responsibility. TQC results in job enlargement as cell members undertake new self-inspection tasks and participate in quality improvement activities. With TQC there are savings on labour and raw materials: fewer quality control inspectors, fewer rework hours and less material wasted (Schonberger, 1982, pp. 36–7).

Minimum waste is the third component of the Japanese production model. Waste is eliminated or at least minimized by just-in-time (JIT) production. As the name suggests, it is a hand-to-mouth mode of manufacture which aims to produce the necessary components, in the necessary quantities, at the necessary quality, at the necessary time. It is a system in which stocks of components and raw materials are kept to a minimum; ideally, they are delivered in a matter of days or even hours before use in the manufacturing process. A number of beneficial outcomes have been posited to stem from just-in-time production. At a lower or superficial level, JIT reduces inventory and scrap (Schonberger, 1982). Advocates of JIT argue that when components are produced in small quantities, just-in-time, any defects are discovered quickly and the production of large amounts of substandard work is avoided. At a higher level, JIT attempts to modify employee behaviour and to secure increased employee commitment. Total quality control management may stand alone or may operate in tandem with cellular and just-in-time production. The core elements of the Japanese model of production are summarized in Figure 3.6.

There is considerable debate amongst academics as to whether or not Japanese production methods are part of a new, distinctive system of manufacturing. Do they constitute a significant departure from existing job design principles, Taylorism and human relations (see, for example, Oliver and Wilkinson, 1988; Wood, 1991)? One of the authors, Bratton (1992), has argued elsewhere that the concept of Japanization is a helpful abbreviation for a range of Japanese management practices now being adopted by European and North American managers. The term describes a coherent and distinctive managerial strategy which seeks to enlist employees' ingenuity, initiative and cooperation at the point of production, in order to attain corporate goals (profitability and commitment).

To help you understand the diverse components of the Japanese model, we have developed a theoretical framework for examining the concept of Japanization. Our model is based principally on two recent contributions to the debate on Japanese-style management: Oliver and Wilkinson's (1988) theory of 'high dependency relationships', and Guest's (1987) HRM model. As Figure 3.7 shows, our model has six major components: a set of manufacturing techniques, a set of dependency relationships, a set of HRM policies, a set of supplier

Techniques	Outcomes
Cellular Technology ——————————→	Flexibility
Total Quality Control ——————————→	Quality Product
Just-in-Time ——————————→	Minimum waste

Figure 3.6   Core elements of the Japanese production model

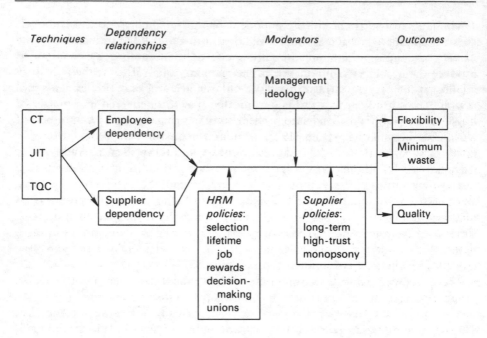

Figure 3.7   A model of Japanese industrial management

Source: Bratton, 1992.

policies, a managerial ideology, and a series of outcomes. We shall examine the main dimensions of the model.

The set of manufacturing techniques are cellular technology (CT), just-in-time (JIT), and total quality control (TQC). The principles of these production methods have already been discussed. Japanese manufacturing processes, it is alleged, create a complex web of high dependency relations which calls for adroit management. The cellular system implies a low level of substitutability and a heightened dependency on a multi-skilled workforce. Also TQC heightens dependency when the safety net of the safety inspectors is removed. Further, just-in-time is vulnerable to delays and stoppages. If the company is operating on zero or minimum inventory, late delivery or stoppages due to strikes quickly affect the manufacturing process. As Oliver and Wilkinson point out: 'A mere work-to-rule or overtime ban could be as disastrous for a company operating a JIT system as could a strike for a company not doing so' (1989, p. 135).

Implicit in our model is the need for a set of 'moderators' to counterbalance the company's dependency on its workforce and suppliers. The organization needs to develop mechanisms that exert sufficient influence over employees and suppliers to prevent them exploiting the organization's dependency (Oliver and Wilkinson,

1988). A set of HRM policies is designed to promote a high degree of employee commitment and to minimize the likelihood of industrial stoppages. A unique set of supplier–buyer policies aims to generate a reciprocal obligation between the buyer and the supplier. Another dimension to our model is a managerial ideology which also acts as a moderator. Analyses of large Japanese companies have often conceptualized the corporation as a 'community', and theorists have focused on how workers are socialized into complying with the rules and norms of the 'corporate community'. Dore (1973) identified a multiplicity of ways that the employment relationship entailed obligations beyond the exchange of labour and cash in both the British and the Japanese factories he studied. Japanese workers in large corporations are constantly reminded by management of the 'competition' in the product market. The notion of corporate 'competitiveness' is an ideology that acts to regulate corporate members' behaviour independently from the actual market conditions outside the company. The Japanese approach to job design is characterized by cooperativeness, group problem-solving, and attitude control (what may be described as the social organization of work), and the system is characterized by a sophisticated production planning. But the social organization of work constitute a sophisticated control system of employee behaviour. For example, Burawoy (1979) has given an account of how workers in self-organized teams created a work culture that reproduced the conditions of workers' own subordination.

A study of engineering companies in the north of England found evidence of the 'coercive culture system'. Operators working in the cells perceived a moral obligation to work hard, to 'put a full day in', because of peer-group pressure or clan control. The cell members had increased autonomy but the management had increased control through a computerized production system. Management control can therefore be conceptualized by the term 'computer-controlled-autonomy' (Bratton, 1991).

Finally, the outcomes or goals of the system are flexibility both in terms of workforce skills and tasks, minimum waste, and minimum quality defects as they arise in production. Some may question our model of Japanese management: is it a description of what actually exists even in Japan, or is it a set of manufacturing and employment practices that organizations should implement? Is it a theory or a helpful way to organize a complex social phenomenon, such as 'Japanese management'?

A number have acknowledged that models of Japanese manufacturing and employment practices may be based on myths. According to Whittaker (1990) there are 'multiple' challenges to Japanese-style employment; for example, lifetime employment and the *nenko* payment system are undergoing reform in Japan. The Japanese government has been prodding companies to reform their employment policies in the light of an ageing population. For example, a Labour Ministry report said that the practice of lifetime employment should be changed to mirror changing attitudes about work and careers, and applauded the growing trend in which mainly young Japanese opt to change jobs, often frequently, rather than sign up for lifetime employment at a major corporation.[7]

The fact that Japanese employment practices are changing in Japan should not surprise us. A mature capitalist society is a highly complex and dynamic arrangement and perhaps the only thing that is constant is change itself. Moreover, in the light of empirical evidence, we should be careful not to dismiss Japanization as insignificant (see, for example, Oliver and Wilkinson, 1988). Although current *practice* in job design may be still some way behind the theoretical models examined in this chapter, in our view the Japanese model is a perspective to job design worthy of serious study because it is affecting the way managers approach job design and human resource management in the workplace today. Jurgens' (1989) study of the automobile industry illustrates that a large number of Japanese management concepts have been adopted by US, British and German automobile companies and interest in the Japanese model is more than a 'passing fad' (1989, p. 204).

The review of the research reported here testifies that for avant-garde managers on both sides of the Atlantic, the Japanese model represents the state-of-the-art for job design. In our view, the model (Figure 3.7) is a useful framework for organizing the complexities of Japanese management practices and can be judged by its usefulness in identifying key aspects of management innovations in job design and HRM practices. It is best conceptualized as an 'ideal-type' which can form the basis of experimentation for western organizations. It does not necessarily follow that all elements of the model must, or can, be applied to every workplace. Indeed, there is evidence that the transfer of Japanese industrial management into British and North American organizations has been highly selective (Jurgens, 1989), and many British companies that have redesigned jobs do not fully appreciate the high dependency relationships implicit in the Japanese model (Oliver and Wilkinson, 1988); further, Japanese job-design practices have been installed alongside traditional adversarial industrial relations systems (Bratton, 1992).

■ Implications of Japanese-style job design

On the second important question, the impact of Japanese-style management is subject to debate, as is the concept of Japanization itself. For HRM practitioners, attention has focused on the need for HR development (see Chapter 9), and the need to synchronize human resource management and labour relations to Japanese-style manufacturing strategy (Oliver and Wilkinson, 1988). Much debate has also centred upon alternative scenarios of 'upskilling' and 'deskilling' of workers. According to Piore and Sabel (1984), Japanese work arrangements exemplify 'the re-emergence of the craft paradigm'. This interpretation of the Japanese-model has its critics. Observers of changes in work structures employing a sociological perspective have asserted that Japanese production regimes do not reverse the general deskilling trend inherent in capitalist production systems. A further defining characteristic of the Japanese approach to management, critics argue, is its tendency to increase the intensity of work (Turnbull, 1986; Sayer, 1986; Tomaney, 1990). In addition, the changes in work organization attempt to offer management 'new' solutions on the back of the old (Thompson, 1989). For others the outcomes of Japanese-style job design are less deterministic; whether such practices 'upskill' or 'deskill' workers depends, amongst other things, on a number of factors such as batch-size, managerial choice and negotiation.[8]

	Motivation assumptions	Critical techniques	Job classification	Issues
Scientific management	Motivation is based on the piecework incentive system to pay. The more pieces the worker produces the higher the pay.	Division of tasks & responsibilities. Task analysis. 'one best way'. Training. Rewards.	Division of tasks & of 'doing' & 'control' leads to many job classifications.	Criteria of motivation may be questioned. No role for unions. Cooperation costs. Product inflexibility.
Job enrichment	Motivation is based on social needs and expectations of workers. To increase performance focus on achievement, recognition, responsibility.	Combining tasks. Increase accountability. Create natural work units. Greater responsibility.	Some supervisory tasks are undertaken by workers as the 'control' is shifted downwards.	Criteria of motivation may be questioned. Undefined union role.
Japanese management	Motivation is based on teamwork or 'clan-like' norms & the organization culture. Performance and motivation are social processes in which some workers try to influence others to work harder.	Intensive socialization. Lifetime employment. Consensual decision-making. Non-specialized career paths. Seniority-based pay.	Requires fewer job classifications because of flexibility and a degree of autonomy.	Criteria of motivation may be culture-bound. Collaborative union role. Work intensification.

Figure 3.8   Three approaches to job design

■ Summary

The way work is designed is critical for human resource practitioners. Job design affects both an organization's competitiveness and the experience and motivation of the individual and work group. This chapter first examined the meaning of work in contemporary western society and proceeded to evaluate alternative job-design strategies including scientific management, job enrichment and Japanese job design concepts, which are summarized in Figure 3.8. The chapter has also described different perspectives on job design and located work and job design within a wider context not normally covered in more prescriptive accounts of HRM.

■ Key concepts

- Work
- Scientific management
- Job enrichment
- Job Characteristic Model
- Group technology

- Job design
- Human relations movement
- Job enlargement
- Fordism
- Japanization

Discussion questions

1. What is meant by the term 'work'?
2. Explain the limits of Taylorism as a job design strategy.
3. 'Job rotation, job enlargement and job enrichment are simply attempts by managers to control individuals at work.' Do you agree or disagree? Discuss.
4. Students often complain about doing group projects. Why? Relate your answer to autonomous work teams. Would you want to be a member of such a work group? Discuss your reasons.
5. 'The notion of "Japanization" is a "chaotic conception". "Japanization" is a useful framework for organizing the complexities of Japanese management practices.' Critically evaluate these two statements. Discuss your reasons.
6. Explain the typical Japanese work structure, as you would picture it, in terms of the job characteristic model.

■ Further reading

Knights, D. *et al.* (eds) (1985), *Job Redesign Critical Perspectives on the Labour Process*, Aldershot: Gower.

Pahl, R. E. (ed.) (1988), *On Work*, Oxford: Blackwell.

Piore M. J. and Sabel, C. F. (1984), *The Second Industrial Divide*, New York: Basic Books.

Thompson, P. (1989), *The Nature of Work* (2nd ed.) London: Macmillan.

Whittaker, D. H. (1990), *Managing Innovation: a study of British and Japanese Factories*, Cambridge: CUP.

Wicken, P. (1987), *The Road to Nissan*, London: Macmillan.

Wood, S. (ed.) (1989), *The Transformation of Work*, London: Unwin Hyman.

■ Chapter case study   Wolds Insurance plc.

Wolds Insurance plc. is a large insurance company that employs 1850 people in its branches throughout the UK. The company's head office is in Manchester where it was established in 1928.

The Underwriting department at the Newcastle branch consists of thirteen clerks, of whom one is a section head and one a head of department. The nature of the work in the department has fundamentally changed over the last twenty years from book-keeping, and an accounting process to clerical processing. There are various types of policy, the main difference being between 'commercial' and 'personal'. The vast majority of policies taken out are personal. Until late 1991, the underwriting department was divided into personal and commercial sections, but in January 1992 these were combined. Although clerks vary in the mix of commercial and personal policies they deal with, the variety in the work of each clerk is small.

Before 1988, the process of policy issue at branch level was manual with the premium being calculated by the use of manuals and charts. Details of the policy would be sent to Head Office and issued from there. Head Office introduced a mainframe computer for this process in 1983, but the procedure at branch level remained much the same until mid-1988, when the VDTs were installed in the underwriting department.

At first the department was not 'on-line' and premiums still had to be calculated manually. Policy details, however, were to be keyed in directly and the VDT was used to check the details of any given policy. In 1989 the system went 'on-line', details of the policy being keyed in direct at branch level. In 1991, the computer was programmed to calculate premiums automatically. Management's aim was to computerize as many policies as possible through complex programming and standardization of product. This reduced the processing time: for the majority of policies it was necessary only to transfer details from form to screen and to use the right classification as specified in the manual. Before on-line computerization a clerk could do 35 policies a week and after computerization 80 policies a week could be processed.

Clerical staff numbers were reduced to a third inside three years and the previously separate departments of commercial and personal were combined into one. The division of work in the branch was divided into four functions: underwriting, claims, cash, and accounts. In addition, the clerks were divided into two types of employee: those knowledgeable on insurance, capable of answering enquiries and dealing with non-standard cases and those who processed routine policies. In terms of knowledge required, standardization had reduced the differences between the policies and for some had reduced the knowledge required. Many of the policies are now offered on a 'take it or leave it' basis and the processing of the policy is routine and repetitive, requiring little knowledge of insurance. Details of the customer and cover required are keyed into the computer in the specified order and the premium is calculated automatically. Some knowledge of insurance is still required nonetheless for dealing with the enquiries.

The underwriting clerks are beginning to show signs of frustration, as much of their working day is spent on routine processing. There is also tension between the clerks doing the routine processing and those clerks working on the non-standard and more interesting cases. These factors are resulting in serious morale problems, high absenteeism and increasing mistakes in the processing. The manager of the department and the HR manager realize that changes are needed, but it is not clear to them how to improve the situation.

(The case is based on 'Skill, deskilling and new technology in the non-manual labour process.' by Heather Rolfe, in *New Technology, Work and Employment*, Vol. 1, No.1, 1986, pp. 37–49.)

Assignment

You have recently been appointed HR assistant at Wold Insurance. You have been asked by June Cole, the HR manager, to consider ways of 'enriching' the work of the underwriting clerks. Prepare a written report focusing on the following questions:

(a) What symptoms suggest there is something wrong in the underwriting department?

(b) Using the job design concepts discussed in this chapter, suggest how to improve the clerical jobs in the underwriting department.

You may make any assumptions you feel are necessary, providing they are realistic and you make them explicit, in your response.

■ References

1. An AEU convener discussing the changes in job design and quoted in Bratton, 1992, p. 165.
2. Smith, Michael (1989), 'Team spirit makes workers happier at Lucas', *Financial Times*, 31 January.
3. McDougall, Bruce (1991), 'The Thinking Man's Assembly Line', *Canadian Business*, November.
4. *Labour Research* (1991), 'The Widening of the Pay Divide', January 1991.
5. *Labour Research* (1990), Workplace Death – Who To Blame', September.
6. Turnbull, P. (1986), 'The "Japanisation" of production and industrial relations at Lucas Electrical', in *Industrial Relations Journal*, Vol. 17, No. 3.
7. 'Annual Labor Report Applauds Job Hopping and Predicts Fewer Services for Consumers', *Asahi Evening News*, 1 July 1992, p. 4.
8. See Bratton, J. (1992), *Japanization at Work*, London: Macmillan, for a review of the arguments and evidence.

CHAPTER 4

Employee Health and Safety

In Britain today more people die from occupational disease than from accidents at work but nearly half the working population has no access to an occupational health service.[1]

There is a fair amount of air contamination on the [factory] floor. Ventilation is poor. It's far too hot. There is a build up of fumes. We get people complaining of headaches. Dermatitis is a problem, that's been linked to the coolant we use . . . We are supposed to have safety representatives, but it's become so lax.[2]

■ Chapter outline

Introduction
Health and Safety and the HRM cycle
The importance of health and safety
Health and safety legislation
Occupational health problems
Role of management
Summary

Chapter objectives

After studying this chapter, you should be able to:

1. Explain the benefits of a healthy and safe workplace.
2. Discuss some key developments in occupational health and safety.
3. Describe the major health and safety legislation in Britain.
4. Identify some contemporary health and safety hazards in the workplace.
5. Summarize the health and safety responsibilities of management and employees.

■ Introduction

The need to develop and maintain a healthy and safe work environment for employees is an important management function. Health and safety legislation and regulations provide part of the legal context of HRM. But, health and safety is not simply about supplying hard hats and goggles or adequate ventilation. It is not only a technical issue. Above all health and safety raises the question of economic costs and power relations. As Sass (1982, p. 52) emphasized:

> In all technical questions pertaining to workplace health and safety there is the social element. That is, for example, the power relations in production: who tells whom to do what and how fast. After all, the machine does not go faster by itself; someone designed the machinery, organized the work, designed the job.[3]

The management of health and safety is influenced by a variety of factors, internal and external to organizations, including: economic costs, government, trade unions and public opinion. The economic cost of occupational health and safety to the organization is double-edged. On the one hand, health and safety measures which protect employees from the hazards of the workplace can conflict with management's objective of containing production costs. On the other hand, effective health and safety policies can improve the performance of employees and the organization, by reducing costs associated with accidents, disabilities or illness.

As in other aspects of the employment relationship, government legislation and the health and safety inspectorate influence managements' approach to health and safety. The Health and Safety at Work etc. Act (HASAWA), 1974, for instance, requires employers to ensure the health, safety and welfare at work of all employees. Furthermore, since the passing of the Single European Act in 1987, an organization's health and safety policies are also influenced by EC Directives. In Britain, the HM Inspectors of Factories enforce the law on health and safety, but they also influence the management of occupational health and safety through their additional role as advisors and educators. Growing public awareness and concern about 'green' and environmental issues has had an affect on occupational health and safety. Organizations have had to become more sensitive to workers' health and general environmental concerns. Manufacturing, for example, 'environment friendly' products and services and using ecologically sustainable processes present a continuing challenge to all managers in the nineties. Survey data also appear to confirm that managers in British workplaces are having to deal with health and safety issues unilaterally (Millward *et al.* 1992, pp. 162–3). New laws and the rising cost of health are important reasons why employee health and safety should not be marginalized, and why we have included the topic in Part 1 of this book, as part of the context of HRM. However, there is another important reason why management needs to pay more attention to health and safety. It is this: if strategic HRM means anything, it must encompass the development and promotion of a set of health and safety policies to protect the organization's most valued asset, its employees.

■ Health and safety and the HRM cycle

The employer has a duty to maintain a healthy and safe workplace. The health and safety function is directly related to the elements of the HRM cycle: selection, appraisal, rewards and training. Health and safety considerations and policy can affect the *selection* process in two ways. It is safe to assume that in the recruitment process potential applicants will be more likely to be attracted to an organization that has a reputation for offering a healthy and safe work environment for employees. The maintenance of a healthy and safe workplace can be facilitated in the selection process by selecting applicants with personality traits that decrease the likelihood of an accident. The *appraisal* of a manager's performance that incorporates the safety record of a department or section can also facilitate health and safety. Research suggests that safety management programmes are more effective when the accident rates of their sections are an important criterion of managerial performance. Safe work behaviour can be encouraged by a *reward* system that ties bonus payments to the safety record of a work group or section. Some organizations also provide prizes to their employees for safe work behaviour, a good safety record or suggestions to improve health and safety. *Training and HR development* play a critical role in promoting health and safety awareness among employees. The HASAWA (1974) requires employers to provide instruction and training to ensure the health and safety of their employees. Studies indicate that safety training for new employees is particularly beneficial because accidents are highest during the early months on a new job.

On the question of the importance of occupational health and safety: while economic cost and HRM considerations will always be predominant for the organization, the costs of ill-health and work-related accidents are not only borne by the victims, families, and their employers. Clearly, the costs of occupational ill-health and accidents are also borne by the taxpayer and public sector services. The NHS, for example, bears the costs of workplace ill-health and accidents. Reliable estimates of the total costs of occupational ill-health and accidents are incomplete, which is perhaps symptomatic of the low priority given to this area of work in the UK. A Health and Safety Executive (HSE) document admitted that: 'Although occupational diseases kill more people in the UK each year than industrial accidents, there is only limited information about them'. An unofficial estimate of occupational disease and accidents in Britain, at 1986/7 prices, has estimated the total cost at between £1.5 and £2.2 billion.[4]

This chapter explains why a working knowledge of occupational health and safety is important for every manager in general, and its importance to HRM functions in particular. After giving a brief history of occupational health and safety, we review health and safety legislation in Britain, and draw some comparisons with the legislation elsewhere. The chapter also discusses several contemporary health and safety problems including occupational stress, smoking, alcoholism and drug use, and AIDS. The chapter then proceeds to examine what managers can do to develop, promote and maintain a healthy and safe workplace.

The World Health Organization defines 'health' as 'a state of complete physical, mental and social well-being, not merely an absence of disease and infirmity'.[5] According to this definition, managers are immersed in one of society's greatest challenges: the design and maintenance of a work organization that is both effective in meeting business objectives and healthy and safe to its employees. It is unfortunately true that, until relatively recently, the attitude of managers and employees towards accident and safety did not promote a healthy or safe workplace.

The traditional approach to safety in the workplace used the 'careless worker' model. It was assumed by most employers, the courts and accident prevention bodies that most of the accidents were due to an employee's failure to take safety seriously or to protect her/himself. The implication of this is that work can be made safe simply by changing the behaviour of employees by poster campaigns and accident prevention training. In the past, the attitudes of trade unions often paralleled those of the employers and managers. Early trade union activity tended to focus on basic wage and job-security issues rather than safety. Trade union representatives used their negotiating skill to 'win' wage increases, and health and safety often came rather low down in their bargaining priorities. If union representatives did include health and safety as part of their activities, it was often to negotiate the payment of 'danger' or 'dirt' money, over and above the regular wage rate. According to Eva and Oswald (1981, p. 33) the tendency for union officials was 'to put the onus on to inspectors and government rather than to see health and safety as part of the everyday activity of local union representatives'. Among employees dangerous and hazardous work systems were accepted as part of the risk of working. Lost fingers and deafness, for instance, were viewed as a matter of 'luck' or the 'inevitable' outcome of work. In the early 1970s, a major investigation into occupational health and safety concluded that 'the most important single reason for accidents of work is apathy'.[6] There is a paradox here. When there are major disasters on land, air and sea involving fatalities, society as a whole takes a keen interest. Yet, although every year hundreds of employees die and thousands receive serious injuries in the workplace, society's reaction tends to be muted.

In the 1960s, something like a thousand employees were killed at their work in the UK. Every year of that decade about 500 000 employees suffered injuries in varying degrees of severity, and 23 million working days were lost annually on account of industrial injury and disease. Such statistics led investigators to argue that 'for both humanitarian and economic reasons, no society can accept with complacency that such levels of death, injury, disease and waste must be regarded as the inevitable price of meeting its needs for goods and services' (Robens, 1972, p. 1). Since the Robens report, there has been a growing interest in occupational health and safety. Moreover, it has been recognized that the 'careless worker' model does not explain occupational ill-health caused by toxic substances, noise, and badly designed and unsafe systems of work. Nor does this perspective highlight the importance of job stress, fatigue and poor working environments in contributing to the causes of accidents. A new approach to occupational health and safety, the 'shared responsibility' model, assumes that the best way to reduce levels of occupational accidents and disease relies on the cooperation of both employers and employees; a 'self-generating effort' between 'those who create the risks and those who work with them' (Robens, 1972, p. 7).

In the late 1970s, the British TUC articulated a 'trade union approach' to health and safety that emphasized that the basic problem of accidents stems from the hazards and risks which are built into the workplace. The trade union approach argued that the way to improve occupational health and safety was through re-designing organizations and work systems so as to 'remove hazards and risks at source.'[7] A Health and Safety Executive (HSE) document would seem to support this approach by stating: 'Most accidents involve an element of failure in control – in other words failure in managerial skill . . . A guiding principle when drawing up arrangements for securing health and safety should be that so far as possible work should be adapted to people and *not vice versa*'. (TUC, 1989)[8]

Trade unions can have a different approach to health and safety as Figure 4.1 depicts.

Statistics show that during 1987–8, for instance, 525 employees were killed and 33 746 suffered major injuries at work. A survey conducted in the Sheffield area

Figure 4.1   A trade union view on health and safety

Source: Eva and Oswald, 1981.

found that one in three people sitting in a General Practitioners' waiting room had suffered ill-health as a result of past employment and 10 per cent were consulting their physician about a work-related illness.[9]

■ The importance of health and safety

Apart from the humanitarian reasons, there are strong economic reasons why managers should take health and safety seriously. In considering the economics of an unhealthy and unsafe workplace it is necessary to distinguish between costs falling upon the organization and costs falling upon government funded bodies, such as hospitals.

According to the Central Statistical Office's annual Social Trends survey, UK employees take more days off sick than any other country in the European Community apart from the Netherlands. In 1991, on average about 2.7 per cent of the working week is lost through illness or injury in the UK, compared to under 1 per cent in Greece. It is not difficult for an organization to calculate the economic costs of a work-related accident. An accident is an unforeseen or unplanned event that results in an injury and material damage or loss. The list of cost headings, shown in Figure 4.2, demonstrates that designing and maintaining a safe work environment can improve productivity by reducing time lost due to work-related accidents, as well as avoiding the costs present in every work-related accident and illness.

There are also indirect costs associated with work-related accidents. In the example cited in the Robens Report, the costs arising from an accident involving a fork-lift truck which was driven too fast round a factory gangway corner is calculated (Figure 4.2). The indirect costs include: overtime payments necessary to make up for lost production; cost of retaining a replacement employee; a wage cost for the time spent by HRM personnel recruiting, selecting and training the new employee and, in less typical cases, the cost associated with loss of revenue on orders cancelled or lost if the accident causes a net long-term reduction on sales, and attendance at court hearings in contested cases. The economic costs of work-related accidents, and the techniques for assessing them, require further research. A Canadian study, however, suggests that indirect costs of work-related accidents could range from 2 to 10 times the direct costs (Stone and Meltz, 1988: 502). Recent case studies conducted by the Health and Safety Executive indicate that the cost of industrial accidents can be as high as 37 per cent of associated profits and 5 per cent of operating costs (quoted in *Personnel Management Plus*, February 1993). A healthy and safe work environment helps to reduce costs and improve organizational effectiveness. If work-related illnesses and accidents can be transposed on to the balance sheet the organization can apply the same management effort and creativity to designing and maintaining a healthy and safe workplace as managers customarily apply to other facets of the business. As Robens stated: 'accident prevention can be integrated into the overall economic activity of the firm' (1972, p. 140).

1. *Cost of wages paid for the time spent by injured workpeople:*   £
    (a) assisting the injured person, or out of curiosity, sympathy etc., or
    (b) who were unable to continue work because they relied on his aid or output
    In category *(a)* 6 employees lost on average 20 minutes: 13.46
    In category (b) 3 workers lost on average 60 minutes:............................   20.19

2. *Cost of material or equipment damage:*
    In this instance the casing of a 5 HP electric motor was cracked beyond repair and
    replaced by a new motor: 400.00
    Installation cost: 100.00

3. *Cost of injured worker's time lost:*
    Treatment for abrasion on leg. 2 hours lost at £6.73 per hour.....................   13.46

4. *Supervisor's time spent assisting, investigating, reporting, assigning work,*
    training or instructing a replacement and making other necessary adjustments:
    One and a half hours at £8.00 ....   12.00

5. *Wage cost of decreased output by injured worker after return to work:*
    4 days at 2 hours/day light work: 56.00

6. *Medical cost to the company:*
    (A reduction in accidents does not necessarily mean lower expenses for running
    the works medical centre)...   35.00

7. *Cost of time spent by administration staff and specialists on investigations or in the*
    processing of compensation questions. H.M. Factory Inspector reports, insurance
    company and Department of Health and Social Security correspondence etc.
    Low in this case:..   50.00

                                                                          TOTAL: 700.11

Additional Charges
Other cost elements not applicable to this accident but which must be considered in others include:
Overtime necessary to make up for lost production.
Cost of learning period of a replacement worker.
A wage cost for the time spent by supervisors or others in training the new worker.
Miscellaneous costs (includes the less typical costs, the validity of which will need to be clearly
shown with respect to each accident):
— renting equipment
— loss of profit on orders cancelled or loss if the accident causes a net long-term reduction in sales
— cost of engaging new employees (if this is significant)
— cost of excess spoilage of work by new employees (if above normal)
— attendance at court hearings in contested cases.
Costs such as these are present in nearly every accident.

Figure 4.2   The cost of an accident

Source: Robens, 1972:189. The original figures have been adjusted for inflation. Used with
permission.

Besides improving productivity and reducing costs, maintaining a healthy and
safe work environment helps to facilitate employee commitment to quality and to
improve industrial relations. One of the side effects of a proactive health and
safety policy is that it leads to improved productivity and quality. Collard (1989)
reports that in two foreign companies studied, a CAP (cost and productivity)
programme was continually emphasized by top management and 'one major

aspect of this was the highest standards of housekeeping' (1989, p. 4). Further, it is argued that employee and union–management relations can be improved when employers satisfy their employees' health and safety needs. Increasingly trade unions have been focusing their attention on health and safety concerns. In some cases, new provisions covering health and safety have been negotiated into collective agreements. When employers take a greater responsibility for occupational health and safety it can change employee behaviour and employees might take a less militant stance during wage bargaining if management pay attention to housekeeping.

A major challenge to HRM professionals is to provide a healthy and safe work environment for employees. Humanitarian and economic reasons dictate such a policy but, as we have already stated, there is also a pervasive portfolio of legislation, regulations, codes of practice, and guidance notes dealing with occupational health and safety and, as with other employment law, the human resource practitioner has taken on the role of advising managers on the content and legal obligations of this.

■ Health and safety legislation

The history of occupational safety legislation can be traced back to the Industrial Revolution and the early factory system in the eighteenth century. The conditions of employment in the new factories were appalling. Dangerous machinery, long hours of work, and poor diet caused physical deformity, as indicated by this 1833 testimony:

> I can bear witness that the factory system in Bradford has engendered a multitude of cripples, and that the effect of long continued labour upon the physique is apparent not only in actual deformity, but also, and much more generally, in stunted growth, relaxation of the muscles, and delicacy of the whole frame.'[10]

The early conditions of employment have to be related to their context before they can be evaluated historically. It must be remembered that employment standards were low before the process of industrialization began. Comparisons of conditions of employment and health and safety provisions must begin from here, not from late twentieth century standards. Many employment practices in the early factories were inherited from the pre-industrial era. An example of this is child labour. In the new factories children worked for their parents, collecting wastes and tying threads, as they had done at home. These children were necessarily involved in the same hours of work as the adults for whom they worked. Family labour was a bridge between the conditions of employment in the pre-factory world and the new factory system. Family labour was not automatically abolished by the early Factory Acts. Early legislation attempted to regulate the hours of work and employment conditions of women and children.

Up to the 1820s, the main pressure for imposing a minimum age and for limiting the hours of factory work came from humanitarians, and some enlightened employers, such as 'the philanthropic Mr Owen of New Lanark' (Mathias, 1969). The 1802 Health and Morals of Apprentices Act was designed to curb some of the abuses of child labour. This Act applied only to pauper apprentices in the factories; it restricted hours of work to twelve, prohibited night work, and provided for instruction in the 'three R's'. Inspection was to be by a magistrate appointed by the local justices of the peace.

Enforcement of the 1802 Factory Act was ineffective since the inspectors were 'generally well disposed to the mill-owner' (Gregge, 1973, p. 55). The 1833 Factory Act outlawed the employment of children under 9, limited the hours of work of children between 9 and 13 to eight hours per day, and appointed four government factory inspectors to enforce the legal requirements. An Act of 1844 imposed limited requirements for guarding dangerous machinery in textile mills where women and children were employed. The early safety legislation as confined to textile factories and affected the conditions of employment for women and children only. No limitations were imposed on adult men in the textile factories, and it was not until the 1870s that safety regulations extended to cover non-textile factories, such as pottery, match-making, iron and steel making, railways and shipping. During the period 1850 to 1900, Factory Acts were amended, tightened and extended to new industries due to a combination of factors, including social reformers, the inspectorate and, more significantly, campaigning by a growing and more militant trade union movement. Eva and Oswald (1981) assert that many of the work stoppages and campaigns, and the occasional 'mob riot', were over a variety of issues in which safety at work played a part. The introduction of safety regulations was painfully slow. Progress was hindered by consistent opposition from the majority of employers who claimed the Factory Acts would make British industry uncompetitive. In 1856, for instance, employers succeeded in *lowering* the standards for guarding machinery where women and children worked. The 1867 Factory Act extended safety laws beyond the textile mills, and even began to abandon the myth that safety law's only purpose was to protect women and children; adult male employees were considered, theoretically at least, capable of protecting themselves (Hobsbawm, 1968). The 1901 Factories and Workshops Consolidation Act introduced a more comprehensive health and safety code for industrial workplaces. The 1901 Act drew together five other statutes passed since 1878, and was followed in its turn by a large number of detailed regulations. It remained the governing Act until the Factories Act of 1937. The subsequent Acts of 1948 and 1959 added some new provisions but produced no fundamental changes in the scope and pattern of the legislation. Industrial safety legislation was consolidated by the Factories Act of 1961.

The 1961 Factories Act defined a 'factory' as any premise in which two or more persons are employed in manual labour in any process for the purpose of economic gain. One aspect of the definition – a place cannot be a factory unless it is one in which *manual* labour is performed – caused some litigation. The first Part of the Act is concerned with general provisions affecting the health of the factory employee. Thus, the Act establishes minimum standards in factories on cleanliness, space for employees to work in, temperature, ventilation, and lighting. The Act laid down very specific standards: for example, a factory will be deemed to be overcrowded if the amount of cubic space is less than 400 cubic feet for every employee in the workroom. The basic rule for temperature is that after the first 30 minutes the temperature should not be less than 60 degrees Fahrenheit (15.5 degrees Centigrade) in rooms where much of the work is done sitting and does not involve serious physical effort.

Part II of the Act lays down general requirements aimed at promoting the safety of factory employees. The Act governs the fencing of machinery in factories. Section 14(1) provides:

> 'Every dangerous part of any machinery . . . shall be securely fenced'. There are further requirements relating to lifting equipment, floors and gangways, access to the workplace, ventilation and inflammable gas. The Act also contains general welfare provisions such as the adequate supply and maintenance of washroom facilities, and a statutory reporting system for accidents and industrial diseases.

The *Mines and Quarries Act, 1954*, provides a comprehensive and detailed code governing safety underground and in quarries. The rise in employment in the service sector and the growth of white-collar trade unionism help explain the extension of legal protection to office and retail employees. The *Offices, Shops and Railway Premises Act, 1963* extended to these premises protection similar to that provided for factories. The general provisions follow that of the Factories Act 1961 and deal with cleanliness, lighting and temperatures, and so on. The Factories Act 1961 and the Offices, Shops and Railway Premises Act 1963 were the principal provisions on health and safety before the subsequent Health and Safety at Work etc. Act, 1974.

■ Health and Safety at Work etc. Act, 1974

□ (i) THE ROBENS REPORT

Occupational health and safety came under detailed scrutiny in the early 1970s by a government appointed committee, chaired by Lord Robens. In the 1960s, white-collar trade unions pressed for health and safety legislation to be extended to cover employees in laboratories, education, hospitals and local government who were not covered by any of the earlier statutes. In 1968, the Labour Government set up the Robens Committee on Safety and Health at Work to review the whole field and to make recommendations. The Robens Committee's wide-ranging report criticised attitudes and the existing state of health and safety law. To summarize the findings of the Committee:

- Despite a wide range of legal regulation, work continued to kill, maim, and sicken tens of thousands of employees each year. The Committee considered that the most important reason for this unacceptable state of affairs was *apathy*.

- There was *too much law*. The Committee identified eleven major statutes which were supported by nearly 500 supplementary statutory instruments. The Committee believed that the sheer volume of law had become counter-productive.
- Much of the law was often *obscure, haphazard, and out-of-date*. Many laws regulated obsolete production processes. Further, the law focused on physical safeguards rather than preventive measures such as training and joint consultation.
- The provision for *enforcement* of the existing legislation was fragmented and ineffective. The Committee felt that the pattern of control was one of 'bewildering complexity.'
- Existing health and safety law *ignored large numbers of employees*. Over 8 million workers in communication, education, hospitals and local government were not covered by any statutes prior to 1974.

The Committee made four main proposals to improve occupational health and safety:

1. The law should be rationalised. A unified framework of legislation should be based upon the employment relationship (not on a factory or mine). All employers involved with work or affected by work activities (except domestic servants in private homes) were to be covered by the new legislation.
2. A self-regulating system involving employers, employees and union representatives should be created to encourage organizational decision-makers to design and maintain safe work systems and help employees to take more responsibility for health and safety. The basic concept should be that of the employer's duty to his/her employees; employers should design and maintain safe and healthy systems of work; and the concomitant duty of the employee is to behave in a manner that safeguards her/his own health and that of her/his co-workers.
3. A new unified statutory framework setting out general principles should be enacted.
4. A new unified enforcement agency headed by a national body with overall responsibility should be established, and should provide new, stronger powers of sanction.

The Labour Government lost the 1970 general election before the Committee completed its research. In 1972, the Robens Committee published its report and the Conservative Government introduced a new Bill in Parliament. Two years later, the Conservatives lost the general election. In 1974, the Labour Government re-introduced a similar Bill which became the Health and Safety at Work etc. Act, 1974, which the next section examines.

HRM IN PRACTICE 4.1

Firms turn blind eye to health and safety

by Kate Lowe

More than half of Britain's bosses have failed to implement new health and safety measures required under UK law.

In interviews conducted for the *Personnel Today* Reader Panel 54 per cent of personnel specialists said their firms failed to meet new European requirements.

The laws, which came into force on 1 January this year, cover health and safety issues such as manual handling, computer screens and general conditions in the workplace.

When asked what measures their firms had taken to prepare for the laws, one in five personnel specialists said their company had provided some form of training.

About 14 per cent said their firms had amended existing policies or introduced procedures. A further 13 per cent said their companies had carried out workstation assessments.

Just 6 per cent said they had studied the regulations and 1 per cent said their firms had allocated funds.

"The Government and the Health and Safety Executive have done very little to enforce these regulations. It is now clear many employers have exploited this," said general secretary of general union GMB John Edmonds.

Health and Safety Commission chairman Sir John Cullen warned the 25 per cent who have taken no action to get moving. But he was reluctant to commit the HSE to immediate action.

"There is no way the inspectorate is going to take enforcement action against firms right away," he said.

"It will be checking companies have a plan in hand to comply with regulations."

Head of employment relations at Anglia Polytechnic University Professor Patricia Leighton said the results raised a serious credibility issue.

"These regulations had the potential to considerably improve health and safety law. Companies will not feel they are at risk if they are mixed messages coming from a variety of sources, she said."

From the start, the regulations, introduced to bring the UK into line with the rest of Europe, have caused controversy.

Earlier this year GMB chiefs threatened to take the Government to court over the regulations claiming the Government had failed to fully implement the European safety directives in UK legislation.

Source: Personnel Today, April 1993. Used with permission.

⌐ **(ii) The Health and Safety at Work etc. Act, 1974**

The complete coverage of this complex Act is outside the scope of this chapter. The approach we have adopted is to highlight the salient features of the Act so that the student of HRM can become familiar with some important principles and terminology. The main duties on employers are contained within Section 2 of the Act (Figure 4.3).

☐ (iii) EC legislation

In the 1990s, EC directives under *Article 189* of the *Treaty of Rome* are an important source of health and safety legislation. Directives are binding, although member states can decide upon the means of giving them legal and administrative effect. In the UK this is usually in the form of regulations. The *Noise at Work Regulations, 1989*, is an example of a European directive that was enacted in 1990. Regulations are normally published with associated approved codes of practice and guidance notes. EC directives have covered a wide range of health and safety issues such as asbestos and the control of major industrial accident hazards, and the HR specialist needs to be appraised of EC health and safety legislation. As a result of EC legislation, as of 1 January 1993, all British workplaces will be legally and financially responsible for ensuring that health and safety regulations are implemented. The implications for HRM and health and safety specialists are formidable. The Health and Safety Commission stated: 'Accidents and ill-health are never inevitable; they often arise from failures in control and organization. A central requirement in the regulations is for a risk

General duties

2.– (1) It shall be the duty of every employer to ensure, so far as is reasonably practicable, the health, safety and welfare at work of all his employees.

(2) Without prejudice to the generality of an employer's duty under the preceding subsection, the matters to which that duty extends include in particular–

  (a) the provision and maintenance of plant and systems of work that are, so far as is treasonably practicable, safe and without risks to health;

  (b) arrangements for ensuring, so far as is reasonably practicable, safety and absence of risks to health in connection with the use, handling, storage and transport of articles and substances;

  (c) the provision of such information, instruction, training and supervision as is necessary to ensure, so far as is reasonably practicable, the health and safety at work of his employees;

  (d) so far as is reasonably practicable as regards any place of work under the employer's control, the maintenance of it in a condition that is safe and without risks to health and the provision and maintenance of means of access to and egress from it that are safe and without such risks;

  (e) the provision and maintenance of a working environment for his employees that is, so far as is reasonably practicable, safe, without risks to health, and adequate as regards facilities and arrangements for their welfare at work.

Figure 4.3   The Health and Safety at Work, etc. Act, 1974, section 2: the duties on employers

assessment in order to help the employer decide what health and safety measures are needed'.[11]

■ Occupational health problems and issues

Many employees would probably say they were not healthy if the World Health Organization definition of health quoted above was used as a benchmark. This section examines several health problems that are of special concern to today's HRM practitioners: job stress, alcohol abuse, smoking and AIDS.

■ Job stress

The term 'stress' in now part of the regular vocabulary of managers and employees. While some stress is normal to life, if stress is repeated or prolonged individuals experience physical and psychological discomfort. The experience of work can lead to a variety of symptoms of stress that can harm employees' health and job performance. Figure 4.4 illustrates some common symptoms of stress.

Much research into job stress has tended to focus on 'executive burnout' and on individuals in the higher echelons of the organizational hierarchy. However, stress can affect employees at the lower levels of the hierarchy. A US study found that the two most stressful jobs were a manual labourer and a secretary. In another US study researchers found that the incidence of first heart attack was 2.5 times greater among skilled manual employees than among senior management grades. In fact, the rate increased the lower the occupational grades.[12] A US health organization also found that women in clerical occupations suffer twice the incidence rate of heart disease as all other female employees.[13] In addition to the physical and psychological disabilities, occupational stress costs individuals and business considerable sums of money. For example, in 1991 it was estimated that occupational stress cost Canadian business annually over £7 billion in absenteeism, disability payments, replacement payments and lower productivity.

Tension and anxiety	Sleep problems
Anger and aggression	Digestive problems
High blood pressure	Chronic worry
Inability to relax	Irritability and boredom
Excessive alcohol and/or tobacco use	Uncooperative attitudes
Forgetfulness	Increased accidents
Increased absenteeism	Reduced job satisfaction

Figure 4.4   Typical symptoms of stress

☐ Causes of stress

Occupational stress occurs when some element of work has a negative impact on an employee's physical and mental well-being. For example, work overload and unrealistic time deadlines will put an employee under pressure and stress may occur. Job stress cannot be separated from personal life. For example, illness in the family or divorce put an employee under pressure and lead to stress. Factors that cause stress are numerous and their relationships complex. However, researchers identify two major types of stressors: work-related factors and individual factors.

A variety of work-related factors can lead to stress: role ambiguity, frustration, conflict, job design and harassment. *Role ambiguity* exists when the job is poorly defined, uncertainty surrounds job expectations and where supervisory staff and their subordinates have different expectations of an employee's responsibilities. Individuals experiencing role ambiguity will be uncertain how their performance will be evaluated and will experience stress. *Frustration*, a result of a motivation being blocked to prevent an individual from achieving a desired goal, is a major stressor. A clerical employee, trying to finish a major report before finishing time, is likely to become frustrated by repeated PC breakdowns that prevent the completion of the goal. Huczynski and Buchanan (1991) draw on Swedish research to illustrate the frustration of information technology:

> Office workers who used to wait happily for hours while folders were retrieved from filing cabinets now complain when their computer terminals do not give them instant information on request . . . Stress arose mainly from computer breakdowns and telephone calls which interrupted their work. The employees never know how long these interruptions would last, and had to watch helplessly while their work piled up. So they worked rapidly in the mornings in case something stopped them later. (1991, p. 352)

Interpersonal and inter-team *conflicts* are another source of occupational stress. When employees with different social experiences, personalities, needs and points of view interact with co-workers disagreements may cause stress. A further cause of stress in the workplace is the *design of jobs*, that is, their content, structural environment, and physical demands. Jobs that have a limited variety of tasks, are repetitive, have low discretion and are highly controlled do not activate employees upper level needs, particularly achievement and self-actualization, and may cause stress. Karasek (1979) argued that the most stressful jobs were those that combined high workload and low discretion.[14] Craig (1981)[15] also identifies job design as a stressor:

> Countless office staff work in high bureaucracies which have been described as 'honeycombs of depression'. The work you're doing can make you sick: work under pressure of time, to keep up the production quotas or deadlines, work that 'drives you crazy' because it's so boring . . . Office workers frequently keep tablets in their desks to get through the days, or take frequent days off. They then go to their doctor, where the problem is treated as a personal one, in isolation.[16]

Sexual and racial *harassment* at work is another source of stress. Sexual harassment can range from unwanted propositions and sexual innuendo to attempted physical contact or rape. It can be difficult for an HR manager to convince employees and other managers to take sexual harassment seriously. It is often viewed as a 'joke'; something to do with 'chatting-up' attractive female co-workers or bottom pinching. However, sexual harassment is about power relationships. It is about harassment aimed at women by men who occupy positions of power. It is, as one writer put it: 'a new, formal title for an age-old predicament, the boss-man with anything from a lascivious line of chat, to wandering hands, to explicit demands for sex as a reward for giving you, the women, work'.[17]

Sexual harassment is extremely stressful; it is also unlawful. The legal concept of 'detriment' is important here sexual harassment is a 'detriment' *per se*, it can lead to an employment-related detriment to the female employee and, as such, it has serious implications for management.[18] In 1986, the European Parliament passed a resolution on violence against women. As a consequence it commissioned a report on *The Dignity of Women at Work*. This report led to the adoption of the EC code of practice, Figure 4.5. HR professionals have to take appropriate action to prevent sexual harassment and to inform employees of the consequences of sexual harassment. Racial harassment in the workplace can also

This defines sexual harassment as "unwanted conduct of a sexual nature" affecting "the dignity of women and men at work". It defines harassment as largely subjective, in that it is for the individual to decide on whether conduct is acceptable or offensive.
■ The code says that member states should take action in the public sector and that employers should be encouraged to:
■ issue a policy statement;
■ communicate it effectively to all employees;
designate someone to provide advice to employees subjected to harassment;
■ adopt a formal complaints procedure; and
■ treat sexual harassment as a disciplinary offence.
   The code obliges member states to make a report on the measures taken to implement it by 1994.

Figure 4.5   The EC code on sexual harassment

cause stress. It can range from racist jokes or verbal abuse to racist graffiti in the workplace or physical attacks on black employees. No matter how subtle it is, racial harassment is extremely stressful, it can damage black employees' health, and presents a major challenge for managers.

Individual factors causing stress are equally varied and complex. Individual factors that can produce stress include: financial worries, marital problems, pregnancy, problems with children, and death of spouse. In 1992, a record number of mortgages were foreclosed in Britain, doubtless causing considerable stress. A major personal factor that can cause stress among working women is the 'dual role' syndrome; the additional burden of coping with two jobs; the paid job and the unwaged 'job' at home (cooking, housework and shopping, etc). As Craig (1981) puts it: 'The pressures on working mothers are enormous. Feeling guilty because you're not an ideal stay-at-home mum . . . get the breakfasts, get the shopping done, go to the launderette, fetch the kids from school, do the ironing, clean the house. A carefully worked out timetable can be upset and life thrown into chaos when your lunch hour is switched or you're required to do overtime without notice.[19]

A general and widely recognized cause of stress is a person's personality. For example, 'Type A' personalities, that is, those individuals who are highly competitive, set high standards, place considerable emphasis on meeting deadlines and are 'workaholics', tend to have a higher propensity to exhibit symptoms of stress (McShane, 1992). Figure 4.6 illustrates work-related and individual causes of stress.

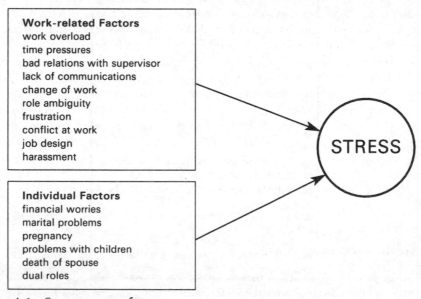

Work-related Factors
work overload
time pressures
bad relations with supervisor
lack of communications
change of work
role ambiguity
frustration
conflict at work
job design
harassment

Individual Factors
financial worries
marital problems
pregnancy
problems with children
death of spouse
dual roles

STRESS

Figure 4.6   Some causes of stress

Figure 4.7   Stress caused by the 'dual-role' syndrome

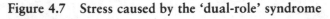

Source: Personnel Management Plus, April 1992. Used with permission.

Until recently, job stress has been considered to be a personal problem. Today, it is recognized that stress is a major health problem at work, and it is a general management responsibility to provide the initiative to eliminate or reduce the causes of stress. At organizational level, attention to basic job design principles can alleviate the conditions that may cause stress. At the individual level, HR professionals have conducted workshops on stress management to help the individual employee to cope with stress and avoid over exposure to stress-causing situations. Workshops designed to change 'life-styles' by promoting healthy eating and fitness, while helping employees relieve the strains caused by job stress, cannot eliminate the source of stress. Like other occupational hazards, stress needs to be controlled at source. As discussed, stress arises from a variety of sources and it is important for HR managers to identify priorities and investigate ways of dealing with the problem. Management should look at the design of jobs (see Chapter 3) and organization structure, and conduct detailed surveys to identify priorities for action. Figure 4.8 shows some of the specific actions individuals and HR practitioners can take to alleviate occupational stress.

■ Alcohol and drug abuse

A recent estimate indicates that in England and Wales there are approximately 3 million excessive drinkers and 850 000 problem and dependent drinkers. About one in 25 of the population in England and Wales, and possibly as high as one in ten in Scotland, may be personally affected by severe alcohol-related problems.[20]

Individual Strategies	Organizational Strategies
Physical exercise	Meeting with employees to discuss extent of stress
Hobby	
Meditation	Conduct a survey and inspect workplace for stress-causing factors
Group discussions	
Assertiveness training	
	Improve job and organizational design
	Improve communication
	Develop a stress policy and monitor its effectiveness
	Train managers to be sensitive to the causes and early symptoms of stress.

Figure 4.8   Action to reduce occupational stress

It has been estimated that in 1989 one in ten employees in Britain may have a drink problem. Excessive consumption of alcohol is both a health problem and a job performance problem in organizations.[21] In alcohol abuse, behavioural problems range from tardiness in the early stages to, in the later stages, prolonged absenteeism. A US study estimated that problem drinkers are absent from work, on average, 22 days per year and are at least twice as likely as non-alcohol drinkers to have accidents.[22] The direct and indirect costs of alcohol abuse to employers include the costs of accidents, lower productivity, poor quality work, bad decisions, absenteeism, and managers' lost time in dealing with employees with an alcohol problem.

Employers have been advised to have a written statement of policy regarding alcohol abuse, which can be discussed and agreed with employees and, where applicable, union representatives. The policy should recognise that alcohol abuse is an illness and it should be supportive, rather than punitive, otherwise employees will hide their drink problem as long as possible. The Health and Safety Executive (HSE) in a paper, 'The problem drinker at work', advocates that a policy should encourage an employee who believes he/she has a drink problem to seek help voluntarily, and, subject to certain provisions, have the same protection of employment and pension rights as those granted to an employee with problems that are related to other forms of ill-health. Research in Scotland estimated that 20 per cent of employers had a policy to deal with the problem drinker. In addition to preparing a policy, management can devise a procedure for dealing with alcohol abuse. To encourage employees to seek advice, it is suggested that the procedure should be separate from the discipline procedure. Finally, the HRM department is advised to establish links with an external voluntary organization to obtain help and develop an employee assistance programme.

■ Smoking

It has been estimated that of the 600 000 deaths in the UK each year, 100 000 are caused by tobacco.[23] 90 per cent of all deaths from lung cancer and chronic bronchitis are smokers. 40 per cent of heavy smokers (over 20 cigarettes a day) die before retirement age compared with only 15 per cent of non-smokers.[24] One North American manager calculated the cost of smoking to his company at about £1.5 million per year, or £1500 per smoker. This figure was estimated by putting a money value to such items as the time each employee spends smoking (estimated at 30 minutes each day), absenteeism due to smoking related illness, property damage and additional maintenance.[25] Smoking increases employers' costs as Figure 4.9 (money that 'goes up in smoke') shows. Recent research has highlighted the health risk of 'second-hand smoking' (inhaling other people's smoke). In 1988, a government report estimated the risk of lung cancer for a non-smoker inhaling other people's smoke to between 10 and 30 per cent.

In the past, employers have restricted employees smoking in order to reduce fire risks or to comply with hygiene standards. To reduce the risks and costs associated with smoking, to appease non-smokers, and to deter possible legal action from employees suffering from polluted air caused by smoking, many organizations now have established policies on smoking at the workplace. The Civil Service, for example, has recently restricted smoking in Inland Revenue offices. Management and union representatives at British Telecom agreed to ballot employees on their views on a smoking ban. The result was a 3 to 1 majority in favour of a smoking ban in common work stations. The company

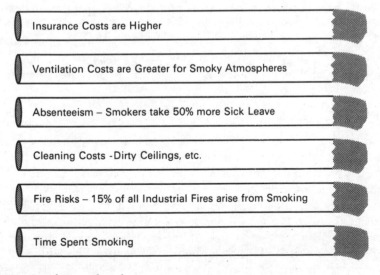

Insurance Costs are Higher

Ventilation Costs are Greater for Smoky Atmospheres

Absenteeism – Smokers take 50% more Sick Leave

Cleaning Costs -Dirty Ceilings, etc.

Fire Risks – 15% of all Industrial Fires arise from Smoking

Time Spent Smoking

Figure 4.9   Smoking-related costs

£15,000 'passive smoking' settlement

A CONSULTANT physician at the London Chest Hospital found that passive smoking "played an important part" in the bronchitis of Veronica Bland, who won an out-of-court settlement from her employer last month.

Although Stockport Metropolitan Borough Council's insurers decided not to test Bland's case in court, paying a £15,000 settlement, the key points of her claim are known.

Supported by local government union Nalgo, Bland said the council was liable for her bronchitis because it failed to ensure "sufficient and suitable ventilation" in her office in line with section 7 of the 1967 Office, Shops and Railways Premises Act.

Bruce Piper, legal officer for Nalgo, said the case rested on three points: the council's statutory responsibility under the Act, the causal link between passive smoking and Bland's illness and, significantly, evidence that the council must have known of the risks which passive smoking presented as long as 10 years ago.

Bland had been working for the council since 1979, and a smoking policy was not introduced until shortly before she began her action in 1990.

However, in 1983 the National Local Government Committee of the TUC urged branches to push for restrictions on smoking at work.

In the same year Gwent County banned smoking unless an entire section voted to opt out. Piper said it would be hard for a large employer to claim it was unaware of the risks presented by passive smoking.

The 1990 IPM guide 'Smoking policies at work', points out that in 1988 the 'Fourth report of the independent scientific committee on smoking and health' confirmed the risks to non-smokers of tobacco smoke.

Between July 1988 and September 1989 Bland worked close to seven colleagues who smoked continually. She estimates that in this time she inhaled smoke from the equivalent of 150 cigarettes every day plus smoke from those visiting the office.

Source: Personnel Management Plus, February 1993. Used with permission.

---

set up a union/management working party to examine the details of implementation. Many employers believe that they would face hostility from employees if they implemented a non-smoking policy. Companies that have implemented non-smoking policies report increased awareness of the health risks of smoking and little employee or union resistance. A government report found that: '79% of smokers interviewed acknowledged the right of non-smokers to work in air that is free of tobacco smoke (and not surprisingly, 84% of non-smokers and 78% of ex-smokers also thought so'.[26] HRM professionals agree that successful non-smoking policies require consultation with employees. In a unionized workplace it requires a joint approach by management and union.

■ AIDS

I was not trained to manage fear, discrimination, and dying in the workplace.[27]

A textbook on human resource management for the 1990s would be incomplete if no reference were made to society's most recent menace, AIDS (Acquired Immune Deficiency Syndrome). AIDS is caused by a virus called Human Immune-deficiency Virus (HIV) that attacks the body's immune system. The World Health Organization estimated the number of people affected with AIDS might total 500 000 to 3 000 000 in 1993. In Britain, by the end of March 1992, a total of 5782 cases of AIDS had been reported, and 17 494 individuals had been reported HIV-positive. The fear of catching HIV can create problems for human resource managers. Employees might refuse to work with a person with AIDS. As one North American human resource manager explained: 'No matter how sophisticated or educated you are, AIDS can trigger irrational things in people . . . There's a big potential for disruption. It could close a plant down.'[28]

Recently a North American chain store manager had to call in the Red Cross to explain to distraught employees that AIDS cannot be transmitted through normal contact in the workplace. This happened when an employee developed AIDS and died. Six months later employees were still refusing to use the drinking fountain or the toilet (see Chapter Case Study). Employee performance and morale plummeted as employees went into a panic. Companies that have encountered the problem of managing AIDS in the workplace have found that it is better to expect a problem and be proactive in educating employees about the issues AIDS raises. As with any HRM policy, it requires a clear endorsement from top management down. The chairman of Levi Strauss, Robert Hass, confirms the need for senior management support: 'This (AIDS) is frequently viewed as something that the personnel department should take care of, but there has to be support from the top. You can't do it with one flyer.'[29] As attitudes and legal considerations change, AIDS has important implications for HRM policy and practices.

■ Role of management

Perhaps, more than any other HR activity, health and safety offers the HR manager an opportunity to be more proactive than reactive. This, if effective action was followed through, would increase the HRM department's contribution to improving the health and safety of the organization's employees. There are a number of strategies that can be used by organizations to ensure a healthy and safe workplace and ensure compliance with legal requirements. This section does not aim to be prescriptive, offering advice on what HRM managers should be doing. The strategies summarized in Figure 4.10. are intended primarily to generate discussion on the implications of health and safety on management

1. **Design**	safe and healthy systems of work
2. **Exhibit**	strong management commitment
3. **Inspect**	workplace for health and safety problems
4. **Establish**	procedures and controls for dealing with health and safety issues
5. **Develop**	training programmes
6. **Set up**	health and safety committees
7. **Monitor**	safety policies
8. **Draw up**	action plan and checklist

Figure 4.10   Strategies to improve health and safety in the workplace

practices, and how health and safety measures can be reconciled with broader management objectives.

■ Design safer systems of work

The most direct approach to ensuring a safe and healthy workplace is to design systems of work that are safe and without risk to health. This can often only be done satisfactorily at the design, planning and/or purchasing stage. It may be far more difficult to modify existing machinery or systems of work, to eliminate or reduce hazards, than it is at the investment stage Thus, management must take cognizance of long-term organizational changes to control hazards. Simply trying to persuade employees, for instance by poster campaigns, to adapt their behaviour to unsafe systems of work is unacceptable. The Health and Safety Executive (HSE) maintains that the basic problem of accidents stems from hazards inherent in the workplace: 'Most accidents involve an element of failure in control – in other words *failure in managerial skill* [our emphasis]. A guiding principle when drawing up arrangements for securing health and safety should be that so far as possible work would be adapted to people and not vice versa.' As managers identify processes, machines and substances that are hazardous to the health and well-being of employees, they must modify the process to eliminate or reduce the hazard and risk 'at source'. In some cases, robots can perform hazardous tasks, such as paint spraying and welding. The provision of protective equipment is the typical means used by organizations to reduce physical hazards, and it is also an employer responsibility.

■ Exhibit commitment

Senior management carries the prime responsibility under the Act (1974) for ensuring a safe and healthy workplace. The Robens Committee believed that 'apathy' was a major cause of workplace accidents. No matter how much activity on health and safety is initiated by HR professionals, health and safety should be an integral part of every manager's responsibility, from the chief executive officer down to the lowest level supervisor. Anything less than total support from top management raises questions about the sincerity of the organization's commitment in the eyes of employees, government agencies and the public at large. To exhibit commitment managers' salary and promotion might be tied to a satisfactory safety record and compliance. Larger organizations have also appointed specialists in the area, including health and safety officers, safety engineer and medical technicians. If the safety officer is to be effective s/he must be given adequate authority in the management hierarchy to make changes and implement changes.

■ Inspect the workplace

Another proactive approach to the management of health and safety is regular formal inspections of the workplace: regular monitoring of the work environment and regular physical examination of employees. For example, construction sites and manufacturing plants requires regular inspections to check the application of safety standards and relevant laws. In some manufacturing processes frequent monitoring of air quality , levels of dust and noise is needed. Organizations may monitor a wide range of matters relating to employees' health, from routine eye tests and chest X-rays to screening for breast/cervical cancer and incidents of infertility and abnormal childbirths. A 'health' survey of employees can also help identify hazardous and unhealthy processes.

We can identify three main types of formal inspection: accident, special and general. *Accident inspections* will follow an accident or dangerous incident ('near miss') in the workplace. *Special inspections* might concentrate on a particular work-station, system of work or hazard. The safety committee might decide that it is necessary to examine the training of fork-lift truck operators or dust problems; this would be the first step in a plan of action. A comprehensive survey of the entire workplace is the purpose of *general inspections*. In a unionized workplace these inspections are frequently conducted jointly with the union safety representative. The *SRSC* (Safety Representatives and Safety Committees) *Guidance Notes* recognize the advantages in formal general inspections being jointly conducted by the employer or manager and union safety representative:

> The safety representatives should coordinate their work to avoid unnecessary duplication. It will often be appropriate for the safety officer or specialist advisers to be available to give technical advice on health and safety matters which may arise during the course of the inspection.[30]

The Sutcliffe system

Sutcliffe Catering is one of a rising number of firms putting health and safety at the top of the agenda. Tim Ring reports

The cost of health and safety is rising rapidly. Not only are insurance companies bumping up their premiums well beyond the rate of inflation, but new laws, like the EC health and safety directives introduced in January, have added to the statutory burden on employers.

Yet despite the financial, legal and moral risks of failing to tackle health and safety, *Personnel Today* research earlier this year found more than half of UK companies had failed to implement EC laws.

Many firms are put off by the amount of time it takes to set up health and safety programmes. Certainly, Sutcliffe Catering, which has just introduced a safety programme which more than complies with the requirements, began planning its scheme 18 months ago, well before the regulations were on most companies' agendas.

Even under previous legislation, Sutcliffe felt by tightening up its safety training it could benefit from reduced management time spent dealing with accidents, fewer insurance claims and therefore lower premiums.

Sutcliffe is one of the UK's biggest contract catering companies, running staff canteens for firms like Ford and ICL. Its 20,000 staff mostly work in kitchens where there are dangers such as knives, food and fat to spill, cookers and gas rings.

In the last year the Health and Safety Executive recorded 3,500 accidents in Britain's workplace kitchens resulting in three or more days' sick leave.

Sutcliffe group personnel director Peter Davies says European legislation and the hike in employer liability premiums prompted him and hygiene and safety director David Barnes to review safety training 18 months ago.

What emerged was a Quality Through Safety training programme which is being progressively introduced to all staff.

The programme demands the ultimate price — qualifying is a condition of employment. It is also unusual in being delivered to manual workers predominatly through distance learning.

Sutcliffe had to create the course itself, as it found no existing material for the catering business. Hygiene manager Sue Cummins, helped by agency Vis A Vis, carried out much of the work.

Sutcliffe chose distance learning because it was surprisingly successful with an earlier hygiene course.

Staff spend an average of 15–20 minutes a day over six weeks working through the training material. At the end they take a multiple choice exam marked independently by the Institution of Occupational Safety & Health. Sutcliffe saw outside validation as essential in giving the programme credibility.

The training material was prepared by Barnes' group, based in Bristol, made up of Cummins and three other environmental health officers.

The team trained senior Sutcliffe managers in each of the firms's eight regional operating companies; each company typically has one personnel manager and one training manager with three field training officers who administer the programme. Those trainers in turn train the catering managers who run the scheme themselves.

By the end of April in a typical regional company, two out of three of the unit managers had been trained and between 10 and 20 per cent of staff had begun the course. Trowbridge was the first unit to pass with a 100 per cent pass rate.

While success in the programme is a condition of employment, Barnes expects all staff to pass it sooner or later and staff can resit the test each year.

"Staff do have silly accidents and we know the areas of concern. You can put up posters and run courses – they mean something at that moment, but then they go away. This way it remains in their minds," he says.

The measure of the programme's success will be its impact on the company's annual accident statistics.

Source: *Personnel Today*, June 1993. Used with permission.

Thorough preparation, including designing a comprehensive set of checklists covering all aspects of the workplace, is essential if managers are to discover physical health hazards.

■ Establish procedures and controls

A health and safety policy is likely to fail unless there are effective procedures and controls established. The procedures for handling health and safety problems need to meet some basic requirements:

(a) allow employees and union representatives to talk *directly* to the managers who can make decisions;

(b) operate without undue delay;

(c) be able to handle emergency problems; and

(d) permit discussion about long-term decisions affecting health and safety.

Clearly, these recommendations have important implications for HRM policy and action. Let us briefly examine these considerations. Problems might occur if line managers are expected by senior management to be responsible for safe working practices, but at the same time are denied the authority to make decisions and implement changes. In principle, organizational procedures should ensure that the responsibility of each level of management for health and safety is matched by the authority at that level of management to make decisions. The appointment of a safety officer may be a necessary prerequisite to establishing effective procedures and controls, but it is not sufficient. The position must be placed into the management hierarchy with clear lines of reporting and accountability, which will enable procedures for raising problems to operate, without undue delay, and avoid other managers absolving themselves from responsibilities.

It is recommended that the committee on health and safety include key departmental managers, employees and union representatives. At best, committees can be a vehicle for discussion and the strategic planning of health and safety. At worst, they can degenerate into a 'talking shop' which will draw scepticism from the rest of the workforce. HR specialists and line managers must perceive their rewards, or a significant proportion of them, as contingent upon the success of a health and safety programme. To evaluate that success, monthly, quarterly, and annual statistics need to be reported directly to the senior management team.

■ Develop training programmes

One way to obtain compliance with health and safety regulations is through enhancing employees' knowledge, understanding and commitment, which can be achieved through health and safety programmes. The purpose of safety training is generally the same as that of any other training programme: to improve job knowledge and skills and to ensure optimum employee performance at the specified level. In health and safety training, specified performance standards include attention to safety rules and regulations regarding safe work behaviour. Like any other training, health and safety training should be developed systematically. First, problems or training needs are identified by inspection, by accident reports, and through discussion at the health and safety committee. Next, the planning, execution and evaluation of the training take place (see Chapter 9).

The HASAWA (1974) imposes a duty on employers to provide training to ensure a healthy and safe workplace. Research suggests that safety awareness training programmes only have a short-term effect on employees' behaviour. This would suggest that after employees complete their safety training at the orientation stage, the HR department should organize regular refresher courses. Experience suggests that line managers, supervisors, and safety representatives need to be exposed to regular training. Top management support is a key ingredient in the availability and success of health and safety training. Studies suggest, however, that the number of representatives attending TUC health and safety courses has fallen (Booth, 1985).

■ Set up health and safety committees

As already noted, the HASAWA requires employers to establish safety committees where this is requested by a safety representative. Where these committees are not initiated by the union, organizations often have safety committees which have employee members and are chaired by the safety or HRM specialist. Making the committee effective is mainly in the realm of senior management. A safety committee may develop into a 'talking shop' with no effective decision-making authority. To avoid this, a senior member of the management team, with executive authority, should be a member of the Committee.

The functions of the Committees, their terms of reference, depends on individual company policy, relevant safety legislation and the employee/union relations situation. The *SRSC Guidance Notes* suggest the following terms of reference:

(a)   The study of accident and notifiable diseases statistics and trends, so that reports can be made to management on unsafe and unhealthy conditions and practices, together with recommendations for corrective action.

(b)   Examination of safety audit reports on a similar basis.

(c)   Consideration of reports and factual information provided by inspectors of the enforcing authority appointed under the Health and Safety at Work Act.

(d)   Consideration of reports which safety representatives may wish to submit.

(e)   Assistance in the development of works safety rules and safe systems of work.

(f)   A watch on the effectiveness of the safety content of employee training.

(g)   A watch on the adequacy of safety and health communication and publicity in the workplace.

(h)   The provision of a link with the appropriate inspectorates of the enforcing authority.

(Reg 9, pp. 37–8)

Employers or their representatives are primarily responsible for compliance with health and safety laws. The existence of these committees does not diminish the employer's duty to ensure a healthy and safe workplace. The work of the safety committees should supplement management's arrangements for regular and effective monitoring for health and safety precautions; it cannot be a substitute for management action.

A critical study of the implementation of the Safety Representatives and Safety Committees Regulations has been undertaken by Walters (1987). The findings from his small sample of cases in the print industry suggest that the joint regulation of health and safety is based on the assumption of trade union organization and power in the workplace. With an inimical economic and political environment in the eighties, this power diminished and the SRSC Regulations have had a very limited direct effect on the joint regulation of health and safety in the workplace: 'It is only in the large workplaces that any significant application of the SRSC Regulations with regard to joint inspections, provision of information and time off for training seems to have been made' (Walters, 1987, p. 48).

The authoritive study by Millward *et al.*, however, indicates that in spite of the hostile industrial relations climate of the 1980s, joint health and safety committees were just as likely to exist in 1990 as in 1984. In 1990, 23 per cent of managers reported joint committees specifically for health and safety issues, in 1984 it was 22 per cent (Millward *et al.*, 1992, p. 162). Another finding which is relevant to the point that increasingly managers seem to be assuming responsibility for health and safety issues unilaterally, is that health and safety committees were much less commonly found in non-unionized workplaces in 1984 then in 1990, and the decline in health and safety representatives was particularly marked in the service sector. Table 4.1 shows the arrangements for dealing with health and safety in Britain, for each broad sector in the economy.

TABLE 4.1 Arrangements for dealing with health and safety, 1984 and 1990.

	All establishments		Private manufacturing		Private services		Public sector	
	1984	1990	1984	1990	1984	1990	1984	1990
Joint committee for health & safety	22	23	33	32	15	18	23	25
Joint committee for health, safety & other matters	9	9	15	10	7	8	9	11
Workforce representatives. no committee	41	24	25	20	39	16	52	40
Management deals, consultation with employees	–	5	–	3	–	5	–	5
Management deals, without consultation with employees	–	37	–	34	–	51	–	14
Management only, consultation	22	–	22	–	34	–	10	–
Other answer	6	2	5	1	5	1	7	4
Don't know/not answered	*	*	*	*	–	–	*	*

Source: Adapted from Millward et al., 1992, p. 161. Used with permission.

■ Monitor policy

Safety specialists argue that the safety policy should reflect the employer's commitment to develop safe systems of work, and to pursue a healthy work environment. Apart from giving details of the specialist safety services provided by the organization, the safety policy also outlines the safety responsibilities of all levels of management within the hierarchy. This part of the safety policy is particularly important for identifying which member of the management hierarchy should be involved when a health and safety problem arises in the workplace.

There is a growing awareness that, in practice, many employers are 'turning a blind eye' to new health and safety requirements. Furthermore, many safety policies are not that helpful in practice because of failure to monitor their relevance to workplace arrangements, inadequate training, and supervisors and safety officers lacking authority to make decisions. The TUC is critical of safety policies, arguing that 'many safety policies are just pious blue-prints which look good but are either ignored or unworkable'.[31] A proactive approach would involve HRM professionals regularly checking to ensure that safety policy, management procedures and arrangements work, and are changed to suit new developments or work structures in the workplace.

■ Draw up action plan

HRM professionals can be more proactive in the area of health and safety by developing an 'action plan' and checklist (Figure 4.11)

■ Summary

Employee health and safety is an important aspect of HRM. Organizations should provide a safe and healthy workplace for their human resources. This chapter has examined the role of health and safety in organizations and the development of legislation. Job stress, alcoholism, smoking and AIDS are health problems discussed in this chapter. Trade unions have attempted to secure improvements in health and safety at work through collective bargaining and, at times, through direct action by work stoppages; unions have also pressed for some stringent health and safety legislation. European Community directives will be an important source of health and safety regulations in the 1990s. With such developments in the law, and a growing awareness of health and safety hazards, it is likely that HRM professionals will face challenges and greater responsibilities in this area during the foreseeable future.

HSE OHS checklist for employers
Preventing occupational ill health

	Yes	No	Uncertain
■ Do I know whether any of my operations involve a health risk?	□	□	□

eg exposure to skin irritants such as solvents, poor working practices when using harmful materials, exposure to excessive noise, exposure to harmful dusts, fumes or gases, frequent heavy lifting or carrying.

| ■ Do I take account of any specific regulations or recommendations applying to these risks? | □ | □ | □ |

eg specific regulations covering work with lead and asbestos

| ■ Are all the risks that have been identified adequately controlled? | □ | □ | □ |

eg through improved workplace design engineering controls or by using personal protection

| ■ Is the effectiveness of controls being assessed and monitored? | □ | □ | □ |

eg by regular environmental monitoring. possibly backed up with health checks

Placement and rehabilitation

	Yes	No	Uncertain
■ Do I know whether any of my operations carry specific health requirements?	□	□	□

eg good eyesight or colour vision

| ■ Do I know whether any of my operations present a hazard to people with a particular problem? | □ | □ | □ |

eg dusty conditions may be unsuitable for some workers with chest problems

| ■ Do I take these factors into consideration in a clear and fair way at recruitment and subsequently? | □ | □ | □ |

eg by ensuring that the specific health requirements for a job are assessed and people are not turned down because of irrelevant health conditions

| ■ Am I prepared to modify working arrangements where practicable to accommodate employees with health problems? | □ | □ | □ |

eg by rearranging working hours, adjusting the height of work surfaces.

First aid and treatment

	Yes	No	Uncertain
■ Do my first aid procedures comply with the *First Aid at Work Regulations?*	□	□	□

See HSE guidance booklet HS (R)II

| ■ Have I considered my first aid needs for coping with illness at work, and made appropriate arrangements? | □ | □ | □ |

eg emergency on call arrangements with a local doctor or nurse

| ■ Have I considered whether any additional treatment services would be cost-effective in my operation and if so, made suitable arrangements? | □ | □ | □ |

eg regular visits to the workplace by physiotherapists or dentists to aviod workers having to take time off for appointments

Health promotion

	Yes	No	Uncertain
■ Have I considered whether the benefits of health education, employee assistance or counselling programmes would justify their introduction, and have I introduced such programmes?	□	□	□

eg programmes aimed at improving diet and reducing smoking and problem drinking. The workplace can be an ideal location in which to encourage employees towards healthier living

| ■ Do I know whether screening tests are available that could improve the health of my staff by detecting treatable illness at an earlier stage, and if so, have I arranged for them to be carried out? | □ | □ | □ |

eg arrangements with local health authorities or others for cervical smears to be carried out at the workplace

Information, instruction and training

	Yes	No	Uncertain
■ Do my employees understand any health risks involved in their work and how to minimise them?	□	□	□

| ■ Have my employees received sufficient instruction and training in how to avoid ill health? | □ | □ | □ |

eg hygiene procedures and correct use of personal protective equipment

If you answered NO or UNCERTAIN to any of these questions you need help

Figure 4.11   Checklist for health and safety

Source: Reproduced with permission from: *Review Your Occupational Needs – employers' guide*, HSE, HMSO, 1988.

■ Key concepts

- 'Careless worker' model
- Self-regulatory
- Robens Report
- 'as far as practicable'

- Safety committee
- Safety policy
- 'as far as reasonably practicable'

Discussion questions

---

1. Explain the 'careless worker' model.
2. 'Spending money on health and safety measures is a luxury most small organizations cannot afford.' Build an argument to support this statement. Build an argument to negate it.
3. Explain the role of an HRM specialist in providing a safe and healthy environment for employees.
4. Explain the symptoms and causes of job stress, and what the organization can do to alleviate it.
5. 'Employers with poor safety records often have poor written safety policies.' Do you agree or disagree? Discuss.
6. Explain how training can improve occupational health and safety.
7. 'Stress on women both inside and outside the work organization is a huge challenge.' Discuss.

■ Further reading

Codrington, C. and Henley, J. S. (1981), 'The industrial relations of injury and death', *British Journal of Industrial Relations*, November.

Cooper, C. L. and Smith M. J. (eds) (1985), *Job Stress and Blue Collar Work*, Chichester: Wiley.

Craig, M. (1981), *Office Workers' Survival Handbook*, London: BSSRS Publications.

Eva, D. and Oswald, R. (1981), *Health and Safety at Work*, London: Pan Books.

Health and Safety Commission (1976), *Safety Representatives and Safety Committees*, London: HMSO.

Smith, I. T. and Wood, J. C. (1989), *Industrial Law* (4th ed.), London: Butterworths, Ch. 11.

Robens, Lord (1972) *Report of the Committee on Safety and Health*, London: HMSO.

▌ Chapter case study   Managing AIDS at
▌ Johnson Stores plc

Gwen Fine is the HRM manager at Johnson Stores plc, a large department store located in SE England. One Monday morning in January, Norman Smith, a trainee manager in the hardware and electrical goods department, walked into Gwen's office, sat down and broke the news that he was terminally ill. But that was not all he said. He rambled on about a friend who had died of AIDS. Both of them knew what he was trying to say, but neither knew how to express it. Finally, Norman stopped and asked: 'You know what it is, don't you?' 'Yes, I do,' replied Gwen. 'It's a terrible thing in our society.' Norman went on to tell her that he could expect to live two more years, at best. Later that morning, Gwen reflected on the meeting with Norman and felt ashamed of her insensitive comment. She confided in a close co-worker her feelings: 'What a stupid, impersonal thing to say,' she chided herself. 'The man is dying.'

Norman was on sick leave for six weeks following the meeting in early January with Gwen Fine; a doctor's note described his illness as shingles. The staff in Norman's department were an understanding group and carried the extra work. In February, Norman phoned Gwen Fine with good news. He was feeling better and the store could expect to see him back at work the following Monday.

When Norman walked into the store his co-workers were overwhelmed by the stark change in his appearance. 'My God, he looks terrible,' Gwen thought when she met him later in the day. At 43, Norman was a handsome man. Yet he had lost 30 pounds since Gwen had last seen him. Dark rings circled his eyes, and his cheeks were sunken. His tall frame seemed unsteady as he leaned on a walking stick he was now carrying. The illness had also caused unsightly skin eruptions and irritation on his legs.

Norman was confident, until returning to work, that he could keep his condition private. He had offered himself as a 'guinea pig' to a group of specialist doctors searching for an AIDS cure at the regional hospital. The treatment demanded Norman leave the store once a week. 'Why are you always going to the hospital?' his co-workers began asking. Rumours began to circulate in the store about Norman's illness, focusing on his sexuality and the possibility he had AIDS. Co-workers began behaving differently to him. Staff in his department avoided Norman and attempted to ostracize him. Employees in the store also refused to use the water fountain, cups in the canteen, or the toilet. As another department manager stated: 'The linking of Norman's illness to AIDS triggered irrational things in people and Johnson's entire employees simply panicked. People are totally misinformed about AIDS.'

The reaction from Norman's co-workers began to affect morale and cause disruption. In April, three long-serving employees in the hardware and electrical department requested a transfer. The sales in the department fell sharply in the first quarter. Shortly after the release of the quarterly sales figures, Gwen Jones received an E-mail message from her boss, Stan Beale, the store's general manager, requesting an urgent meeting to discuss Mr Norman Smith.

(*Note:* the names of the characters and the company are fictitious, but the case is based on a true story taken from 'Managing Aids: How one boss struggled to cope', in *Business Week*, February 1993.)

Assignment

---

1. If you were in Gwen Jones' position would you have handled the case differently? Explain.
2. Drawing on the concepts in this chapter, and your own research, what policy or procedural changes could be instituted at Johnson Stores plc to prevent such disruption in the future?

■ References

1. Dr J. Cullen, Chair of the Health and Safety Commission (1986) and quoted in (1989) *Workplace Health: A Trade Unionists' Guide*, London: Labour Research Dept, p. 2.
2. Andrew, a machine operator at Servo Engineering, quoted in Bratton, Japanization at Work, 1992: 124.
3. Quoted in Giles, A. and Iain, H. C. (1989), 'The Collective Agreement' in J. Anderson *et al.* (eds), *Union–Management Relations in Canada* (2nd ed.) Ont: Addison-Wesley.
4. (1989), *Workplace Health: A Trade Unionists' Guide*, London: Labour Research Dept, p. 3.
5. Quoted in Kinnersly (1987), *The Hazards of Work*, London: Pluto Press, p. 1.
6. Robens, Lord (1972), *Safety and Health at Work* (Cmnd 5034) p. 1.
7. TUC (1979), The Safety Rep and Union Organization, London: TUC Education, p. 10.
8. TUC (1979), The Safety Rep and Union Organization, London: TUC Education, p. 10.
9. *Workplace Health*, p. 2.
10. Witness to the Factories' Inquiry Commission, 1833, and quoted in F. Engels (English edn, 1973), *The Condition of the Working Class in England*, London: Progress Publishers, p. 194.
11. Quoted in Sigman, A., 'Back on the agenda', *Personnel Management Plus*, February 1993.

12. See Fletcher, B. *et al.* (1979), 'Exploding the myth of executive stress' in *Personnel Management*, May, and quoted in Craig, M., *Office Survival Handbook*, London: BSSSRS, p. 10.
13. Haynes, S. G. and Feinleils, M. (1980) 'Women, work and coronary heart disease, prospective findings from the Framingham Heart Study', in *American Journal of Public Health*, 70, February, and quoted in BSSRS, p. 10.
14. Huczynski, A. and Buchanan, D. *Organisational Behaviour*, London: Prentice-Hall, 1991, p. 311.
15. *Office Survival Handbook*.
16. Ibid. p. 10.
17. Raeburn, Anna (1980), *Cosmopolitan*, August, and quoted in BSSR, p. 19.
18. Smith, I. T. and Wood, J. C. (1989) *Industrial Law* (4th ed.) London: Butterworths, pp. 83–4.
19. *Office Survival Handbook*, p. 18.
20. Quoted in (1983), *Bargaining Report*, London: Labour Research Department, December.
21. *Workplace Health*, p. 27.
22. Filipowicz, C. A. (1979), 'The Troubled Employee: Whose Responsibility?', *The Personnel Administrator*, June. Quoted in Stone, T. H. and Meltz, N. M., (1988), *Human Resource Management in Canada* (2nd ed.), Toronto: HRW, p. 529.
23. *Workplace Health* p. 29.
24. From 'Smoking – the Facts', Health Education Council.
25. Falconer T., (1987), 'No Butts About It,' *Canadian Business*, February.
26. From 'Smoking attitudes and behaviour', HMSO, quoted in (1984), *Smoking at Work*, London: TUC, p. 62.
27. Lee Smith, a former executive of Levi Strauss & Co., quoted in (1993), 'Managing Aids: How One Boss Struggled to Cope', *Business Week*, 1 February, p. 48.
28. *Business Week*, 1 February 1993, pp. 53–4.
29. *Business Week*, 1 February 1993, pp. 53–4.
30. SRSC Guidance Notes, paragraph 18.
31. TUC (1986) *Health and Safety at Work: TUC Course Book for Union Reps* (4th ed.), London: TUC, p. 163.

PLANNING AND SELECTION

CHAPTER 5

Human Resource Planning

Real manpower planning in any organisation is to do with ability in handling 'people'.[1]

Of comprehensive and systematic manpower planning fully integrated into strategic planning there exist few examples at the present time.[2]

Strategic personnel planning . . . must be far sighted, but action based; imaginative and flexible but conceptually bound; authoritative but not authoritarian; and meet business needs but not ignore the needs of its employees.[3]

■ Chapter outline

Introduction
Manpower planning
Human resource planning
Career management
Competencies
Summary

Chapter objectives

After studying this chapter, you should be able to:

1. Understand the different approaches to Manpower Planning.
2. Explain the difference between Manpower Planning and Human Resource Planning.
3. Explain the growing importance of career management in organizations.
4. Understand the use of competency-based approaches to planning individual development.

■ Introduction

In Chapter 2, we argued that external conditions and pressures for change are having a considerable and continuing impact on the way that an organization manages its human resources. The nature of the changes has led to the recognition of people as the source of competitive advantage. If identical non-people resources, in the form of raw materials, plant, technology, hardware and software, are available to competing organizations, then differences in economic performance between organizations must be attributed to differences in the performance of people.

For senior managers in an organization, whose task it is to plan a response to such pressures, the attraction, recruitment, utilization, development and retention of people of the required quantity and quality for the present and the future ought now to rival finance, marketing and production in the construction of strategic plans. However, the evidence currently available (Nkomo, 1988) would suggest that HRM/Personnel Managers still have only a limited input into the planning process at strategic levels and that the nature of this input is essentially to help in the formulation of plans based on decisions already determined. This would suggest that human resource information is used to ensure that people do not constrain or have an adverse impact on the business plan already decided. The more such business plans are based on figures and mathematical models, the greater the need for information about people to be expressed in a similar fashion. On paper at least, the plan for people will 'fit' the plan for the business. The growth of Manpower Planning techniques through the 1960s which provided such information, and their incorporation into comprehensive computer models, was a key factor in the personnel function's development and acceptance at some strategic planning meetings.

Over the years, however, while theoretical development has multiplied the number and sophistication of manpower planning techniques, the activity has slid in and out of favour at strategic levels. This was partly because the data and the computer models failed to live up to expectations with the possibility that personnel departments were unable to make use of the theoretical advances. It was also because the people issue fluctuated in importance. Thus in times of relative full employment, people and their skills were important because of their scarcity. During the years of recession in the 1980s the manpower plan was used to slim down the workforce, while the demographic issues of the late 1980s appeared to make people important again.

Human resource planning (HRP) is based on an assumption that people do not fluctuate in importance. The emphasis on quantities, flows and mathematical modelling, which appeared to be the main concern of manpower planning, is at least complemented by, and progressively superseded by, a qualitative view of people whose performance lies at the core of business strategy. We have also shown that performance lies at the core of the HRM cycle. HRP therefore will be concerned with the development and provision of a framework which allows an organization to integrate key HR activities so that it may meet the needs of employees and enhance their potential *and* meet the performance needs of business strategy.

This chapter will look at the transition from manpower planning driven by techniques towards human resource planning as an aspect of HRM.

■ Manpower planning

Manpower planning owes its importance, however fluctuating, to the importance of business strategy and planning in many organizations. It is worth, just for a moment, paying attention to the process of planning at this level. A plan represents one of the outcomes from a process which seeks to find a solution to a defined problem. There have been many attempts to rationalise this process to provide a set of easy-to-follow linear steps so that efficient decisions can be made to formulate a plan from a choice of alternatives prior to implementation. Plans therefore represent the precise articulation of an organization's strategy, produced as a result of a rational consideration of the various issues which affect an organization's future performance before making a choice of the action required. In this process senior managers will conduct an appraisal of both internal and external situations using a range of techniques to assess the organization's strengths and weaknesses and the threats and opportunities – the so-called SWOT analysis. Formally the emphasis will be on data which can be quantified and this is not surprising, since the planning process itself is an organization's attempt to pre-empt and deal with identified problems and uncertainty, and numbers are certain, precise and simple to comprehend. This image of certainty and control is one that gives comfort to many senior managers, despite the doubts expressed by some academics (Mintzberg, 1990) about the reality of the process.

If business strategy and plans find their expression in measurable financial, marketing and production targets, the manpower plan represents a response of the personnel function to ensure that the necessary supply of people is forth-coming to allow the targets to be met. The rationalized approach to manpower planning and the key stages are shown in Figure 5.1. The manpower plan can therefore be expressed in a way that matches the overall business strategy and plan. In theory at least, a manpower plan can show how the demand for people and their skills within an organization can be balanced by supply.

The rationalized approach leading to a balance of demand and supply can be found in some of the definitions and explanations of manpower planning over the last 20 years. According to Smith (1980, p. 7), manpower planning means:

1. Demand work – analysing, reviewing and attempting to predict the numbers, by kind, of the manpower needed by the organization to achieve its objectives.
2. Supply work – attempting to predict what action is and will be necessary to ensure that the manpower needed is available when required.
3. Designing the interaction between demand and supply, so that skills are utilised to the best possible advantage and the legitimate aspirations of the individual are taken into account.

In 1974 the Department of Employment had defined manpower planning as:

> strategy for the acquisition, utilisation, improvement and preservation of an organisation's human resources.[4]

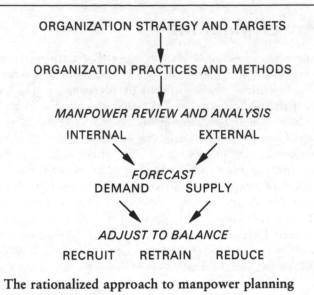

Figure 5.1   The rationalized approach to manpower planning

This definition was broad and general enough to cover most aspects of personnel management work. Four stages of the planning process were outlined:

1. An evaluation or appreciation of existing manpower resources.
2. An estimation of the proportion of currently employed manpower resources which are likely to be within the firm by the forecast date.
3. An assessment or forecast of labour requirements if the organisation's overall objectives are to be achieved by the forecast date.
4. The measures to ensure that the necessary resources are available as and when required, that is, the manpower plan.

Stages 1 and 2 were linked in the 'supply aspect of manpower' with stage 1, being part of the 'normal personnel practice'. Stage 3 represents the 'demand aspect of manpower'. There were two main reasons for companies to use manpower planning: first, to develop their business objectives and manning levels; and second, to reduce the 'unknown factor'.

While equilibrium can serve as an ideal, organizations will be composed of a variety of supply and demand problems throughout their structure, which planning will need to bring into overall balance at optimum levels. The movement towards equilibriums involves a variety of personnel activities such as recruitment, promotion, succession planning, training, reward management, retirement and redundancy. The complexity of the interaction of these factors in the context of the aims of optimization and overall equilibrium made manpower planning a suitable area of interest for operational research and the application of statistical techniques. In this process, organizations could be envisaged as a series of stocks and flows as part of an overall system of resource allocation. Models of behaviour could be formulated in relation to labour turnover, length of service, promotion flows and age distributions. These variables could be expressed as mathematical and statistical formulae and equations allowing solutions for manpower decisions to be calculated. With the growing use of computers, the techniques and models became more ambitious and probably beyond the comprehension of most managers. In large organizations there was a growth in the number of specialist manpower analysts who were capable of dealing with the complex processes involved.

In the UK, the Institute of Manpower Studies (IMS) based at Sussex University has been a principal advocate of manpower modelling. According to the Institute (Bennison, 1980, p. 2), the manpower planning process involves:

a. determining the manpower requirements; how many people;
b. establishing the supply of manpower;
c. developing policies to fill the gap between supply and demand.

The Institute favours a flexible approach where plans are developed, based on an understanding of the whole manpower system. The first step in manpower analysis is to describe the present manpower system and set its expected objectives. The system can be drawn as a 'collection of boxes and flows representing the way that manpower behaves in the organisation' (Bennison, 1980, p. 5). Planners can assess the critical 'decision points' for manpower policy. For example, decisions for the recruitment and promotion of managers can occur in a meaningful way using statistical planning techniques where the 'practical limits of variation' (Bennison, 1980, p. 17) can be defined for factors such as levels of labour turnover at particular points, technology development impact and forecasts for growth. If possible, the relationship of the factors to the decisions will be quantified, allowing the generation of promotion paths under different assumptions of demand and supply.

The IMS and others involved in the development of models and techniques would be the first to accept that manpower planning is more than 'building a statistical model of the supply of manpower' (Bennison, 1980, p. 2). An emphasis on the models at the expense of the reality of managing and interacting with people was bound to be greeted with suspicion; certainly by employees and their representatives, but also by managers 'forced' to act on the results of the calculations. It may be argued that the manpower analysis is there to serve as an aid to decision-making, but the presentation of data and an inability to deal with the ever-increasing complexity of models was always likely to result in the manpower analysis being 'seen' as the plan. The domination of equations which mechanistically provide solutions for problems based on the behaviour of people may actually become divorced from the real world and have a good chance of missing the real problems. Hence the bad reputation of manpower planning. Cowling and Walters (1990, p. 6), reporting on an IPM survey of human resource planning, found that few respondents attributed benefits of planning to increasing job satisfaction/motivation (33.5 per cent), reducing skills shortages (30.2 per cent) and reducing labour turnover (22.4 per cent). Of the respondents who used computers, 3.3 per cent reported a use for job design and 9 per cent for job analysis. These are all vital areas of concern for any organization – areas which are at the heart of HRM approaches.

There have also been a number of doubts about the connection between the business plan and the manpower plan. In a survey of US firms by Nkomo (1988), while 54 per cent of organizations reported the preparation of manpower plans, few reported a strong link between this activity and strategic business planning. Pearson (1991, p. 20) reports the problem for manpower planners where business objectives may be absent or where they may not be communicated. Cowling and Walters (1990, p. 6) found that 58.4 per cent of respondents faced a low priority given to planning compared with immediate management concerns. The authors conclude, 'Of comprehensive and systematic manpower planning fully integrated into strategic planning there exist few examples at the present time'.

There have been a number of attempts to make manpower planning techniques 'user-friendly' to non-specialists. Thus the fall-out from theoretical progress in manpower analysis has been the application of techniques to help with particular problems in the workplace.[5] Bell (1989, p. 42) argues that personnel managers understood the concept of manpower planning even if line managers and corporate planners did not, and that they were able to use basic techniques. Some personnel managers have been able to use manpower planning techniques to help them understand and deal with 'real' manpower problems, for example, why one department in an organization seems to suffer from a dramatically higher labour turnover than others, or why graduate trainees are not retained in sufficient numbers. This can be seen as part of a continuing search by the personnel function to find areas of expertise that would legitimise its position and prove its value. In this approach, manpower plans and policies serve as initiators of operations, and techniques are used to monitor the progress of operations and to raise an awareness of problems as they arise. There is an attempt to use manpower information as a way of understanding problems so that action can be taken as appropriate. The disproportionate influence of the plan as a solution is replaced by an attention to planning as a continuous process. In this way personnel managers have been practising what Fyfe (1986, p. 66) refers to as 'the diagnostic approach to manpower planning'. This approach builds on and broadens the rationalized approach to identify problem areas, and tries to understand why they occur. The theoretical idea of a balance of demand and supply and equilibrium can only occur on paper or on the computer screen. The more likely real-life situation is one of continuous imbalance as a result of the dynamic conditions facing any organization, the behaviour of people and the imperfections of computer models. The diagnostic approach is based on the following thesis:

> before any manager seeks to bring about change, or reduce the degree of imbalance, he or she must be fully aware of the reasons behind the imbalance (or the manpower

HRM IN PRACTICE 5.1

Computer firm scraps contracts

by Gaby Huddart

Computer giant ICL has torn up working agreements at three of its plants in a company-wide drive towards flexible contracts.

Under the plans, the firm, which has recently been examining ways to increase flexibility across the workforce, will bring in personal contracts and throw out regular working hours.

"We are exploring more flexible ways of working," personnel director of ICL Europe, Andrew Mayo told *Personnel Today*.

"In some areas, we now have groups of teleworkers working from home and we are outsourcing groups of staff," he said.

In the latest development ICL has told 2,000 staff at its manufacturing and supply division their overtime agreement will be axed at the end of August.

The new practices, overtime rates and contracts that will replace the old system are detailed in a booklet, *Competitive Working Practices*, sent to all staff.

Weekend overtime will be cut by 25 per cent. Shift pay will also be reduced and supervisors can no longer expect extra cash for their first hour of overtime.

"To enable the business to grow we have to be competitive in every aspect and that includes people," said personnel manager for manufacturing and supply Mike Campbell.

Hours will vary week to week under contracts.

Source: Personnel Today, 15 June 1993.
Reprinted with permission.

---

problem) in the first place. Unless managers understand more about the nature of manpower problems, their attempts to control events will suffer from the hit-and-miss syndrome. (Fyfe 1986, p. 66)

Figure 5.2, on the following page, shows the stages of this process.

By comparison with the rationalized approach, manpower problems using a diagnositic approach, are to be identified and explored so that they can be understood with the data used to help in this process and the speed of the computer providing support at an early stage. The rationalized approach will seek to minimize the time spent on such matters, preferring instead to focus on problems that can be easily defined or that most closely match ready prepared solutions which may be difficult to challenge. For example, in the rationalized approach, organization practices and methods – which include the division of labour, the design of work, the technology used, the relationships between departments and groups and the degree of management supervision – will precede the manpower review and be taken as a set of 'givens' in the ensuing

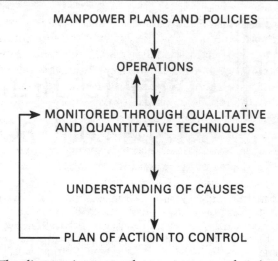

Figure 5.2   The diagnostic approach to manpower planning

calculations. Yet these may be the very factors which lie at the heart of manpower problems. Thus a national clearing bank which faces a problem of retaining bank clerks may respond to this imbalance by stepping up recruitment and/or increasing pay. A diagnostic approach however would mean becoming aware of this problem by monitoring manpower statistics such as wastage and stability, and obtaining qualitative data by interviewing staff. The interviews may reveal concerns with job satisfaction and career paths open to bank clerks, reflecting the aspirations of staff which are not being met by current bank practices. Rather than express these aspirations openly for fear of conflict with management, many staff prefer to seek employment elsewhere. The loss of skilled labour has important cost implications and, in the face of continuing shortages of skilled workers, a diagnostic approach to retention can provide a significant pay-off. Bevan (1991) provides a guide to some of the reasons for high staff turnover. Significantly, but not unexpectedly, pay was not the only issue. Among the main factors identified were:

- job not matching expectation for new employees;
- lack of attention from line managers and lack of training;
- lack of autonomy, responsibility, challenge and variety within the work;
- disappointment with promotion and development opportunities;
- standards of management including unapproachable, uncaring and distant behaviour and a failure to consult.

These are all complex factors reflecting general areas of concern, but which require solutions that are specific to the context of each organisation. In the case of the national clearing bank example, the organization could respond to the diagnosis in various ways. For example, management could accept the problem and do nothing except lower the quality of recruitment to bank clerk positions so that, hopefully, those staff would be less likely to have career aspirations. Hardly very progressive and not very complex, but certainly an option. However, more likely would be an attempt to improve the work environment and work practices so as to provide avenues for greater job satisfaction and personal growth. This may have implications for job design, department structure and management style, creating a tension that will have to be resolved. In this way, manpower planning becomes integrated into the whole process of management of the employment relationship which itself plays a proactive part in affecting organization, strategy, structure and practices. Importantly, manpower planning has a part to play in bridging the gap between the needs of the organization (as defined by senior management) and the needs of individual employees. This theme will be explored later in the chapter.

While the diagnostic approach to manpower planning will have an incremental impact, the changes that it will bring about will accumulate in the organization's value system and mould its response to larger and more significant human resource problems. A good example is provided by responses to the decline in the number of young people entering the workforce. The number of 16- to 19-year-olds in the UK has been falling, from 3.7 million in 1982 to 2.6 million by 1994. In the late 1980s it was predicted that such a decline would cause labour markets to tighten all over the UK, particularly in those areas where organizations had already faced constraints on production posed by shortages of skilled workers. Atkinson (1989, p. 22) has outlined a range of responses to this problem based on three characteristics:

a. sequential – 'introduced only slowly as the full seriousness of the shortage problem becomes apparent to firms';
b. hierarchical – 'with more difficult/expensive responses deployed only when easier/cheaper ones have proved inadequate';
c. cumulative – 'they . . . will build on each other'.[6]

Figure 5.3 shows the pattern of responses adopted by different organizations. The model sees a progression from tactical responses, starting with doing nothing (Quadrant 1) and competing for the diminishing supply of labour (Quadrant 2), to more strategic ones, identifying new and substitute supplies of labour (Quadrant 3) and improving the use and performance of existing workers (Quadrant 4). The latter two quadrants have important implications for the nature of the employment relationship and the approach to manpower planning. It is somewhere between Quadrants 3 and 4 that, we would suggest, Human Resource Management and Human Resource Planning begins.

■ Human resource planning

Human resource planning (HRP) can now be seen as an aspect of human resource management (HRM) where HRM, to use David Guest's phrasing, 'is carefully

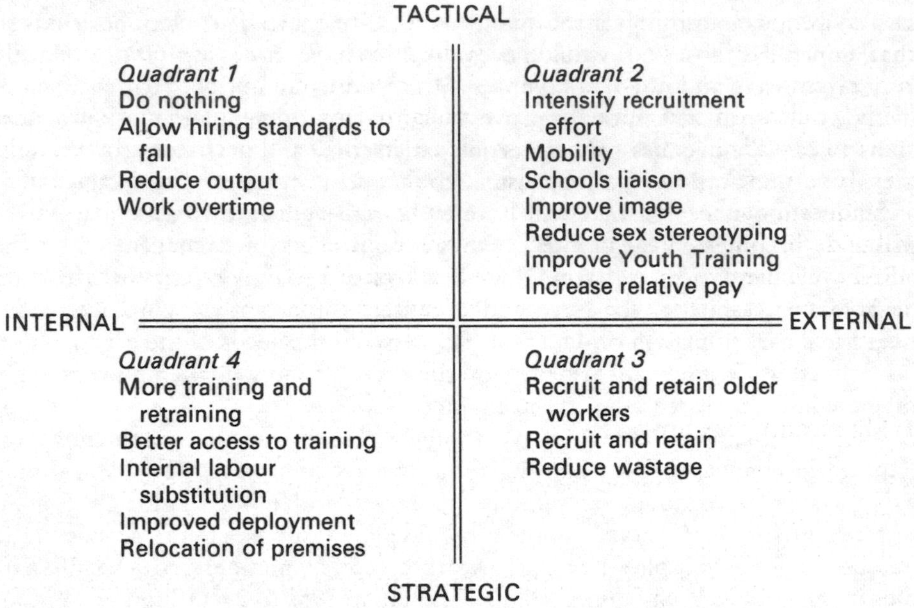

TACTICAL

Quadrant 1	Quadrant 2
Do nothing	Intensify recruitment
Allow hiring standards to	effort
fall	Mobility
Reduce output	Schools liaison
Work overtime	Improve image
	Reduce sex stereotyping
	Improve Youth Training
	Increase relative pay

INTERNAL ══════════════════════════════════════ EXTERNAL

Quadrant 4	Quadrant 3
More training and	Recruit and retain older
retraining	workers
Better access to training	Recruit and retain
Internal labour	Reduce wastage
substitution	
Improved deployment	
Relocation of premises	

STRATEGIC

Figure 5.3   Patterns of responses to the demographic downturn

Source: Adapted from Atkinson, 1989. Used with permission.

defined to reflect a particular approach to the management of people in organisations' (1989, p. 48). The replacement of the term Manpower Planning by HRP, as has happened in many organizations, may not actually amount to very much difference. The key point is that HRP will occur as a consequence of senior management's belief that people represent the source of competitive advantage and that the continuing development of those people will be a vital feature of strategy in both its formation and its implementation. How quickly senior managers adopt such a belief is highly problematic. Certainly, the external factors that we identified in Chapter 2 may have a significant influence, however the impact will vary. For example, highly bureaucratic organizations may have great difficulty in responding quickly to external pressures. Such organizations are designed and structured to deal with a certainty that will be repeated time and time again. Any variation will be resisted and forced into standardized responses. For such organizations, the manpower issue is concerned with the 'right number of people in the right place at the right time'. The task of the manpower plan will be to identify and supply required quantities of people with appropriate 'standardized' skills. This is the thinking that still dominates the minds of many managers in UK organizations. Even where it becomes recognized that standardized responses do not satisfy new demands, such an organization is more likely to revise its standardized response than fundamentally to reform its view of the employment relationship. Indeed, as Guest (1989, p. 50) suggests, a HRM approach is just one of a variety of approaches to the management of people in organizations, and it is 'not always the most sensible policy to pursue'.

HRP builds on and develops the rationalized and diagnostic approaches to manpower planning that we have already identified in this chapter. It certainly may involve the use of manpower modelling, simulations and statistical techniques, but these will be set within an overall approach to planning which will underpin the package of interdependent policies and activities that form the HRM cycle that we identified in Chapter 1. Figure 5.4 shows a representation of the HRP process. There are a number of features in this process which give HRP a distinctive flavour.

■ Plans and planning

HRP is seen as a continuous and cyclical process incorporating an HR Plan. This allows a distinction to be made between processes to produce a plan and the activity of planning as part of a problem-management process. Kolb (1982, p. 109) conceives the process of 'problem management', drawn from the theory of experiential learning, as proceeding through a series of stages in a cycle[7]. The

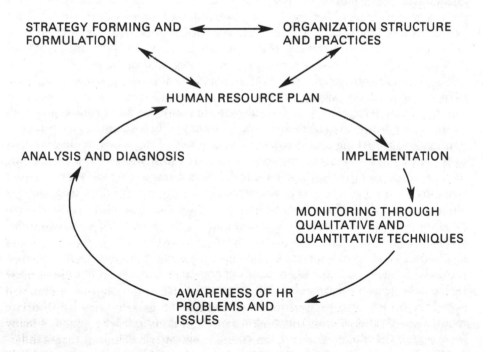

Figure 5.4   A model of HRP

idea of a cycle is particularly appropriate to HRP. The cycle is full of tensions, for example, between analysing and diagnosing HR issues and problems and implementing a solution, between awareness of the issues and problems and generating a plan. HRP involves the creative use and resolution of such tensions. Thus the use of rationalized models and techniques to produce a plan is countered by the need for an awareness of HR issues and problems. Without the awareness, a plan may be based on false and outdated assumptions about the behaviour of people. Awareness without a plan however has no impetus and direction for action.

■ Tactics and strategy

In the diagnostic approach to manpower planning, quantitative planning techniques are used in combination with qualitative techniques to identify and understand the causes of manpower problems. The information can then be used to generate solutions equal to the complexity of the problems. We also saw that such an approach had the potential to affect organization structure, job design and work practices. Organizations could also work out short term tactics to deal with external manpower issues like skills shortages and a decline in the number of young people in the labour market. In both the diagnostic approach and the rationalised approach, manpower plans are established with reference to a predetermined strategy for the long term – although doubts have already been expressed about the reality of such a link. An HRP approach can draw upon a less deterministic view of strategy that can provide a vital interdependent link between HRP, organisation structure and strategy. Mintzberg (1978, p. 935) has criticized definitions of strategy as an explicit, rationally predetermined plan as incomplete. For Mintzberg, strategy is a 'pattern in a stream of decisions'. The source of such patterns may be formulations of conscious and rational processes expressed by senior managers as intended strategy but also emergent, probably unintentional, learning and discoveries as a result of decisions made gradually over time. Included in this latter process of strategy formation will be the learning of and from employees through their interaction with the organisation's structure, work processes and suppliers/clients/customers.[8] Realised strategy will be a result of both intended and emergent processes. Diagnostic techniques of planning will tap some of this learning and, in the context of an HRM value system, learning will feed through into strategic decisions. As we will see in later chapters, this view of awareness and understanding emerging from the HRP process is fundamental to generating the energy to keep the HR cycle moving and to the achievement of desirable HR outcomes such as commitment and high performance. It is also a requisite of such approaches as Total Quality Management. Tactics adopted in the short term as a response to HR problems and issues form part of the emerging stream of decisions, and senior managers who are able to absorb the understanding gained from such a process will be able to declare an intended strategy that will reflect the vision held by the whole organization.

■ External and internal labour

The rationalised approach is based on a neutral view of the sources of supply for forecasted demands for labour. Based on an assumption of the interchangeability of workers, the main consideration will relate to costs. Thus it may be cheaper on balance to recruit workers from outside the organization and save on the costs of training those workers already employed. Similarly, the aim of minimizing costs was a key factor for many years in the process of deskilling work so that workers who left, 'wastage', could be easily substituted by new recruits.

In traditional manufacturing organizations, the restrictive practices of craft-based trades unions based on time-served apprenticeships and demarcation was seen by management as justification to seek opportunities to deskill the work over the years where possible. A deskilling strategy was not always possible or desirable (see Chapter 3) and in the face of skills shortages, managers began to pay more attention to keeping scarce workers, using a diagnostic approach to manpower planning.

The HRP approach takes this process several stages further. Accepting that vital skills may not be available in the external labour market, the focus shifts to workers already employed and their potential for further development allied to the need for flexibility. Previous attention to the 'right' number of people is superseded by attention to the 'right' kind of people. This of course requires further explanation.

Academics working in the fields of sociology and labour economics have developed a theoretical framework, referred to as *labour market segmentation*, to classify and explain the ways in which organizations seek to employ different kinds of labour. Loveridge (1983, p. 155) has developed a classification based on the following factors:

a. the degree to which workers have flexible skills which are specific to an organization
b. the degree to which work contains discretionary elements which provide stable earnings

The classification helps to explain how and why some organizations will adopt different approaches to the management and planning of the employment relationship for different groups of employees. Thus workers in the primary internal market would include those with important and scarce skills which are specific to a particular organization; an organization would be anxious to retain such workers and develop their potential. It would be such employees who would form the focus for the application of the full range of HRM activities. On the other hand, some workers operating in the secondary internal market will be deemed by management to be of less importance, except in their availability at the times required by an organization. Such workers would include part-time, seasonal and, increasingly, home-workers. An organization would wish to recruit and retain those employees deemed by management to be the kind of workers who could be trained to the organization's requirements, but there would be less

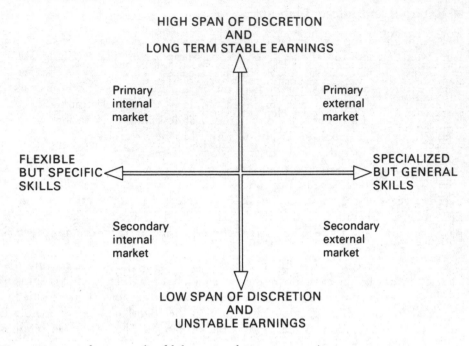

Figure 5.5   A framework of labour market segmentation

Source: Loveridge, 1983. Used with permission.

interest in applying the whole package of HRM policies. Workers operating in the external markets would be considered to be someone else's concern. Atkinson and Meager (1985, p. 2) have presented a model of a flexible firm which:

> draws into a simple framework the new elements in employers' manpower practices, bringing out the relationships between the various practices and their appropriateness for different companies and groups of workers.

The model identifies four types of flexibility:

a. functional – 'a firm's ability to adjust and deploy the skills of its employees to match the tasks required by its changing workload, production methods and/or technology';

b. numerical – a firm's ability to adjust the level of labour inputs to meet fluctuations in output;

c. distancing strategies – the replacement of internal workers with external sub-contractors, that is, putting some work; such as running the firm's canteen, out to contract;

d. financial – support for the achievement of flexibility through the pay and reward structure.

The flexible firm will achieve these flexibilities through a division of its workforce into a 'core' group surrounded by 'peripheral' groups. The core group would be composed of those workers expected to deliver functional flexibility and would include those workers with firm specific skills and high discretionary elements in their work. The peripheral group would be composed of a number of different workers. One category might be directly employed by a firm to perform work with a low discretionary element. Another category would be employed as required on a variety of contracts, for example, part-time, temporary and casual workers. This category might also include highly specialised workers such as consultants. The final category would be composed of trainees on government financed schemes, some of whom may be prepared for eventual transfer to the core group.

This flexible firm has been subject to much debate during the 1980s and 1990s. The model has been criticized (Pollert, 1988, p. 281) as being unsupported by the evidence and as presenting a self-fulfilling prediction of how such a firm should be created. The evidence however showed a confused picture. At the time of the 1987 Employers' Labour Use Strategies Survey (Hakim, 1990, p. 162), only a small minority of employers had a conscious core/periphery manpower strategy. However an ACAS survey (1988), in the same year, found a growing range of flexible working practices. This would suggest that in the late 1980s there were many organizations adopting flexible working practices in an *ad hoc*, unplanned and, occasionally, opportunistic manner. Hakim has praised the model of a flexible firm as a 'simplified synthesis' of key ideas whose achievement was to 'reveal the inner logic of existing labour strategies, to disclose the implicit structure of segmented labour markets' (1990, p. 180). Consciously or unconsciously, planned or unplanned, many organizations have continued the move towards flexibility although the shape of the flexible firm is still emerging. (See HRM IN PRACTICE 5.1 and 5.2 for two examples.)

■ Career management

We argued in Chapter 1 that HRM values reflect a unitarist perspective on the employment relationship, with the assumption that there is common interest between management and workers. Senior managers in organizations that claim they are adopting a people-oriented HRM perspective will seek to match the needs of the organization and the needs of individual employees. Except for senior managers themselves, some commentators would doubt that this could ever occur. However, as we have shown above, it is quite possible for managers to learn and discover the needs of individuals and groups of employees through the HRP process and for this understanding to affect the perception of organization needs. There will also be many other occasions, both formal and informal, when the matching of individual and organization needs will be considered, for example, selection, performance appraisal, coaching, counselling and mentoring. Such considerations will form the dynamics of HRM and the

HRM IN PRACTICE 5.2

Credit house allows staff to stay at home

by Steve Lodge

The severe shortage of IT staff has forced a NatWest subsidiary to pilot teleworking.

Credit house Lombard North Central plans to try out teleworking among specialist staff by September.

"As long as the economics do not go out of the window it will be worth it. Specialists are difficult enough to recruit in the South East but we are in the Crawley area of zero unemployment," said John Field, deputy director of group and banking services.

Teleworking will also help solve pressures on office space as well as staff dissatisfaction with commuting, the company believes.

Initially computer development, technical authors, organisation and methods, and internal auditing staff will work from home.

The feasibility study in Lombard's 1,000-employee head office revealed that teleworking was not cost effective for all jobs, particularly at the lowest levels.

"It becomes a management problem. If you have teleworkers you are putting trust in people," he said.

"You need to have control mechanisms but be able to strike a balance."

Field added that not all staff might want to work from home, even if their job was suited to teleworking.

"We are not putting people under pressure to try it. If it does not work for them we will not stop them from coming back to work," said Field.

The organisation plans to extend teleworking down to clerical workers as and when technology costs come down. Field says that by then teleworkers will probably be able to work in a satellite office.

Source: Personnel Today, 26 June 1990.
Reprinted with permission.

---

functioning of an HR cycle. Thus data gathered about low morale may provide the rationale for a training intervention which may provide the capability and impetus for new kinds of work at higher levels of task complexity. Over a longer period of time, such processes require organizations to meet demands from employees for career management.

Mayo (1991, p. 69) has defined career management as follows:

> The design and implementation of organizational processes which enable the careers of individuals to be planned and managed in a way that optimizes both the needs of the organization and the preferences and capabilities of individuals.

The term 'career' is one that is most usually applied to managerial and professional workers. In the terminology of the flexible firm, it would be these groups that would constitute an organization's core workforce. Many organizations have responded to the career aspirations of such workers through HRP policies and processes such as succession planning, secondment, 'fast-track' development, and a vast array of personal- and management-development activities. Such responses have been based on the dubious assumption that only managers and professional employees have the potential for career development. An HRM view is that a greater number of employees have the potential for development, although the extension to the core workforce, to whom this view may apply, will vary between different organizations. You might question whether the idea of a career can be extended to a larger number of employees. After all, not everyone can be 'promoted' through the organization hierarchy even if they had the potential to do so. This is a view that is often presented to justify the status quo and to limit the resources devoted to employee development. However, it is a view based on a traditional and increasingly stagnant concept of career. As many organizations have discovered, continuous personal development is possible among large groups of employees if limiting factors that prevent the exposure of employees to new opportunities and experiences for development can be removed. Limiting factors may include organization structure and climate, and the design of work. In this sense, the term 'career' is extended to apply not only to movement through pre-defined stages such as those found in professions or organization hierarchies, but also to personal growth and development through the employees' interaction with their work environment. This view matches Hirsh's 'developing potential' emergent model of Succession Planning where 'in a person based approach, posts can be considered as ephemeral and may be designed around people' (1990, p. 18).

Through HRP, an organization will aim to provide a framework for the integration of career-management activities and processes. Within this framework, the HRM cycle shows the links between the key HR activities that are required for integration. However, the dynamics of career management will depend on the process for bridging the multiple and possibly conflicting demands of the organization and the needs and aspirations of employees. Verlander (1985, p. 20) has proposed a model of career management based on career counselling between employees and their line manager. The main elements of this model are shown in Figure 5.6. The model highlights the importance of the role of line managers in HRM processes. The nature of this role, and the skills required, will be explored further in Chapters 7 (Performance Appraisal) and 9 (Human Resource Development).

■ Competencies

In embracing an idea of development and careers for all employees, many organizations have sought a language that could enable discussions about the performance, capabilities and aspirations of individuals to take place on the basis of a common understanding of terms. In recent years, such understanding has been achieved by the development of competency-based approaches.[9] A

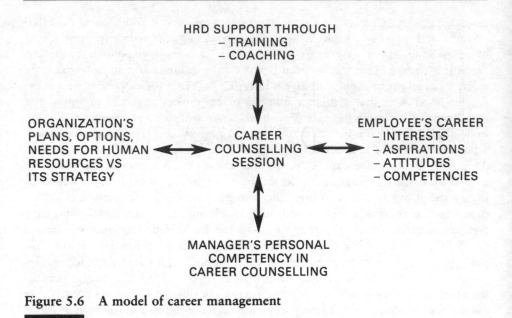

Figure 5.6   A model of career management

Source: Adapted from Verlander, 1985.

competency is concerned with the *Underlying characteristics of a person*, which lead to *competent or effective work performance* if (i) *he/she is in the right post* and (ii) *the organization is right*.

Between underlying characteristics and work performance comes behaviour and it is behaviour which has formed the focus for definitions of competency most recently. Thus Woodruffe (1992, p. 17) gives the following definition of competency:

> A competency is the set of behaviour patterns that the incumbent needs to bring to a position in order to perform its tasks and functions with competence.

Because competency is concerned with behaviour that is relevant to the job, and the effective or competent performance of that job, the identification of clusters of competencies carries considerable potential for assessment and development purposes within an organization.

The analysis of behaviour should be able to identify and isolate dimensions of behaviour that are distinct and are associated with competent or effective performance. Whilst the analysis is concerned with visible and overt behaviour, it is highly likely that it will also identify some of the underlying characteristics that feed into behaviour, for example, skills, knowledge, values, attitudes, motivation, perception, and creativity. Once identified, competencies can provide a user-friendly starting point for the assessment and development of

Cash sweetener tempts staff to go part time

by Anna Smith

British Airways is offering 6,000 Heathrow ground staff an extra six months' pay if they switch to part-time work.

The airline has also promised to protect pension rights of anyone over 50 years' old who accepts the deal.

"What we are finding is we need more flexible resourcing within the organisation," said human resources director Valerie Scoular.

"Rather than thinking of full-time staff we could actually manage with more part-time people," she added.

The airline has introduced two schemes to tempt ground staff away from full-time contracts.

One scheme, called Wind Down, is geared to staff over the age of 50 who want to reduce the hours they work in the run-up to retirement.

Alongside pension rights protection they will receive a lump sum payment equivalent to six months' salary.

Staff under the age of 50 will receive the lump sum only under the second scheme, Switch Down.

Employees were asked to tell the firm by the end of March whether they were prepared to give up their full-time jobs.

According to officials, take-up has been good and the schemes are likely to go ahead.

British Airways is the latest in a string of employers to switch staff from full-time to part-time working.

But unlike others, such as retail chain the Burton Group, it is giving staff a choice rather than offering redundancy as the only alternative.

Scoular said the airline, which lost 4,600 jobs between 1990 and 1992, would need flexible staffing to avoid compulsory redundancies.

National secretary for civil air transport at general union the TGWU George Ryde said he supported the schemes as long as they are voluntary.

"Our only concern is controlling it so it doesn't become exploitative," he said.

Source: Personnel Today, May 1993. Used with permission.

---

people in an organization. They will be derived from the work that people do, the organisation that they are in, what is regarded as competent and effective and, most importantly, the people they are. The following is a list of competencies developed for managers at W.H. Smith (Jacobs, 1989, p. 32):

- Written communication
- Oral communication
- Leadership
- Team membership
- Planning and organization skills

- Decision-making
- Motivation
- Personal strength
- Analytical and reasoning skills

While the spread of competency-based approaches is limited mainly to managers in larger organizations, the potential of competencies for integrating HRM processes for all employees is now being recognized.

■ Summary

Human resource planning is more than just the sophisticated application of quantitative manpower planning techniques for the forecast of demand and supply flows into, through, and from organizations. It is an inseparable part of an organization's overall approach to the management of its human resources. This chapter has outlined the way early approaches to manpower planning had limited and fluctuating popularity. However, through problem-solving diagnostic approaches, planning techniques could be used to learn about employee problems and explore possible solutions that had the potential ultimately to affect organization strategy. HRP is a continuation and extension of this process, which fully recognises the potential of people and their needs in the development of strategies and plans.

■ Key concepts

- Manpower planning
- Planning techniques and modelling
- The diagnostic approach
- Human resource planning
- Labour market segmentation
- The flexible firm
- Core and periphery workforce
- Career management
- Competencies

Discussion questions

1. 'When an organization is mapping out its future needs it is a serious mistake to think primarily in terms of number, flows and economic models.' Discuss.
2. How is HRP linked to Corporate Planning?
3. What would be your response to the publication of figures which showed an above-average turnover of students in a University/College Department?

4. What are the implications of labour segmentation for the management of people?
5. Should organizations faced with shortages of skilled labour 'poach' these workers from other organizations by bidding up wages?
6. What is meant by the 'flexible firm'? Explain the implications of the flexible firm for the management of human resources.

■ Further reading

Bramham, J. (1989), *Human Resource Planning*, London: IPM.

Cowling, A. and Walters, M. (1990), 'Manpower Planning – where are we today?', *Personnel Review*, Vol. 19, No. 3, pp. 3–8.

Fyfe, J. (1986), 'Putting people back into the manpower planning equations', *Personnel Management*, October, pp. 64–9.

Hakim, C. (1990), 'Core and periphery in employers' workforce strategies: evidence from the 1987 ELUS survey', *Work, Employment and Society*, Vol. 4, No. 2, pp. 157–88.

Jacobs, R. (1989), 'Getting the measure of managerial competence', *Personnel Management*, June, pp. 32–7.

Nkomo, S. M. (1988), 'Strategic planning for human resources – let's get started', *Long Range Planning*, Vol. 21, No. 1, pp. 66–72.

■ Chapter case study   Career management at JJJ Bank plc

You are required to read the following case study and prepare responses to the questions that follow. Please attempt to illustrate your responses with examples.

JJJ Bank is one of the UK's major clearing banks. Over the last decade, the Bank has faced an environment that is increasingly competitive and fast moving. The Bank has been undergoing a major strategic review of its structure and activities. A key belief has been that greater responsibility for the development and delivery of activities should be passed to front-line employees. Successive voluntary redundancy programmes had made for a relatively young workforce.

Hitherto, career development had equated to promotion through a 17-grade structure. Hence, prior to the redundancies, such promotion could be expected through the grades every 2 to 3 years. Fairly simple manpower planning techniques now reveal a slowing-down in the number of future promotions. A formal integrated career management framework does not currently exist.

Recently, a series of one day workshops concerning career management at JJJ plc was held by the HR manager for a random selection of managers and employees. One of the key issues highlighted was that career progression was seen as a 'gradist' concept due to the number of grades. This was seen to reduce emphasis on career management issues such as developmental job moves, sideways job moves, rewards for on-the-job and self-directed development, promoting an entrepreneurial job culture based on knowledge, experience, skill and opportunity and evolution of a flatter, more flexible, organization structure. It soon became clear that there was little congruence between the fast-moving environment which the Bank now faced and career management. Perhaps most important of all, line managers did not often promote development, seeing it as the role the HR function to develop people and manage careers.

In a follow-up survey of all staff, some of the key findings were as follows:

- When looking at career issues in the organization, it is suggested that
  - line managers are not willing to develop staff, particularly 'on the job';
  - the organization does not readily promote development or on-the-job development;
  - the organization does not help people manage their own careers;
  - the organization does not often explain career options open to people;
  - the organization needs to devote more resources to helping people to manage their development and career planning.

- There is an overall belief that it is important to work for an organization which
  - allows people to build their own career;
  - encourages personal development;
  - allows people to develop by experiencing different fields of work';
  - allows people to develop their existing competencies and skills;
  - provides information on career development;
  - regards career development as important.

Further research about the criteria used for promotions revealed that while individuals wanted promotion decisions to take into account their career development, they believed that they were promoted on the simple basis of suitable vacancies being available. Furthermore, with regard to whom the system promoted, women felt that expediency was favoured over and above career development.

Questions

1. What are the key issues in the management of careers in this organization?
2. What suggestions would you make for improving career management in this organization? What are the key roles and responsibilities?
3. How could a competency framework help this organization plan and manage careers?

■ References

1. Fyfe, John (1986), 'Putting people back into the manpower planning equations', *Personnel Management*, October.
2. Cowling, Alan and Walters, Mike (1990), 'Manpower Planning – where are we today?', *Personnel Review*, Vol. 19, No. 3.
3. Stenhouse, David (1986), IPM National Conference, October.
4. Department of Employment (1974), *Company Manpower Planning*, Manpower Papers, No. 1.
5. See particularly John Bramhams' books, *Practical Manpower Planning*, London: IPM (1988), and *Human Resource Planning*, London: IPM (1989).
6. The subsequent recession from 1990 disturbs the flow of Atkinson's model but the principles can be recycled for other HR issues to show how manpower planning can break through into organization strategy.
7. The theory of experiential learning will also be a feature of Chapter 11 on Human Resource Development
8. See Chapter 9, 'Strategy and HRD'.
9. There has in recent years been some confusion over the two terms 'competence' and 'competency'. The term competence is usually associated with the development of standards for the outcomes of performance for a particular role or job. In the UK a competence-based framework has been established by the National Council for Vocational Qualifications (NCVQ). National Vocational Qualifications (NVQs) are being developed to fit the framework for all occupational areas. Each NVQ is expressed in outcomes terms with standards in the form of appropriate performance criteria. This chapter concentrates on organization-determined competencies.

CHAPTER 6

Recruitment and Selection

Recruitment is the biggest single challenge facing personnel managers in the 1990s.[1]

events of the nineties will create such demands for change upon organisations that many will go under. And the major reason they will do so is that they fail to recruit and retain the people they need to help them change.[2]

We didn't want the traditional 20-minute interview, and the you-go-to-the-same-football-match-as-me-so-you-must-be-okay line.[3]

■ Chapter outline

Introduction
Recruitment, selection and the HRM cycle
Attraction
Selection interviews and techniques
Summary

Chapter objectives

After studying this chapter, you should be able to:

1. Understand the place of recruitment and selection in HRM
2. Explain the nature of attraction in recruitment.
3. Explain the effectiveness of interviews as a selection technique.
4. Understand the place of recruitment and selection as a stage in the formation of the employment relationship.

■ Introduction

Towards the end of the 1980s recruitment and selection were seen as two of the key issues facing organizations as they prepared for the 1990's. Continuing skills shortages and the prospect of a significant decline in the number of young people (the so-called 'demographic time bomb') would, according to Curnow (1989, p. 40), mean that 'recruitment is moving to the top of the personnel professional's agenda' and that the 1990's would be 'the era of the recruiter' (see also Table 1.1,

Chapter 1). Such would be the difficulties in recruiting and retaining staff, many organizations would require a 'radical response' (Herriot, 1989, p. 35). It would only be those organizations with recruitment skills equal to the enormity of the challenge that could possibly survive. With a shift in power to those with skills to sell, employers would also be compelled to see the attraction and retention of workers as part of the evolving employment relationship, based on a mutual and reciprocal understanding of expectations. Recruitment followed by selection would be vital stages in the formation of such expectations, with an emphasis on a two-way flow of communication. Employees would be selecting an organization and the work on offer as much as employers would be selecting employees. Traditional approaches, that attempt to attract a wide choice of candidates for vacancies before screening out those that do not match the criteria set in job descriptions and personnel specifications, would be too one-sided.

For a short time at least, a number of organizations did react to the impending shortages along the lines suggested. Some organizations began to adjust and widen their recruitment criteria in order to increase the numbers of recruits (Hendry et al, 1988, p. 38). One consequence in the UK was an improvement in the quality of youth training, with the guarantee of employment on the completion of training in order to attract diminishing numbers of young people. However, many of the changes adopted could be seen as tactical adjustments only. By the end of the 1980's, recession had already begun and power in the labour market swung back to employers, except in continuing cases of skills shortages. Swings in power from buyers of labour to sellers of labour and vice versa will be a continuing feature of labour market conditions in the future; organizations will tactically make adjustments according to the changes. However, the nature of the tactics employed in an organization will be determined by management's philosophy of its approach to the management of people leading to wide variations in recruitment and selection practices.

There have been a number of other pressures, outlined in this book, which have forced organizations to reconsider and develop their recruitment and selection practices as part of a strategic approach to HRM. As we have already seen, organizations have responded to the pressures that they have faced by attempting to utilise and develop the potential of the people they employ but different groups of workers may be viewed in different ways. Thus employees seen as part of the *primary internal market* (See Chapter 5) will become the focus for measures intended to bring about increased motivation, increased acceptance of responsibility, deepened skills and greater commitment. Such employees become part of an organization's core workforce, and recruitment and selection represent the entry point activities. Seen in this way, emphasis may be placed on admitting only those applicants who are likely to behave, acquire skills and show 'attitudinal commitment' (Guest, 1989, p. 49) in line with the requirements of an organization's strategy. Thus recruitment and selection criteria will be adjusted and techniques employed accordingly. Many organizations have adopted a range of sophisticated recruitment and selection techniques in order to identify and admit the 'right' people. Once they are in, employees may be able to move on to the HRM cycle as part of a progression and development of a career within that organization. In theory, employees could be moving round the cycle several times during their working lives and thus subject to recruitment and selection processes on more than one occasion in the same organization. Expenditure on more advanced approaches to recruitment and selection would be part of a package of HRM activities. Because employees would be seen as central to an organization's strategy, they would be subject to a whole range of HRM policies in an attempt to benefit from their potential and to reduce the possibility of losing talent through poaching by other organizations. Employees forming the *secondary internal market*, seen as less important and less central to an organization's activities would be subject to less screening at the point of entry with attention paid mainly to possession of the basic skills required. Such employees would be recruited and selected by more traditional and cheaper methods.

Variations in practice, however, are bound by the law of the land. Recruitment and selection have been notorious areas for prejudice and subjective influence and these could well result in infringements under legislation dealing with discrimination. In the UK the key legal provisions are contained in the Sex Discrimination Act, 1975 (amended 1986), and the Race Relations Act 1976. Both acts disallow discrimination and in general there are two forms of discrimination which are against the law:

a. Direct – where workers of a particular sex, race or ethnic group are treated less favourably than other workers, for example, a policy to recruit only men to management posts.
b. Indirect – where a particular requirement apparently treats everyone equally but has a disproportionate effect on a particular group and the requirement cannot be shown to be justified. For example, a job advert which specified that applicants should be 1.85 metres tall might unjustifiably result in a low proportion of female applicants.

Under certain circumstances, however, both acts allow for discrimination on grounds of genuine occupational qualifications. For example, under Section 7(2) of the Sex Discrimination Act, it is possible to recruit a man only when 'the essential nature of the job calls for a man for reasons of physiology (excluding physical strength or stamina) or, in dramatic performances or other entertainment, for reasons of authenticity, so that the essential nature of the job would be materially different if carried out by a woman'.

In general, personnel departments have played a key role in bringing organization practices relating to recruitment and selection in line with the provisions of the law. Certainly, there are few examples of direct discrimination, although indirect discrimination is more difficult to uncover and eliminate. There are other forms of discrimination which are not covered by the law, for example, age and sexuality, and instances where existing law is not rigorously enforced, for example, disability.

■ Recruitment, selection and the HRM cycle

If HRM is concerned with the development of an integrated package of policies towards the management of people which are designed to utilise and develop the potential of those people, then recruitment and selection represent vital stages in the determination of which employees will be able to benefit from such policies. Watson (1989, p. 125) refers to recruitment and selection as:

> the processes by which organizations solicit, contact and engender interest in potential new appointees to vacant positions in the organization, and then in some way establish their suitability for appointment.

Watson goes on to note that this definition does not include the process of negotiating the terms on which new employees are to be admitted into an organization, and that it is the task of management to influence this process to the advantage of the organization. We have already mentioned that, under different labour market conditions, power in this process will swing towards the buyers or sellers of labour, employers and employees respectively. It is therefore important to understand that the dimension of power will always be present in recruitment and selection, even in organizations that purport to have an HRM focus. Much will depend, however, on the extent to which the overall management philosophy supports and reinforces an HRM strategy which focuses on the utilisation and the development of new employees once they have gained entry to an organization.

Throughout this book we have referred to the HRM cycle as a representation of the elements of HRM policy areas. While the policies will be designed to achieve particular organization targets and goals, those policies will also provide an opportunity for individual needs to emerge and to be satisfied. This view assumes that organization targets and goals and individual needs can coincide, with mutual benefits to both sides of the employment relationship. While many commentators would doubt that such mutuality could ever occur on the basis of equality, and that organization needs, as determined by senior management, would always take precedence, we have already argued that through HRM activities individual needs may influence the perception of organization needs. An HRM approach requires a people-oriented focus and the utilization and development of their potential. Recruitment and selection processes will therefore aim to attract and admit those whom management view as the 'right' people for such an approach. There will clearly be a wide variety of interpretations of such a view of people among different organizations. However at a general level, we can use some of the literature to point to the outcomes an HRM approach is intended to achieve, and work backwards to gain some understanding of the kind of employees organizations with an HRM strategy may be seeking to attract.

In Guest's (1989, p. 49) model of HRM (see Figure 1.5, Chapter 1) the HRM outcomes may provide some guidance.

☐ **(i) STRATEGIC INTEGRATION**

This is concerned with:

1. the integration of HRM into strategic planning;
2. the coherence of HRM policies across policy areas and across hierarchies;
3. the acceptance and use of HRM practices by line managers.

We have already mentioned in Chapter 5 on HRP that deterministic views on strategy and strategic planning are somewhat problematic. Further, Mintzberg's (1978, p. 935) view of strategy as a 'pattern in a stream of decisions' allows us to place HRM in an interdependent position in relation to decision-making on objectives, structure, job design and work processes. Such decisions will clearly affect the quantity and quality of recruits. The acceptance of HRM as a major aspect of strategy will generate systems to ensure coherence throughout an organization, and appropriate actions by line managers. Both coherence and actions will be a function of the set of values that permeate an organization, often referred to as culture, that serve to reward and reinforce management actions.

☐ **(ii) COMMITMENT**

In recent years there has been a great deal of attention paid to the concept of commitment, particularly organizational commitment. Mottaz (1988, p. 468) views organizational commitment as

> an affective response (attitude) resulting from an evaluation of the work situation which links or attaches the individual to the organization.

In his review of the literature on commitment, Mottaz groups the factors which determine this attitude into two categories – individual characteristics and organizational characteristics. Individual characteristics might consist of demographic or status variables such as age, tenure, education and gender, and personality factors such as work values and expectations. Organizational characteristics include factors such as task characteristics, pay, promotion opportunities and social involvement. However there seemed to be little overall agreement on the relative impact of the factors on commitment. Mottaz goes on to establish and test a model of organizational commitment based on the notion of exchange, where individuals attach themselves to an organization on the basis of their work values composed of specific skills, desires and goals in return for work rewards – the extent to which individuals can use their skills, satisfy desires and achieve goals. The model therefore focuses attention on the individual characteristics (values) and organizational characteristics (rewards) where organizational commitment is determined by the degree of fit between values and rewards. Among Mottaz's conclusions, and of significance for recruiting and selecting for commitment, is the finding that workers with high work values and high work standards will require levels of work rewards to match these standards. Focusing on individual characteristics alone in recruitment and selection will not ensure commitment as an outcome. In order to attract potential employees for an HRM approach requires management to examine work rewards on offer in the form of interesting and meaningful work and a supportive environment as well as good pay and promotion/development prospects.

□ (iii) FLEXIBILITY

In Chapters 3 and 5 we made reference to the terms of Atkinson and Meager (1985, p. 2). In particular, the term 'functional flexibility' implies the recruitment of employees to form a core group which possess or is able to acquire the skills required to enable an organization to respond and cope with rapid change. The progress of 'functionally flexible workers' is shown in Figure 6.1.

Flexible employees have the potential continuously to learn new skills, that is, to broaden the range of skills possessed and deepen understanding and performance in existing areas of work. The latter would include taking increasing authority and responsibility for work performance. This multi-skilled workforce forms the basis of new forms of organization structure and job design implied in HRM organizations (see Chapter 3).

□ (iv) QUALITY

Total Quality Management (TQM) is one the key sets of ideas and practices associated with HRM and particularly the Japanese influence on HRM. Many

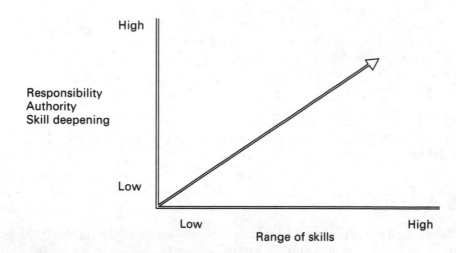

Figure 6.1   The progress of functionally flexible workers

organizations have espoused 'Quality' as a key objective; however there has been much disappointment over its progress in the UK and the USA.[4] Senge[5] reports the frustration of Dr Edwards Deming, one of the founding fathers of TQM, 'with the inability of American management to grasp the messages of the worldwide quality movement'. In particular Deming criticises the way managers may see TQM as the application of a range of statistical techniques in order to understand and measure physical processes, whilst neglecting their responsibility in the management and development of people. Wilkinson et al. (1991, p. 31) argue that while there are many similarities between TQM and HRM, short-term considerations such as costs may interfere with implementation. Management may become preoccupied with the achievement of 'hard' results and neglect 'softer' aspects such as employee development, motivation and commitment. As many organizations seek to revise their approaches to TQM, the focus will shift towards the 'softer' aspects and the developable qualities of recruits.

It is clear that the desirable HR outcomes, underpinned by culture, will enable organizations to form a loose model of the kind of employees it would wish to attract through recruitment. While it may be possible to state most clearly the more objective or 'hard' parts of the model, in the form of academic and vocational qualifications and/or previous experience, many organizations pursuing an HRM approach have begun to pay far more attention to values, personality and attitudes of potential employees. This image itself will be projected from the organization into the labour markets, as will knowledge about the system of selection for potential candidates. For example, the selection process for production teams at Toyota's UK plant in Burnaston, Derbyshire included:

- a five-page application form with questions on personal values;
- tests of numeracy, attitude and ability to learn;
- a video-interactive test of learning;
- a targeted behavioural interview lasting 75 minutes;
- a simulated production-line test;
- references and medical;
- a final interview.[6]

The image and selection system did not seem to worry 20 000 applicants for 400 jobs. HRM IN PRACTICE 6.1 provides a further example of a shift to a 'soft' model for recruitment.

■ Attraction

Whatever the image projected, organizations pursuing an HRM approach will be aiming to create and maintain an internal labour market. Indeed the organization's commitment to such a process will form part of its evolving value system and make the access to the market even more attractive to those outside it. For

example, in November 1992 management and unions at the Rover Group in the
U.K. began a new agreement, the New Deal, which would underpin a philosophy
of 'success through people'. Key features of the New Deal include:

- recognition of Rover as a single status company;
- continuous improvement to be a requirement for everyone;
- flexibility subject to ability to do the job;
- maximum devolution of authority and accountability to individuals and
  teams;
- establishment of a single grade structure;
- a common bonus scheme related directly to company performance;
- a good working environment;
- life-time employment;
- constant open and honest two-way communications throughout the
  company;
- training/re-training and development opportunities open to all;
- participation by all to improve continuously processes and company
  performance;
- continued recognition of trade unions;
- arbitration, in the unlikely event of any grievance or dispute not being
  resolved, through company/trade union procedure.

The New Deal at Rover is clearly designed to bring about increased
motivation, increased acceptance of responsibility, deepened skills and greater
commitment from workers already employed within the organization. Indeed it is
vital to the operation of an internal labour market that new work opportunities
are made available to the existing workforce, and recruitment and selection
comes initially from within. Thus the main beneficiaries of the evolving
philosophy of an HRM organization will be those already employed. The
enhanced focus on the internal market will also increase the attraction of the
organization among workers in the external markets and form part of the image
projected.

Images projected, values and information on espoused goals will interact with
workers in the external labour markets, including both employed and unemployed. This interaction will determine the degree of attraction to an organization on the part of potential recruits. Think about an organization you would like
to work for. What images, values and information about that organization came
into your mind?

Schneider (1987, p. 437), using a theory of interactional psychology, has
proposed an Attraction–Selection–Attrition framework to explain differences
between organizations that are due to the attraction of people to organization
goals, their interaction with goals, and 'if they don't fit, they leave'. The proposed
framework is shown as Figure 6.2. Schneider uses the findings from vocational
psychology to argue that people are attracted to an organization on the basis of
their own interests and personality. Thus people of similar types will be attracted

Bistro chain puts personality first

FIRM PUTS PEOPLE SKILLS AHEAD OF QUALIFICATIONS

by Gillian Drummond

A restaurant chain has opened its doors to jobhunters in a campaign to attract managers.

Potential recruits met managers of TGI Friday's at a two-day event in London last week.

The open days marked a change in direction for the American-style bistro chain, part of brewing group Whitbread.

It is putting CVs to the side and concentrating on recruiting people for their personality rather than their skills.

"People are so often hired for their skills and fired because they don't fit in. We're trying to get round that," said human resources manager Alison Finnigan.

"You set up interviews and the candidates may have wonderful CVs, but they can't tell you about a person's personality.

"We're looking for people with a non-autocratic leadership approach who can interact with people. Then we look at their business acumen," she said.

Market research by the company shows customers think staff are the most important element when visiting restaurants.

The open days included videos and slide shows about the company.

According to Finnigan the initiative was designed as a two-way exercise.

"We wanted people to come along, talk to the managers and see what it's like to work at TGI Fridays."

The 10-restaurant chain hopes to use the open days to recruit 12 managers and attract future candidates.

Source: Personnel Today, 19 May 1992.
Reprinted with permission.

---

to the same place. Furthermore, the attraction of similar types will begin to determine the place. Following selection, people who do not fit, due to error or misunderstandings about the reality of an organization, will result in an attrition from that organization. At the heart of the framework are organizational goals out of which the structures and processes will emerge which will form the basis for attraction decisions.

In recruitment the manifestation of values, ethos and desired image will usually take the form of advertising and other recruitment literature, including glossy brochures that are often aimed at graduates. In recent years, the undoubted expertise that exists within the UK advertising industry has been utilised in company recruitment. The utilitarian approach that focused on specifying job

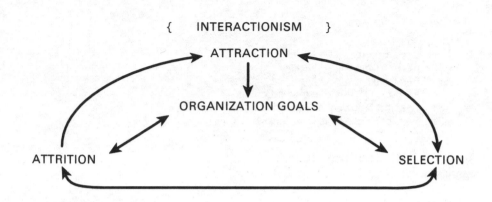

Figure 6.2   An attraction–selection–attrition framework

Source: Schneider, 1987.

details, terms and conditions is being increasingly superseded by advertising that attempts to communicate a message about the company image (see HRM IN PRACTICE 6.2). There has been a marked shift towards recruitment adverts that are creative and reflect the skills normally used in product marketing. Recruitment advertising is now fully established within the advertising mainstream.[7]

Images presented in recruitment adverts and brochures will only form part of the attraction. There is not a great deal of evidence that it is entirely effective. In any case, such advertising can be expensive and an organization will take account of a number of other factors in forming its recruitment plans and choice of media. These might include the following:

a. costs;
b. time to recruit and select;
c. labour market focus, e.g. skills, profession, occupation;
d. mobility of labour – geographic and occupational;
e. legislation on Sex Discrimination, Race Discrimination and Disability.[8]

A further manifestation of the image to which recruits will be attracted is a description of the actual work that potential employees will be required to do. The traditional way of providing such information is though the form of a Job Description. Job Descriptions are usually derived from job analysis and describe tasks and responsibilities that make up a job. Against each description, there would normally be the specification of standards of performance. A typical format for a job description is given in Figure 6.3.

In addition to a description of a job, there would be some attempt to profile the 'ideal' person to fill the job in the form of a Personnel Specification. It is accepted

JOB DESCRIPTION

Job Title
Department
Responsible to:
Relationships
Purpose Of Job/overall Objectives
Specific Duties and Responsibilities
Physical/Economic Conditions

Figure 6.3   Job description format

that the ideal person created may not exist in reality and that the specification would only be used as a framework within which a number of candidates could be assessed. A common format for a personnel specification is the Seven-Point Plan based on the work of Alec Rodger (1970), shown as Figure 6.4. An alternative to the Seven-Point Plan is Munro-Fraser's Five-Fold Grading System (1971) shown as Figure 6.5. In both forms of personnel specification, it is usual to indicate the importance of different requirements. Thus certain requirements might be expressed as essential and some as desirable.

Both job descriptions and personnel specifications are key elements in the traditional repertoire of personnel managers, and they are likely to remain so in one form or another. Over the years, various attempts have been made to develop and fine-tune techniques and practices. One such development is the shift of emphasis in job descriptions away from specifying tasks and responsibilities and towards results to be achieved (Plachy, 1987, p. 56). In the UK such a shift has received an impetus from the development of a framework of National Vocational Qualifications (NVQs). Such qualifications are *competence-based* and stress items of work performance as outcomes[9] with specified performance criteria. While the development of NVQs has been subject to some criticism (Ashworth and Saxton, 1990, p. 3) there will be increasing pressure on

PERSONNEL SPECIFICATION

Physical Characteristics
Attainments
General Intelligence
Special Aptitudes
Interests
Disposition
Circumstances

Figure 6.4   Seven-point plan

FIVE-FOLD GRADING SYSTEM

Impact on Other People
Qualifications and Experience
Innate Abilities
Motivation
Adjustment

Figure 6.5   Five-fold grading system

organizations to incorporate NVQs and the competence-based approach into personnel and HRM activities.

For some commentators the whole business of job descriptions, however formed, means too much bureaucracy (and NVQs have been seen by some organizations as too bureaucratic) and the preservation of layers of organization hierarchy. We have already emphasised that an HRM approach implies a people-oriented focus that allows the potential of all employees to be developed and utilized. Job Descriptions may represent a barrier to such a focus if they reinforce unnecessary layers of hierarchy and responsibilities are protected as status symbols.[11] The abolition of Job Descriptions in the UK is not particularly widespread[11] and some descriptive expression of the work to be done will always be an important part of the flow of information to potential recruits. However the drive towards flexibility and changing work practices will see new forms of such descriptions in the future.

In Chapter 5 we explained how many organizations have developed *competencies* (as distinct from NVQ competence referred to above) as a starting point for the assessment and development of people. Competencies – which are usually written specifically for each organization, reflecting the nature of work carried out – values and culture have the potential for integrating HRM activities for all employees. It has been argued (Feltham, 1992, p. 92) that using competencies will allow organizations to free themselves from traditional stereotypes in order to attract applicants from a variety of sources. Stereotypes of the 'ideal' person may be contained within Personnel Specifications and despite warnings, organizations may be reinforcing the stereotype in their recruitment practices. Competencies appear to be more objective, have a variety of uses in attracting applicants, and will allow an organization to use more reliable and valid selection techniques.

■ Selection interviews and techniques

As we have seen, it is usual for an organization that wishes to recruit new employees to define criteria against which it can measure and assess applicants. Increasingly however such criteria will be set in the form of behavioural characteristics and attitudes which cannot be easily measured. Rather than trust to luck, organizations will turn to more 'sophisticated' selection techniques.

Underlying the process of selection and the choice of techniques are two key principles:

1. Individual differences – Attracting a wide choice of applicants will be of little use unless there is a way of measuring the ways people differ. People can differ in many ways such as intelligence, attitudes, social skills, physical characteristics, experience and so on.
2. Prediction – Recognition of the way people differ must be extended to a prediction of performance in the workplace.

Selection techniques will to varying degrees meet these principles of measuring differences and predicting performance. Increasingly organizations may use a variety of techniques, and statistical theory is used to give credibility to techniques that attempt to measure people. Some commentators would suggest that this credibility is 'pseudo-scientific' and that many limitations remain with many selection techniques. Two statistical concepts have been of particular importance in selection, reliability and validity.

Reliability. This refers to the extent to which a selection technique achieves consistency in what it is measuring over repeated use. For example, if you were being interviewed by two managers for a job in two separate interviews, you would hope that the interview technique would provide data so that the interviewers agreed with each other about you as an individual. Alternatively, if a number of candidates are given the same selection test, you would want to have some confidence in the test providing consistent results concerning individual differences between candidates. The statistical analysis of selection techniques normally provides a reliability coefficient, and the higher the coefficient (the closer to 1º0), the more dependable the technique.

Validity. This refers to the extent to which a technique of selection actually measures what it sets out measure. There are different forms of validity but in selection the most important is *criterion validity*, which measures the results of a technique against criteria; this may be the present success of existing employees (*concurrent validity*) or future performance of new employees (*predictive validity*).

In practice validation is a complex process and would require an organization to conduct studies with large numbers of candidates. By the time such studies were completed, it is highly likely that the work from which some of the criteria were derived would have changed. Validity is also related to the particular environment and context in which performance is carried out. Such problems have not stopped many organizations using tests and other selection techniques which have been validated elsewhere.

Of all the techniques used in selection, the interview is the oldest and most widely used. Various attempts have been made to classify interviews, and it may be useful to point out some of the categories that have been developed:

HRM IN PRACTICE 6.2

Firm woos quality people

by Gaby Huddart

A recruitment campaign for Barclays Life aims to change public perception of jobs in the sector as well as attract applications.

The campaign, which so far has included six advertisements, shows what kind of people work for Barclays Life. It also includes comments from staff about why they find the job at Barclays Life rewarding.

"The advertisements show a broad cross-section of the Barclays Life sales force, so people get an idea of the breadth of people working at Barclays Life," said the director of Barkers, the firm which designed the campaign, Andrew Young.

"We're trying to change what people think of the life assurance business and get professional people interested in working in the sector," he added.

The advertisements emphasise the complexity of financial products and the abilities staff need to be able to sell them.

The company wants ambitious people who are good communicators to apply. At present the industry is not renowned for such staff, said Young.

"We want to show it's a good career and to raise the image of Barclays Life and the industry in general."

The company wants to expand its sales force in preparation for the end of the recession and has received 1,000s of applications in response to the campaign.

"We don't want quick-buck salesmen but quality people and that is what we're getting," said Barclays Life communications manager Yvonne Ridley. She said the company chose Barkers to design the campaign after a three-way pitch and is pleased at the way the Barclays Life image is being conveyed.

The campaign has appeared in the broadsheet national newspapers, the *Daily Mail*, *Daily Express* and the *Grocer* magazine.

"We wanted a broad national campaign but did not appear in the tabloids because we are not aiming at that market," said Young.

Source: Personnel Today, 18 May 1993.
Used with permission.

(i)   *Information elicited*. Interviews have a specific focus and require information at different levels:
  - An interview may focus on facts. The style of the interview will be direct, based on a question and answer session.
  - An interview may focus on subjective information once factual information has been obtained.
  - There may also be a focus on attitudes and subconscious information, requiring intensive probing techniques and involving qualified psychologists.

(ii) *Structure*. Interviews may vary from the completely structured based on planned questions and responses, to the unstructured allowing complete spontaneity by an applicant and little control by the interviewer. A compromise between the two extremes is most likely where an interviewer maintains control by the use of guide questions but allows free expression on relevant topics.

(iii) *Order and involvement*. The need to obtain different kinds of information may mean an involvement from more than one interviewer. Applicants may be interviewed serially or by a panel.

In 1949 Wagner (1949, p. 17) carried out the first comprehensive review of research associated with the employment interview. Wagner noted that from 174 sets of ratings that were reported, reliabilities ranged from a correlation coefficient of $r = 0.23$ to 0.97, with a median of $r = 0.57$. Validity, from 222 results obtained, ranged from $r = 0.09$ to $r = 0.94$, with a median of $r = 0.27$. Wagner considered such results to be not particularly high. This pattern continued for the next four decades and the interview as a selection technique became a subject for intense research and examination. In their 1965 review, for example, Ulrich and Trombo (1965, p. 100) agreed that the interview seemed deficient in terms of reliability and validity and were forced to conclude that judgements about overall suitability for employment should be made by other techniques.

There have been two lines of research to examine the reasons behind such poor results for the selection interview.[12] The first line focuses on the processing of information by interviewers leading to a decision on acceptance or rejection. The second focuses on the skills of effective interviewing. Table 6.1 gives a summary of this research.

By 1982 Arvey and Campion (1982, p. 281) were able to report less pessimism about reliability and validity when interviews were conducted by boards (panels) and based on job analysis and job information. In particular, reference was made to the success of situational interviews (Latham *et al.*, 1980, p. 422) where interview questions are derived from systematic job analysis based on a critical incident technique. Questions focus on descriptions of what an applicant would do in a series of situations. Responses are judged against benchmark answers that identify poor, average or excellent employees. In addition to situational interviews, Harris (1989, p. 696) reports on other new developments in interview format which rely on job analysis. These include behaviour description interviews, which assess past behaviour in various situations, and comprehensive structured interviews, which contain different types of question, for example, situational, job knowledge, job simulation and work requirements. Such developments have resulted in an enhanced effectiveness for the selection interview and improved scores for reliability and validity. For example, brewers Joshua Tetley improved its selection of pub managers by identifying the characteristics of successful pub managers from the life themes of existing managers. These were developed by focusing on successful situations and highly productive managers.

18 themes were identified including critical thinking, assertiveness, and stamina, and these were used to construct interview questions and the indicative responses of successful pub managers. Thus in asking questions about a candidate's leisure time activities, the interviewers would listen for responses that indicated stamina and fitness because there was a clear correlation between these and success in pub managing. Lunn (1987, p. 45), Tetley's Personnel Director, reported 'clear evidence that the system provides us with people who have the talent for making a real contribution to the success of the company'.

TABLE 6.1   Summary of research on selection interviews

A. Processing of Information

Pre-Interview	Use of application forms and photographs to reject on grounds of sex, scholastic standing and physical attractiveness.
First impressions	Decisions made quickly leading to a search for the rest of the interview to support the decision. Negative information will be heavily weighted if the decision is rejection but a positive early decision may lead to warm interviewer behaviour.
Stereotypes	Interviewers may hold stereotyped images of a 'good' worker against which applicants are judged. Such images may be personal to each interviewer and potentially based on prejudice.
Contrast	Interviewers are influenced by the order in which applicants are interviewed. An average applicant that follows below-average applicants may be rated above average. Interviewers may compare applicants against each other rather than against objective criteria.
Attraction	Interviewers may be biased towards applicants they 'like'. This attraction may develop where interviewers hold similar opinions and attitudes to applicants.

B. Skills of Interviewing

Structure	Variation in interview structure affected reliability, with low scores for unstructured interviews.
Questions	Interviewers may use multiple, leading, embarrassing and provocative questions.
Listening	Interviewers may talk more than listen, especially if they view the applicant favourably. Interviewers may not be 'trained' to listen effectively.
Retention and Interpretation	Interviewers may have poor recall of information unless guides are used and notes are made. Interviewers have difficulty in interpreting information.

It is interesting at this point to note that much of the progress in interviews as a selection technique has occurred where organizations have sought to identify behaviour and attitudes that match their models of employees to be selected. This has required an investment in more sophisticated techniques of analysis.

Traditional job analysis techniques allow models of jobs in terms of task and responsibilities to be produced. Organizations faced with change and seeking to employ workers whose potential can be utilized and developed will increasingly turn to techniques of analysis that will produce inventories of characteristics and behaviour associated with effective performance in the present and the future. This brings us back to competencies.

Lists of competencies which provide organization-specific characteristics and behaviour are developed through the use of sophisticated analytical techniques, and can provide the raw material for selection techniques that have a good record of reliability and validity, for example, psychometric tests, biodata, situational interviews. Increasingly an organization may use competencies to draw up a range of selection techniques by which to assess the competencies identified. Techniques may be combined and applied together at events referred to as Assessment Centres. While for most organizations that have developed lists of competencies, such approaches have only been applied to the selection of managers, organizations can use mixed techniques in the selection of all employees. The combination of techniques will allow the assessment of competencies and job related skills and knowledge.

Have any of your colleagues applying for graduate training programmes been 'through' an Assessment Centre? What was their reaction to this process? How a selection technique appears to those subjected to it, its face validity, is not important in a technical sense, but could be important in attracting good applicants to an organization. If your colleagues relayed negative reactions to you about their experience of selection techniques with one organization, this may affect your image of it. Techniques that may be effective from an organization's perspective may be seen as negative and unfair by applicants. In work carried out by Mabey and Iles (1991, p. 50) on the reactions of MBA students to selection and assessment techniques, interviews were rated fair and useful while tests left many feeling negative. However the combination of techniques in an Assessment Centre was seen as fair and useful in that the event allowed for the use of objective techniques and the opportunity for a dialogue between the applicant and the employer. The findings remind us of the dilemma facing organizations in the 1990's. That is, while it is increasingly important to select the 'right' kind of employees using a suitable range of techniques, there is also a danger that in using such techniques, the organization may simultaneously manage to alienate the very candidates it wants to attract.

The view of recruitment and selection practices as features of a dialogue goes some way towards Herriot's (1990, p. 34) idea of 'front-end' loading processes as a development of the social relationship between applicants and an organization. Both parties in the relationship are making decisions during recruitment and selection and it would be important for an organization to recognize that high

New code on psychological testing lays down best practice guidelines

A NEW code on psychological testing will be published by the IPM next month. It will replace the code on occupational testing first published in 1988.

The code has been radically revised and updated to take into account the huge development which has taken place in occupational testing, says Angela Baron, policy adviser on employee resourcing.

"The new code differs form the old one by setting out what we consider to be best practice in the use of test," she says. "It lays down specific guidelines for practitioners using psychological tests, and the training required for using them. It does not provide the knowledge or information necessary for practitioners to carry out testing."

The code will be circulated to members with their copies of *PM Plus* next month. It states that its purpose is to ensure that proper consideration is given to the appropriateness of using tests, that they are used in a professional manner relevant to the employment context and that equality of opportunity is maintained. It also specifies that tests should be carried out by trained people and that those tested should be informed of the reasons for the test and of the results of it.

The code sets out the minimum level of conduct required or personnel professionals involved in testing. These requirements include that while tests can be used for recruitment and selection, training and development and counselling, results should not, as a general rule, be used as the sole basis for decision-making on an appointment.

On training, the code specifies that everyone responsible for the application of tests should be trained to the level of competence recommended by the British Psychological Society and should hold the society's statement or certificate of competence in occupational testing (level A).

Those using personality questionnaires must receive further training to understand the background to personality testing. A level-B certificate from the BPS should be available by the end of the year.

Before using psychological tests, the code says, professionals should determine that they are relevant and that the people administering them are competent to carry out the tasks.

Practitioners should also lay down policy on confidentiality, who will have access to the results and whether they will be kept for management purposes. Feedback should also be given unless there are strong reasons against.

Users should satisfy themselves that a test has been rigourously developed, that it is valid, is not biased against any group, is acceptable to those taking it, and has been effectively used in similar circumstances.

They should also ensure that test results are restricted to those with a genuine need to know them.

Candidates must be informed that tests will be conducted and if results are stored on computer, under the Data Protection Act 1984, they must be informed that the data is held and the purposes for which it will be used.

On personality questionnaires, the code states that these are most useful in providing an 'added dimension to decision-making'. They should not, in general, be used as screening devices and should never be used as the primary basis for selection.

The code reminds practitioners that tests should be constantly monitored for validity and that they should be updated and verified at least every five years. It also warns that copyright laws prohibit the reproduction of test materials without the express permission of the supplier.

Further, transfer of pencil and paper tests on to computer is not only an infringement of copyright, but users risk obtaining flawed results from tests not specifically developed for computer use.

Source: Personnel Management Plus, June 1993. Used with permission.

quality applicants, attracted by their image of an organization, could be lost at an early stage unless applicants are supplied with realistic organization and work information. Applicants have a picture of expectations about how the organization will treat them, and recruitment and selection represents an opportunity to clarify the picture. One method of developing the picture, suggested by Herriot (1989, p. 48), Realistic Job Previews (RJPs) which can take the form of case studies of employees and their work, the chance to 'shadow' someone at work, job sampling and videos. The aim of RJPs is to enable the expectations of applicants to become more realistic. Work by Premack and Wanous (1985, p. 706) found that RJPs lower initial expectations about work and an organization, causing some applicants to de-select themselves but RJPs also increase levels of organization commitment, job satisfaction, performance and job survival among applicants who continue into employment.

■ Summary

This chapter has examined the nature of recruitment and selection for organizations that are pursuing an HRM approach to the management of people. It is essential that such organizations see that whatever the state of the labour market and their power within it, contact with potential recruits is made through the projection of an image that will impact on and reinforce the expectations of potential recruits. Such images are used by recruits to self-select in the initial stages. Organizations now have the ability to construct models of the kind of employees they wish to recruit, and to identify how far applicants match their models using acceptably reliable and valid techniques of selection. However, recruitment and selection are also the first stages of a dialogue between applicants and the organization that forms the employment relationship. Failure to appreciate the importance of the formation of expectations during recruitment and selection may result in the loss of high quality applicants and set the initial level of the employment relationship at such a low level as to make the achievement of desirable HRM outcomes most difficult.

■ Key concepts

- Recruitment
- Attraction
- Selection
- Image projection
- Attrition

- Reliability
- Validity
- Job descriptions
- Personnel specifications
- Face validity

Discussion questions

1. 'Recruitment is the biggest single challenge facing Personnel Managers in the 1990's.' Discuss.
2. Decision-making in selection has become a two-way process. How can the decisions of applicants be improved?
3. How can the predictive validity of the employment interview be improved?
4. Should Job Descriptions be abandoned?
5. '. . . appeal to their guts instead of just their brains.' How far do you agree with this view of graduate recruitment.
6. What information do you expect from an organization in recruitment?

■ Further reading

Cook, M. (1988), *Personnel Selection and Productivity*, Chichester: Wiley.

Curnow, B. (1989), 'Recruit, retrain, retain: personnel management and the three Rs', *Personnel Management*, November, pp. 40–7.

Herriot, P. (1989), *Recruitment in the 1990s*, London: IPM.

Makin, P. J. and Robertson, I. T. (1986), 'Selecting the Best Selection Techniques', *Personnel Management*, November, pp. 38–43.

Smith, J. M. and Robertson, I. T. (eds) (1989), *Advances in Selection and Assessment*, Chichester: Wiley.

Watson, T. (1989), 'Recruitment and Selection', in Sissons, K. (ed.), *Personnel Management in Britain*, Oxford: Basil Blackwell.

■ Chapter case study   Best-u-Do Stores plc

You have been invited by Best-u-Do plc, a large DIY retail organization that recruits substantial numbers of graduates, to design a recruitment campaign and selection procedures.

The company has become very aware of the importance of recruiting young people and that its image is one of elitism. That is, in the past only potentially high-flyers have been recruited and selected. It is also aware that it has failed to attract or retain graduate employees in sufficient numbers. Recent surveys showed that the glossy brochure was 'unimpressive', and exit interviews indicated that the graduates' aspirations were not being monitored or met.

The management very much wants to change its image with graduates and has asked you to provide a detailed presentation of proposals.

Task

Working in groups of 3 or 4, research and prepare a presentation for the management of the company on how it should amend its approach to the recruitment and selection of graduates. In particular, you should consider:

(a) the work expectations of recent graduates (what will *you* expect from an employer in the first few years of employment?);
(b) how the organization should conduct its recruitment and selection (e.g. image, attraction, techniques of selection);
(c) how graduates can be retained in an organization (Refer back to Chapter 3 to consider job design, and Chapter 4 to consider health and safety issues).

Be prepared to justify your proposals and provide details of current practice from other organizations.

■ References

1. Curnow, B. (1989), 'Recruit, retrain, retain: personnel management and the three Rs', *Personnel Management*, November, pp.40–7.
2. Herriot, P. (1989), *Recruitment in the 1990s*, London: IPM.
3. Bryan Jackson, Director of Human Resources at Toyota's Derby plant. Quoted in *Guardian*, 17 December 1992, p. 18.
4. There have been a number of reported successes too. See for example, 'The problem with the post' in *Guardian*, 6 February 1993, p. 40.
5. Senge, P. (1991), 'Transforming the Practice of Management', paper presented at the Systems Thinking in Action Conference, 14 November.
6. Bryan Jackson, quoted in *Guardian*, 17 December 1992.
7. There are even awards for recruitment adverts sponsored by *Personnel Today* and *The Independent* newspaper.

8. See Paddison, L. (1990), 'The Targeted Approach to Recruitment', *Personnel Management*, November, pp. 54–8.

9. NVQ competences that specify outcomes should not be confused with 'competencies' examined in Chapter 5.

10. A keen advocate of the abolition of job descriptions is US management 'guru', Tom Peters.

11. Although see Griffiths, J. (1992), 'Honda reaches accord in UK', *Financial Times*, 9 November, p. 10.

12. For an extensive coverage of the research see Arvey, R. D. and Campion, J. E. (1982), 'The Employment Interview: A Summary and Review of Recent Research', *Personnel Psychology*, Vol. 35, pp. 281–322; and Harris, M. M. (1989), 'Reconsidering the Employment Interview: A Review of Recent Literature and Suggestions for Future Research', *Personnel Psychology*, Vol. 42, pp. 691–726.

PART 3

REWARDS AND DEVELOPMENT

CHAPTER 7

Performance Appraisal

A great deal depends on the extent to which you have a good relationship with your boss, as a team. I, now, have a super boss and we work very well together. The comments on my appraisal depend not on an hour's discussion, but on a whole year's interaction. But if you get off badly with your first two managers, you may as well just forget it.[1]

Perhaps the least liked managerial activity is doing the annual performance appraisal.[2]

■ Chapter outline

Introduction
Assessment, appraisal and control
From control to development
Appraisal techniques
Summary

Chapter objectives

After studying this chapter, you should be able to:

1. Critically explain the purpose and uses of appraisal.
2. Explain contrasting approaches to appraisal.
3. Explain the use of appraisal in employee development.
4. Understand the use of different assessment and appraisal techniques.

■ Introduction

Of all the activities in the HRM cycle, performance appraisal is arguably the most contentious and least popular among those who are involved. Managers do not seem to like doing it, employees see no point in it, and, personnel and human resource managers as guardians of an organization's appraisal policy and procedures have to stand by and watch their work fall into disrepute. Remarkably, despite the poor record of appraisal within organizations, it is an accepted part of management orthodoxy that there should be some means by which performance can be measured, monitored and controlled (Barlow 1989, p. 499). Appraisal therefore acts as an information-processing system by which progress towards objectives can be monitored and errors spotted, including the identification of under-achievers whose weaknesses can be corrected efficiently and rationally. Indeed a failure to show that management is in control would be regarded as highly ineffective by those with an interest in the affairs of an organization. As a result, appraisal systems have for some time served to prove that the performance of employees is under control or to give the appearance of control. As Barlow (1989, p. 500) has stated: 'Institutionally elaborated systems of management appraisal and development are significant rhetorics in the apparatus of bureaucratic control'. It might be that the idea of control is at the heart of the problem of appraisal in organizations.

The relation of employee appraisal to other key dimensions of the HRM cycle is shown in Figure 1.7 (p. 28). The information relative to an employees' job results and behaviour can lead to human resource development activities. Performance appraisal data can determine employee rewards and are also used to validate predictors in the selection process.

This chapter will seek to explain why appraisal systems have continuously failed to find respect among employers and employees alike. However, it will also explore how, within an HRM approach, appraisal has the potential to reverse past trends so that it is viewed less as a threat and a waste of time and more as the source of continuous dialogue within organizations between organizational members.

■ Assessment, appraisal and control

Assessment is the process by which data are collected and reviewed about an individual employee's past and current work behaviour and performance. This allows *appraisal*, which can be seen as an analysis of overall capabilities and potential, allowing a decision to be made in line with a purpose. In reality both assessment and appraisal are likely to be combined and this can mean that the two terms may be synonymous in many organizations.

There are a variety of declared purposes for appraisal and the most usual rationalization and justification for appraisal is to improve individual performance. However under such a broad heading come a number of more focused reasons. Phil Long's (1986) survey at least reveals what many organizations claim they hope to achieve. Table 7.1 shows why companies in the UK review performance. In many organizations appraisal will take place formally at predetermined intervals and will involve a discussion or interview between a manager and individual employees. The purposes of such discussions can be broadly categorised into

TABLE 7.1 Why companies review performance

	%
To assess training and development needs	97
To help improve current performance	97
To review past performance	98
To assess future potential/promotability	71
To assist career planning decisions	75
To set performance objectives	81
To assess increases or new levels in salary	40
Others – e.g. updating personnel records	4

Source: Long, 1986.

(i) the making of administrative decisions concerning pay, promotions and careers, work responsibilities;

(ii) the improvement of performance through the discussion of development needs, identifying training opportunities and the planning of action.

Both categories of purpose require judgements to be made. In the first category, a manager may be required to make a decision about the value of an employee both in the present and the future, and this may cause some discomfort. Several decades ago, McGregor (1957, p. 89) reported that a key reason why appraisal failed was that managers disliked 'playing God', which involved making judgements about the worth of employees. Levinson (1970, p. 127) thought that managers experienced the appraisal of others as a hostile and aggressive act against employees which resulted in feelings of guilt about being critical of employees.

Making judgements about an employee's contribution, value/worth, capability and potential has to be considered as a vital dimension of a manager's relationship with employees. Although the occasion may be formally separated from the ongoing relationship, appraisal activities and decisions will be interpreted by an employee as feedback and will have a potentially strong impact on an employee's view of 'self', for example, self belief and self esteem. What is particularly interesting is the way individuals respond to feedback, because there is no simple formula for how feedback can be used to motivate people, even though managers may be quite convinced, in their own minds, that there is. We do know however that feedback has a definite influence in demotivation![3] Try a test on yourself: make a list of what motivates *you* to work and make another that indicates what demotivates you. It is likely that the latter will be longer, covering a wide range of factors. Thus there is always a danger in any situation when a manager has to provide feedback to employees that the outcome will be demotivated employees. The seminal study that highlighted this possibility was carried out by Meyer, Kay and French (1965,

p. 123) at the General Electric Company. Although this work was carried out in the mid-1960s, it is remarkable how the lessons have been forgotten and the mistakes uncovered at that time have been repeated many times over in many organizations. The study looked at the appraisal process at a large plant where appraisal was judged to be good. There were 92 appraisees in the study who were appraised by their managers on two occasions over two weeks. The first interview discussed performance and salary, the second discussed performance improvement. The reactions of the appraisees was gathered by interviews, questionnaires and observation. It was discovered that while interviews allowed for general praise, criticism was more specific and prompted defensive reactions. Defensiveness by appraisees involved denial of shortcomings and blaming others. On average 13 criticisms per interview were recorded and the more criticism received, the more defensive the reaction of the appraisee. The study revealed that the defensive behaviour was partly due to most appraisees rating themselves above average before the interviews – 90 out of 92 appraisees rated themselves as average or above. It was also found that, subsequent to the interviews, criticism had a negative effect on performance. A summary of some of the conclusions from this study is set out in Table 7.2.

The last conclusion in Table 7.2 gives emphasis to the role of managers as developers of their employees on a continuous basis. It is a role which will be explored in more detail in Chapter 9, Human Resource Development. However, it is worth stating at this point that assessing and appraising are likely to occur on both formal and informal occasions, and the latter will occur far more often than the former. Employees are able to accept criticism if it is useful and relevant to them and the work they are doing. Feedback provided in this way has a strong chance of improving performance and, crucially, provides an opportunity for a continuing dialogue between managers and employees out of which will emerge joint understanding of individual development needs and aspirations. As many managers and employees have found, where the informal and continuous processes are operating effectively, this will make the formal appraisal less isolated and less prone to negativity. The extent to which employees are able to accept feedback will vary to a considerable extent amongst employees, and managers will need to be able to cope with such variations. That is, they will

TABLE 7.2   Summary of findings from Meyer, Kay and French study

---

- Criticism often has a negative effect on motivation and performance
- Praise has little effect – one way or another
- Performance improves with specific goals
- Participation by the employee in goal-setting helps produce favourable results
- Interviews designed primarily to improve performance should not at the same time weigh salary or promotion in the balance
- Coaching by managers should be day-to-day and not just once a year

---

need to 'know' their people as individuals and this itself will be a reflection of the development of managers.

As has already been mentioned, it is an accepted part of management orthodoxy that there should be some means by which performance can be measured, monitored and controlled (Barlow 1989, p. 499), and that appraisal systems provide evidence that management is in control. Randell (1989, p. 160) points out that most appraisal schemes in the UK are underpinned by a 'performance control approach' to appraisal. Figure 7.1 provides the key stages of this approach. It is argued that the control approach is an outcome of the drive towards rationality and efficiency in our organizations. Certainly such beliefs may become part of a set of taken-for-granted assumptions that dominate life in organizations, and may also be difficult to challenge. Organization leaders, managers and employees may often be unaware of the ways in which such beliefs lie behind their actions. Thus, even though the experience of appraisal in organizations is very mixed, to say the least, it would be tantamount to heresy radically to alter its orientation towards the control of performance. However, an HRM approach requires the risk to be taken, and this may first of all require an awareness by managers of their taken-for-granted beliefs.

Gareth Morgan's *Images of Organization* (1986) has provided an examination of the way metaphors lie at the foundation of our ideas and explanations about organizations. In this book Morgan draws on the literature that highlights the role of metaphor in explaining complex phenomena, like organizations, by the crossing of images and language. Thus an organization may be crossed with the image of a machine and this may be very useful in understanding what happens and what should happen in organizations. However, metaphor only provides a partial view of a phenomenon and not a whole view, for example, an organization may be compared with a machine or said to have machine-like

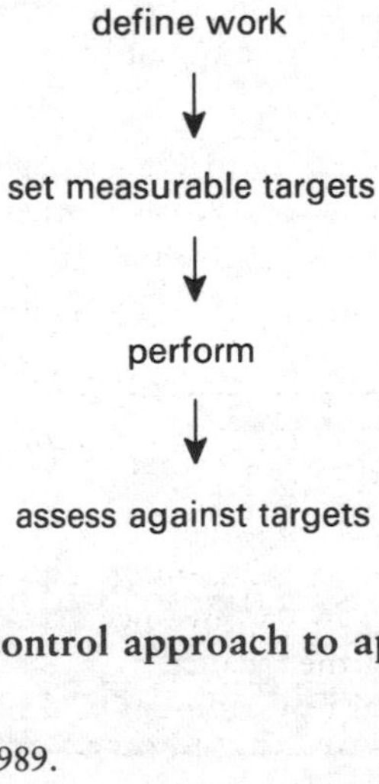

define work

↓

set measurable targets

↓

perform

↓

assess against targets

Figure 7.1   A performance control approach to appraisal

Source: Adapted from Randell, 1989.

qualities, but it is not and will never be a machine. A danger occurs however when the metaphor, in this case a machine, becomes a taken-for-granted assumption. In such cases the partial explanatory power of the metaphor may be taken as a whole and the organization may be seen literally as a machine! This is not as ridiculous as it sounds because much of the language of organizations, and many of the processes developed, can be related back to an assumption of an organization as a machine. Henry Mintzberg (1989, p. 339) has argued that the form of structure called 'machine bureaucracy' has dominated thinking about how organizations should be constructed and that terms like 'getting organized', 'being rational', and 'achieving efficiency' represent evidence of this domination. As Mintzberg has written: 'I believe that to most people . . . what I am calling machine bureaucracy is not just *a* way to organize, it is *the* way to organize; it is not *one* form or structure, it *is* structure' (Mintzberg 1990, p. 340, original emphasis).

We should not be surprised therefore to find an attachment by many managers to the idea of control in appraisal, and the perception by employees that they are being controlled by appraisal systems. Barlow (1989, p. 500) takes the argument further. He points out that appraisal serves to make rational, simple and static a relationship between managers and employees which is ambiguous, complex and dynamic. Ambiguity, complexity and dynamism cannot be eliminated in reality, and thereinlies the falseness of the experience of appraisal. For many employees, appraisal is just not seen as relevant. The following reflect the opinions of managers about appraisal, gathered in a field study in a sector of the petrochemicals industry.

> Successful types are spotted early on. You usually find that it would seem those people are going to start moving fast. I think we're talking about a fairly small percentage in the fast-moving track, because one always has to consider the constraints of availability of positions for people to move to: you actually have to have slots available for them. There is a strong element of being in the right place at the right time. Or being *known* by your managers so that they can earmark slots for you.

> I think success is having the ear of higher management. To be noticed by higher management, and having opinions asked for, often. It's being able to influence the decision-maker in a department. And I think an awful lot depends on being in the right place at the right time.

> If we were asked for a good man, we certainly wouldn't go hunting through appraisal forms. We'd do it by personal knowledge and I suppose, to some extent, by rule of thumb. *Appraisal forms are no use.* It's what's left out rather than what's put in that's important. (Barlow, 1989, pp. 505–507)

In this section, we have discussed the espoused purposes of appraisal and how some of the research evidence has indicated that in reality appraisal may be less than effective in the achievement of these. The problem may be due to the way appraisal processes are formulated, based on an explicit or implicit performance control orientation. If we refer back to some of the HRM approaches and the outcomes of flexibility, quality and commitment, we can see that organization leaders and managers will need to ask themselves some fundamental questions on the purpose of appraisal and the nature of organization control mechanisms.

From control to development

It is highly unlikely that the pressure for rationality, efficiency and control on organizations will disappear overnight. The questioning of underlying principles that is required for the development of a culture that supports and reinforces the ideas and practices of HRM can be a painful process. For example, it may be difficult to resist the requirements of financial controllers to show conformity to standardised budgets, and so on. However, this would be just the kind of critical resistance that would indicate to employees the desire of senior managers to implement an HRM strategy. At the heart of such a strategy therefore is the willingness to move from an approach to management based on control, as exemplified by traditional performance appraisal, towards one based on gaining employee commitment.

Walton (1985, p. 79) has written about the disillusionment with the apparatus of control which assumes low employee commitment and mere obedience. He reports on a number of organizations that have attempted to move towards a work-force strategy based on commitment. In recent years the drive towards leaner and flatter organization structures has meant the removal of layers of supervision and an investment, both psychologically and physically in harnessing the potential of employees. In Chapter 6 we referred to the Mottaz's (1988, p. 468) model of organizational commitment and the finding that workers with high work values and high work standards will require levels of work rewards to match these standards. Such workers are unlikely to be satisfied with static work tasks and standards. Their high expectations will lead to a desire for continuous development, and through such development organizations will be fulfilling the strategy of harnessing the potential of their employees. Assessment and appraisal serve as the fulcrum of such a process. The contrast between control approaches and commitment could not be greater for managers: the former involves a concentration on techniques, the latter a shift towards attitudes, values and beliefs.

A developmental approach to appraisal that attempts to harness potential would for many organizations mean a spread in the coverage of appraisal systems to all employees who form the Primary Internal Labour market. For many years, discussions of potential and prospects for development have been confined to managers only. This provided a strong signal to the rest of the organization that only managers were worthy of such attention with the implicit assumption that non-managers cannot develop. Table 7.3 shows the results of Long's (1986) survey for the Institute of Personnel Management, of grades of employee whose performance was regularly reviewed. While the figure for manual workers is

TABLE 7.3   Grades of employee and performance reviews

	%
Directors (board level)	52
Senior management	90
Middle management	96
Junior management	92
First line supervisor	78
Clerical/secretarial	66
Skilled/semi-skilled	24
Professional/scientific/advisory	55
Others	7

small compared to other grades, 24 per cent represented a large rise from 2 per cent in 1977. It is likely that this trend has continued as more organizations have attempted to harmonize conditions between different grades of employees and adopt HRM ideas.

In the shift towards a more developmental approach, the suspicion that surrounded control approaches may remain. Harper (1983, p. 69) suggests dropping the word 'appraisal' because it puts employees on the defensive. Instead, he recommends a shift towards future-oriented review and development which actively involves employees in continuously developing ways of improving performance in line with needs. The outcome could be a set of objectives to be achieved by individual employees. Such objectives may be concerned with immediate performance against current tasks and standards, but they might also be concerned with a variety of work and personal changes, for example, change of standards, task, job and career. Once employees are encouraged to pay attention to their progress at work, the organization must be able to respond to their medium- and long term career aspirations (see Chapter 5). The manager's role will be to resolve the inevitable tension that will result between individual goals and the manager's interpretation of organization goals. How can data about employees be gathered for development purposes?

The performance of a work task can be presented as a relationship between means and ends (Ouchi, 1979, p. 843). The means take the form of the attributes, skills, knowledge and attitudes of an individual employee which are applied to a task in a specific situation. The ends are the outcomes, taking the form of results achieved which may be measurable quantitatively or qualitatively against an explicit or implicit standard or target. Between means and ends is the behaviour of the individual in a 'transformation process', as shown in Figure 7.2.

While all phases of this process can be the focus of appraisal, particular attention to behaviour in the transformation process will reveal how an individual has applied aptitudes and attitudes to a task, taking account of all aspects including time and place, machinery and equipment, other employees and other circumstances – for example, the presence of a manager or a customer. The

MEANS   →   TRANSFORMATION PROCESS   →   ENDS

→

- knowledge   applied to task   - results
  and skills   - measurements
- attitudes   - standards

Figure 7.2   The performance of work as a transformation process

attention to how an employee performs will provide rich data on current effectiveness and potential for further development. For example, if we assume that a worker has been trained to complete a basic task, attention to the transformation process will provide data on a number of issues. The first time the worker completes the task, assessment of process reveals nervousness until completion, when the results achieved can be compared against a standard. The nervousness can be corrected by adjustment to his skills and practice until confidence is gained. Further attention to process reveals that once confidence is gained, the worker performs with some sense of rhythm and flow that achieves perfect results. Given static conditions and standards, this is as far as the worker can go in this task. He can continue to perform with confidence but after some time this becomes too easy. This feeling prompts the worker to ask for some adjustment; at first this may be to the work targets and then to an extension of tasks within the job. The important point is that ease within the transformation process, assessed by the worker, leads to developmental adjustments.

Continued attention to process may eventually result in a further range of adjustments, such as increased responsibility through job enlargement and job enrichment, and a reconsideration of future direction within the organization. On the way, the organization may benefit from rising efficiency and effectiveness, including better standards. Through attention to the behaviour of a worker in the transformation process, data can be provided for a whole gamut of developmental decisions over time, starting with adjustments to reach minimum standards, to career changes and progression. Figure 7.3 shows a representation of this development starting at the centre with attention to immediate performance and extending outwards to career changes and progression. Individual employees are able to set targets, objectives and goals for each stage through appraisal.

A number of techniques have been developed which allow for the appraisal of behaviour and performance. These can be used in addition to techniques that measure the inputs (means) and outcome (ends) of the transformation process. The ability to employ various techniques in appraisal will depend on a number of contingencies. William Ouchi (1979, p. 843) has provided a model which specifies these and allows a choice of techniques to be made. Figure 7.4 has been adapted from Ouchi's work. This model can be used to reconcile the dilemma that organizations may face in appraisal: that is, between the desire to maintain

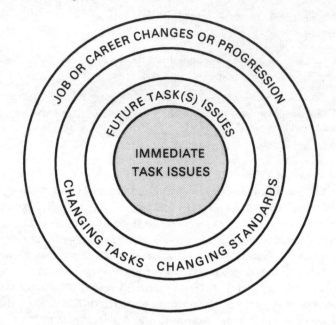

Figure 7.3   Developmental decisions

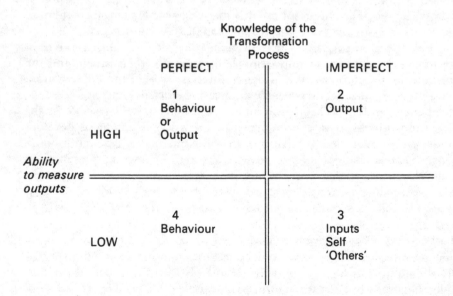

Knowledge of the
Transformation
Process

PERFECT   ‖   IMPERFECT

	1 Behaviour or Output		2 Output

HIGH

*Ability
to measure
outputs*

	4 Behaviour		3 Inputs Self 'Others'

LOW

Figure 7.4   **A framework for the design of organizational control mechanisms**

Source: Adapted from Ouchi, 1979.

control and the desire to foster a developmental emphasis. Bureaucratic forms of control depend on the feasibility of measuring desired performance: 'the ability to measure either output or behaviour which is relevant to the desired performance is critical to the "rational" application of . . . bureaucratic forms of control' (Ouchi 1979, p. 843).

In Ouchi's model, if an organization has either the ability to measure outputs of behaviour or has a high understanding of the transformation process involved in production, the organization could opt for bureaucratic control and base appraisal on either behaviour or output measurements or both. Thus in Cell 1, typical of traditional manufacturing and service organizations where work process steps can be clearly stated, both behaviour and output techniques can be used. In Cell 2 only outputs can be appraised successfully, perhaps because work processes cannot be observed, for example, sales workers. In Cell 4 employees' behaviour can be observed but outputs are more difficult: this may be due to groups of employees producing group outputs or measurable outputs produced over a long period of time, for example, research workers. In all the above cases, the logic of control may be extended to tie appraisal to some form of performance or merit-related-pay system (see Chapter 8). However in Cell 3 there is imperfect knowledge of transformation and low ability to measure outputs, making bureaucratic control virtually impossible. Ouchi refers to this cell as a 'clan', based on a ritualised, ceremonial or 'cultural' form of control arising from shared attitudes, values and beliefs. Most professional workers would fit most of the time into this category. Appraisal is seen as control only in the sense of reinforcing the values of trust and allowing individuals to identify their own development needs. Behaviour, while difficult to observe formally, can be observed by those present at the point of production. For example, those able to observe the performance of a university lecturer are the students being taught and the lecturer him/herself. A university can bureaucratically control who becomes a Lecturer through its selection processes, hence it is possible to assess 'inputs', for example, qualifications and other attributes. However once installed, the performance of a lecturer is much more difficult to assess rationally. It can however be assessed and appraised by the lecturer him/herself through self-appraisal and by others, for example, students and/or peers. As will be shown below, such forms of appraisal are not without their problems, especially if organizations wish to exert bureaucratic control. However such techniques can be highly productive in allowing the development focus of appraisal to emerge and fostering a culture which supports this. Increasingly, as we have shown, control based on shared values and beliefs which attempts to engender commitment, high trust and continuous development amongst all employees lies at the heart of HRM strategies. Therefore, the appraisal techniques suggested in Cell 3 may form part of a repertoire of techniques even where it is possible to employ the performance control techniques of Cells 1, 2 and 4. How organizations can manage the process and the conflicting demands will now be examined.

■ Appraisal techniques

We have shown that there is considerable pressure on organizations to adopt performance control approaches to appraisal, and that even in organizations that espouse an HRM orientation, beliefs that emphasise rationality and efficiency may become part of a set of taken-for-granted assumptions. Clearly an organization which desires to develop appraisal with a development focus will need to challenge such assumptions. The result is likely to be the emergence of sophisticated models that make use of multiple techniques that satisfy the demands of multiple users. In Chapter 8, Reward Management, we will examine how appraisal can have a key impact on decisions on remuneration within organizations. However, in the interests of equity, such decisions will need to be taken on the basis of decisions which are both reliable and valid (See Chapter 6).

If we refer back to our earlier analysis, we saw that quite a record had been established to show the problems of appraisal. These stemmed mainly from the way systems were established as a way of evaluating employees by their superiors for a variety of purposes, for example, improving performance, pay, promotion, and so on. Over the years, a large battery of techniques has been made available to organizations. Some of these techniques carry validity and reliability scores suggesting greater 'objectivity', for example, psychometric tests. However what cannot be escaped is that all employees will have an opinion on how well they are performing, the rewards they desire and deserve, and the training they require. That is, whatever techniques of appraisal are employed, self appraisal will always be there too. Where the emphasis of appraisal is on evaluation and performance control it is only to be expected that differences will exist between an individual's self appraisal and the appraisal of his/her superior. Campbell and Lee (1988, p. 303) suggest a number of discrepancies between self and supervisory appraisal:

  (i)   Informational – disagreement about work to be done, how it is done, and the standards to be used in judging results.
  (ii) Cognitive – behaviour and performance are complex and appraisers attempt to simplify this complexity. Different perceptions will result in disagreement between appraisers and appraisees.
  (iii) Affective – the evaluative nature of performance control appraisal is threatening to appraisees and triggers defence mechanisms, leading to bias and distortions in interpreting information. Appraisers also may find appraisal threatening.

All of the above would suggest that self appraisal in an environment of evaluation and control is not effective and this is not surprising. However Campbell and Lee suggest that: 'such pessimistic conclusions do not rule out the possibility that self appraisals can be used as important developmental and motivational tools for individuals' (1988, p. 307).

We have already shown that employees are able to observe their own performance and obtain data for appraising strengths and weaknesses and identifying future goals from the processes of working. We have also shown that such observations may allow the organization to benefit from rising efficiency and effectiveness including better standards. Allowing employees to appraise themselves for development purposes is an acceptance of the values of such a process for individuals and the organization. The extent to which employees are able to appraise themselves objectively becomes a question of how willing they are to seek and accept feedback from their work behaviour and the environment that they are in. Employees can learn to appraise themselves and will treat it as part of their own development, if they can see the value of it for themselves rather than as a manipulative management tool. HRM IN PRACTICE 7.1 shows the efforts of the HR Department at Nationwide Building Society to help employees assess themselves for career development.

Self appraisal for development will not occur unless it is set in an environment that facilitates and encourages such a process. Where a positive experience from self appraisal is gained, employees may then be willing to share their thoughts on the process with others. This may take the form of peer or team appraisal (Edwards and Sproull, 1985, p. 28) or upward appraisal. An example of upward appraisal is shown in HRM IN PRACTICE 7.2. Feedback may also be sought from a variety of other sources, including customers and suppliers. This places appraisal in the context of ideas concerning continuous learning and development, with the focus on the individual as a self-directing learner. This in turn could form the focus for whole programmes of development which include self, peer and upward appraisal, rather than seeing appraisal as a distinct and separate process. In addition, employees throughout an organization will be able to make more effective use of the techniques of appraisal. These Techniques can fall into three categories: inputs; results and outcomes; and behaviour.

■ Inputs

This is a broad and potentially vague category which has been traditionally concerned with listing traits or personality attributes. Typical attributes might be dependability, loyalty, decisiveness, resourcefulness, stability, etc. Because such attributes may be difficult to define, there will be little agreement among different users of lists of measures of their presence in employees. In Chapter 6, Recruitment and Selection, we referred to the issue of reliability. The use of personality attributes in assessing and appraising can lack reliability, giving rise to charges of bias, subjectivity and unfairness. This is normally the case when managers attempt to measure their employees in appraisal interviews. However, they may have a developmental use where employees are able to apply such measurements in a form of self assessment.

Psychological tests can also provide information on the personalities of employees and their IQs. A large industry has been established to provide reliable and valid tests for organizations, and many are used in appraisal, especially for managers at various points in their careers. In many organiza-

Self assessment and career development at Nationwide Building Society

HRM IN PRACTICE 7.1

As part of an exercise to examine the effectiveness of self assessment processes in career development, Nationwide Building Society ran a series of workshops for employees. The workshops were structured on a 2.5 days plus 1 day follow-up basis. The workshops particularly focused on the use of 'hands on' self assessment techniques such as

- Introduction to a model of career management
- Introduction to Personal Construct Psychology with one-to-one work on a repertory grid
- Group feedback
- Kolb's Learning Style Inventory
- Session on the use of the 'I Ching' as a catalyst for change introducing the conception of right brain thinking

- Personal action plans followed by a one day follow-up two months later

Three workshops were run covering 36 employees between the ages of 26 and 47. At the two month follow-up the following results were obtained by questionnaire:

87% found the workshops of positive or considerable benefit

96% claimed it was a totally new form of appraisal and development, suggesting it was more holistic and unlike traditional appraisal -'this would last'.

75% said that their career plans were more considered and focused than they would ever have been and believed that career objectives were more meaningful and realistic.

tions, managers attend Development Centres where assessment tests and exercises are used to provide a report on individual strengths and limitations, and suggested development activities. There may be, however, conflicting views on the use of such processes. Table 7.4 shows the responses by questionnaire of 31 managers six months after they had attended a Development Centre in a large financial services organization in the UK.

■ Results and outcomes

The results and outcomes of behaviour provide the most objective techniques of providing data for appraisal. When available, measurements can be taken at different points in time and comparisons made with targets, if set. Typical measurements might relate to production, sales, numbers of satisfied customers or customer complaints. We can also include in this section the achievement of standards of competence as contained within National Vocational Qualifications

Federal Express employees appraise their managers

Personnel executives from some of Britain's top companies have heard how regular, **in depth appraisal of bosses by their subordinates** can be the key to better management – and improved financial performance. The power of "reverse appraisal" was revealed at a presentation hosted by the Work Research Unit of ACAS (the Advisory Conciliation and Arbitration Service) near Hinckley. Delegates were part of a network of companies using ACAS services, representing the automotive, aerospace, brewing, food, electronics, chemical and financial services industries. The presentation was made by Federal Express Business Logistics UK, part of the US-based $8 billion FedEx Corporation, which invites all 93,000 employees worldwide to take part in regular SFA (survey-feedback-action) sessions to appraise the performance of the people managing them and the company as a whole. Employees at all levels are then involved in setting goals which workgroups and workgroup managers are charged to achieve. "Even our chief executive has to go through regular SFA appraisals each year with his board, as I do with the management team with whom I work", explained Tony Pattemore, managing director of FedEx Business Logistics UK, which employs 1,050 people and has grown in turnover from £7 million to £45 million since 1986. "SFA is now a central part of our *business* policy rather than a personnel policy. It is a fundamental as measuring financial performance". Survey-feedbcak-action has been operated by FedEx in the USA for ten years and in the last four years within the UK. The programme embodies the following principles:

- *Survey:* every FedEx employee is asked to complete a detailed questionnaire asking how they feel about the way the company is managed in general, and specific questions about the performance of the manager to whom they are responsible. Questionnaires are completed in company time, supervised by trained "invigilators", and are sealed and sent to be analysed at FedEx headquarters in Memphis, Tennessee. All replies are guaranteed confidentially and the UK response rate over four years has increased from 69 per cent to "nearly 100 per cent".

- *Feedback:* questionnaires are returned to local workgroups and their managers with an analysis of their results, which remain anonymous – the programme is carefully designed, so that particular views cannot be "traced" to individuals. The analysis produces both a picture of the individual workgroup/manager relationship and a broader picture of what people think about the company's management as a whole.

- *Action:* workgroups and managers discuss the results (in company time) and agree plans of action to improve specific matters. The progress of each action plan is then monitored monthly to assure that goals are achieved. On a wider scale, feedback results are used to influence company strategies, e.g. internal communications policies, training and personal development programmes.

Mr Pattemore explained: "In the early stages there were concerns about confidentiality and some people were reluctant to make their views known, but this problem has very largely been overcome. We have demonstrated that action plans result in real changes, which has increased the willingness of people to participate. Fears that the programme might put unreasonable pressure on managers have been allayed by training and support, and it is clearly understood that, where managers needed help to improve an area of concern, the company will provide it. Managers realize that in a service business like business logistics the key to our success is the quality and motivation of our people, and they recognize the importance of SFA in gaining total commitment", said Mr Pattemore. "The bottom line of the SFA programme is that it helps us provide our customers with better service – and the quality of our service is what gives us a competitive edge in the marketplace".

Source: Executive Development, Vol. 5, No. 2, 1992. Reproduced with permission.

(NVQs). A growing number of organizations, such as Boots the Chemist, are attempting to include NVQs as targets for their workforce.

It is not surprising that most measurements are quantifiable although many organizations will attempt to modify quantification with qualitative measurements or comments. The attractiveness of results and outcomes of behaviour as objective sources of data makes them a feature of most appraisal systems in the UK. Long's (1986) survey found them to be a feature in 63 per cent of organizations. Will such approaches reflect performance-control or development approaches? Key questions will relate to how objectives, targets and goals are set, how managers and employees will interact in work towards their achievement, and the use made by employees of measurements as feedback in order to develop further. During the 1960s, there was a growth in schemes of Management by Objectives (MBO), designed to control the performance of

TABLE 7.4   Responses of managers six months after attending a development centre

QUESTION	YES	NO
Did the development centre help you to address development needs?	6	25
Did the development centre help you learn more effectively on the job?	0	31
Did the development centre promote you development on the job?	6	25
Did the development centre help find out strengths and limitations?	18	13
Has the development centre helped you manage your career more effectively?	10	21
Has the development centre helped you understand the competencies you need?	27	4
Has the development centre made you a better manager?	9	22

managers and stimulate them as regards their development. If this could be achieved, the needs of managers and the organization could be integrated. However, such schemes soon came under attack and many fell into disrepute. Levinson (1970, p. 134) attacked the practice of MBO as self-defeating because it was based on 'reward–punishment psychology' which put pressure on individuals without there being any real choice of objectives. Modern approaches to objective setting will face similar charges unless managers pay as much attention to the process by which objectives are set as to the content and quantification of objectives and the environment in which employees work towards their achievement.

■ Behaviour

We have already examined how attention to the behaviour of employees in the transformation process will reveal how an individual has applied aptitudes and attitudes to a task and will provide rich data on current effectiveness and potential for further development. Such attention can occur on a continuous basis taking into account both subjective and objective data. Such an approach would form the foundation of any effective development-led appraisal process. Once established, employees may be more willing to accept more codified approaches to rating their behaviour. For example, we have referred to frameworks of competencies associated with effective performance which can provide a user-friendly starting point for the assessment, appraisal and development of people in an organization. In addition to competencies, but closely related, are the use of Behaviour Anchored Rating Scales (BARS) which provide descriptions of important job behaviour 'anchored' alongside a rating scale. The scales are developed (Rarick and Baxter, 1986, p. 36) by generating descriptions of effective and ineffective performance from people who know the job and these are then used to develop clusters of performance and scales. Each scale produced describes a dimension of performance which can be used in appraisal. An example from a scale developed for Planning is shown as Figure 7.5.

Between Excellent and Unacceptable would come the whole range of possible behaviours of varying degrees of effectiveness. Since BARS are based on specific performance and based on the descriptions of employees involved in a particular job, it is claimed that they provide better feedback and a consistent means of improving performance and setting targets. What is particularly interesting is the potential of such instruments as BARS for enhancing self appraisal and allowing a dialogue between employees and 'others' based on more objective criteria.

■ Summary

For organizations that claim to have an HRM approach to the management of people, appraisal has a central place. In the HRM cycle, it is the vital link between

| 7 Excellent | Develops a comprehensive project plan, documents it well, obtains required approval, and distributes the plan to all concerned. |

↑
↓

| 1 Unacceptable | Seldom, if ever, completes project because of lack of planning and does not seem to care. Fails consistently due to lack of planning and does not inquire about how to improve. |

Figure 7.5   A planning BARS

Source: Schneier and Beatty in Rarick and Baxter, 1986.

performance and the processes of rewards and development that are key features in the evolution of a Primary Internal Labour market discussed in previous chapters. Appraisal can be viewed as a process to bridge the gap between an organization and individuals, which allows a flow of information between managers and employees. The flow of information has to be two-way. As with recruitment and selection, organizations may have overall power in the balance of flows. However, failure to allow reciprocal flows in appraisal can have damaging consequences if HRM outcomes are sought. Thus an organization may fail to use appraisal to identify the aspirations and potential of employees, who may in turn prefer to seek fulfilment elsewhere. In addition, appraisal provides an opportunity for feedback from employees to managers on work issues and processes. However, the release of potential and the free flow of information within appraisal systems will require a fundamental shift in values and attitudes and a reform of our view of appraisal as a fragment and separable part of the employment relationship. In this chapter, we have sought to establish that organizations will need to concentrate on creating a learning and developing culture if appraisal is to be accepted by employees as a means of tying the satisfaction of their needs and their development to the objectives of the organization.

■ Key concepts

- Assessment
- Appraisal
- Performance control
- Developmental approaches
- Criticism, praise and feedback

- Transformation process
- Bureaucratic control
- Self, peer, team, upward appraisal
- Learning and development culture

Discussion questions

1. What should be the purpose of appraisal?
2. Should all employees be appraised? How and by whom?
3. Should pay and performance appraisal be linked?
4. How can employees learn to appraise themselves?
5. Do you think students should have more say in appraising and assessing themselves and each other?
6. What do you think is meant by a learning and development culture in an organization?

■ Further reading

Banks, C. G. and Murphy, K. R. (1985), 'Toward narrowing the Research–Practice Gap in Performance Appraisal', *Personnel Psychology*, Vol. 38, pp. 335–45.

Barlow, G. (1989), 'Deficiencies and the Perpetuation of Power: Latent Functions in Management Appraisal', *Journal of Management Studies*, Vol. 26, No. 5, pp. 499–517.

Campbell, D. J. and Lee, C. (1988), 'Self-Appraisal in Performance Evaluation: Development versus Evaluation', *Academy of Management Review*, Vol. 13, No. 2, pp. 302–14.

Fletcher, C. and Williams, R. (1985), *Performance Appraisal and Career Development*, London: Hutchinson.

Randell, G. (1989), 'Employee Appraisal', in Sisson, K. (ed.), *Personnel Management in Britain*, Oxford: Blackwell.

Stinson, J. and Stokes, J. (1980), 'How to Multi-Appraise', *Management Today*, June, pp. 43–53.

■ Chapter case studies

■ Case 1   A mail order company

Appraisals are only carried out for senior staff and the personnel office reminds appraisers that it is time for the annual appraisal. The appraiser completes a form which involves a scalar rating system concentrating on attributes such as drive and energy, moral courage and stability. No objectives are set and the appraisee cannot see the form. Completed forms are sent to personnel after the interview and the forms are then used for succession planning.

■ Case 2   Chartered accountants

Staff work on a series of projects under a system of matrix management with little visible hierarchy. All appraisals are carried out by the Personnel Director. Project Managers summarise the performance of staff after each project (skills, difficulty of task, non-technical demands). This is unseen by staff. The reports are sent to the Personnel Director who develops a file on each member of staff and evens out the variation of ratings among managers.

Before the appraisal interview, the Personnel Director writes a summary of the previous year's performance and this is sent to the appraisee. The interview then involves a discussion, feedback from project managers, counselling and guidance on career development. There is also a discusssion of training needs which the Personnel Director follows up.

■ Case 3   Local authority

Appraisal is carried out on all Administrative and professional staff by section leaders. A six-point scale is used: 1 = outstanding; 2 = very good; 3 = good; 4 = satisfactory; 5 = unsatisfactory; 6 = formal action required. A 5 is common but a 6 is rare.

Forms are not shown to appraisees and if a 6 is awarded, Personnel informs the staff concerned that performance will be monitored over 3 months. A recent survey found evidence that the appraisal system was not trusted and that any attempt to spread the system to manual and clerical grades would be resisted. However the Government is insisting that all employees should be appraised and has threatened to withdraw funding.

■ Case 4   A public relations consultancy

The appraisal process allows staff to review personal and professional development in an informal but structured way with colleagues of their own choosing. Staff work in trios in a peer counselling situation. Each person in the trio takes a turn at the three roles that make up a trio: Consultant; Client; Observer. The work of the trio is initiated by members themselves after initial training in counselling skills, the management of negative feeling and observation skills. There are no forms and no records kept.

Task

Form groups of 3 or 4. For each of the cases, discuss:

(a) the characteristics of the process;
(b) possible strengths and weaknesses;
(c) overall suitability.

For each case, make a summary of the points from your discussion and provide a rationale for any alterations and improvements that you would make.

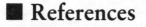

References

1. Barlow, G. (1989), 'Deficiencies and the Perpetuation of Power: Latent Functions in Management Appraisal', *Journal of Management Studies*, Vol. 26, No. 5, pp. 499–517.
2. Tichy N. M., Fombrun, C. J. and Devanna, M. A. (1982), 'Strategic Human Resource Management', *Sloan Management Review*, Vol. 23, No. 4.
3. See Michael Dixon's column in *Financial Times*, 13 January 1993, for a coverage of 'ways of turning people off'.

CHAPTER 8

Rewards Management

Strategy and cultural changes have required radical alterations in the way in which companies handle reward. Indeed, the 1980s have seen a revolution in perceptions about reward and ideas of equity.[1]

There is no such thing as a good pay system; there is only a series of bad ones. The trick is to choose the least bad one.[2]

■ Chapter outline

Introduction
Reward in organizations
Job analysis
Job evaluation
External competitiveness
Establishing pay rates
Alternative rewards systems
Government and pay
Summary

Chapter objectives

After studying this chapter, you should be able to:

1. Explain the key functions of reward management.
2. Explain the importance of job analysis information.
3. Describe the job evaluation process.
4. Describe the key determinants of pay.
5. Evaluate the merits of alternative reward systems.
6. Explain how governments intervene in the pay-determination process.

■ Introduction

Richard Johnston, the human resource director at Flowpak Engineering, decided that a pay structure consisting of a time-rate plus an incentive scheme that was directly linked to individual output was a serious impediment to developing a more multi-skilled workforce. Johnston believed that a time rate system, which offered the employee a fixed wage in return for an unspecified level of performance, would obviate rivalry between co-workers and develop workers' behaviourial skills of cooperation and problem-solving. The time rate, £3.52 per hour, would continue to be influenced by the fairness of the pay as perceived in relation to similar engineering occupations outside the company.

Richard Johnston's experience illustrates the challenges of reward management. Global forces at work today compel managers to improve labour productivity and the quality of their organization's products and services. Social factors impinge on reward management: employee expectations and notions of 'fairness' regarding their pay. Given these pressures, human resource managers seek to design reward structures that facilitate the organization's strategic goals and meet the goals of individual employees.

In most organizations, both private and public sector, an array of pay levels exists. The pay levels in an engineering company differ for different jobs: a skilled machinist might be paid £2 per hour more than an unskilled labourer. Similarly, a supermarket pays different pay rates to checkout operators, department managers and cleaners. An organization's pay structure is the cluster of pay levels associated with jobs in the organization. The pay structure defines the relationships between jobs in terms of pay.

Why do some organizations pay more (or less) than other organizations? Why are different jobs within the same organization paid differently? And why do different employees doing an identical job for the same organization receive different pay? How are these decisions made? How does the government influence reward management? And what effect do trade unions have on pay? Decisions about paying employees for the work they perform are increasingly complex: decisions must be consistent with the organization's goals, with society's values about notions of fairness, and with government legislation.

This chapter discusses some of the important changes that are taking place in reward management. It examines the functions of pay systems, describes different forms of remuneration, and outlines a pay model. Job analysis and job evaluation as techniques for determining different pay rates are explained. The chapter proceeds to examine the determinants of pay, alternative rewards systems, and the role of government in reward management.

■ Reward in organizations

Reward or compensation management is a key element in any discussion of the concept of human resource management. But both these terms have been criticized by scholars who have different perspectives on the debate on human resource management. 'Reward' suggests a special payment for a special act, and 'compensation' suggests payment for an accident or an injury during the course of work (Torrington and Hall, 1987, p. 487). Whilst the term 'reward management' is problematic, we consider that the term best captures the current changes in management assumptions and practice about pay. However, the words 'reward', 'remuneration', and 'pay' are used interchangeably in this text. Reward is defined in the following terms:

> Reward refers to all forms of financial returns and tangible services and benefits employees receive as part of an employment relationship.

Reward is the centre-piece of the employment relationship. The employee and those responsible for reward management have different objectives for the payment contract. For the individual employee the pay cheque at the end of the month is typically the major source of personal income and hence a critical determinant of an individual's purchasing power. The absolute level of earnings determines the standard of living and social well-being of the recipient, and will therefore be the most important consideration for most employees. Employees constantly seek to maximize their reward because of inflation and rising expectations. Further, the axiom of 'a fair day's pay for a fair day's work' raises the question of *relative* income. In most cases what is seen to be 'fair' will be a very rough personalised evaluation.

The organization, on the other hand, is interested in reward management for two important reasons. First, it is interested in the absolute cost of the payment because of its bearing on the profitability or cost-effectiveness. The importance of this varies with the type of organization and the relative cost of employees, so that in a refinery labour costs are minimal, in education or health they are substantial. Second, the organization views pay as a determinant on employee work attitudes and behaviour. Pay may affect an individual's decision to join a company, to work effectively, to undertake training, to accept additional responsibilities, or to join a trade union.

There are three principal objectives of reward management in an organization: to attract and retain suitable employees, to facilitate performance, and to comply with employment legislation and regulations. These objectives have to be achieved within an agreed budget for rewards. First, the reward must be competitive to encourage membership into the organization. In other words, it must attract and retain qualified and competent people to the organization. Rewards that are perceived by prospective members to be inadequate or inequitable will make it difficult for the organization to attract the types of people necessary for success. Second, reward systems are designed and managed to improve productivity and control labour costs. The question of what motivates employees to perform effectively is a difficult one to answer. Amongst practising managers there is a widespread conviction that pay alone motivates workers. This over-simplistic assumption underpins individual wage incentives. Psychological theory and research suggest that the link between individual behaviour and performance is a more complex process.

One of the most widely accepted explanations of motivation is Vroom's (1964) expectancy theory. This approach to worker motivation argues that managers must have understanding of their subordinates' goals and the linkage between effort and performance, between performance and rewards, and between the rewards and individual goal satisfaction. The theory recognizes that there is no universal principle for explaining everyone's motivation, which means that to link performance and reward successfully is difficult to accomplish in practice. Changing the pay system can modify employees' behaviour, which in turn can enhance labour productivity and lower labour costs. In conversation with one of the authors, Richard Johnston explained the benefits of discarding the individual incentive system this way:

> As soon as people realized that there was no personal, peculiar advantage in hiding bits of knowledge, being inflexible, hogging the good jobs, and sticking to their machines and all that . . . it was like suddenly turning the key. (Quoted in Bratton, 1992, p. 171)

The third objective, compliance, means that a reward system should comply with pay legislation. As UK and European Community employment laws change, reward systems may need to be adjusted to ensure continued compliance.

■ Types of reward

The types of reward used will be the result of decisions made concerning the nature of the effort in relation to the reward. Managers are particularly interested in effort-related behaviours, those behaviours that directly or indirectly influence the achievement of the organization's objectives. Figure 8.1 classifies some of these behaviours into four groups: time, energy, competence, and cooperation. To be efficient, managers must ensure that employees turn up for work at the scheduled times; absenteeism and lateness must be minimized. Also, employees must put into the job sufficient energy to complete their allotted tasks within set

Type of Effort	Type of Reward	
Time: maintaining work attendance	Direct	Basic pay Incentive
Energy: performing tasks		
Competence: completing tasks without errors		Merit Overtime
Cooperation: cooperation with co-workers	Indirect	Benefits Paid leave

Figure 8.1   Types of individual effort and reward

time limits. In addition, job incumbents must be competent so that the tasks are completed without errors and above minimum performance standards (performance standard is a minimum acceptable level of performance). Changes in job design (see Chapter 3) require employees to work cooperatively with co-workers to improve the organization's effectiveness.

Figure 8.1 also shows different types of rewards: direct or indirect. Direct types of reward refer to money payments (for example, basic wage or salary, incentives, merit increases and overtime payments). Indirect forms of reward include pensions, private health insurance, and paid time off from work (for example, paid leave for full-time education, JP duties).

In the UK, there are four main types of direct reward system. The basic wage is the irreducible minimum rate of pay. In many organizations it is a basis on which earnings are built by the addition of one or more of the other types of reward. The basic wage is usually determined by a predetermined rate per hour, which tends to reflect the value of the work itself, and generally excludes differences in individual performance. For example, the basic wage for a skilled machine operator may be £3 an hour, for a thirty-five hour week, but operators may receive more because of additional incentive and overtime payment.

A distinction is often made between *salary* and *wage*. A *salary* is a fixed periodical payment to a non-manual employee. It is usually expressed in annual terms, and salaried staff typically do not receive overtime pay. A *wage* is the payment made to manual workers. It is nearly always calculated at an hourly rate. In the 1980s, a number of employers have lessened the divide between salaries and wages by introducing 'single status' payment schemes. This type of payment system is designed to harmonise the terms and conditions of employment between manual and white-collar employees. Common terms and conditions of employment (for example, manual and non-manual employees receive the same number of holidays, sickness benefit, and pensions) were included in the so-called 'strike-free' agreements negotiated in the 1980s in Britain (Bassett, 1987).

An incentive scheme ties pay directly to performance. It can be tied to the performance of an individual or a team of employees. This scheme includes most of the payment-by-results (PBR) systems, as well as commissioned payments to salespeople. Merit pay rewards past behaviours and accomplishments. It is often given as lump-sum payments or as increments to the base pay. Incentive and merit payments differ. While both may influence performance, incentives influence behaviour by offering pay as an inducement. Merit pay, on the other hand, does so by recognizing outstanding *past* performance. The distinction is a matter of timing. Incentive systems are offered prior to the actual performance. Merit pay, on the other hand, typically is not communicated beforehand.

Generally, if employees work beyond the contracted hours they are paid an enhanced rate for the additional hours or overtime. For example, an employee may work from 8am to 5pm for £2 per hour. If the individual works overtime from 5pm to 8pm, the extra three hours may be paid at 'time and a quarter', that is, £2.50 per hour. Overtime working on Saturdays or Sundays may be paid at 'time and a half' or 'double time'.

These four types of pay can make up the total reward package paid to employees and, depending on the size of the organization, the HRM specialist might be responsible for designing and managing all elements of reward management. Systems that distribute pay to employees can be designed in an unlimited number of ways, and a single employer typically will use more than one programme. Current thinking is based on the opinion that pay should be seen as part of the wider relationship between management and employee, and that the reward system adopted should act as a medium for the expression of management style and their attempt to create commitment among the workforce. Current trends reveal attempts to break links with external pressures on the pay system, for example, norms, averages, the 'going rate'. In preference, organizations are shifting the focus towards internally designed factors: performance-linked pay and profit-sharing schemes.

■ Developments in rewards management

The way managers have managed remuneration has undergone significant change in the last decade. A growing number of companies appear to be rewarding their employees, within the same organization and doing an identical job, different levels of pay. Some writers have described these changes in pay practices as 'revolutionary' because they overthrow the old assumption that employees should be paid the same even though their contribution is different, and because this philosophy is being transmitted down through the organization (Curnow, 1986). In the UK, top management pay is increasingly linked to the achievement of business objectives. And for their subordinates too, pay is being geared to individual potential and performance. Performance appraisal, for example, among both non-manual and manual employees is on the increase. In one study, 82 per cent of the organizations surveyed reported using some kind of appraisal scheme (Long, 1986).

In the 1980s, a concerted ideological campaign against automatic annual pay increases by the Thatcher government encouraged a movement towards linking pay to individual performance and the internal dynamics of the business and the local labour markets (IRRR, 1984; Curnow, 1986). Repeated criticisms of national pay bargaining by Government ministers fuelled the debate about its appropriateness. Researchers have chronicled these new developments, such as decentralized collective bargaining (for example, Millward *et al.*, 1992). Two trends have been identified: a significant decline in the influence of multi-employer, national agreements, and a shift towards single-employer bargaining at establishment level and the decentralization of pay negotiations to the level of the business unit, profit centre or plant. It was reported by ACAS that 'it seems, increasingly, companies are organized into separate budget and profit centres, in which unit managers have responsibility for all operations' (1988, p. 12). Millward et al. also reported that between 1984 and 1990, there was a significant fall in multi-employer bargaining over rates of pay. In only about 25 per cent of workplaces was multi-employer bargaining the principal method of pay determination for both manual and non-manual workers (1992, pp. 218–19). Also there appears to have been an increase in alternative or 'creative' reward packages. For instance, the number of companies offering profit-sharing and share ownership schemes to their employees has increased (Pryce and Nicholson, 1988).

■ Rewards and the HRM cycle

By now, it should be clear that reward management is vital to effective management. Brown (1989, p. 25) has stated that: 'The satisfactory management of employment requires the satisfactory management of remuneration as a necessary, if not a sufficient, precondition'. Reward management is directly related to the other elements of the HRM cycle. In the selection process, pay can be a major factor in attracting highly qualified and competent people to the organization. It can also facilitate a low turnover ratio. Pay influences an employee's development and career plan. Performance-related pay can motivate an employee to undertake a course or a training programme. A reward system that directly links pay to performance will require an appraisal system that is both reliable and valid.

To help us examine the complexities of pay, we have developed a framework of reward management. Figure 8.2 contains three basic elements: internal equity, external competitiveness, and the objectives.

The diagram shows two broad policies that any organization must consider in reward management, internal equity and external competitiveness. Internal equity refers to the pay relationships among jobs within a single organization. This policy is translated into practice by the basic techniques of reward management: job analysis, job evaluation, and performance appraisal. The focus is on comparing jobs and individuals in terms of their relative contributions to the organization's objectives. How, for example, does the work of the chef compare with the work of the receptionist, and the waiter? *Job evaluation* is the most common method used to compare the relative values of different jobs inside the organization.

External competitiveness refers to comparisons of the organization's pay relative to the pay of competitive organizations. The organization has three options: to be a pay leader, to match the market rate, or to lag behind what competitive organizations are paying. The determination of the policy on external competitiveness depends on, *inter alia*, labour conditions and the state of the job market and affordability stemming from product market conditions. Our framework also shows that reward packages have explicit or implicit objectives. The balance or relative emphasis between the two basic policies is a key decision to be made in any organization's reward strategy. For example, some organizations emphasize external competitiveness of pay to attract a competent workforce. Other organizations tend to emphasize internal equity of pay, and to place less emphasis on external competitiveness. 'HRM in Practice 8.1' illustrates the problems encountered when internal consistency is ignored.

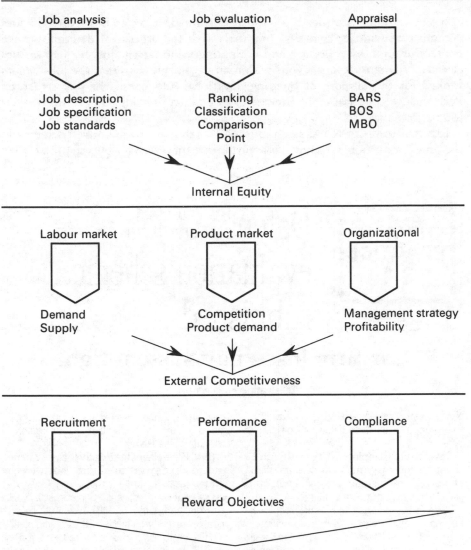

Figure 8.2   A framework for rewards management

Similarly, the policy on external competitiveness is important if the organization is going to attract, retain, and motivate its employees while achieving the other objectives of controlling labour costs and complying with pay legislation. Thus, the two policies, internal equity and external competitiveness, are important components of the concept of human resource management.

Internal equity is typically established through a series of pay techniques commencing with job analysis. Job analysis is the process of determining the content of a job by collecting and evaluating information. Job evaluation uses selected criteria to compare jobs within an organization so that the jobs can be ranked for the purpose of building a rational and consistent pay structure. Performance appraisal is the process of evaluating individuals in terms of their job performance.

External competitiveness is established by reference to job advertisements in the press, or by more systematic labour-market surveys. This information is then

HRM IN PRACTICE 8.1

Defence of job evaluation scheme rubbished

Car firm loses pay system fight

by Heather Falconer

North-west motor dealer H&J Quick has lost a five-year court battle to defend its pay structure.

Five female employees have won their claim for equal pay for work of equal value, effectively rubbishing the job evaluation scheme the firm put forward as its defence.

"We hope the case will make employers approach equal value in a more conciliatory frame of mind," said EOC principal legal officer Elizabeth Whitehouse. "Employers must examine jobs in detail in their evaluation schemes or they will not stand in the way of claims," she said.

The latest tribunal ruling follows a Court of Appeal decision last year that the firm's scheme failed to prevent sexual discrimination because it was not analytical.

"You must break down jobs into their components and assess each one rather than look at whole jobs," Whitehouse said.

Quick's scheme was introduced in 1986 to ward off the women's claims, said personnel manager Bob Heugh.

Six of the claimants lost their cases after an independent expert ruled their jobs were not equal to their male colleagues. Only one successful claimant, a parts clerk, still works for the company, but all five will receive compensation which has still to be decided.

Their success comes as transport union the TGWU begins a campaign for equal pay in the car industry.

National women's secretary Margaret Prosser said there were 380 claims lodged against Jaguar in Coventry and Vauxhall at Luton and claims are being prepared against Aston Martin.

Success could mean rises of up to £1,000 for thousands of female manual workers, mostly sewing machinists.

Source: Personnel Today, 1991. Used with permission.

used to construct a pay structure within the organization. The factors that affect the determination of external competitiveness and pay level include the demand and supply pressures in the labour market, competition for the organization's products or services, and organizational considerations, such as the ability to pay.

While external competitiveness is important, it is internal equity that will often be a priority for HR managers. We have already discussed the notion of fairness in reward, and for employees internal relatives, rather than external comparisons, can be a major source of negative perceptions about reward. To illustrate the importance for managers of achieving internal equity take the following scenario. If two children in the Smith household each receive the same weekly allowance, but their allowance is less than their neighbour's children of similar age, they might grumble but the external differences are generally accepted by the Smith children. However, if at their birthdays, only one child in the Smith family receives an increase in his/her allowance, the internal differences in payment will typically cause an outcry. The point we are making is that generally, there is less scope for error in internal imbalance than external, because any inequities as a result of internal anomalies are more likely to be perceived among co-workers.

So far this chapter has discussed the nature of pay, highlighted some important developments in reward management, and outlined a framework for examining the essential components of remuneration in organizations. The following sections will discuss in more detail the basic components of the model, first focusing on internal equity and the traditional reward techniques of job analysis and job evaluation (appraisal is examined separately in Chapter 7), and proceeding to discuss external competitiveness and the establishment of pay rates.

■ Job analysis

Information technology has made it possible for a word processor, a university lecturer, and an insurance broker to perform different jobs using the same equipment, the computer terminal. If reward is to be based on work performed, a technique is needed to identify the differences and similarities among different jobs in the organization. Observing employees is necessary but not sufficient. Knowledge about jobs and their requirements is collected through job analysis. Job analysis can be defined as:

> The systematic process of collecting and evaluating information about the tasks, responsibilities and the context of a specific job.

Job analysis information informs the HR practitioner about the nature of a specific job. In particular, the major tasks undertaken by the incumbent, the outcomes that are expected, the job's relationships with other jobs in the organizational hierarchy, and job holder characteristics. The basic premise underlying job analysis is that jobs are more likely to be described, differen-

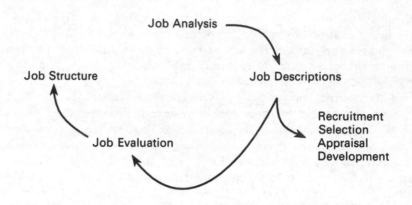

Figure 8.3   Reward actions that rely on job analysis

tiated, and evaluated consistently if accurate information is available to reward managers (Milkovich and Newman, 1990).

Figure 8.3 shows that job analysis information is a prerequisite for preparing job descriptions and for comparing jobs within an organization, job evaluation. Job analysis is also critical for decisions affecting recruitment and selection, appraisal, and employee development. In terms of reward management, unless there is a clear definition of the job and job performance standards it would be difficult to imagine how pay can be linked to individual performance.

■ The process of job analysis

The process of job analysis consists of two main stages: data collection; and the preparation of job descriptions, job specifications and job standards. The process is shown in Figure 8.4. Job analysts collect information about jobs and job holder characteristics. The job information is then used to prepare job descriptions, specifications, and standards.

■ Data collection

Collecting the information involves three tasks: identifying the jobs to be analyzed; developing a job analysis questionnaire; and collecting the data. *Job identification*: to collect information about the firm's jobs, analysts must first identify the jobs within the organization. In stable organizations this can be done from past job analysis reports. The analyst might also have to rely on discussions with workers, the organization chart, or the analyst's knowledge of the organization. To collect data in a systematic way analysts usually develop a *questionnaire* that gathers information about the duties, responsibilities, human abilities, and performance standards of the jobs investigated. Questionnaire design is not easy. There is no one best way to *collect* the data. Analysts make

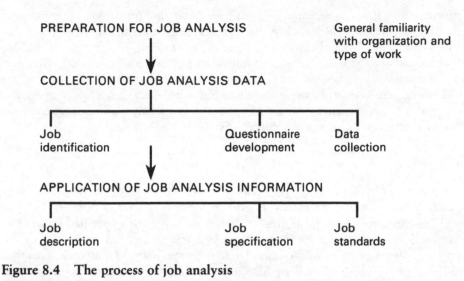

PREPARATION FOR JOB ANALYSIS

COLLECTION OF JOB ANALYSIS DATA

General familiarity
with organization and
type of work

| Job identification | Questionnaire development | Data collection |

APPLICATION OF JOB ANALYSIS INFORMATION

| Job description | Job specification | Job standards |

Figure 8.4　The process of job analysis

trade-offs between accuracy, time, and cost. Figure 8.5 illustrates five different methods of gathering job analysis data.

Let us briefly examine these job analysis methods. A face-to-face interview with the job incumbent is an effective way to gather job information. A major disadvantage with this method is that it is time consuming. Employee-report involves the job incumbent collating the information about his/her job: employees summarize their tasks and activities in the report over a given period of time. Direct observation is a method derived from work-study techniques, and is usually applied to manual occupations. It involves making notes of job-related information. Observation is often regarded as the best method of collecting

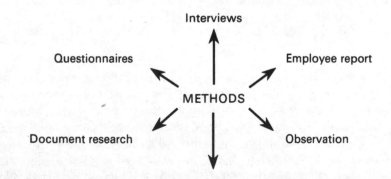

Figure 8.5　Methods of collecting job analysis data

information, and is particularly useful because the trained observer might identify 'unofficial' duties. The method is time consuming, however. An invaluable source of job information will be existing documents, including organizational charts, letters of appointment, and statements of objectives for departments.

Finally, questionnaires can be completed by employees individually or by the job analysts. The advantage with this approach is that it permits a larger sample to be collected quickly, and at a lower cost.

■ Application of job analysis information

The object of collecting job information is to develop job descriptions, job specifications, and job standards. A job description is a written statement that explains the purpose, scope, duties, and responsibilities of a specified job. A job specification is a detailed statement of the human characteristics involved in the job, including: aptitudes, skills, knowledge, physical demands, mental demands, and experience required to perform the job. A job performance standard is a minimum acceptable level of performance.

This completes our discussion of job analysis. The next section examines how job analysis information is used to evaluate jobs in organizations.

■ Job evaluation

British Telecom employs a chief executive officer, departmental managers, technicians, word processors, janitors, and so on. How is pay determined for these different jobs? This question and the techniques employed to answer it lie at the heart of reward management. Our framework for analysing pay shows that the results of job analysis serve as an input for evaluating jobs. Job evaluation is a generic label for a variety of procedures used to establish pay structures inside an organization. Job evaluation can be defined as:

> A systematic process designed to determine the relative worth of jobs within a single work organization.

The technique of job evaluation is concerned with achieving internal equity of pay among different jobs in the organization. The importance of job evaluation to HR managers has increased by the implications of equal pay legislation. European and Canadian equal pay legislation requires, either implicitly or explicitly, that gender-neutral job evaluation schemes be adopted and used to determine and compare the value of jobs within the organization. Thus, it has been argued that job evaluation constitutes the foundation of pay equity (Conway, 1987).

Job evaluation is often misunderstood, so the following three characteristics of all job evaluation schemes are noteworthy with respect to their adequacy for measuring job worth. First, the technique is *systematic* rather than scientific. The job evaluation process depends upon a series of subjective judgements. Job evaluation ratings may be gender biased through the gender linkage of job titles. In one study, for example, subjects assigned significantly lower job evaluation ratings to jobs with a female-stereotyped title – e.g. senior *secretary*-accounting – than to the same job with a more gender-neutral title – e.g. special assistant-accounting (McShane, 1990). Second, selection of the compensable factors is inherently subjective. Criteria for determining job worth often vary between employers, and even between job families within the organization. Thus, 'objective' measurement of job worth is impossible. Third, job evaluation methods differ in their capability to measure differences among jobs. For example, the simple ranking method is less sensitive to changes in job characteristics than the point system.

In addition, it is worth noting that job evaluation is concerned with the job and not the performance of the individual job holder. Individual merit is not assessed. Neither does job evaluation eliminate collective bargaining. It determines the differential gaps between pay; it does not determine pay level. Further, job evaluation produces only a structure of pay rates. Other elements of earnings, such as incentives, are not determined by the method.

■ Job evaluation process

The job evaluation process has the following four steps: gather the data; select compensable factors; evaluate job; and assign pay to the job. Let us look at each of these in turn.

□ 1. GATHER JOB ANALYSIS DATA

Information must be collected through a method of job analysis. In this first step validity should be a guiding principle; that is, the job analyser must accurately capture all of the job content. It is also important for the purpose of job evaluation that similarities and differences among jobs are captured. Ambiguous, incomplete, or inaccurate job descriptions can result in some jobs being incorrectly evaluated.

□ 2. SELECT COMPENSABLE FACTORS

Compensable factors are the factors the organization chooses to reward through differential pay. The most typical compensable factors are skill, effort, knowledge, responsibility, and working conditions.

□ 3. EVALUATE JOB USING EVALUATION METHODS

There are four fundamental methods of job evaluation: ranking, job grading, factor comparison, and point method. The following sub-sections offer some specifics on each of the four methods.

Ranking. Jobs are ordered from least to most valued in the organization. This rank order or hierarchy of jobs is based on subjective evaluation of relative value. In a typical factory we might finish up with the following rank order, Figure 8.6. In this example, the evaluators have agreed that the job of inspector is the most valued of the six jobs listed. Rates of pay will reflect this simple hierarchy. This method has a number of advantages. It is simple, fast and inexpensive. The ranking method will be attractive for small organizations and for those with a limited number of jobs. Obvious disadvantages are that it is crude and entirely subjective, and therefore the results are difficult to defend and legal challenges might make it costly.

Job Grading: also referred to as job classification. As the name suggests, it places jobs in a hierarchy or series of job grades. It is decided in advance how many grades of pay shall be created, and the jobs fall into each grade based on the degree to which the jobs possess a set of compensable factors. The lowest grade will be defined as containing those jobs which require little skill and are closely supervised. With each successive grade, skills, knowledge and responsibilities increase. To illustrate, Grade A includes jobs that require no previous experience, under immediate supervision, with no independent judgement. Grade F contains jobs that require an apprenticeship training, under general supervision, with some independent judgement. In our example in Figure 8.6, the file clerk and the machinist might be slotted into grades A and F respectively. The advantage of this method is that it is relatively simple, quick and inexpensive. A disadvantage is that complex jobs are difficult to fit into the system; a job may seem to have the characteristics of two or more grades.

Factor Comparison: this is a quantitative method which evaluates jobs on the basis of a set of compensable factors. It is a more sophisticated method of ranking in which jobs in the organization are compared to each other across several factors, such as skill, mental effort, responsibility, physical effort and working

Job Title	Rank most valued
1. Forklift driver	1. Inspector
2. Machinist	2. Machinist
3. Inspector	3. Secretary
4. Secretary	4. Forklift driver
5. File Clerk	5. Labourer
6. Labourer	6. File clerk

Least valued

Figure 8.6   Typical job ranking

conditions. For each job, the compensable factors are ranked according to their relative importance in each job. In our example, under the compensable factor heading of 'skill' our six factory jobs are ranked showing the machinist at the top and the labourer at the bottom, Figure 8.7.

Once each benchmark job is ranked on each factor, the job evaluator(s) allocates a monetary value to each factor. Essentially this is done by deciding how much of the wage rate for each benchmark job is associated with skill requirement, how much with mental effort, and so on across all compensable factors For example, in Figure 8.7 of the £7.40 per hour paid to the forklift driver, the evaluator(s) has decided that the job's skill requirements equal £3.00, mental effort is worth £2.40, responsibility equals 90p, physical effort is worth 50p and working conditions are worth 60p. The total £7.40 is therefore allocated among the five compensable factors. This exercise is repeated for each of the benchmark jobs. The advantage with this method is that the criteria for evaluating jobs are made explicit. The main disadvantage is that it is a complex and difficult method to explain to dissatisfied employees. Translating factor comparison into actual pay rates is a somewhat cumbersome exercise, and can be overcome by using a quantitative technique based on points.

Point Method: is also a quantitative method and is the most frequently used of the four techniques. Like the factor comparison method, the point method develops separate scales for each compensable factor to establish a hierarchy of jobs. But instead of using monetary values, as the factor comparison method does, points are used. Each job's relative value, and hence its location in the pay structure, is determined by adding up the points assigned to each compensable factor.

The exercise starts with the allocation of a range of points to each compensable factor. Any number between 1 and 100 points might be assigned to each factor. Next, each of the factors is given a weighting; this is an assessment of how

Job Title	Skill	(£)	Mental effort	(£)	Responsibility	(£)	Physical effort	(£)	Working condition	(£)	Current Wage Rate (£)
Forklift driver	4	(3.0)	5	(2.40)	4	(.90)	2	(.50)	2	(.60)	(7.40)
Machinist	1		2		3		3		3		
Inspector	2		3		1		4		4		
Secretary	3		1		2		6		6		
File Clerk	5		4		5		5		5		
Labourer	6		6		6		1		1		

Note: Rank of 1 is high.

Figure 8.7 Typical ranking jobs by compensable factors

			Factor			
Job Title	Skill	Mental effort	Responsibility	Physical effort	Working conditions	Total
Forklift driver	10	10	10	10	5	45
Machinist	20	15	17	8	10	70
Inspector	20	20	40	5	5	90
Secretary	20	20	35	5	5	85
File clerk	10	5	5	5	5	30
Labourer	5	2	2	17	9	35

Figure 8.8   Point system matrix

important one factor is in relation to the other. For example, in the case of the machinist, if skill is twice as important as working conditions, it is assigned twice as many points (20) as working conditions (10). The results of the evaluation might look like Figure 8.8.

The point values allocated to each compensable factor are totalled across factors, allowing jobs to be placed in a hierarchy according to their total point value. In our example, it would mean that the machinist's wage rate is twice that of the labourer. Such a differential might be unacceptable, but this difficulty can be overcome by tailoring the job evaluation scheme to the organization's pay policy and practical objectives. The point system has the advantage that it is relatively stable over time. And, because of its comprehensiveness, is more acceptable to the interested parties. The shortcomings include the high administrative costs, which might be too high to justify its use in small organizations. A variation of the point system is the widely used 'Hay Plan'. This method employs a standard points matrix, which is applicable across organizational and national boundaries. However, the HR manager should be aware that as far as job evaluation is concerned, there is no perfect system; the process involves subjective judgement.

Moreover, where women are employed care needs to be taken to ensure that gender bias in job evaluation ratings does not exist, for example, by giving higher weighting to physical demands and continuous service in the organization, which tend to favour men. Aspects of the Equal Pay Act are discussed later in this chapter. The focus in this section has been on job evaluation as a technique to achieve internal equity in pay within the organization.

□ **4. ASSIGN PAY TO THE JOB**

The end product of a job evaluation exercise is a hierarchy of jobs in terms of their relative value to the organization. Assigning pay to this hierarchy of jobs is referred to as pricing the pay structure. This practice requires a policy decision on how the organization's pay levels relate to their competitors. The next section is concerned with how employers position their pay relative to what their competitors are paying: the external competitiveness.

■ External competitiveness

While employees' negative feelings concerning internal pay equity might be removed by an effective job evaluation scheme, employees will still compare their pay with those in other organizations and industries. How an organization's pay rates compare to other relevant organizations is known as external competitiveness. Figure 8.2 above shows how an organization's policy on external competitiveness fits into the framework for reward management. The policy expresses the management's intentions regarding their pay levels relative to the pay levels of other organizations competing in the same labour and product markets.

What is the 'going rate'? Can the organization match its competitors? To answer these questions most organizations rely on *wage* and *salary surveys*. Informal or formal pay surveys collect data on what other comparable organizations are paying for comparable jobs. Survey data are used to price benchmark jobs, jobs that are used to anchor the organization's pay scale and around which other jobs are then slotted based on their relative worth to the employer. Evidence suggests that 55 per cent of British employers review newspaper job advertisements, and 71 per cent rely to some extent on informal communications with other organizations, as a means of obtaining comparative pay information.

Once a survey has been conducted, management has three choices: to lead the competition, to match what other firms are paying, or to follow what competitors are paying their employees. Generally high-wage employers are able to recruit and retain a workforce better than low-wage competitors; so decisions regarding external competitiveness and pay level are important because they affect the quality of the workforce as well as operating expenses.

The policy on external competitiveness is determined by a number of economic and organizational factors: first, labour conditions, stemming from competition in the labour market or union bargaining; second, affordability, stemming from product market conditions and the organization's financial state; and third, organizational factors such as the strategic and operating objectives that the organization has established (see Figure 8.2).

■ Labour markets

Managers may typically be heard saying: 'Our pay levels are based upon the market' and, in the 1980s, Conservative politicians insisted that the pay of some public sector employees should to tied to the market' (see HRM in Practice 8.2). Understanding markets requires analysis of the demand for and supply of labour.

HRM IN PRACTICE 8.2

Market factors 'to decide pay of Civil Service'

By Richard Norton-Taylor

The Government yesterday bluntly rejected the unions' argument that the pay of civil servants should continue to be linked to rates in the private sector. It insisted, instead, that the rates should be determined almost exclusively by the market forces of supply and demand.

In a remarkably frank exposition of its approach to the labour market at a hearing of the Civil Service arbitration tribunal it strongly defended its offer of increases of between nothing and $5\frac{1}{2}$ per cent for more than 500,000 whitecollar officials.

The Government's case was put by the Treasury which said: "The Government does not consider that the pay of civil servants, or any other group, should be determined by the needs of the individual. In general terms, pay is a matter for the market place, and social needs are the province of the social security system."

No more money should be given "than is currently needed to recruit, retain and motivate a Civil Service of the required size and calibre." Asked about sagging morale in the Civil Service, Mr Peter Le Cheminant, deputy secretary at the Treasury, said: "Morale cannot be bought."

The Government's offer includes no increase at all for young officials or those at the bottom end of their grades. There was no "management requirement" for an increase because of the large number of applicants for jobs in the Civil Service.

The Treasury said: "The main incentive available to civil servants at present is the possibility of promotion."

The Council of Civil Service Unions is claiming a 13 per cent pay increase, with a £12.50 minimum for the lowest paid. The claim is based on comparable rates in the private sector and increases in the cost of living.

But the Treasury retorted that any reference to indexation in making pay awards "would be entirely contrary to the whole thrust of the Government's economic strategy."

It told the tribunal, chaired by Mr David Calcutt, QC, that it should take account not only of the overall economic situation, but also of demands by other groups in the public sector, teachers and nurses in particular. "The pay settlement for the Civil Service could therefore have an economic importance extending well beyond its direct costs.'

Although the Treasury referred to the Government's promise that it would no cash limit on Civil Service pay in advance of negotiations, it acknowledged that its offer coincided exactly with its 4 per cent guidelines for the public sector.

The hearing will continue today.

Source: Guardian, 20 April 1982. © The Guardian. Used with permission.

The demand for human resources focuses on organizations' hiring behaviour and how much organizations are able and willing to pay their employees. The demand for human resources is a derived demand in that employers require people not for their own sake but because they can help to provide goods and services, the sale of which provides revenue. The supply of human resources focuses on many factors, including the wage rate for that particular occupation, its status, the qualifications of employees and the preferences of people regarding paid work and leisure. Economists inform us that in a perfectly 'free market', the pay level of a particular occupation in a certain geographic area is determined by the interaction of demand and supply. However, most markets, including labour, are not free and have what economists call 'imperfections' on both the demand (for example, discrimination) and the supply (for example, union closed shop) side. The labour market provides a context for reward management and can set limits within which it operates.

■ Product market

Competitive pressures, both national and global, are major factors affecting pay levels. An employer's ability to pay is constrained by his ability to compete, so the nature of the product market affects external competitiveness and the pay level the organization sets. The degree of competition among producers and the level of the demand for products are the two key product market factors. Both affect the ability of the firm to change the prices of its products and services. If prices cannot be changed without suffering loss of revenues due to decreased sales, then the ability of the organization to pay higher rates is constrained. The product market factors set the limits within which the pay level can be established.

■ Organization

Conditions in the labour market and product market set the upper limits within which the pay level can be established. Within most of the European Community, the floor, or minimum, is set by minimum-wage legislation. The conditions in both the labour and product markets offer managers a choice: the pay level can be set within a range of possibilities. The concept of strategic choice emphasizes the role of managerial choice in determining the pay level to be established within an organization. Faced with a range of options, managers might choose to set the pay level relatively high in the range to 'lead' the competition in order to recruit and retain highly qualified people. Further, the organization's profit levels can directly affect its pay levels. For instance, executive salaries are tied to their companies' profits. This general model of the factors influencing the determination of external competitiveness and pay level is presented in Figure 8.9.

■ Establishing pay rates

The pay model emphasizes two basic policy issues: internal equity and external competitiveness. The object of this is to design pay levels and structures that organizational members feel are 'fair', and that will help accomplish management's goals. The appropriate pay level for a job reflects its relative and absolute

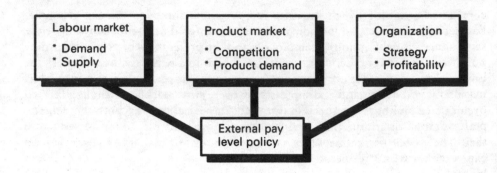

Figure 8.9   A model of factors influencing pay level

worth. The job's relative value to the organization is determined by its ranking by the job analysis and job evaluation processes. The absolute value of a job is determined by what the labour market pays similar jobs. To establish the pay level the two components of the pay model are merged, the job evaluation rankings and the pay survey going-rates.

The results of the job evaluation process and the pay survey are combined through the use of a graph as depicted in Figure 8.10. The horizontal axis depicts an internally consistent job structure base on job evaluation. Each grade is made up of a number of jobs within the organization. The jobs in each category are

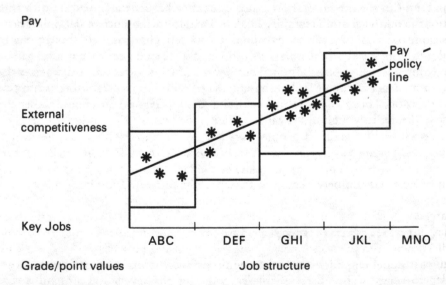

Figure 8.10   The construction of pay levels

considered equal for pay purposes; they have about the same number of points. Each grade will have its own pay range, and all the jobs within the grade have the same range. Jobs in grade 1 (that is, jobs A, B and C), for example, have lower points and pay range than jobs in grade 2 (D, E, and F). The *pay range* defines the lower and upper limits of pay for jobs in a grade. The actual minimum and maximum wage rate paid by the organization's competitors is usually established by survey data. Individual levels of pay within the range may reflect differences in performance or seniority. As depicted in Figure 8.10, organizations can structure their rate ranges to overlap with adjacent ranges a little so that an employee with experience or seniority might earn more than an entry-level person in the next higher pay grade. The job evaluation process helps translate internal equity into practice through job structure.

The midpoint can be determined by pay-survey data from similar jobs. In Figure 8.10, on the vertical axis the pay level policy line has been set to equal the average paid by the organization's competitors for each of the jobs: a matching-competition policy. Management could establish a lag or lead policy by shifting the pay level policy line down or up. Market survey information helps to translate the concept of external competitiveness into pay-setting practice. The pay policy line represents an organization's pay level in the market and serves as a reference point around which pay structures are established. The pay policy line can be raised in response to competitors' pay awards or the cost of living. Thus, pay structures are combinations of external competitiveness considerations and internal equity, and depict pay rates for different jobs within an organization.

Adopting a competitive pay policy is akin to establishing a niche in a product market; there are conventional and new directions in external pay policies. However, there is little empirical evidence of the consequences of these different options (Milkovich and Newman, 1990, p. 198). In the absence of data, the least-risk approach is to set the pay level to match competition, though some organizations set different policies for different occupations and/or skill levels. For example, adopt a lead policy for critical skills, such as computer design engineers; a match policy for less critical skills; and a lag policy for jobs that can be easily filled in the local labour market. Thus, organizations may establish a variety of pay-level policies.

■ Pay and performance

Can reward systems be designed to affect performance? Many of the answers to this question come from theories of motivation and empirical research evaluating strategies to motivate employees. The 'need' theories of motivation emphasize what motivates people, rather than how people are motivated. The two most well-known need theories include Maslow (1954) and Herzberg (1966). Maslow argued that higher-order needs become progressively more important as lower-order needs are satisfied. Herzberg demonstrated that pay takes on significance as a source of satisfaction when it is perceived as a form of recognition or reward. Monetary variables are a key component in the more recent 'process' theories of motivation. For example, Vroom's (1964) expectancy theory grants a prominent role to rewards.

Increasingly British companies attempt to relate pay to performance. The precise methods used vary widely from one firm to another: examples include piecework, bonus schemes, and commission. Piecework (Payment-by-Results) is a reward system in which rewards are related to the pace of work/effort: simply put, the faster an employee works, the higher the output and the greater her/his reward. With the proportional scheme, pay increases in direct proportion to the increase in output.

With the regressive scheme, pay increases proportionally less than output. In contrast, with the progressive scheme pay increases proportionally more than output. In some forms of PBR the reward is based on the performance of a group rather than an individual. A commission is a reward paid on the performance of an individual, typically salaried/sales. The commission earned is a proportion of the total sales and may be added to basic salary.

In 1990 just over a third (34 per cent) of all workplaces in Britain had some form of merit pay, that is, pay that is dependent on the subjective judgement of a superior (see Chapter 7 and Millward *et al.*, 1992, p. 258).

So far we have discussed how jobs are evaluated according to some criteria of internal worth to the organization, and how, based on some combination of internal equity and external competitiveness, jobs are assigned pay grades. Movement within those grades might be based on individual performance appraisal. Although this characterization of reward still dominates many organizational practices, the changed economic climate in which European and North American employers must operate has generated alternative reward systems. Parallel with a growth in alternative reward systems has been a relative decline in some of the more traditional reward practices. It is to some of these alternative pay systems that we now turn.

■ Alternative reward systems

■ All-salaried workforce

Both manual and non-manual employees receive a prescribed amount of money each pay period that is not primarily dependent on the number of hours worked. For example, at Optical Fibres, the UK's leading cable manufacturer, there are no differences between clerical and manufacturing workers on holiday entitlements, pensions, and medical insurance. Every employee – including the plant's general manager – signs on daily in a reception register on arrival and departure; there is no clocking-on and -off (Bassett, 1987).

■ Pay-for-knowledge system

These systems vary pay as a function of the number of different jobs or skills that employees are able to perform competently. Pay increases are tied to learning multiple jobs at ever higher levels of proficiency. Pay-for-knowledge systems (PFKS) reverse the trend towards increased specialization: they encourage functional flexibility and diversification in workers.

This increased functional flexibility gives 'core' workers greater job security. Critics of payment-for-knowledge systems point out the higher training costs, and are sceptical about claims for increased productivity; it flaunts a major tenet of Taylorism, that specialization improves efficiency.

■ Group incentive (gain-sharing) plans

Gain-sharing plans tie pay to performance by giving employees an additional payment when there has been an increase in profits or a decrease in costs to the firm. Incentives are based on a comparison of present profits or costs against historical cost accounting data. Increases in productivity do not necessarily result because employees individually or collectively work harder (that is, work intensification). Typically improvements arise because employees work more smartly, identifying means to perform tasks efficiently without increasing physical effort. The beneficial outcomes arise from what is termed 'group synergy'.

■ Profit sharing

In profit sharing the employer pays current or deferred sums based on company profits, in addition to established wages. Payment can be in the form of current distribution (paid quarterly or annually), deferred plans (paid at retirement and/ or upon disability) or combination plans.

■ Cost savings (Scanlon plan)

Scanlon plans are designed to lower labour costs and distribute the benefits of increased productivity using a financial formula based on labour costs and the sales value of production (SVOP). Payments are typically fairly frequent (for example, monthly). The best-known plan was devised by Joseph Scanlon in the 1930s. The rationale for the Scanlon plan is that psychological growth needs are fulfilled if the employee participates in organizational decision-making while being equitably compensated for participation. The Scanlon plan creates shop-floor production committees in which employees generate suggestions to improve productivity and reduce waste. Screening committees which have both union and management representation act on employee suggestions. Bonuses in the Scanlon plan are paid monthly or quarterly on a plant-wide basis. While many formulas can be used, a common one gives 25 per cent of the benefit of increased productivity to the company and 75 per cent to the employees.

■ Cafeteria-style benefits

'Employee benefits' refer to that part of the total reward package, other than pay for time worked, provided to employees in whole or in part by organization payments (for example, medical, pension). There is some debate regarding employee benefits. For example, do employee benefits facilitate organization performance? Do benefits impact on an organization's ability to attract, retain, and motivate employees? Conventional wisdom says employee benefits can affect recruitment and retention, but there is little research to support this conclusion (Milkovich and Newman, 1990). Following the experience of the 'yuppie' phenomenon, 'designer' compensation arrangements are a vogue. Reward packages in the UK include employee benefits, ranging from membership of health clubs to the use of the company box at Ascot races. Given the absence of empirical evidence on the relationship between employee benefits and performance, and the escalating cost of benefits, benefits are under constant scrutiny by HR managers.

One innovation is cafeteria benefit programmes (CBP). These programmes allow employees to select benefits that match their individual needs. Employees are provided with a benefit account with a specified payment in the account. The types and prices of benefits are provided to each employee in the form of a printout. This programme creates additional administrative costs, but through participation, employees come to understand what benefits the organization is offering. For example, young employees might select dental and medical; older employees might select pension.

All these alternatives represent experiments by organizations to better tie individuals to organization goals, and better to link rewards to individual or group performance in the 1990s.

Further, technical and/or organizational change introduces new products and new methods of production, and the alternative reward systems are designed to encourage functional flexibility and group synergy. At Sanyo (UK), the collective agreement acknowledges the requirement to be flexible: 'all employees are expected to work in any job which they are capable of doing . . . '. And at Inmos, management and unions agree to 'respond flexibly and quickly to changes in the pattern of demand for the company's products and to technological innovation' (Bassett, 1987). Flexibility and common terms and conditions (for all-salaried workforces) are important features of new collective agreements negotiated with Japanese managements and UK unions. To date, there is a lack of data, collected in well-controlled case studies, on the effectiveness of alternative reward systems. One of the authors also reported how a shift from PBR to a standard flat-rate system encouraged flexibility and information sharing (Bratton, 1989).

■ Government and pay

This chapter has dealt with two policy decisions shown in the pay model: internal equity and external competitiveness. In this section the focus shifts to the political and legal context and examines the role government and legislation play in the management of pay. In European states and in North America governments have

Putting the profit motive into practice

Profit-related pay schemes are enjoying a surprising surge in popularity.

By the end of March 1992 there were 2,597 PRP schemes registered with the Inland Revenue, compared to 2,049 schemes in December 1991. The 1991 budget, which made PRP eligible for full tax relief, can partly explain this 25 per cent rise in the number of schemes, but more flexible regulations introduced in 1989 and only now becoming widely known have also had an effect.

One of the first companies to take advantage of this new flexibility was Rhône-Poulene Agriculture Ltd.

Gareth James, the company's personnel director, acknowledges that tax relief is one of the attractions of PRP but warns that the Government could reconsider the scheme if it is hijacked by those who view it as a tax dodge. "I think PRP was set up to motivate people and improve productivity," he says. "But there are signs that it is being used purely for tax-efficiency purposes by some employers."

Gareth James sees little value in fixed bonus arrangements. "A fixed bonus equals fixed motivation and fixed performance," he says. "It isn't a bonus at all but a way of paying salaries."

His company was the first part of Rhône-Poulenc to decide to pull out of the fixed bonus scheme. However, finding an alternative that would apply to all 1,200 employees was no easy task, with five trade unions and a staff association representing interest groups as diverse as hourly paid factory workers, technical and scientific staff, engineers and support staff.

James says: "We wanted something that would not be divisive, but we are talking about an incredibly heterogeneous population because of the nature of what we do and because of our mixed missions."

The search began for a bonus pay scheme that would be simple and therefore readily understood by all employees. "We wanted to focus on profit because we think that is something most people understand," says James. "It is actually a very simple concept, compared to added value, which is much more complicated."

It was also important that employees should feel they 'owned' the new bonus scheme, and so, James set up a bonus consultation group made up of representatives of each of the company's six bargaining units.

The consultation process involved trade-offs and compromises on both sides.

The proposals that finally emerged from this consultation process were significantly different from those originally put forward, but they had the approval of both management and employee representatives.

Because the proposed new bonus scheme involved changes to terms and conditions of employment, it was put to a secret ballot of all employees, with results that were more encouraging than the management team had dared to expect – a 92 per cent turn-out, with 82 per cent voting in favour.

So far GMB union members have every reason to be happy with a deal which last year gave them a bonus of 12 per cent of gross earnings – worth 13.5 per cent to standard tax payers.

Introduced at the beginning of 1991, the PRP scheme triggers a bonus when operating profits are 10 per cent below budgeted levels. At that point the bonus represents 2 per cent of earnings. A further 3.5 per cent bonus is triggered when budgeted operating profits are reached. "So if the company doesn't make the target, people lose 1.5 per cent of their previously guaranteed bonus and if we just hit budget they are no better or worse off than before," James explains. "The money only begins clocking up for above budget improvement, which is true profit improvement."

The knowledge that real profit improvements will be reflected in pay packets has proved to be a powerful employee motivator, according to James. He describes visible efforts to reduce waste and cut costs and tells of a group of employees in a manufacturing area who worked out how much profit each ton of their production had contributed to the bonus scheme. The scheme is also contributing to teambuilding across the organisation and to employees' sense of belonging, he says.

Communication is crucial to maintaining this level of motivation.

Source: Personnel Management Plus, August 1992. Used with permission.

a profound impact, both directly and indirectly, on employees' reward. In the UK, the direct effect on pay is through legislation, such as the Equal Pay Act 1970 and the Equal Pay (Amendment) Regulation 1983, which requires equal pay for equal work (*Garland* v. *British Rail Engineering Ltd*, 1983). In this regard, 'pay' includes any other benefit, whether in cash or in kind, which an employee receives directly or indirectly in respect of an individual's employment. When considering pay organizations within the European Community, systems must take account of Article 119 of the Treaty of Rome, which requires equal pay for equal work. Through such laws, governments in the West intervene directly in the pay-setting process.

Government can also affect reward management by introducing pay control programmes. These typically aim at maintaining low inflation by limiting the size of pay increases. Pay controls can vary in the broadness of the application and in the stringency of the standard. The broadness of the application can include all employees, public and private, or focus on one particular group, for instance civil servants. The standard for allowable pay increases can range from zero to increases equal to some price change or productivity measure. Throughout the 1980s in Britain, the Conservative government used its control of public sector pay to try to influence pay trends in the wider economy. The Conservative government's approach to public sector pay was summarized in 1990 by Norman Lamont, then Chief Secretary to the Treasury, when he said that the government had used a 'combination of pressures' to 'reproduce the discipline which markets exert in the private sector'.[3]

In addition, government has an indirect influence on the pay-setting process as depicted in Figure 8.11 above. Government actions often affect both the demand and supply of labour; consequently, wages are also affected. Legislation can restrict the supply of labour in an occupation. For instance, a statute that sets minimum age limits would restrict the supply of young people. Government also affects the demand for labour. The UK government is a dominant employer; consequently it is a major force in determining pay levels in and beyond the public sector. Government fiscal and monetary policies that affect the economy indirectly affect market forces which, in turn, influence pay. The reward techniques (performance appraisal, job evaluation) and the outcomes of those techniques (pay levels, pay structures) must be designed to be in compliance with the laws passed by parliament and the European Community. This responsibility falls on the HR specialist. Given the importance of equal pay legislation for reward management, the final section examines important issues of pay equity.

■ Equal pay legislation

> Discriminatory employment practices are a manifestation of prejudicial patterns of behaviour in society generally.[4]

The concept of equal pay for women is in conflict with the view that employees' pay should be dictated by the supply and demand of labour. Equal pay legislation, therefore, curtails market forces. Equal pay legislation has existed in the UK for over two decades. Let us look briefly at the development of the UK legislation.

In 1919, the International Labour Organization (ILO) made the concept of equal pay for work of equal value one of its founding principles. In 1951, the ILO passed Convention 100: 'Each member shall . . . ensure the application to all workers of the principle of equal remuneration for men and women workers for work of equal value'. In 1972, the UK became bound to EEC Article of the Treaty of Rome:' Each Member State shall . . . maintain the application of the principle that men and women should receive equal pay for equal work'. The Equal Pay Act, 1970, inserted into contracts of employment an implied term, the 'equality clause'. The equality clause enforced equal terms in the contract of employment for women in the same employment; it required the elimination of less-favourable terms where men and women are employed on like work, and where the work has been rated as equivalent by a job evaluation assessor in the same employment.

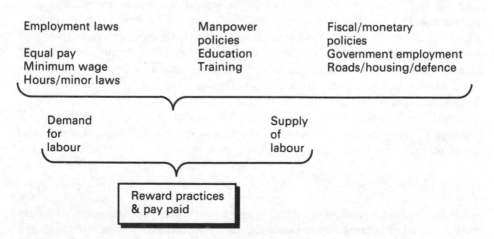

Figure 8.11   Indirect government influence on rewards management

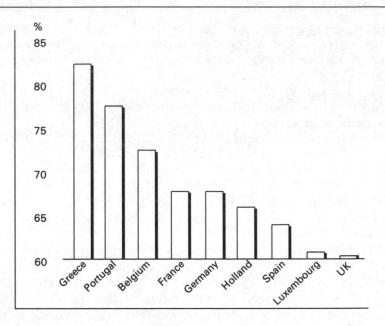

Figure 8.12   Women's pay as a percentage of men's, EC countries (non-manual employees in retail sector)

In the early 1990s statistics revealed that although Britain had the second highest rate of female employment in Europe, at 52 per cent, the earnings gap between women and men has narrowed since 1979. In 1991, women non-manual employees earned 63 per cent of non-manual men's pay, compared to 58 per cent in 1979. The pay gap is particularly significant in retail distribution, and banking and finance. In these sectors, Britain had the widest earnings gap in Europe at 53 per cent and 61 per cent respectively for employees (EOC, 1992), see Figure 8.12. For women manual employees the change has been from earning 59 per cent to 62 per cent of equivalent men's pay.[5] Although women's average earnings did improve over the period 1970–85, the fact remains that after 20 years of equal pay legislation in Britain, women still earn, on average, less than two-thirds of men's average earnings.

Equal pay legislation has failed to address the problem of occupational segregation, that is, the gap between the kinds of jobs performed by men and those performed by women.

■ Pay equity

In 1982, the European Court held that the UK's Equal Pay Act did not comply with Article 119 of the Treaty of Rome, because equal pay was available for work of equal value only where the employer had chosen to conduct a job evaluation study. There was no way a woman could compel her employer to carry out such a

HRM IN PRACTICE 8.4

Merit pay schemes discriminate against women, says report

APPRAISAL schemes and merit pay systems, which are used by around 50 per cent of British companies are often biased against women.

This is the conclusion of an Institute of Manpower Studies report, funded by the Equal Opportunities Commission, which examines merit schemes in a finance company, a local authority, a manufacturer and a catering organisation.

Sexual stereotypes still prevail, according to the report, with managers often valuing different attributes for men and women.

Managers in the finance company were found to rate intelligence, dynamism, energy and assertiveness as important for males, while thoroughness, organisation, dependability and honesty were valued more highly for females.

Discrimination is most obvious, it says, where staff are set qualitative objectives which can be subjectively assessed. Widening of line management responsibility to cover reward systems has also increased management discretion.

"There may be very strong business reasons to devolve responsibility to line managers but unless companies realise the implications they could be building discrimi-

nation into the system," says Stephen Bevan, one of the authors of the report.

Merit schemes are common in the private sector and are spreading in the public sector, particularly as the Citizen's Charter involves the introduction of performance pay for civil servants, teachers and other state employees, IMS points out.

Bevan warns employers that many merit pay schemes may be illegal and may breach the European Court's ruling in the Danfoss case. Where merit rises are unequally distributed between the sexes, this ruling states that the burden of proof is on the employer to show that discrimination has not occurred.

"Companies are poor at monitoring performance pay against any criteria, but particularly in terms of equal opportunities," says Bevan. He advises employers to monitor gender bias in appraisal schemes and to check access to training and promotion.

'Merit pay, performance appraisal and attitudes to women's work' is published by the IMS, Mantell Building, University of Sussex, Falmer, Brighton BN1 9RF.

Source: Personnel Management Plus,
November 1992. Used with
permission.

---

study. Consequently, the Equal Pay Act was amended by the 1983 Equal Pay (Amendment) Regulations, which meant that even where there is no 'like work' or non-discriminatory job evaluation, if the women's work is of 'equal value' to that of a man, the equality clause entitles her to corresponding conditions to the man. The new Regulations were first tested in the case of *Hayward* v. *Cammell Laird Shipbuilders Ltd.* (1987), where a cook – supported by her trade union and the EOC – established her work as of equal value to that of men working in the shipyard as insulation engineers, painters, and joiners. Conway (1987) argues that ' The equal value concept recognizes that occupational segregation persists and that the concomitant undervaluation of "women's" work is responsible for a large part of the earning's gap'.

The time, legal expenses and the bad publicity for the company might provoke the proactive-thinking HR practitioner to avoid such legal judgements and seek pay equity through enlightened decisions or collective bargaining. Equal pay for women will not be guaranteed by collective bargaining and legislation alone however, for, as Wedderburn observes, pay equity will be secure 'only when its justice is adequately understood and practised by men'. (1986, p. 503).

■ Pay equity and job evaluation

All legislation requires, either implicitly or explicitly, that gender-neutral job evaluation schemes be adopted or developed, and used to determine and compare the value of female-dominated and male-dominated jobs. Thus, job evaluation constitutes the foundation of pay equity. It is critical that job evaluation schemes are designed and applied with the least possible amount of bias, particularly gender bias.

■ Summary

This chapter has stressed that rewards management is central to the activities of HR managers. An effective compensation system is designed to satisfy employee needs and reinforce job behaviour consistent with organizational objectives. No single best compensation system exists. The design of reward systems is contingent on the organizational and environmental context in which they must operate.

The framework for the pay model we have developed in this chapter emphasizes two fundamental policy issues: internal equity and external competitiveness. The model provides a useful framework for examining the techniques and issues surrounding reward management. Job evaluation, which seeks to ensure that the job structure is based on the content and relative contribution of the work, ideally should be seen as a technique to achieve internal fairness or equity in pay. Empirical evidence testifies that job evaluation contains subjective elements, however. Organizations can use pay-survey data to position their rewards: either to lead, to match, or to lag behind their competitors, depending upon external and internal pressures. This chapter has also documented the interest in alternative pay systems and the relative decline in some of the more traditional compensation practices. Finally, we have explored how government intervenes both directly and indirectly in the pay determination process. Keeping up-to-date and complying with pay legislation is the prime responsibility of HRM specialists.

■ Key concepts

- Job analysis
- Point method
- Internal equity
- Government

- Job evaluation
- Pay model
- External competitiveness
- Pay equity

Discussion questions

1. What can a pay system do for (a) an organization, and (b) an employee?
2. What is job analysis? Why is it desirable and what problems are associated with its use?
3. What does job evaluation have to do with internal equity and efficiency?
4. You are a manager, and the annual wage negotiations are being concluded. Management has acceded to the trade union's demand for a 15 per cent wage increase, and is now considering whether prices should be increased by 15 per cent to cover this increase. You are asked to comment. Without considering changes in other possible variables, what would your comments be in the following circumstances?
   (a) Your firm's only product is one popular make of car.
   (b) Your firm has a world patent on a new computer game which has made all previous designs redundant, and this is your only product.
5. 'Equal pay for women will be secure only when its justice is adequately understood and practised by men' (Wedderburn, 1986). Do you agree or disagree? Discuss.

■ Further reading

Brown, W. (1989), 'Managing Remuneration', in K. Sisson (ed.), *Personnel Management in Britain*, Oxford: Blackwell.

Bowey, A. M. and Thorpe, R. (1986), *Payment Systems and Productivity*, London: Macmillan.

Curnow, B. (1986), 'The Creative Approach to Pay', *Personnel Management*, October.

McShane, S. (1990), 'Two tests of direct gender bias in job evaluation ratings', *Journal of Occupational Psychology*, 63, pp. 129–40.

Rollins, T. (1988), 'Pay for performance: Is it really worth the trouble?', *Personnel Administrator*, Vol. 33, No. 5.

Saxby, M. (1987), 'Integrated Job Evaluation', *Management Services*, December.

Schwab, D. and Grams, R. (1985), 'Sex-related Errors in Job Evaluation; A Real-World Test', *Journal of Applied Psychology*, Vol. 70, No. 3.

Smith, I. (1983), *The Management of Remuneration*, London: IPM.

Spencer, S. (1990), 'Devolving Job Evaluation', *Personnel Management*, January.

Veres, J. (1900), 'Job Analysis in Practice: A Brief Review of the Role of Job Analysis in Human Resource Management', in Ferris, G. *et al.* (eds.), *Human Resource Management: Perspectives and Issues* (2nd ed.) London: Allyn & Bacon.

Woodley, C. (1990), 'The cafeteria route to compensation', *Personnel Management*, May.

■ Chapter case study   Blueflame Appliances plc

Blueflame Appliances plc manufacturers domestic gas fires for the European and Canadian markets. The industry is highly competitive, with Belgian and Dutch manufacturers claiming 55 per cent of the market. Blueflame Appliances has grown in size during the last three years. New product lines, including the 'log' open-fires, have been introduced and new designs and colours have been added to existing products.

The company is planning to introduce a series of important changes which will have a significant effect on the way the firm is organized and the actual work people do. These changes include the introduction of self-managed teams, self-inspection by production workers, and expensive new machinery which must be operated (24 hours) as against the present system which is a five-day week plus overtime on weekdays and some Saturdays. The production and inventory control system will also be computerised.

Blueflame Appliance is viewed as a good company to work for. Management believe strongly in employee training and the pay rates for the manual and non-manual employees match the rates paid by competitors.

Wages for the manual employees are based on 'domestic negotiations between Blueflames Alliances' management and the General, Municipal Boilermakers (GMB) shop stewards, within the nationally negotiated rates for engineering employees. In addition, the manual employees are on an individual payment-by-results (PBR) system.

The quality control inspectors, first-line supervisors and production controllers – the technical grades – have staff status and their salaries are negotiated separately by the Manufacturing, Science and Finance Union (MSF).

Over the last decade, changes in the demand for different skills by the company have produced an irregular pay structure. Some differentials have widened, others have narrowed. Employees with similar qualifications and skills are paid different rates in different sections of the factory. In addition, among the production workers, the high bonus earners are reluctant to transfer to different machines and are opposed to alterations in the reward system that threaten to reduce their earnings.

There is no doubt that the changes in the manufacturing process will demand greater commitment and flexibility from the manual employees, and a new role for the technical grades. The senior management is fully aware of the limitations of the current reward system, and is supportive of some radical changes in this area. At a recent planning meeting, the plant manager, Mr T. Olesen, asked the human resource manager to explore possible alternative reward systems for the manual production employees. He would like to promote flexibility among different trades, commitment to team-working and self-inspection, and he is anxious to improve labour productivity and quality.

At the monthly union–management consultative meeting the engineering manager raised the possibility of job evaluation for the manual and technical grades. In reply, the senior MSF steward identified a number of concerns with job evaluation. Specifically, she said that 'job evaluation was not objective and was pro-management', and that job evaluation would be 'gender-biased and favour male employees at the expensive of female workers'.

The human resource manager said that although she did not agree with it, she quite understood the point the MSF union representative was making. Subsequently, it was agreed that the human resource department should produce a document outlining a job evaluation scheme appropriate for the company and addressing the unions' concerns.

As the assistant human resource manager you have been given the task of drafting two reports: one to the plant manager, Mr T. Olesen, and the other to the MSF representative, Mrs Y. Whincup, and other members of the union-management consultative committee.

Task

Your report to Mr T. Olesen should:

(a) Outline the merits and limitations of the present reward system for the manual workers; and

(b) identify an alternative reward system for Blueflame Alliances' employees.

Your report to Mrs Y. Whincup and the union–management consultative committee should:

(a) Explain how the company would address the union's concerns if a job evaluation was implemented; and

(b) outline the most appropriate job evaluation method justifying your choice.

■ References

1. Curnow, Barry (1986) 'The creative approach to pay', *Personnel Management*, October.
2. Richard Johnston, a practising HR manager, quoted in Bratton, J. (1992) *Japanization at Work*, London: Macmillan, p. 171.
3. Quoted in 'Future uncertain for public sector pay', in *Bargaining Report*, Labour Research Department, May 1991.
4. Smith, A., Craver, C. and Clark, L. (1982), *Employment Discrimination Law* (2nd ed.) p. 1, and quoted in Lord Wedderburn (1986), *The Worker and the Law* (3rd ed.) 1986, p. 447.
5. These figures are based upon two reports: *Women and Men in Britain 1991*, published by the Equal Opportunities Commission (1991) and the Department of Employment's 1991 *New Earnings Survey*.

CHAPTER 9

Human Resource Development

Only by drawing on the combined brainpower of all its employees can a firm face up to the turbulence and constraints of today's environment.[1]

If the training and development of its employees is not afforded a high priority, if training is not seen as a vital component in the realization of business plans, then it is hard to accept that such a company has committed itself to HRM.[2]

Training? It's a joke . . . as a setter operator you can be asked to do a job that you have never done before. And, the only training you get is maybe fifteen minutes with a setter.

■ Chapter outline

Introduction
Establishing HRD
Implementing HRD
Strategy and HRD
HRD and the line manager
Summary

Chapter objectives

After studying this chapter, you should be able to:

1. Discuss the place of Human Resource Development (HRD) within HRM strategies.
2. Explain the requirements of a successful HRD policy.
3. Explain how an HRD policy may be implemented.
4. Explain principles of learning and their role in HRD.
5. Outline the purpose of evaluation in HRD.

■ Introduction

Within most formulations of HRM, training and employee development represent the vital if not the pivotal components. Keep (1989, p. 111) argues that the case for a strategic approach to Training and Development is easily made if human resource management is to have any meaning above an empty 'buzz phrase'. Usually retitled to *Human Resource Development* (HRD), an organization's investment in the learning of its people acts as a powerful signal of its intentions. First of all, the replacement of the words 'training cost' with 'investment' should allow everyone involved in HRD to take a longer term view, particularly with respect to the outcomes of HRD where the continuation of viewing training as a short term cost has persistently acted as a powerful break on many training strategies throughout the modern age. Secondly, HRD acts as triggering mechanism for the progression of other HRM policies that are aimed at recruiting, retaining and rewarding employees who are recognised as the qualitative difference between organizations. Thirdly, if it is an HRM strategy to engender the conditions whereby loyalty and commitment towards an organization's aims can be encouraged, HRD carries the prospect of unleashing the potential that lies within all workers, thus getting the ideas out of the heads of workers into the heads of bosses, allowing employees to contribute to and indeed transform strategy.

Inspiration for western organizations to reap the benefits of HRD has come inevitably from the success of Japanese companies (see Bratton, 1992). In their examination of Japanese personnel and training policies, Brown and Read (1984, p. 53), highlighted the conviction of Japanese management that business success based on high standards of performance was dependent on a trained and constantly updated workforce. Manpower and training policies were always constructed in the same context as business plans and strongly related to them. The HRM cycle that has been highlighted in this book is based on an idealised Japanese organization as the prototype of worker loyalty. The cycle prescribes the integration of HRM activities to create an internal labour market.

While the cycle highlights the pivotal place of development, context will limit and constrain the design of policies, their implementation and the extent to which the HRD elements of the cycle can be integrated in reality. Guest (1989, p. 50) refers to the 'cement' that binds the system to ensure successful outcomes to HRM policies. Included in the 'cement' are both the support of senior managers and leaders and a culture that reinforces HRM. Thus the processes linking performance, appraisal and development would be carried out effectively by line managers 'as part of their everyday work', resulting in the assessment of needs for job improvement and career development. Development activities would be evaluated not only to prove that they were worthwhile in terms of outcomes expected, but also to allow employees to transfer learning into their work as it is currently defined, and to redefine work and responsibilities in the light of new capabilities and competences.

There have been two important features of Japanese 'cement' which have been particularly emphasised as distinctive in Japan but often absent in western organizations, causing the cycle to come to a halt. The first of these is the Japanese presumption in larger organizations of life-time employment for core workers. Dore and Sako (1989, p. 76) have outlined how life-time employment allows Japanese organizations to recruit employees for a career rather than for a job which may soon become obsolete. Employees are expected to retrain and indeed many employees undertake courses of self study in order to continue their learning. Employees are therefore carefully selected as much for their ability to learn as for their current repertoire of skills. Once recruited, employees become worth investing in although the form of this investment may be more subtle than a large training budget. Secondly, line managers are fully involved in the development of their subordinates to such an extent that the differentiation between learning and working becomes virtually impossible to discern (and include in a budget). There is an emphasis on informal learning which line managers regard as part of their job and a responsibility on which they will be valued. It is the acceptance of this responsibility by line managers, more than any other within the HRM cycle, that carries the potential to produce the HRM outcomes of loyalty, flexibility, quality and commitment so earnestly desired by many UK organizations. Not the least of these outcomes is that HRD activities of the more formal kind, such as courses, are likely to prove their worth, but also the transfer of learning into the workplace can alter the nature of work itself and the relationships between managers and employees.

■ Establishing HRD

It is doubtful whether the senior management of many western organizations would be willing to commit to such an idea as life-time employment (although see the terms of the New Deal at Rover in Chapter 6). Indeed, commitment in Japan to this principle may itself be changing. However, if employees are worth investing in, some consideration is required of why this may be the case including some understanding of the potential that may lie within all employees and a consideration of the work that they do. Discussion of an employee's potential, and his/her prospects for development, is usually confined to an organization's managerial cadre. The various models that have been produced in the literature focus almost solely on the development of managers, with the implicit assumption that non-managers cannot develop or their potential is limited. For example, Hall (1986, p. 235) provides a progressive model of career growth and effectiveness through an integration of task and personal learning shown as Figure 9.1.

Managers, as well as mastering the knowledge and skills required to improve their work performance in the short term and their adaptability in the long term, should also have the chance to assess themselves through an exploration of attitudes towards career and personal life. Such an assessment will determine suitability for higher positions within organizations. Progression continues towards 'being truly one's own person . . . to being a self-directed, self-aware organizational leader'. (Hall, 1986, p. 252)

If models of development and fulfilment of potential have been reserved for the élite ranks of managers, the rest of the workforce has faced a more limited and

	Task Learning	Personal Learning
Short Term	Improving performance-related knowledge, skills and abilities skills and abilities	Resolving issues regarding attitudes toward career and personal life
Long Term	Improving adaptability	Developing and extending identity

Figure 9.1   Task and personal learning dimensions in career effectiveness

Source: Hall, 1986.

restricted framework. Nowhere in the industrialised West is the restriction on development more in evidence than in the UK, where Taylorist–Fordist approaches to control, through job design and the deskilling of jobs in order to reduce training costs, continue to hold sway in many organizations. In Chapter 7 we referred to the role of metaphor in understanding organizations and how the machine may come to be seen as the ideal way of organizing. Marsick (1987) has written of a 'paradigm' of workplace training and development represented by an organization ideal of a machine. A paradigm can be thought of as a 'framework' of thinking which provides an explicit or implicit view of reality (Morgan, 1980, p. 606) based on fundamental assumptions about the nature of reality. Marsick argues that the machine ideal causes jobs to be seen as parts co-ordinated by a rational control system, where performance can be measured as observable behaviour, and which is quantifiable and criterion referenced. Attitudes are important only in so far as they can be manipulated to reinforce desired performance. Each individual has a responsibility for his/her part but no more and has to work against a set standard. Learning is based on a deficit model which assesses the gap between the behaviour of employees and the set standard. Training attempts to close the gap by bringing employees up to the desired standard or competence but not beyond. There is little place for the consideration of attitudes, feelings and personal development.

A further implication of the above ideal may be a subservience of learning and training to accounting procedures which measure the cause and effect relationships between training programmes and output and profit in the short term. If a relationship cannot be shown, there will be pressure to provide the proof or cut the cost of the training. Even where organizations espouse an HRD approach, all too often sufficient amounts of the machine ideal remain in place, and hidden from view, to present an effective and powerful barrier to organization learning. Sadly, a number of public service organizations are being encouraged, and indeed required, to adopt the approaches associated with the 'efficient' mechanistic paradigm with the accompanying debilitating effect on skill levels and learning, for example, schools, universities and hospitals.

The accumulation of deskilling combined with standardised products for mass markets that are no longer mass but increasingly fragmented, has resulted in what

Finegold and Soskice (1988, p. 22) see as a self-reinforcing cycle of low quality products and low skills. They argue that as a nation the UK's failure to educate and train its workforce to the same levels as its competitors is both a cause and a consequence of a relatively poor economic performance. It is a cause because the absence of a well-educated and trained workforce has restrained the response of UK organizations to changing world economic conditions; and it is a consequence because the mass production techniques of UK organizations for many years signalled a demand for a low-skilled workforce. It is not difficult to see how such signals feed into attitudes towards learning outside organizations. For example, there has been in the UK, until the recession of the 1990s, a comparatively low staying-on rate in full-time education compared to other countries, and the examination system protects A-levels as an academic 'gold standard', despite efforts to raise the status of vocational education. There has been a great deal of effort in the UK to change attitudes towards training, the most recent being based on local initiatives through Training and Enterprise Councils (TECs)in England and Wales and Local Enterprise Companies (LECs) in Scotland. However it is unlikely that the TECs and LECs alone will have an impact on the forces that maintain the low quality/low skills equilibrium in the UK Action is required from within organizations.

Fonda and Hayes (1986, p. 47) have shown how some organizations can actually ask 'Is more training really necessary?' in their outline of a range of training and development models that are suited to organizations' intentions in relation to their environment. Their models of 'Ad Hoc' – meeting HRD needs as they arise, and 'Planned Maintenance' – HRD carried out to keep the organization in shape but not seen as making a central contribution, assume stable and predictable product markets and unchanging skill requirements. In both cases training is not central and may not exist.

By contrast, Japan and other countries in the Far East, and the competitive European nations, have long rejected Taylorist–Fordist methods of control and the waste of employee talent implied. Quickly adapting production methods with new technology, employees have been seen as assets to train and develop, and the national structures of education and training have responded accordingly. Furthermore, as layers of managers were removed as organizations sought leanness and fitness, employees could be allowed a greater role in decision-making and an opportunity to enhance their knowledge and skills.

A number of researchers and writers have highlighted the distinction between eastern and western mindsets. The 'Japanese mindset' has its roots in the philosophy of Confucius and the religions of Buddhism and Shintoism. In Japanese organizations, eastern culture has generated quite different attitudes to those found in the UK. Aspects of this include: the cultural axiom of wa, meaning harmony and synergy, organic imagery; and diffuse orientation – start with generalities and context before closing in on details.

Hampden-Turner (1990, p. 173) has examined how Asian countries are benefiting from the brainpower of their employees, and how eastern values allow organizations to see complementarities and connections rather than narrow targets such as profit. Thus products have been targeted that 'will supply the knowledge and skills to make other products and develop the economy's human resources at the same time'. Further products will be considered in relation to its 'family' and place in a generation of related products. This fundamental view results in a different role for cost accountants. Japanese organizations, and Asian organizations in general, also come under less pressure from external financial pressures with the result that organizations are more often 'owned' by employees. There is less equity in a Japanese organization's financing and less pressure to show short term results and pay high dividends. Shareholders prefer growth, leaving more flexibility for investment, research and HRD. This contrasts sharply with the short-termism in the UK and the power of 'cost control' ideas and techniques.

The implications are clear. Breaking out of the low quality product/low skill equilibrium requires a challenge to the very mindset that transformed western economies once in the past. That mindset is now a burden, as many organizations have discovered to their cost as markets flowed to the East. A policy of HRD has to reflect the strategy of senior managers who are able to view their organizations in a variety of ways. Seeing people as being 'worth investing in' means being able to ward off the competing pressures that might challenge this view, whilst at the same time providing the support for a value system that we might call a learning environment. In such an environment, key participants are able to respond to calls for the spread of HRD activities throughout the workforce and ensure their success. Many of the scenarios deal with a freeing-up of organizational relationships and a removal of barriers to learning. Of particular importance are the actions of managers at all levels in supporting learning and turning around an aversion to risk-taking towards opportunity spotting. The HRD approach identifies and utilizes what the Japanese have called the 'gold in workers' heads'. Thus managers learn to recognise the value of front line employees who have the closest contact with customers and are thus first to learn about new needs and desires.

In recent years many organizations have been attracted by the idea of a learning company or learning organization. However, little is known about how such organizations may achieve this status. As Pedler, Boydell and Burgoyne (1988, p. 1) noted in their 1988 Learning Company Project Report,

> The Learning Company is the new frontier and the scouts are busy bringing back reports. . . . Many people are talking about it but no-one has yet claimed to be able to offer a working model of what a Learning Company is.

Various definitions have been presented and these can provide some help in understanding the concept. Pedler, Boydell and Burgoyne's (1988, p. 3) definition is: 'an organization which facilitates the learning of all its members *and* continuously transforms itself'. Peter Honey (1991, p. 30) suggests that: 'creating a learning organization is simple but not easy. It requires you to take continuous improvement seriously and actively encourage people within your sphere of influence to do the same'.

We should also take care with any definition. Much of the language used in discussions about the concept of the Learning Company represents a clear challenge to many of our ideas about companies and their relationships with the rest of society. The challenges require a preparedness to face up to fundamental attitudes and the sources of such attitudes – much easier said than done! However, if the Learning Company represents something of an ideal or a vision, then the gap between reality and the vision may generate a natural or 'creative' tension which can provide the energy for a change in the direction of the vision (Senge 1990, p. 9). HRM IN PRACTICE 9.1 shows how one organization in the U.K. has already started this process.

■ Implementing HRD

Models of training and development have shown a remarkable tendency to match the conventional wisdom of how organizations should be run. Depending on the resources committed to their activities, trainers have had to justify the commitment by adherence to prescriptive approaches. Traditionally workers learnt their jobs by 'exposure' to experienced workers who would show them what to do ('Sitting by Nellie'). Undoubtedly much learning did occur in this way, but as a learning system it was haphazard, lengthy and bad habits could be passed on as well as good ones. In some cases, reinforced by employers' tendencies to deskill work, workers were unwilling to give away their 'secrets' for fear of losing their jobs. Most importantly, line managers did not see it as their responsibility to become involved in training employees, and the range of forces referred to above acted to prohibit any consideration of valuing employee potential.

In the 1960s, following their establishment by the Industrial Training Act 1964, the Industrial Training Boards encouraged a systematic training model. The approach was widely adopted and became ingrained into the thinking of most training practitioners. The approach was based on a four stage process shown as Figure 9.2. The approach neatly matches the conception of what most organizations would regard as rationality and efficiency. There is an emphasis on cost effectiveness throughout: training needs are identified so that wasteful expenditure can be avoided, objectives involving standards are set, programmes are designed and implemented, outcomes are evaluated, or more precisely validated, to ensure that the programme meets objectives originally specified and organization criteria. There is a preference for off-the-job learning, partly because of the weaknesses identified by the 'sitting by Nellie' approach, and partly to formalise training so that it is standardised, measurable and undertaken by specialist trainers. The trainer can focus on the provision of separate training activities that avoid the complexity of day-to-day work activities and make evaluation all the more easy.

Over the years the basic elements of this systematic training model have remained and most organizations that claim to have a systematic and planned approach to training would have some representation of it. There have also been

HRM IN PRACTICE 9.1

Rover learning business

For a number of years the company has conducted employee attitude surveys. These consistently revealed that our employees did not feel that best use was made of their talents and that they were prepared to rise to greater challenges than we put in front of them. They felt that they were not well enough informed about opportunities for involvement, development and progression within the business. In responding to those very serious and clearly articulated statements, several thrusts for progress have been undertaken. The first has seen the establishment of Rover Learning Business. Rover Learning Business is a "business within the business". It has its own chairman, managing director, executive committee and board of governors. Its primary aim is to provide a top quality learning and development service to all employees as customers, regardless of geography and with equal opportunity. It is committed to providing assistance to everyone wishing to develop themselves. It attempts to change the emphasis from "training", which most people still regard as having something done to them, to "learning" – doing something for themselves.

Clearly, the learning opportunities within any business are widespread. The emphasis within RLB's title on the word "learning" was intentional, designed to bring about that switch of emphasis such that self-development and acceptance of responsibility by the individuals and their line manager should be the way forward rather than the traditional route. Rover Learning Business provides learning packages and consultancy within the company. Its first product, launched in May 1990 was the "REAL" programme (Rover Employees Assisted Learning), under which any employee is entitled to receive up to £100 a year for pursuing virtually any kind of learning programme. The emphasis has been very much on saying "Yes" to proposals put forward by employees rather than having a list of restrictions, although in order to ensure compliance with tax regulations there have had to be a number of rules and policies put in place. But these have been very much to a necessary minimum.

Courses in "in-shore navigation", sheep husbandry, outward-bound team events, Japanese, swimming, have all been approved. The criterion is only that it is a legitimate learning experience, receipted and delivered by a recognized body.

Language training and system/software appreciation have proved most popular. In the second year of operation some who undertook personal interest courses have switched to more academically demanding programmes. The learning culture is starting to take hold.

The intent has been to establish a more populist approach to learning and development, emphasizing that careers can be something pursued not only by a relatively small band of professional and managerial employees but also by any one of our employees who feels so motivated to take up the challenge. The personnel mission statement sets out the objectives for Rover to create that kind of learning environment.

Source: D. Bower (1993) 'The Learning Organization', *Executive Development*, Vol. 6, No. 2, pp. 4–7. Reprinted with permission.

IDENTIFY TRAINING NEEDS
AND
SPECIFY OBJECTIVES

↓

DESIGN A PROGRAMME

↓

IMPLEMENT A PROGRAMME

↓

EVALUATE TRAINING

Figure 9.2   A four-stage training model

a number of refinements by advocates of a more realistic and more sophisticated model. Kenney and Reid (1986, p. 14) have presented a planned six stage training cycle with evaluation occurring at all stages. The training cycle can be applied at all levels of an organization. Donnelly (1987, p. 4) argues that in reality senior management may abdicate responsibility for training policy to training departments, with a consequent potential for widening the gap between training and organization requirements. Essential prerequisites for any effort to implement a training model are a consideration of budgets, attitudes, abilities and culture/climate. A key requirement of training activity is that it should be relevant and 'reflect the real world'.

Bramley (1989, p. 6) also argues that the training sub-system may become independent of the organization context. He advocates a cycle that is open to the context by involving managers in analysing work situations to identify desirable changes, and designing and delivering the training to bring the changes about. Evaluation occurs throughout the process with an emphasis on managers taking responsibility for encouraging the transfer of learning, that occurs during training, into workplace performance. Bramley's Effectiveness Model is shown as Figure 9.3.

The refinements to the basic model of the systematic approach to training advocate taking a more sophisticated view of training and this essentially involves taking account of reality or organization context. Implicit in the models are the inherent limitations of organization reality that may prevent the models from operating or maintain training activity at a low level. Thus the reality may be little consideration for training in relation to organization strategy and a culture which emphasises short term results against set standards. In the Bramley model, the limitation may be a refusal by managers to become involved in training by neither identifying needs in relation to situations nor supporting the transfer of learning. These are both features of an organization's learning climate and are necessary and essential conditions of implementing an HRD approach.

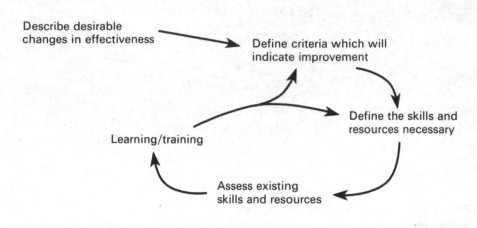

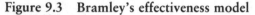

Figure 9.3   Bramley's effectiveness model

Taylor (1991, p. 264) has argued that it is possible to present two views of why systematic training models may not match organizational reality. In the first, the Rehabilitative Critique, it is argued that the systematic model's concepts are sound and can be used as a heuristic device and an approximation to reality. The models serve to highlight the problems to be overcome at each stage by refining techniques. For example, in identifying training needs, trainers may not have access to the 'real' learning needs of the organization because of a lack of access to information and low credibility with senior managers. The refinement would be for trainers to raise the profile of training. The Radical Critique, however, argues that the systematic model is based on flawed assumptions and is merely a 'legitimising myth' (1991, p. 270) to establish to role of the trainer and to allow management's right to define skill within the employment relationship. For example, it is often assumed that training is in everyone's interest. However, in times of rapid change, the definition of skill and the redesign of work which determines and is determined by employee learning, may lead to a divergence of interest between employees and management and unbalance the employment relationship between them. Taylor (Taylor, 1991, p. 273) concludes that while systematic models may have helped to 'professionalise' the training activity and to provide a simple and easily understood explanation of training procedures, such models are incomplete and really only suitable for organizations operating in stable environments where goals can be clearly set, outcomes measured and mere compliance obtained from employees. However, according to Taylor, 'Continued adherence towards what is still essentially a mechanistic procedure may well prevent trainers tapping into the more nebulous but powerful organizational forces such as mission, creativity, culture and values' (Taylor, 1991, p. 273). Such forces will need to be considered and understood in any HRD approach and will form a vital part of the remainder of this chapter.

■ Strategy and HRD

Persuading the senior managers in an organization to integrate HRD into strategy would seem to be an essential prerequisite of successful HRD. How this is actually achieved is undoubtedly easier said than done. There is also the problem of the strategic planning process itself. Over the years, particularly in the West, both managers in organizations and writers have viewed the process as deliberate and purposeful. Senior managers scan the environment, develop alternative goals aligned with mission, and formulate business plans and policies. Thus it would seem that the extent to which HRD becomes a feature of strategy depends on the ability of senior managers to sense important environmental trends and signals in HRD terms, that is, learning for employees. Pettigrew, Sparrow and Hendry (1988, p. 29), in a model of factors which trigger and drive training activity, identify the external forces which may begin the process. Technological and market changes may signal a skills gap, government requirements on health and safety may force training to be considered, or financial support from external agencies may act as a pump-priming mechanism. Crucially, the model recognises the importance of a 'positive culture for training' and the existence of 'Training Champions' among senior managers who contribute to a company philosophy that supports training in espoused terms at least. While crucial, this view of strategy places great reliance on the ability of senior managers to deliberate on the factors which include HRD action through plans and policy.

This is however a top down view of the process. Mintzberg (1987, p. 66) provides a view of strategy-making which can foster learning within an organization if senior managers allow it. Strategies can emerge from the actions of employees:

> A salesman visits a customer. The product isn't quite right, and together they work out some modifications. The salesman returns to the company and puts the changes through; after two or three more rounds, they finally get it right. A new product emerges, which eventually opens up a new market. The company has changed strategic course. (Mintzberg, 1987, p. 68).

Through the employees' interaction with production processes, customers, suppliers and clients, both internal and external to their organization, employees can monitor, respond to and learn from evolving situations. If the information can flow, strategies can be 'formed' by such interactions as well as deliberately 'formulated'. The whole process requires the reconciliation of emergent learning with deliberate control. Senior managers must be able to use the tension between the two processes of deliberate and emerging strategy-making, and resolve the dilemma to 'craft' a strategy for the real world. If they can only see strategies in deliberate planning terms they not only run the risk of such strategies becoming unrealised, but also waste the learning that can emerge from their employees. Integrating HRD into strategy therefore requires the development of the senior management team so that the dilemma to be resolved between control through planning and emergent learning becomes an acceptable form of their thinking.

■ HRD and line manager

Even if senior managers become 'Training Champions' and begin both to 'form' and 'formulate' strategy by resolving the dilemma of control through planning and emergent learning, such commitment to HRD has to be translated into the structures, systems and processes that might be called a learning climate. Paul Temporal (1978, p. 93) has identified the learning climate in an organization as being composed of subjectively perceived physical and psycho-social variables which will fashion an employee's effectiveness in realising learning potential. Such variables may also act as a block to learning. Physical variables cover the jobs and tasks an employee is asked to do, the structure within which they are set, and factors such as noise and the amount of working space. Of particular significance is the extent to which the work contains learning and the extent to which work can be adjusted in line with employee learning. Psycho-social variables may be more powerful. These include norms, attitudes, processes, systems and procedures. They appear within the relationships in which an employee is involved, for example, with superiors, peers, subordinates, customers and suppliers. Few organizations pay any attention to their learning climate and yet any attempt to implement strategies and policies of HRD and HRM are inevitably doomed unless the learning climate can be influenced to provide support.

At the heart of the learning climate lies the line manager/ employee relationship. If we examine the activities that are involved in HRD, we can see just how important this relationship is. Figure 9.4 shows HRD elements drawn from the HRM cycle. As separate items, the activities may be carried out efficiently. However, HRD requires integration, and the key to achieving this lies in the thoughts, feelings and actions of line managers. The separation of the elements is for analysis only; each is embedded within the learning climate. Organizations that are able to fuse the elements together so that their separation is virtually untraceable within a supportive learning climate will come closest to the successful development and implementation of an HRD policy. A number of roles have been associated with managers to support the fusion, including coach, counsellor and mentor. A brief examination of the elements will highlight the key features of these roles.

In Chapter 7, Performance Appraisal, a distinction was made between performance control (Randell, 1989, p. 160) approaches to assessment, and appraisal and developmental approaches. The latter may use sophisticated techniques such as behaviour anchored ratings scales or competencies combined with self appraisal and feedback from 'others', including line managers, in order to foster a development and learning culture which we can now place alongside our current analysis of the learning climate. Some organizations are also seeking

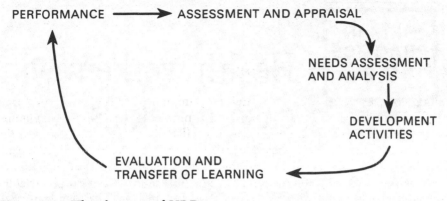

Figure 9.4   The elements of HRD

to establish a link between rewards and skills within jobs (see HRM IN PRACTICE 9.2). Line managers will be involved in the assessment and appraisal of employees on a continuous basis. Where this occurs in a climate of mutual trust and support and an absence of fear, this is likely to release a flow of information about all aspects of workplace performance. Employees who are closest to their work are able to identify their own problems, the problems of their work, and the opportunities for development for themselves and their work. Continuous review both affects and is affected by the learning climate and releases a flow of information allowing integration with the next element of the HRD cycle, needs assessment and analysis.

In the systematic model of training, needs assessment and analysis is concerned with identifying gaps between work performance and standards of work/ performance criteria which have a training solution. Training needs can exist and be identified throughout an organization. Boydell (1976) has identified three possible levels: organization; job/occupation; and individual.

In theory, needs are identified at corporate or organization levels and feed through to individual levels. Once again, the approach reflects a mechanistic view of organizations and people within it. In particular, there is an emphasis on the flow of information down the hierarchy to individuals whose training needs are assessed against standards as defined by others. Each person has a responsibility to perform against the standard and to receive appropriate training if they are unable to do so. This is clearly a reflection of the planned and deliberate formulation of strategy referred to above. While this may be entirely appropriate in environments where current performance is defective or standards and criteria of performance are unchanging, it is unlikely to release the talents of employees. A call for a consideration of emergent strategy at senior management levels requires needs assessment and analysis to be utilised, not only to identify deficiencies against standards but also to identify opportunities for learning

HRM IN PRACTICE 9.2

Health workers win cash for skills

by Anna Smith

A northern health authority is ditching national wage rates in favour of skills-based pay.

West Cumbria Health Care, which becomes a trust next month, is regarding all its jobs according to the skills required for each one.

The pay scheme, which managers and union representation have worked on together, coincides with a joint agreement on terms and conditions for the new trust.

"The implementation of the conditions will not be a breach of the public sector pay limits," said personnel director Ken Hutchinson.

"But they are a radical departure from Whitley rules," he added.

Existing staff will be offered skills-based contracts, although they have the right to remain on Whitley Council conditions.

In future staff will be recruited under the new terms.

The trust plans to develop performance-related pay which will measure the performance of all staff against the skills laid down for their jobs.

West Cumbria Health Care has been a leader in selling locally negotiated contracts to staff.

More than eight in 10 nursing auxiliaries have accepted contracts outside the national system.

This latest move extends the skills-based concept to managers, nurses and midwives, professionals like physiotherapists and support staff like porters and cleaners.

"Thirteen per cent of the workforce is already outside Whitley so we hope that experience will encourage others," said Hutchinson.

Source: Personnel Today, 9 March 1993.
Used with permission.

---

and development. This may involve as much an assessment of work practices and products produced, structures, systems, processes and relationships – that is, the learning climate – as of individuals.

Emerging from a consideration of needs will be plans for development activities. These may take the form of on-the-job or work based opportunities supported by line managers, or off-the-job courses run by specialists, which may or may not lead to paper qualifications, and open/distance learning activities. Whatever the form of development activities undertaken, the key questions concern whether and how learning will actually occur, and whether learning can be integrated into workplace behaviour and sustained. The learning climate is the source of some of the answers to these issues in a most powerful way.

First of all, will learning occur and how? Throughout the twentieth century there have been many ideas concerning learning. A distinction is usually made between 'associative learning or behavourism' and 'cognitive learning'. The main differences between the two traditions are summarised in Figure 9.5. We can see

Associative Learning	*Cognitive Learning*
Learning in terms of responses to stimuli; 'automatic' learning	Insightful learning
Classical conditioning (Pavlov's dogs)	Thinking, discovering understanding, seeing relationships and meanings
Operant/Instrumental conditioning	New arrangements of previously learned concepts and principles

Figure 9.5   Traditions of learning

how the nature of the work that employees are required to perform will lead to the acceptance of a particular view of learning. It will also underpin much of a line manager's understanding of human behaviour and motivation. Thus the reduction of work into low-skilled and repetitious tasks will favour associative and behaviourist views of learning even where, in the initial phases of learning, knowledge and understanding is required. The main thrust of the learning is to produce behaviour that can be repeated time after time in relatively unchanging conditions. This matches very closely the form of learning required for task learning identified in Figure 9.1 above by Hall (1986, p. 235). More complex work favours the need for knowledge, understanding and higher-order cognitive skills, underpinned by cognitive learning theories. However, the acquisition of knowledge and understanding also requires an outlet for action through behaviour in the workplace.

Modern theories of learning contain elements of both associative and cognitive learning but most importantly emphasise the process of learning and its continuity. This has resulted in a great deal of attraction for such theories in organizations pursuing HRD policies. Kolb (1984, p. 42) has provided an integrated theory of experiential learning where learning is prompted through the interaction of a learner and his/her environment. The theory stresses the central role of individual needs and goals in determining the type of experience sought and the extent to which all stages of learning are completed. For learning to occur all stages of a learning cycle should be completed. However, individual learners will have an established pattern of assumptions, attitudes and aptitudes which will determine effectiveness in learning. Kolb's Learning Cycle is shown as Figure 9.6.

According to Kolb, learning occurs through the grasping of experience and the transformation of it. The transformation of the impact of experience on the senses (CE), through internal reflection (RO), allows the emergence of ideas (AC) that can be extended into the external world through new actions (AE). Unless the process can be completed in full, learning does not occur and individuals may not begin the journey to qualitatively finer and higher forms of awareness, which may be called development.

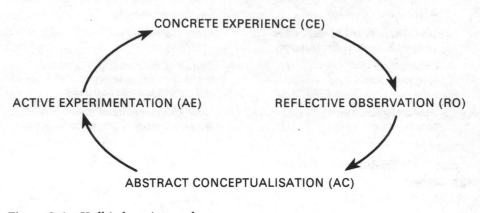

Figure 9.6   Kolb's learning cycle

Source: Kolb, 1984.

The variables that have already been identified as the learning climate of an organization are significant since they will influence and add to the intrinsic or internal blocks to learning 'owned' by each person. Temporal's (1978, p. 93) classification of these blocks is:

Perceptual   where the learner is unable to see what the problem is.

Cultural   where the learner cuts him/herself off from a range of activities through the acceptance of norms regarding what is 'done' or 'not done', is right or wrong.

Emotional/   where the learner feels insecure in certain situations, which
Motivational   causes reluctance to take action based on the learner's ideas and beliefs.

Intellectual   where the learner has not developed the right learning skills, the mental competence to resolve problems and approach situations correctly.

Expressive   where the learner has poor skills of communication.

The source of these internal blocks to learning lies in the combination of conscious, subconscious and unconscious beliefs within each person that particular processes, required for the completion of the learning cycle, can be carried out. The release of talent and potential that lies within each employee will require learners to overcome barriers to learning by their own efforts and the support and encouragement of a positive learning climate. The learning cycle, therefore, contains the seeds for continuous learning and development in the workplace. However it can also serve to highlight factors which prevent continuous learning, such as the learning climate and the role of line managers. In particular, line managers may be crucial in determining the extent to which knowledge, skills and understanding gained in development activities can be transferred into workplace behaviour and performance. This shifts our attention to evaluation.

The systematic model of training places evaluation as the last stage of a four stage model. Although a number of writers have pointed out the value of evaluation at each stage of the model (Kenney and Reid, 1986; Donnelly, 1987), the image of evaluation encompassed by many trainers is that of a final stage added on at the end of a training course. In such cases, evaluation serves to provide feedback to trainers so that small adjustments and improvements may be made to activities, or to provide data so that expenditure on training may be justified. Given the precarious standing of training in many organizations, the collection of data by evaluating activities is a vital process in establishing the credibility and value of training.

In an HRD approach, such battles should have been largely fought and won. That is, managers at all levels should see employees as worth investing in and HRD as vital to organization survival and prosperity. This is not an excuse to avoid evaluation. On the contrary, evaluation is part of a continuous process acting as an important link throughout learning by providing feedback to those involved, for example, trainers, employees and managers. The purpose of evaluation is primarily to enhance learning and contribute to the positive transfer of learning from development activity to workplace behaviour and performance. Once again, we see the over-riding importance of the learning climate and the abilities and attitudes of individual learners, because if transfer does not occur, development activities will be seen to be of little value in the eyes of employees and managers alike.

Baldwin and Ford (1988, p. 65) have provided a model of the transfer process shown as Figure 9.7. The model specifies six crucial linkages in the transfer of training. For example, we can see that new skills can be learnt and retained but support and opportunity to use the learning must be provided in the work environment. Baldwin and Ford (1988, p. 93) draw on research to identify support activities by line managers to include goal-setting, reinforcement activities, encouragement to attend, and modelling of behaviours.

The responsibility of the line manager for the development of his/her employees has come to be seen as the linchpin in HRD and HRM and the route towards continuous employee development. However, while many organizations might espouse such a policy, there has so far been insufficient evidence of widespread practice and acceptance of these responsibilities by managers. Leicester (1989, p. 53) found an absence of implemented continuous development policies, but in organizations where managers had been trained in interpersonal skills and had an explicit responsibility for managing people, employees were more likely to be fully trained: 'not just for the job . . . but continuously prepared for a work performance that is a regular contribution to corporate success. In this sense, training begets training: only a fully trained management will create and continue to maintain a properly trained workforce'(Leicester, 1989, p. 57).

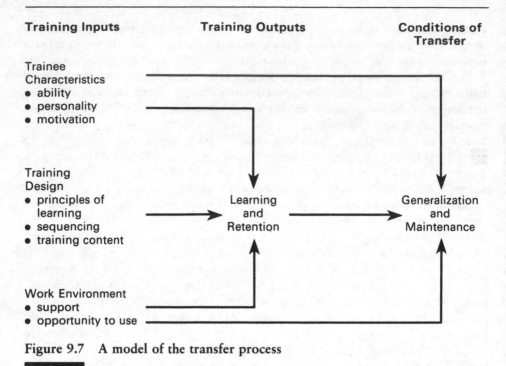

Figure 9.7   A model of the transfer process

Source: Baldwin and Ford, 1988.

■ Summary

This chapter has sought to highlight some of the key features of an HRD policy as part of an integrated HRM strategy. It will be apparent that a fundamental shift of responsibility for employee development passes to line managers and employees themselves. This will require a different role for trainers as a separate group and function. In many organizations, trainers have become 'facilitators' of learning and 'change agents' in fostering a supportive learning climate. There has been clear progress in many organizations and a great deal of energy devoted to the development of a learning workforce. We noted in Chapter 6, Recruitment and Selection, how the assessment of ability to learn may be a feature of an organization's selection activities. We also noted that this may influence the expecatations of employees. In such organizations, learning and development become key features of the employment relationship, and the provision of resources and support for HRD activities an accepted part of working life. It is not difficult to imagine in such circumstances the creation of a virtuous cycle of continuous development and enhanced performance. However, in many other organizations in the UK, there remain significant barriers to HRD, most notably the attitudes of managers and employees. Low expectations, lack of confidence and self belief and negative memories of learning from school can all play a role in preventing individuals from taking opportunities for further development. Employees may also be adversely influenced by the attitudes of fellow workers. Thus the adverse learning climate within a group may counter attempts by managers to foster a positive learning climate. Negative attitudes to HRD remain the key issues to be addressed in the years to come.

■ Key concepts

- Human resource development
- Low quality product
  – low skill equilibrium
- The Learning Company
- Systematic training model

- Learning climate
- Learning cycle
- Learning transfer
- Line manager responsibility
- Emergent learning

Discussion questions

1. What is the relationship between strategy and HRD?
2. What have been the main benefits of a systematic approach to training? What are the criticisms of the systematic model for an organization pursuing an HRD policy?
3. How will your learning at school/college be transferred to work?
4. What is a 'Training Champion'?
5. How can employees be motivated to learn? Who should be responsible? Do we all learn in the same way?
6. What kind of learning skills will organizations require in the future?

■ Further reading

Baldwin, T. T. and Ford, J. K. (1988, p. 65), 'Transfer of Training: A Review and Directions for Future Research', *Personnel Psychology*, Vol. 41, pp. 63–105.

Bramley, P. (1989), 'Effective Training', *Journal of European Industrial Training*, Vol. 13.

Cooke, J. and Knibbs, J. (1987), 'The Manager's Role in Staff Development', *Journal of European Industrial Training*, Vol. 11, No. 1, pp. 5–8.

Keep, E. (1989), 'Corporate Training Policies: The Vital Component', in Storey, J, (ed.), *New Perspectives in Human Resource Management*, London: Routledge, pp. 109–25.

Leicester, C. (1989), 'The Key Role of the Line Manager in Employee Development', *Personnel Management*, March, pp. 53–7.

Pedler, M., Burgoyne, J. and Boydell, T. (1991), *The Learning Company: A Strategy for Sustainable Development*, Maidenhead: McGraw-Hill.

■ Chapter case study   ABC Publishers plc

■ Background

ABC Publisher plc is a publisher of educational literature. The market is very competitive and continuing growth depends on the success of its 15 Sales Staff, organised into two teams to cover the UK.

Training and development for staff is accommodated through a formal scheme covering all personnel. The development of each employee is formulated through discussions with immediate superiors. The content of discussions is recorded and nominations for training are then forwarded to the HR manager who will liaise between departments and the HRD department.

■ Programme X

Programme X was a course on general sales and marketing skills aimed at all sales staff. The course, constructed by trainers after consultation with the personnel manager and the sales team managers, involved 13 days 'off-the-job' training in two blocks: Part 1 – 10 days; and Part 3 – 3 days. Part 2 of the programme involved the production of a work-based project worked on over three months between Parts 1 and 3 of the programme. Projects were presented in Part 3 of the programme. The project involved the selection of an activity within each participant's sales area which provided an opportunity of improved sales or enhanced customer service.

Topics covered in Part 1 included:

Finance in ABC;
Effective sales management;
Customer management;
Presentation skills;
Negotiating skills.

There were various attempts to evaluate the programme but the main purpose was to obtain information to enable the programme to be improved. HRD staff were also required to report to the HR Manager on the success of the programme.

Prior to Part 1, a briefing session was held at the HRD Centre for all participants. The content of the course was outlined and pre-course reading distributed. The sales team managers were encouraged to conduct their own briefing although no record or check was made on this. Recent interviews with participants suggested that such briefing sessions were rare.

At the end of Parts 1 and 3, participants were offered the opportunity to express reactions to the programme through qualitative comments on each topic covered and the completion of ratings scales on the performance of HRD staff and overall value of the programme.

The projects were meant to be selected in consultation with sales team managers and findings were then presented to other participants on the course in Part 3 of the programme. Feedback was provided at the end of the presentation and in written form by HRD Staff. Interviews with participants, however, suggested that the implementation of proposals made in projects was haphazard. At the end of Part 3, the participants returned to work and many felt that while the programme had been useful, there had been little impact on their performance.

Questions

1. Comment on this organization's approach to the training and development of sales staff.
2. Why did the programme have little impact on the performance of the staff?
3. What would be your suggestions for improving the impact of HRD activities in this organization? Consider the role and responsibilities of:

   a. Senior managers
   b. Sales team managers
   c. HR manager and HRD staff
   d. Sales staff.

■ References

1. This line is taken from an often-quoted text by Konosuke Matsushita of Matushita Electric. The full quotation is as follows:

   We are going to win and the industrial west is going to lose out. There is nothing you can do about it, because the reasons for your failure are within yourselves. With your bosses doing the thinking while the workers wield the screwdrivers, you are convinced deep down that that is the right way to run a business. For you, the essence of management is getting the ideas out of the heads of the bosses and into the hands of labour.

   The survival of firms today is so hazardous in an increasingly unpredictable environment that their continued existence depends on the day-to-day mobilisation of every ounce of intelligence. For us, the core of management is the art of mobilising and putting together the intellectual resources of all the employees in the service of the firm. Because we have measured better than you the scope of the new technological and economic challenges, we know that the intelligence of a handful of technocrats, however brilliant they may be, is no longer enough to take them up with a real chance of success.

Only by drawing on the combined brainpower of all its employees can a firm face up to the turbulence and constraints of today's environment.

2. Keep, E. (1989), 'Corporate Training Policies: The Vital Component', in Storey, J. (ed.) *New Perspectives in Human Resource Management*, London: Routledge, pp. 109–25.

3. Quoted in Bratton, J. (1992), *Japanization at Work*, London: Macmillan, p. 109.

4. Reports on the death of life-time employment in Japan's large organizations have been exaggerated, although recession in 1992/3 has resulted in some reforms such as redeployment of workers or the offer of training and finance for workers to set up their own businesses. See Leadbeater C. (1993), 'Tough Middle Age for Lifetime Jobs', *Financial Times*, 13 January.

EMPLOYEE AND LABOUR RELATIONS

CHAPTER 10

Communications and Employee Participation

The way forward is to run your business mainly on trust, not to police them [employees]. I don't seem to sign anything any more and this is the way it should be.[1]

People actually know who the managing director is now . . . He is actually trying to communicate.[2]

Previously we had very formal joint consultations. We have stopped that too. The only thing that's at all formal is when occasionally we have to negotiate something like an annual wage deal . . . What we do now is, we get them [shop stewards] in and have a chat. We don't keep minutes.[3]

■ Chapter outline

Chapter objectives

After studying this chapter, you should be able to:

1. Explain why managers might want to increase employee participation.
2. Describe the different dimensions of employee participation.
3. Explain different approaches to improving communications in organizations.
4. Summarize the structure and operation of joint consultation committees and some obstacles to the consultation process.

■ Introduction

In January 1993, it was reported that Lloyds Bank had given a promise to its 40 000 employees it would be honest and open with them whether the news was good or bad. Lloyds Bank introduced an employee communication 'charter'. Another large business, ICL (UK), used its team briefing system to communicate to its workforce the rationale behind the company's announcement of a pay freeze in late 1992. Employee communication and participation is another theme that has figured prominently in the HRM model. The two cases of Lloyds Bank and ICL (UK) are part of the evidence confirming the substantial increase in methods to improve communications between managers and employees and other initatives, such as quality circles and formal and informal consultative meetings to raise employee involvement and commitment (Millward *et al.*, 1992). Evidence has been produced from a number of case studies about the *nature* of employee participation (for example, Marchington, 1987). The majority of studies of employee participation have focused on the private business sector. With a few notable exceptions, the public sector, and particularly local government employee participation policies, have gone largely undocumented (Perkins, 1986). The call for greater employee participation is not new; it has a long history (Brannen *et al.*, 1976). Four key features that influence workers' participation have been identified: the pattern of industrial relations, the views of the main interested parties, the importance of personnel policy, and legislative context (Guest, 1986).

British industrial relations are based on the traditions of voluntarism, centring on collective bargaining. Voluntarism means a preference by managers, trade unions and the government for the voluntary regulation of the employment relationship, and a preference for a non-legalistic form of joint regulation or collective bargaining. However, the tradition of voluntarism has been increasingly circumscribed since the 1960s and 1970s by Labour governments and, in the 1980s, by Conservative government legislation and the decline of traditional industrial sectors, formally the 'bastions' of British trade unionism. These trends reduce the capacity of trade unions to take radical initiatives to extend workers' participation and control through collective bargaining.

The views of the principal 'actors' in the industrial relations system are also determinants of employee participation. There is a consensus among employer groups and the Conservative government of the early 1990s which can be summarised as follows: employee involvement is desirable; the aim of employee involvement is to promote workers' interest in the success of the organisation, and policies for involvement should be directed at the workforce as a whole. Support for extending employee participation generally comes from human resource managers. However, various writers have expressed serious doubts about how much influence human resource managers are able to exert in practice over major personnel policy formation (Guest, 1986).

The legislative context further affects the nature and extent of employee participation. The 'legislative push' for new systems of employee participation has diminished since 1979. The 1975 Employment Protection Act gives limited rights to union representatives to obtain certain information from their employers. The 1974 Health and Safety at Work Act encourages employee participation. The 1982 Employment Act requires certain companies to include a statement in the annual report describing the action taken during the year to introduce, maintain or develop employee involvement. However, in terms of changing actual practice and encouraging participation, the law is likely to be marginal (Marchington and Wilding, 1983, p. 35). The renewed interest and policy initiatives supported by the government and many employers adopting, either implicitly or explicitly, a HRM paradigm, tend to centre on the voluntary development of employee involvement. The major machinery for this is direct communication with employees and problem solving at the point of production. There is little evidence of any extensive employee participation in policy formulation. In practice, to date, participation is limited to policy implementation.

■ Employee participation and HRM

A central concept of strategic HRM is the individual employee-oriented approach to participation. The techniques developed in the 1980s span a number of different spheres of the employment relationship and the HRM cycle: job design, for example, quality circles; rewards, for example, profit-related pay; employee communication programmes; and decision-making. There are two interrelated aspects of the contemporary debate on the HRM approach to employee participation. First, there is the argument that participation fundamentally transforms the climate of the employment relations because it leads not only to changes in worker behaviour, but more significantly to long-term changes in employee attitudes, for example, increased employee commitment to organizational goals, and that these in turn will result in gains in labour productivity and quality. Second, there is the argument that employee participation techniques, by promoting the individual employee rather than employees' collective bodies, deliberately undermine the role of the trade union representative.

This chapter examines these two themes. The chapter defines and seeks to clarify the terms which have been used in the debate on employee participation. It therefore begins by defining 'employee participation'; the meaning of the term is quite elastic. It goes on to explain the growth of interest in HRM directed at 'employee participation'. The nature of participation in organizations and some obstacles to participation are also discussed.

■ The nature of employee participation

A review of the literature reveals that the terms 'employee participation' and 'employee involvement' have different meanings. In essence, participation involves employees exerting a countervailing and upward pressure on management control, which need not imply unity of purpose. Employee involvement, in contrast, is perceived to be a 'softer' form of participation, to imply a commonality of interest between employees and management, and stresses that involvement should be directed at the workforce as a whole and not restricted to trade-union channels. As Guest (1986) states: 'involvement is considered to be more flexible and better geared to the goal of securing commitment and shared interest' (1986, p. 687).

When people talk about participation or involvement, they are reflecting their own attitudes and work experiences, and their own hopes for the future. Managers tend to talk about participation when in fact they mean consultation. For example, the CBI believes that: 'Employees at all levels must understand and appreciate the economic and commercial realities of operating in today's highly competitive trading climate' (ACAS, 1987). Consultation in practice usually means a structure for improving communications, usually 'top-down' communications. Employees and union representatives when offered consultation believe they are about to be given participation. For example, 'in order to play their full part they [employees] need to be provided with full information and *real opportunities* [our emphasis] to influence decisions which affect their working lives' states the TUC.[4] Differing expectations amongst employees will affect their attitude, their propensity to participate, and ultimately the success of participation techniques in the organization. Therefore, a vital first step, if there is to be any meeting of minds, is to create a common language and conceptual model.

Definitions of employee participation or involvement do not always reflect the range of possibilities, from some small degree of influence to 'total control'. For instance, Salamon defines participation as a

> philosophy or style of organizational management which recognizes both the need and the right of employees, individually or collectively, to be involved with management in areas of the organisation's decision making beyond that normally covered by collective bargaining. (1987, p. 296)

The process of employee involvement should provide employees with the opportunity to influence and, wherever possible, take part in decision making on matters which affect their working lives. Charlton (1983) has suggested that the most prevalent classification is that which differentiates direct from indirect participation. The term 'direct' is used to refer to those forms of participation where individual employees, albeit often in a very limited way, are involved in the decision-making processes which affect their everyday work routines. Direct participation, such as briefing groups or the creation of new work organisation arrangements (self-managed teams), is viewed as a device to increase labour productivity and implicitly to improve job satisfaction. On the other hand, indirect participation is used to refer to those forms of participation where representatives or delegates of the main body of employees participate in a variety

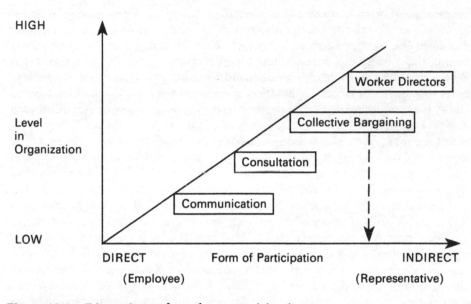

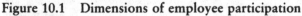

Figure 10.1   Dimensions of employee participation

of ways in the decision-making processes within the organization. Indirect forms, such as joint consultation, widening the content of collective bargaining and 'worker directors', are associated with the broader notion of 'industrial democracy' (Brennen, et al. 1976; Bullock, 1977).

Conceptual models have been provided by Salamon (1987). Figure 10.1 depicts an adaptation of such models and shows the relationship between three constituent elements: the forms of participation, direct and indirect; level; and the scope of participation. Figure 10.1 illustrates that there are four possible referents of the term participation. Those meanings are participation through the communication of information, extended consultation, collective bargaining, and worker directors. It is outside the scope of this chapter to examine the wider debate on worker directors and industrial democracy. Participation through communication and consultation are directly pertinent to HRM techniques. Employee participation through the process of collective bargaining is examined in Chapter 12. Before examining participation techniques in detail, the following section addresses the question: why the enthusiasm for employee participation?

■ Management and attitude change

Management has continually to address two interlinked problems with regard to human resources: control and commitment. Fox (1985) argues that faced with the management problem of securing employee compliance, identification and commitment, management have adopted a range of employment strategies including employee communication and participation. The current enthusiasm for employee participation and improved communications needs to be viewed within the context of a management HRM strategy, the purpose of which is to secure employee support, involvement and commitment to facilitate change, and so ensure the most effective operation of the organisation. Commitment means individual employees identifying with the organization's gaols, which, in turn, increases motivation and satisfaction, and enhances performance. A new buzz-word for these changes is employee 'empowerment'. The involvement–commitment cycle is depicted in Figure 10.2, and is the reverse of the vicious circle of control discussed by Clegg and Dunkerley in the early 1980s (see also Huczynski and Buchanan, 1991, pp. 306–309).

The management view of employee involvement is based on a perception of consensus. The BIM assumes for instance, that there is a 'community of interest between employer and employee in furthering the long term prospects of the enterprise'. Consequently the main purpose of employee involvement is to 'achieve a greater commitment of all employees to the definition and attainment of the objectives of the enterprise' (BIM, 1977, p. 1). The CBI puts forward a similar view: 'a company with good relations is more likely to succeed than one where the workforce remains uninformed and uncommitted . . . (employees) need to be fully informed about their company's opportunities and problems in order to achieve the united effort needed to beat the competition' (ACAS, 1987).

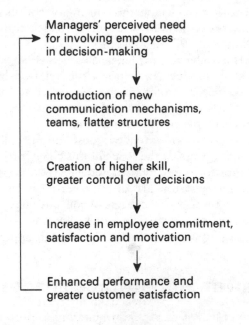

Figure 10.2   The involvement–commitment cycle

The Advisory, Conciliation and Arbitration Service (ACAS) sees employee involvement as a key to improved efficiency: 'if you do involve people and get some sort of identification with the aims of the organisation, people feel committed and involved. They will work more effectively and the organisation will become more successful and that's in everybody's interests.'

HR theorists have put forward two reasons why organizations introduce employee involvement schemes. First, employee involvement presents a socially acceptable management style. Development of employee communications and involvement will be encouraged because generally companies desire to project 'a socially responsible stance on such issues' (Marchington and Wilding 1983, p. 32). Second, the justification for introducing employee involvement stems from the perennial managerial problems of efficiency, harmony, and problems associated with alienation. (Williams, 1979; Guest, 1986). These managerial problems may be poor quality work, strikes, higher labour turnover or absenteeism, and management sees a solution in the introduction of employee involvement (Charlton, 1983, p. 76). Participation may not only improve the quality of a decision but also its chances of successful implementation on the factory floor (Marchington; 1982, p. 157). The interest in employee participation largely stems from the perceived benefits, such as attitudinal changes amongst the workforce, and in turn the improvement in organisational effectiveness, quality of product or service. This view is captured in a statement by Bassett that the new industrial relations of the 1980s has seen a development in trade union leaders' attitudes that rejects the 'idea of the employer as an enemy, the replacement of the class struggle with the struggle for markets' (1987, p. 174). Surveys of British employers have shown that the reasons most frequently cited for the introduction of profit-sharing schemes are to promote worker identification and commitment to the organization. The reduction of traditional 'them and us' feelings is cited as one of the major expected benefits of wider share ownership, and similarly Bratton (1992) cited 'greater cooperation' and positive shopfloor 'attitudinal changes' stemming from the creation of self-managed manufacturing teams.

Research on employee participation in local government in the north of England, by one of the authors, attempted to assess the value management placed on employee involvement. The question was posed: to what extent can employee participation/consultation 'improve the quality of service(s) and performance' and 'good industrial relations' within the authority along a simple four-point qualitative scale: 'large extent', 'limited extent', 'not at all', and 'don't know'. The large majority of local authorities responding to our questionnaire acknowledged that employee participation and consultation had an important contribution to make in improving the quality of the service(s) and performance and industrial relations. The strongest endorsement from management for employee consultation was in the area of industrial relations. Almost all the respondents (95 per cent) agreed that employee consultation can make a positive contribution to good industrial relations both for manual and non-manual employees.

Although there is strong empirical evidence that shows employee participation techniques lead to positive attitudes towards the organization and work, some writers remain sceptical. Kelly and Kelly (1989), for example, question whether the techniques associated with the 'new industrial relation' have made much impact on 'them and us' attitudes in industry, and call for further research. We believe that there is sufficient evidence that shows employee participation techniques can result in positive attitudes towards organizational goals and job satisfaction, and that without employee participation an organization cannot maximize the potential of its human resources. The remainder of this chapter deals in some detail with the different forms of participation most closely identified with HRM: communication and consultation.

■ Employee communication

The exchange of information and the transmission of meaning is the very essence of an organization.[6] Information about the organization – its production, its products and services, its external environment and its people – is essential to management and employees. Communication is the process by which information is exchanged between a sender and a receiver.[7] The communications process in organizations is a complicated one: complicated by organizational characteristics such as hierarchy, and complicated by the fact that individual employees have idiosyncrasies, abilities and biases. Nevertheless, communications within organizations are central for the other processes of power, leadership, and decision-making.

The role of communications for the organizational centre of control can be seen in studies of managers and their work. American writers have found that managers spend an overwhelming amount of their time in communications. Some writers estimate that 80 per cent of the time of managers is spent on interpersonal communications. In other words, the business of managers is communications. The internal characteristics of an organisation affect the centrality of communications. For example, the more the company's manufacturing and human resource management strategies empower people and are idea-orientated, the more important communications become. Information is transmitted through an organization so that appropriate decisions can be made by the communications system. This section discusses the human resource department's role in managing the communication system. Generally, the size of the organization will affect how sophisticated the communication system is. In small organizations, the system might be informal and subject to frequent management intervention; in large organizations, on the other hand, specialists may serve as employee communications managers. Most organizations use a mixture of formal and informal ad hoc arrangements to communicate to their employees.

Organizational communication has been defined by ACAS (1987, p. 3) as:

The systematic provision of information to employees concerning all aspects of their employment and the wider issues relating to the organization in which they work.

To be effective, communication must take place regularly, it must be a two-way process to give employees the opportunity to participate, and it should involve all members of the management team including first-line supervisers. Writers on communication have also stressed that:

- there should be commitment from senior management to communication;
- management should take the initiative in devising and maintaining the communication system;
- a combination of written and face-to-face channels of communication is best;
- messages should be in a form which can be readily understood;
- information should be perceived to be relevant to employees;
- messages should be consistent with actions;
- training in basic oral and written communication skills increases the effectiveness of the system;
- the communication system should be monitored and evaluated.

■ Problems that organizations face

There are challenges which must be taken into account when HR managers try to devise a communication system that will work to the benefit of everyone concerned.

□ DISPARATE GEOGRAPHICAL LOCATIONS

In large organizations, for example a hospital or a local authority, there might be multi-sites or plants that create a problem of contact and consistency in the communication system.

□ LARGE VARIETY OF SKILL GROUPS

A large public organization such as a local authority is responsible for different types of employees: refuse collectors, social workers, environmental officers. This might mean that there is no community of interest and no common corporative objective which normally binds employees together. Considerable time and effort may have to be spent on identifying relevant information for each of the skill groups and in disseminating it to them. It also indicates that there are challenges in centralizing and coordinating the communication system in such organizations.

☐ **EMPLOYMENT ARRANGEMENTS**

The growing tendency to employ part-time workers creates challenges in ensuring that face-to-face communication takes place with all employees. Added to this is the fact that certain groups of employees, for example sales representatives, might spend a large proportion of their time away from their office.

☐ **FINANCIAL CONSTRAINTS**

In a highly cost conscious business environment, HR managers may face a challenge justifying the cost of practising effective communication, for example an employee news bulletin. In a study conducted by one of the authors, a respondent said that: 'communications is unfunded and undervalued'.[8]

■ The extent of organizational communication

As previously mentioned, the evidence from UK national survey investigations suggests an increase in the extent of organizational or workplace communication during the 1980s (Daniel and Millward, 1983; Batstone, 1984; Millward and Stevens, 1986; Millward *et al.*, 1992). In 1980, Daniel and Millward asked both management and union representatives to assess the amount of information given on three broad areas: pay and conditions of service; human resource requirements; and the financial position of the organization. Trade union representatives were also asked how useful they found the information received from management in negotiations. Managers assessed rather differently the amount of information they gave on the three broad areas. Pay and conditions of employment were the subject of more communication, while the financial position of the company was the subject of least communication. Managers tended to assess the information they gave more highly than the union representatives assessed the information they received (Daniel and Millward, 1983, p. 148). However, for both managers and union representatives there was a general tendency for the information given to be assessed more highly in larger establishments.

Since the early eighties, one writer argues that as part of a 'logical development' many companies facing intense competitive pressures not only have attempted to draw upon their employees' skills and knowledge more fully, but also have disclosed more information to employees to highlight the organization's problems and to enlist their co-operation in overcoming them (Batstone, 1984, p. 261). In a study of communication in local authorities in the North of England, it was reported that communication tended to be 'good' in the smaller Authorities, employing fewer than 2000 employees. 29 per cent of the local authorities falling in the 'below 500' category reported communication was 'good'. In contrast, only one Authority with over 20000 employees reported communication was 'good'.[9] The implication is that size is a factor affecting the success of communication between management and their subordinates. The 1982 Employment Act which required certain companies to include a statement in the annual report describing the action taken during the year to introduce, maintain or develop employee involvement has had no impact on communication in the local authorities surveyed.

In 1990, Millward and his research team probed for evidence of mechanisms managers had introduced for involving employees or their representatives in the activities of their workplaces.

Overall, the findings show that more methods of communication were being used simultaneously in 1990 than in 1984: over the period 1984 to 1990, the average number of methods used by management to communicate with or consult employees was up from 2.0 to 2.4 (1992, p. 168). In the case of employee involvement, the findings show a substantial increase in initiatives to raise employee involvement, up from 35 per cent to 45 per cent (1992, p. 176). A more detailed examination of the 1990 survey is to be found in the following sections.

■ Information disclosed by management

The two issues that are the subject of most communication are terms and conditions of employment and major changes in working methods or work organization, whilst investment plans were the least commonly reported as the subject of a lot of communication. In 1984, managers in organizations with recognized unions reported giving more information on all topics than the managers in organizations without recognized trade unions (Millward and Stevens, 1986, p. 155). In this author's survey of local authorities, respondents reported that information disclosed to the workforce is largely limited to health and safety and internal vacancies. With the exception of internal vacancies and promotions, manual employees tended to receive more information than their colleagues in the non-manual areas (Bratton and Sinclair, 1987).

The sort of information disseminated by management is shown in Table 10.1. Overall, the findings reveal that information relating to wage costs and human resource development (training) received are most frequently disclosed by management. Another interesting finding is that UK-owned establishments are less likely than their foreign-owned counterparts to disclose information to their employees: around 50 per cent of UK-owned establishments gave their workforce information on at least one of the items listed in Table 10.1, compared with 60 per cent of foreign-owned establishments.

■ Methods of communication

Communication is the process by which information is transmitted between a sender and receiver. The organization has three basic methods of transmitting information, as depicted in Figure 10.3. Verbal communication ranges from a casual conversation between two employees to a formal speech by the managing

TABLE 10.1   Information given to employees or their representatives, by ownership in the private sector, 1990 (percentages)

	All establishments	UK-owned establishments	Foreign-owned establishments
Wage costs	25	27	36
Training received	25	23	28
Accidents	25	21	31
Employee sickness/absenteeism	24	23	29
Labour productivity	20	21	32
Occupational health	18	17	21
Skills/qualifications	15	15	8
Number of resignations	14	11	7
Gender mix	11	7	2
Ethnic mix	10	5	2
None of the above	44	48	36

Source: Adapted from Millward *et al.*, 1992, p. 174. Used with permission.

director. In face-to-face meetings the meaning of the information being conveyed by the sender can be expressed through gesture or facial expressions, what is referred to as non-verbal communication. Written communication ranges from a casual note to a co-worker to an annual report. Electronic mail systems and video machines have revolutionized written and verbal communication in organizations.

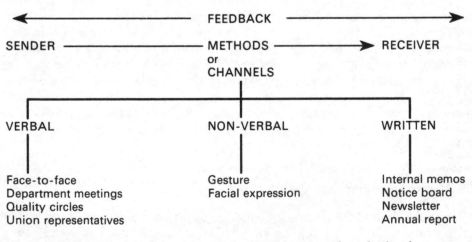

Figure 10.3   A model of the communication process and methods of communication

■ Two-way communication

Much of the literature on organizational communication is prescriptive, providing an analysis of what constitutes good practice. Communication can flow in three directions: downward, upward, or horizontally, as depicted in Figure 10.4. Communication that flows from one level of the organization to a lower level is a downward communication. When we think of managers communicating with subordinates, the downward pattern is the one we usually think of. Upward communication flows to a higher level in the organization. Upward communication keeps managers aware of how employees feel about their jobs and the organization in general. Communication that flows between employees at the same level in the organization is a horizontal communication. This type of communication includes communication between co-workers in different departments or divisions of the organization, or between co-workers in the same team. Formal communication follows the organization's chain of command or hierarchy. The organization's informal communication network, the grapevine, is not based on hierarchy but on social relationships. The grapevine is an important means through which employees fulfil their need to know about the organization. For example, new employees generally digest more information about the company informally from their co-workers than from formal orientation programmes (McShane, 1992).

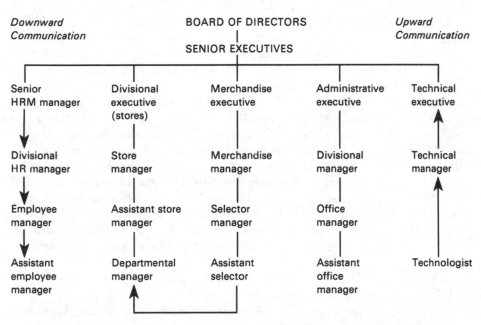

Figure 10.4 **Downward, upward, and horizontal organizational communication in a retail store**

The literature tends to emphasize the importance of communication being a two-way process: upward and downward communication flows. The most common forms of two-way communication are 'suggestion schemes', attitude surveys, and employee appraisals. However, the popularity of the 'two-way' concept should not blind us to the fact that the dominant orientation is still downward communication. In addition, two-way communication should not be confused with consultation. The aim of the two-way process is often only to ensure that employees have understood the message and does not necessarily imply that employees' reactions, feelings, and criticisms will have any effect upon the decision making process. This might be true even where briefing groups, which we discuss below, have been installed. In organizations where there is a commitment to participation there will be other structures and processes whereby employees are involved more directly in decision making. Thus, in reality, communication systems are an essential prerequisite to genuine employee participation, but often fall short of being a form of it.

The systematic use of the management chain, regular meetings between junior managers and their subordinates, suggestion schemes, newsletters, and opinion surveys were all cited as the channels managers use to communicate with their subordinates (Millward *et al.*, 1992). The most observable change between the 1984 and 1990 large-scale surveys was regular meetings between junior managers and their immediate subordinates, a rough substitute for team briefings, up from 36 per cent to 48 per cent. Other changes included regular newsletters, up from 34 per cent to 41 per cent; surveys or ballots, up from 12 per cent to 17 per cent; and suggestion schemes, up from 25 per cent to 28 per cent. The findings also show great variation in the use of these methods between sectors of the British economy, see Table 10.2. Overall in 1990, 90 per cent of workplaces surveyed used one or more of these methods (Millward *et al.*, 1992, p. 166). There was also variation with size of the organization, small organizations being least likely to use any of the specified methods. The CBI's 1986 review of fifteen audits they had conducted shows that 65 per cent of employees responded that they did *not* agree that 'There is a good two-way communication here and that management talks and *listens*'. The CBI also reports that 'often excessive reliance is placed on the written word. If this is not reinforced by face-to-face briefing it can be ineffective' (CBI, 1986, p. 425). However, it could be argued that the CBI's report presents a more despondent picture than that prevailing in a majority of organizations, because the organizations on whom they are reporting have probably called in the CBI because a communication problem exists. The lessons to be learnt are clear. There should be a combination of written and face-to-face methods of communication used in an organization and a genuine effort on the part of managers to make the communication two-way.

In our 1987 survey of local authorities we asked about the methods they employed to communicate to their workforce. The majority completing the questionnaire used a combination of departmental meetings (86 per cent); union representatives (86 per cent), and written methods (internal memos/circulars [100 per cent], and notice board [95 per cent]). Two authorities reported that they had

Voice of the people

Last month Lloyds Bank made its 40,000 employees a promise – it will be open and honest with them whether the news is good or bad. Underpinning its pledge are 15 standards for internal communication based on employees' opinions about how the bank has acted in the past.

Some, like the first, are not radical. "Top management will undertake to explain the rationale, the facts and the pros and cons of the decisions they take which affect us and the way we work together," it says.

The second sounds like good management sense. "We shall all be candid and open with each other. Admitting our mistakes and learning from them is a key part of this."

But in a company where lifetime employment is becoming a thing of the past and staff are frightened to speak out, these pledges represent a huge cultural leap.

In place of a paternalistic banking culture, Lloyds is spelling out employees' right to give constructive feedback to their bosses and top management without fear of reprisal.

"We've tried to get across the point that each of us has a responsibility in creating an open environment," says communications and quality manager Paul Rudd.

It seems, for all the talk about empowerment and involvement, most British companies have yet to move beyond simply informing employees as and when they choose.

A study, by internal communication consultancy Smythe Dorward Lambert, looks at what has happened to communication during the last two turbulent years. Its conclusions will make sobering reading for personnel managers who thought the age of empowerment had come.

It finds little evidence for the E-word being anything more than a 1990s buzz-word. Most companies still put out information which reinforces the company line. Responding to issues raised by staff is not a priority.

"The common theme seems to be that feedback and empowerment should take place on a need-to-happen basis as designated by senior management and in a form with which they, and not necessarily their employees, are happy," the report's author Nick Andrews concludes.

It reveals widespread frustration among communication professionals with top management teams who pay lip-service to communication and then fail to deliver. Of those surveyed, nearly 40 per cent say they lack proper support.

"Commitment and backing is given only when it is convenient," says one respondent, a manager in a public utility.

Written communication policies are more common than they were two years ago – just over four in 10 companies have them. But the report says most communication still adds up to a series of ad hoc firefighting measures rather than something built into mainstream decision-making.

Smythe Dorward Lambert thought the radical changes in most businesses in the last two years might have prompted companies to formalise their communication with employees. But it concludes this has not happened.

Less than 40 per cent of those surveyed say communication was carefully planned to help them through changes while 43 per cent confirm it took place in a piecemeal way. Nearly 10 per cent admit it was planned as an afterthought.

A mere 5 per cent say internal communication allowed employees to contribute to the changes going on around them.

"This implies change within organisations is still seen as being imposed on employees rather than a process in which all employees participate," says Andrews.

Despite the dismal findings, Andrews holds out hope for the future. He believes a growing number of employers realise internal communication means more than just informing employees, and involvement and eventually empowerment must come into the equation.

He points to organisations, like Lloyds Bank and Texaco, which have moved away from mission statements handled down from on high. He believes the future lies in the sorts of charters they have drawn up, which grant employees rights and set new expectations.

Source: Personnel Today, February 1993. Used with permission.

'no regular planned method' of communication. Again, the channels by which information was communicated to employees tended to vary according to the size of the authority. The use of departmental meetings and briefing groups tended to be more prevalent in authorities employing fewer than 2000 employees. Authorities with 30 000 plus employees tended to use trade union representatives, internal memos and notice boards.

■ Briefing groups

Briefing groups are considered an effective way of passing information downward and upward through the hierarchy – that is, of increasing the two-way communication flow. A briefing group is a group of employees which are called together regularly and consistently in order that decisions and policies, and the reasons for them, may be explained to other employees. Those briefed communicate in turn to their own briefing group so that information is systematically passed down the management line. Briefing groups are designed to convey understanding of the information to organizational members through face-to-face communication.

Another important aspect of briefing groups is that the system supports and develops the leadership role of management. As Perkins states, 'Briefing groups reduce the oft-stated problem of union representatives becoming the source of information because the system relies on regular briefing of supervisory staff and them taking on the role of work-group communicators' (1986, p. 32). Opposition from trade unions to team briefing stems from the perceived threat to the shop stewards' traditional leadership role within the organization. A team briefing is seen by the unions as an attempt to by-pass established consultative and negotiating procedures. In North America team briefing has been used as part of a union-avoidance strategy (see Chapter 11). If an organization does decide to adopt team briefing, support from top management is essential. Further, to be effective team leaders need to be trained; they need to be aware of the objectives of the system and learn how to run briefing sessions.

■ Monitoring the communication system

Monitoring is essential for maintaining and improving the effectiveness of the communication system. However, the monitoring of communication effective-

TABLE 10.2 Some methods used by management to communicate with their employees, 1984–1990 (percentages)

	All establishments		Private manufacturing		Private services		Public sector	
	1984	1990	1984	1990	1984	1990	1984	1990
1 Regular meetings of workgroups	–	35	–	23	–	33	–	45
2 Regular meetings of junior management	36	48	24	31	34	47	46	62
3 Regular meetings of senior management	34	41	37	38	33	40	33	46
4 Management chain	62	60	58	57	58	58	69	65
5 Suggestion scheme	25	28	15	14	25	31	31	31
6 Regular newsletters	34	41	24	22	33	44	41	52
7 Surveys or ballots	12	17	10	7	11	17	14	24
Other methods	8	13	8	11	8	13	8	16
None of these	12	9	17	14	15	11	7	4

Source: Adapted from Millward *et al.*, 1992, p. 167. Used with permission.

ness is not well developed in most organizations. The 1987 survey of local authorities found that the overwhelming majority, 95 per cent, of the respondents did not monitor. And, the one authority that did employ monitoring methods employed fewer than 400 people.[10] The joint ACAS, CBI and TUC survey of communication also found that 50 per cent of their respondents did not monitor the effectiveness of their communication system. They further added that 'the availability of management resources and associated costs appeared to be the critical factor in determining whether or not any evaluation of the communication process between management and the workforce was carried out'.[11]

Clear objectives must be established and reasonable measures of them developed. Measures of communication effectiveness might include:

- the extent of employee co-operation;
- information on employee perceptions of the employee–management climate, collected by an organizational survey;
- absence and labour-turnover levels.

This information is valuable only if there is some basis of comparison. Therefore, the data must be broken down by employee constituency, by factory or site, or by a time period. Comparing information enables the HR manager to identify where objectives have been achieved and where they have not. It also indicates where to look for the causes of problems in the achievement of communication objectives.

■ Joint consultation

In its simplest form consultation may take the form of an informal exchange of views between a group of employees and their manager on an incoming piece of machinery or a reorganization of the office. However, where the size of the organisation makes access for employees to management problematic, then more formal structures need to be created. Joint consultation has been defined as:

> Involving employees through their representatives in discussion and consideration of relevant matters which affect or concern those they represent, thereby allowing employees to influence the proposals *before* [our emphasis] the final management decision is made (IPM, 1981).

Joint consultation, on the other hand, differs from collective bargaining or joint regulation because the latter utilizes the processes of negotiation and agreement between representatives of management and employees. We can develop the difference between joint consultation and joint regulation further. The difference between joint consultation and collective bargaining appears to rest on the notion that both conflict and a common interest are inherent elements of the employment relationship which need to be handled in different ways. Consultation may be viewed as a means of promoting action when there are no

HRM IN PRACTICE 10.2

Communications network support

Within an hour of computer company ICL announcing a pay freeze for workers in the UK late last year its line managers were organising team briefing of nearly all 14,000 staff.

This might have been an easy achievement for an organisation with all its staff in one company, but ICL has numerous subsidiaries, joint ventures and a large number of staff based in the field.

Like many large businesses, ICL has devolved many of its activities, and with them personnel management, to a growing number of subsidiaries. But it is working hard to maintain standards and a common approach across all divisions.

Personnel director of ICL UK David Wimpress is clear about lines of communication and authority in the company. He believes when instruction from the top is unavoidable, as in the pay freeze and a decision to reduce staff numbers by 4 per cent this year, communications should be as rapid, and thorough, as possible.

Outside these occasions, and providing a few key rules are not broken, ICL's subsidiaries are given as much freedom as possible to implement their own personnel policies.

"The way forward is to run your businesses mainly on trust, not to police them," says Wimpress.

It would not be easy to police ICL.

Half of ICL's UK staff work in subsidiary companies. These go under separate names and operate at arm's length.

"The old ICL was very much a large company with the paraphernalia of large-scale bureaucracy. Now our divisions embrace core values but have a degree of freedom," says Wimpress.

One way ICL UK has devolved power to its new subsidiaries is by slashing staff numbers at head office. Staff levels at head office have plummeted from 750 to just 50.

But communication between the company's head office and its subsidiaries remain regular.

The firm also reinforces the links between its separate companies and the main business by appointing its directors to the boards of subsidiaries.

Alongside team briefings, ICL uses a cascading system of internal computer mail. Important memos can be cascaded quickly through the terminals of management to staff. Nearly all staff have access to a terminal.

For the past year office-based staff have recieved audio cassettes every four months and field staff every two months.

There is also an annual employee opinion survey across the whole company. Subsidiaries are able to tailor it to include questions specific to their business, but there are a few key questions which all employees are asked.

These focus on the effectiveness of managers, the frequency of team briefings and whether staff feel they have a clear set of objectives.

Other characteristics of working at ICL are universal. There is a handbook of company policies, including equal opportunies, and a slim volume called *The Management Framework* which outlines the company's commitment to customer care.

Another initiative found across the company is its Investing in People scheme, launched five years ago, which offers performance pay, regular staff appraisal, objective setting and career planning.

Source: Personnel Today, March 1993. Used with permission.

obvious conflicts of interest, whereas joint regulation or collective bargaining is a means of reconciling divergent interests. However, Salamon believes that every aspect of the employment relationship has the potential for conflict. The distinction between the two approaches to participation is concerned with the 'formal identification of those aspects of the employment relationship in which this conflict should be legitimised and subject to joint agreement by inclusion within the process of collective bargaining' (Salamon, 1987, p. 259). The balance between joint consultation and joint regulation will depend upon the extent and power of workplace trade organisation. Daniel and Millward (1983) found that the existence of Joint Consultative Committees (JCCs) is closely allied to workplace trade unionism: 'consultative committees may tend to become an adjunct to the institutes of collective bargaining where workplace trade union organisation is well established, but provide an alternative channel of representation where it is weak' (Daniel and Millward, 1983, p. 135). In 1990, management appeared to be less enthusiastic about joint consultation (Millward *et al.*, 1992).

■ Model of consultation

Researchers have put forward two different models of consultation. A 'revitalization' model suggests that recent support for consultation has coincided with the increased use of direct employee involvement approaches by employers. This, a number of writers have argued, has the effect, whether planned or not, of undermining collective bargaining and consequently weakening workplace trade unionism (Batstone, 1984; Edwards, 1985). In contrast, the 'marginality' model put forward by some authors suggests that the early eighties witnessed an increased trivialization and marginalization of joint consultation, particularly in organizations confronted by deteriorating economic conditions (MacInnes, 1985; Cressey *et al.*, 1985).

These two models, revitalization and marginality, have been critically evaluated by Marchington (1987). The models of consultation, argues Marchington, do not describe the full range of processes which may take place in the consultative arena. A third model, the 'complementary' model, is proposed, in which joint consultation complements rather than competes with joint regulation or collective bargaining. According to Marchington: 'consultation acts as an adjunct to the bargaining machinery' (1987, p. 340). With this model, collective bargaining is used to determine pay and conditions of employment, whereas joint consultation focuses on issues of an integrative nature and helps to lubricate employment relationships; both processes can provide benefits for employees and the organization.

Evidence has been collected from a number of surveys about the extent of joint consultation since the early seventies (Brown, 1981; Millward and Stevens, 1986; ACAS, 1987; Millward *et al.*, 1992). The majority of the writers are agreed that there has been an increase in the extent of consultation since the early 1970s. Brown (1981), in a survey of manufacturing industry, found that 25 per cent of managers said that their establishments had taken initiatives, between 1975 and 1978, to increase employee involvement. This trend seems to have continued until the mid-1980s. In 1983, Daniel and Millward reported a substantial growth in consultative committees. Establishment size and ownership appeared to be the main characteristics associated with the presence of consultative committees, suggested the researchers: In establishments employing more than 1000 employees, 71 per cent of the managers reported the existence of a consultative committee. In establishments employing fewer than 100 employees the figure was 25 per cent. Further, committees were more likely to occur in the public sector: almost 46 per cent of public sector establishments had them, compared with 33 per cent of private sector establishments (Daniel and Millward, 1983, pp. 130–1). Batstone's survey found that 47 per cent of manufacturing companies reported a policy of increasing employee involvement (1984, p. 263). More specifically, managers in 45 per cent of the establishments said that the shop stewards had become more involved in consultative committees. There was a marked increase in the number of organisations using 'direct' employee involvement strategies: quality circles, autonomous work groups and briefing groups. Such techniques were used in an attempt to secure co-operation for difficult changes (Batstone, 1984, p. 271).

It was also found that between 1980 and 1984, overall the proportion of workplaces with a joint consultative committee remained constant at 34 per cent (Millward and Stevens, 1986, p. 138). In private manufacturing, the proportion of establishments with a joint consultative committee (JCC) decreased from 36 per cent to 30 per cent. Significantly, there appeared to be a relationship between the existence of JCCs and the financial performance of private sector establishments: 'Establishments that were doing better than their competitors were more likely to have joint consultative committees' (Millward and Stevens, 1986, p. 141). The authorities suggest that such a change could indicate a propensity on the part of management to 'experiment with the appropriate forms of employee involvement for their circumstance' (p. 141). Support for Marchington's complementary model, that is, joint consultation operating alongside collective bargaining machinery, was provided by Daniel and Millward (1983) and Millward and Stevens (1986). The 1984 survey found that 'complex consultative structures co-exist with complex collective bargaining arrangements in the public sector in particular' (Millward and Stevens, 1986, p. 143).

By 1990, the situation had changed. The number of establishments reporting the existence of joint consultative committees was down, from 34 per cent in 1984 to 29 per cent in 1990. The picture across broad sectors of the economy is given in Table 10.3. The reduction in the incidence of joint consultative committees (JCCs) is explained by the changing composition of the establishments, the number of larger, more unionized workplaces, rather than management abandoning the JCC model. The finding is significant, argues Sisson, because, given the antipathy towards trade unions throughout the eighties, British management might have been expected to substitute joint consultation for joint regulation (1993, pp. 203–4).

TABLE 10.3   Extent of JCCs by sector, 1984–1990 (percentages)

	All establishments 1984 1990	Private manufacturing 1984 1990	Private services 1984 1990	Public sector 1984 1990
Consultative committee currently exists	34 29	30 23	24 19	48 49
Workplace consultative committee or higher-level committee with local representatives	41 35	33 25	28 25	62 59

Source: Adapted from Millward *et al.*, 1992, p. 152.

As regards the types of activity and the issues dealt with, all three surveys by the Millward team have highlighted that where consultative machinery and collective bargaining machinery exist together there is overlap between consultation and bargaining or joint regulation arrangements (1992, p. 157). The separation of joint consultation from collective bargaining is often attempted by simply excluding from the letter's agenda any item which normally is the subject of joint regulation. Inevitably this means that if the scope of collective bargaining expands, then the scope of joint consultation will reduce. The result can be the creation of the 'canteen, car park, toilet paper syndrome'. This has prompted some observers to characterise the subject matter of Joint Consultative Committees as a 'diet of anodyne trivia and old hat' (MacInnes, 1985, pp. 103–4). However, Millward *et al.* found that in 1990 in manufacturing, production matters were most frequently mentioned, by 18 per cent of respondents, as the most important item to discuss. This was followed by employment issues (12 per cent) and government legislation or regulations (9 per cent) as the third most important issue (1992, pp. 157–8).

In local government it has been recognised that since the participants involved in the consultative and negotiating machinery can well be the same individuals, JCCs may sometimes discuss substantive issues that would normally be negotiable (Perkins, 1986, p. 41). In the public sector, the presence of JCCs at establishment level has increased from 42 to 48 per cent. In a regional survey of both private and public sector organisations, 76 per cent of the respondents reported having joint consultative committees (ACAS, 1987, p. 11). In the survey conducted by one of the authors, almost all (95 per cent) of the local authorities responding to the questionnaire confirmed that it was their practice to consult with trade union representatives and provide joint consultative committees (JCC). Details of the survey are shown in Table 10.4.

Consultation was not, however, always undertaken in a highly formal arrangement. Over 60 per cent of the local authorities replying said that individual counselling of employees on an informal basis took place. Direct

TABLE 10.4   The form of employee involvement in local authorities, 1987

Form	Local Authority (%)
Consultation via trade union reps	95
Joint consultative committee	95
Individual counselling of employees	62
Joint management/employee working parties	57
Suggestion schemes	33
Problem solving groups	14
Quality circles	5

N = 21
Source: Bratton and Sinclair, 1987.

participation schemes, such as problem-solving groups and quality circles, increasingly popular in the manufacturing sector, have not been introduced to a large extent in local government. For instance, only one small authority reported using quality circles (5 per cent). The 1990 survey shows that the proportion of workplaces in the public sector reporting JCCs increased slightly, up from 48 per cent in 1984 to 49 per cent in 1990 (Millward *et al.*, 1992).

■ The structure and operation of joint consultative committees

When choosing a joint consultative structure, or developing an existing one, it is necessary for an organisation to make a number of decisions guided by its aims, philosophy and strategy. Joint consultation is based on a high trust relationship and requires sound and regular information to be communicated to all participating parties (see above). An organization has to decide how much information will be disclosed, by whom and how. Generally, management's role in a consultative structure is to communicate information and be fully involved in the process; otherwise, decisions may be made or agreed upon without their knowledge or support. However, Perkins points out that managements must also be 'involved in their role as employees in the sense that management employees, if they have a duty to consult, also have a right to be consulted with' (1986, p. 48). Finally, the organization will have to have regard to its size and the nature of collective bargaining. Management may adopt either of two broad approaches. It can combine the two processes of consultation and negotiation within the collective bargaining machinery. Alternatively, it can maintain a separate machinery of joint consultation and regulation and simultaneously expand the scope of employee involvement through the joint consultative machinery, without the need formally to concede that these issues are subject to joint determination (Salamon, 1987).

Three main reasons have been identified for the integration of consultative and negotiating machinery within the organization. First, communicating, consulting and negotiating are integrally linked together in the handling of employee relations. Second, trade union representatives need to be fully involved in the consultative process, if only as a prelude to negotiations. Third, as the scope of collective bargaining expands the issues left are otherwise allocated to what may be viewed as an irrelevant process.

Substantive reasons have also been cited for establishing formal joint consultative machinery alongside established collective bargaining structures. First, it may help to overcome organisational complexity which tends to hinder the operation of informed means of consultation. Second, the concept of collective bargaining as dealing with substantive or procedural matters, while consultation is concerned with joint discussion of matters of common interest, forces the two structures apart. Third, regular JCC meetings and the publication of minutes ensure that joint consultation is accorded a proper place in the organizational system and confirms management's commitment and responsibility to consultation with its employees. When there are two sets of arrangements, the terms of reference of the JCC need to be specified by defining both its subject matter and the nature of its authority. An example of joint consultation and collective bargaining structure in the public sector is shown in Figure 10.5.

The subject matter may be defined either in terms of: (a) excluding from its deliberation anything which is subject to joint regulation, that is, substantive and procedural matters; (b) enumerating the items which are to be regarded as matters for joint consultation (for example, a corporate plan, human resource trends, education and training; (c) an ad hoc basis, whether or not an issue should be dealt with in the joint regulation machinery. This method can be used only when union representatives are formally represented within the JCC and able to ensure that there is no management abuse of this privilege (Salamon, 1987).

In the public sector, whilst usually joint consultation and regulation machinery function separately, it is recognised that at lower levels of the consultative machinery substantive issues may be discussed. The main problem is that unless a consultative procedure allows for an element of negotiation, it may become irrelevant and wither (Perkins, 1986).

To ensure the JCC's relevance and survival, management may need to be flexible when interpreting the terms of reference. Finally, when formulating a consultative structure senior management have to decide the level of authority to be vested in the JCC. In this respect, the JCC may be either purely advisory to managements' decision-making or it may have, in effect, a delegated decision. Evidence reveals that the work of the JCCs is usually conducted on a fairly formal basis, with an elected or rotating chair and published minutes. Generally, employee representation on the JCCs in the public sector is union appointed, but it would appear that 'the closer the procedure is to the grass roots the more realistic is individual (employee) representation' (Perkins, 1986, p. 46).

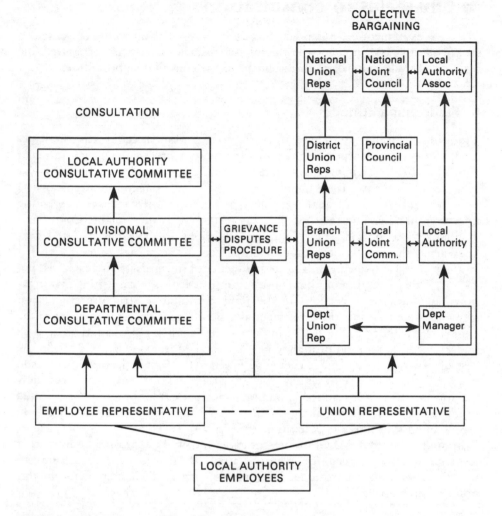

Figure 10.5 **Example of joint consultation and collective bargaining in local government**

On the question of dealing with multi-unionism, the approach varies from one organisation to another. Some organizations aim to bring together all the unions for consultation although they are treated separately for collective bargaining purposes. In local government the division of the consultative machinery for staff, manual, and craft employees is prevalent. This may be appropriate in a highly diffuse organization like local government, where the work of the various departments can be quite distinct, but it does not avoid the possible problems of multi-unionism.

■ Obstacles to consultation

We have examined one potential obstacle in respect of divorcing consultation from collective bargaining; two other major obstacles have been recognised, the attitude of trade unions and management to the consultative procedure.

■ Trade union attitudes

Traditionally, trade unions have distrusted consultation procedures as a management strategy for incorporating union representatives into management forms of control and/or undermining collective bargaining and hence trade union power (Clarke, 1977). As two trade union researchers state: 'Joint consultation came to be seen as at best an inadequate expedient, at worst a positive menace, preventing unions from defending their members as resolutely as they might (Coates and Topham 1980, p. 238). One industrial relations theorist has asserted that 'increasing the involvement only of employees . . . appears to be part of a strategy aimed at reducing the role and influence of stewards' (Batstone, 1984, pp. 264–5). This perception of joint consultation is revealed in case study investigations. In one case, objections to the joint consultative structure from shop stewards were based on the investment and significance that management at the company attributed to the JCC. This support, the union representatives argued, undermined the position of the union' (Bate and Murphy, 1981, p. 395). In the case of a participative management experiment in the DHSS, the principal reason given by the union representing the junior grades for boycotting the new machinery was that it resulted in non-management grades becoming implicated in management decision-making and it 'blurred' the union's traditional role in representing staff interests (Charlton, 1983, p. 74).

In another study, NALGO representatives forcefully expressed concern that joint consultative procedures might be used by management to circumvent traditional collective bargaining machinery. Some of their comments on this point are interesting:

> A system which would undermine trade unions is one where, say, a section of staff actually nominated a member of staff to make comments on their behalf. That would clearly be parallel with the steward's role . . . Some sort of Works Council where a sweetheart system was set up in parallel and which would address people's concerns.[12]

The Nalgo representatives, however, believed that 'participative management is good management' and supported greater workforce involvement, but with the caveat that the traditional role of the steward should not be marginalised. Consultative procedures are more likely to succeed if managers are aware of the fears and potential problems that may confront union representatives sitting on participative bodies. It would be counter-productive for an organization committed to greater employee participation if workplace union representatives

HRM IN PRACTICE 10.3

The key to staff commitment

SWAMPING staff with videos, posters and brochures may seem like an efficient way to get management messages across, but according to new research, it is not slick graphics but a sense of involvement and influence that creates commitment.

The 'Employment in Britain' study, which surveyed 5,000 people last year, points to relatively inexpensive means employers can use to make jobs more attractive and engender greater loyalty without altering pay.

The survey is the most comprehensive national study of employee attitudes undertaken in the last decade.

The study aimed to provide a portrait of workers' priorities, motivations and their attachment to work in general.

The report found that money and job security were important but that real influence over the way work was done and over the organisation as whole was highly valued by employees – and, conversely, was a source of frustration when absent.

IMP director of professional policy John Stevens sees the report as highlighting the importance of participation. "At one time we tended to treat many people in the workforce as semi-detached from the organisation. Competitive pressure, decentralisation and awareness of the need to develop skills, have merged what people want out of work and what employers want out of people. Some industries have been quicker."

The study concludes: "The most powerful influence over a worker's perception of the general quality of management/employee relations was the degree of participation allowed to employees over decisions involving changes in work organisation."

Where people felt their influence was high, 47 per cent said relations with management was very good, but where it was seen to be low only 17 per cent felt that things were going so well.

Very few employers were adopting a participative approach to gaining commitment. Quality circles were shown to have a significant effect. Around 78 per cent of those who took part in such activities thought that these had a great deal or a fair amount of influence on decisions about work practices. "The most striking feature of our data is just how rare it is for employees to be involved in this kind of decision." Only 20 per cent of respondents took part in such initiatives.

The research confirmed the view that pay is not the sole component of motivation and that involvement and a sense of personal development play a vital role.

Good training

Respondents viewed promotion as less important than training: only 11 per cent rated good promotion prospects as 'essential', compared with 27 per cent who felt that good training provision was imperative. The value placed on training was exceeded only by factors such as job security, 'work you like doing' and good relations with a manager.

Meeting aspirations

Examining motivation in its most basic form, the research investigated employees' reasons for working and their commitment to full-time jobs.

Although many claim to cherish a fantasy of winning the pools and giving up work, the study found that most people would work even if there were no financial imperative to do so. Almost 70 per cent said they would prefer to have a job even if there were no financial necessity.

Quality standards

The study examined what influenced their quality standards. Pay incentives were thought to be an important influence on quality standards by fewer than one in 10.

The study says these findings confirm may current personnel practices. "This analysis reinforces the importance . . . of developing 'responsible workers', especially where raising quality standards is a central aim.

Highest-rated jobs

The most satisfying jobs were those involving people, and least satisfying were assembly-line positions. Jobs involving caring for people scored highest. The report says: "The higher the level of social skills required by the job, the greater people's satisfaction with their work."

The other key factor in job satisfaction was age. The least satisfied employees were those between 25 and 34, but after 35 satisfaction was greater with each age group. Women were slightly more satisfied than men at all ages until the 55-plus age group, where women were far more satisfied than their male counterparts.

The workforce of Britain does not want an easy working life, but it does want more control over that life.

Source: Personnel Management Plus, June 1993. Used with permission.

---

were resentful of perceived managerial intention to alienate them (Marchington, 1982).

The potential problems confronting workplace union representatives include: role conflict, loss of contact with membership, and lack of knowledge and expertise, for instance, on interpreting company accounts. When the shop steward is confronted by divergent role expectations, the result is role conflict. It may happen when a steward finds that compliance with one role requirement (for example, representing members at a grievance hearing) may make more difficult the compliance with another (for example, participation in a team examining changes in the organization). Human resource managers can help the union representatives overcome these problems by ensuring that they are given the necessary facilities to keep the channels open between the union and its constituents. For example, in one organization it was found that the stewards were consistently keener on more involvement in the organization of the company than were their constituents and, providing the union representatives did not neglect the 'protective' aspects of their responsibilities, the stewards were free to become more involved in the decision-making process (Marchington, 1980, p. 34).

■ Management attitudes

The other major obstacle to consultation is managerial beliefs and ways of thinking. Managers seek to construct an organizational culture that reflects their ideologies and styles of management and which will reinforce their strategies and control (Gospel and Palmer, 1993). Therefore, it is perhaps not surprising to find evidence that the major obstacle to employee participation is resistance to change by middle and junior management (see, for example, West, 1980; Marchington, 1980). Employee participation, by its very nature, might be expected to pose a threat to the more autocratic manager. It is, argues Rendall, 'the unspoken refusal of a hard core of managers and supervisors to implement change that prevents companies from evolving from authoritarian to participative' (1986, p. 42).

What is clearly apparent in the debate is that participation is a critical component of the human resource management philosophy. Employee participation is characterized by a high trust employment relationship and a more open style of management, one of operating by consent rather than coercion. However, evidence suggests that many managers tend to resist participation because 'it's contrary to their habit-formed ways of thinking and behaving' (Rendall, 1986, p. 42). As is the case with all human resource management policies, the effective implementation of employee participation necessitates management commitment from top to junior level. If key decision-makers in the organization are not fully committed to participation there is a tendency for joint meetings to be 'squeezed out' because of pressure of work. As one industrial relations commentator put it:

> Time is probably a big problem, time and pressure of work . . . making time to do it . . . that's why most things go by the board because everybody is busy . . . Also, it's not just a question of going into meetings . . . need to prepare the brief, think about what you are going to say . . . it's as much time again.[13]

What is apparent from a survey of the empirical evidence is that the attitudinal aspects of employee participation are much more crucial than the 'mechanics' of the various structural configurations of the participatory schemes. Provided organizations are aware of these attitudinal problems amongst managers, they can be ameliorated through training, not just in conventional communication skills, but in the process and dynamics of 'living with employee participation'.

■ Summary

Communication can be thought of as a flow. Communication channels include written, verbal, and nonverbal, each of which has several methods of transmitting information. Communication flows downward, upward, and horizontally in organizations. The role of the human resource management department is to ensure that there are no deviations or blockages in that flow that can cause communication problems. The fewer obstacles that occur in communication, the more that goals, feedback, and other management messages to employees will be received as they were intended.

Employee participation occurs when employees take an active role in the decision-making process in the organization. Employee participation may be formal or informal, direct or indirect, and voluntary or legislated; it may range from a manager exchanging information with an employee or an employee representative on a specific issue, to complete participation in a major investment decision. Greater participation has been identified with HRM philosophy and changes in job design, such as self-managed teams. The terms 'employee participation', 'employee involvement' and 'employee empowerment' have different meanings. Therefore, differing expectations amongst employees and union representatives tend to affect the attitudes of the key players in the industrial relations system, the propensity to participate, and ultimately the success of any experiments in participation. Hence, a vital first step if there is to be any meeting of minds is to create a common language and conceptual framework. Recent studies indicate that British management, to secure employee support and commitment, are adopting HRM-type techniques. Other studies, however, also provide evidence of deep scepticism and concern amongst commentators and practitioners that employee participation and joint consultative procedures might be used by managers to circumvent established collective bargaining machinery, marginalize the role of the workplace union representative and strengthen 'individualism' in the management of the employment relationship. Organizational communication and consultative procedures are more likely to succeed if management is aware of the concerns and potential problems confronting union representatives.

■ Key concepts

- Communication
- Grapevine
- Participation
- Briefing groups

- Non-verbal communication
- Empowerment
- Involvement
- Joint consultation

Discussion questions

1. Describe the communication process, identifying its key components. Give an example of how this process operates with written, verbal and non-verbal messages.
2. Discuss a situation in which you learned some new information from the grapevine and took action on the basis of that information.
3. Identify and discuss different schemes that the HR department manages in order to improve organizational communications.
4. 'Empowerment is a central component of human resource management philosophy.' Do you agree or disagree? Discuss.
5. Explain the difference between joint consultation and collective bargaining.
6. In what ways might employee participation improve decision-making in organizations?
7. 'Joint consultation can be seen as at best an inadequate expedient, at worst a positive menace.' Discuss.

■ Further reading

ACAS (1985), *Workplace Communications*, London: ACAS.

Marchington, M. (1987), 'A Review and Critique of Research on Developments in Joint Consultation', *British Journal of Industrial Relations*, Vol. 25, No. 3, November.

Marchington, M. (1989) 'Joint Consultation in Practice', in Sisson, K. (ed.), *Personnel Management in Britain*, Oxford: Blackwell.

Perkins, G. (1986), *Employee Communications in the Public Sector*, London: IPM.

Townley, B. (1989), 'Employee Communication Programmes' in Sisson, K. (ed.), *Personnel Management in Britain*, Oxford: Blackwell.

▌ Chapter case study   Communications at Forrest Computer Services

In this age of flatter management structures, Forrest Computer Services (FCS) must have one of the flattest. Last year it reduced its management hierarchy almost to pancake proportions when it introduced self-managed teams and abolished all but the most senior management jobs.

Forrest Computer Services has a business team of fourteen senior managers reporting to the three people who make up the board. And below that are a host of manage-less client teams with about fifteen members each and operating as separate commercial units. Teams have to be able to provide a full client support service and draw on all the technical, financial and administrative skills which that requires. Within this framework employees can decide who they want to team up with and teams can elect whether or not they want a leader. Those that have opted for a team leader have not necessarily chosen the person most senior under the older organization. It was a radical reorganization brought about by necessity. The decision followed a massive deficit of £2 million on a turnover of £26.5 million in 1989. It shocked the company which had been growing steadily. Initially it meant slashing costs and therefore staff, so the workforce shrank from 750 to fewer than 500 employees.

But FCS senior management knew they had to do more than cut costs: they had to improve productivity and competitiveness if the company was to stay in an ever tightening market. 'We introduced self-managed teams to build up our client service because that is where we must have the edge', said Forrest's human resource director Carolyn Oliver. 'Every software house can provide the software and systems the clients want: it is the efficiency with which the client is handled that makes the difference and that comes down to the way we are organized,' she said.

Reorganization put a tremendous burden on the human resource department, the way it had to work and the communication system. On top of the reorganization, working practices were completed reassessed – recruitment processes, reward strategies, training and development, and employee participation. On the one hand, it created a free-flowing organization with the flexibility and motivation to react to changes in the market. On the other hand, it bolstered the need for watertight human resource systems to keep this motivated mass from running out of control. Oliver said that the implementation of the plan proved a massive employee participation exercise. In the early weeks there was much misleading and irrelevant information being communicated through the grapevine.

'Top management wanted the ideas to come from the shopfloor. So we brought together twenty people from all levels of the organization bar the most senior, put them into two teams and sent them away for the weekend to thrash out their own ideas of how the company should be organized,' explained Carolyn Oliver. However, this was only the beginning of the consultation process. The next step involved the setting up of employee taskforces to look at the different issues which a reorganization implied. FCS's senior managers disseminated information from the two working parties around the company and asked people to apply for one of the seventy places available on the ten taskforces. About two hundred people applied from the spectrum of jobs and locations in the company.

Six weeks later the taskforces presented their findings to the board. 'They ranged from one extremity to the other. Some liked the way things were and simply wanted to stay put. Others wanted to do away with all senior managers right to the top,' remarked Oliver. Forrest opted for something in the middle – a senior business team with many client teams reporting in. The human resource department had to make the system work. Carolyn Oliver admits frankly that she underestimated the reaction of managers to their sudden loss of power. 'They felt threatened and that their services would no longer be required by the company,' she said. It was a 'hard slog' convincing them that the new-style FCS was for them too, Oliver said. 'You cannot reassure managers by writing to them or making promises in a company newsletter,' she went on to explain.

As all the teams are essentially operating in the same computer services market there was a danger that they would all end up competing against each other, instead of against company competitors. Oliver admitted there has to be a tight coordination of client service teams, close control of the standards they work to, and effective organizational communication. Introducing multi-skilled, self-managed teams also threw up demands from employees for a more permanent system of employee participation in the company.

(*Source:* Adapted from an article, 'Working as a team member', in *Personnel Today*, January 1991.)

Discussion questions

1. What methods could the company have adopted to convince the managers that they had a future at Forrest Computer Services?
2. Should managers try to eliminate the organizational grapevine?
3. Discuss the alternative channels of communication that FCS could have used to disseminate information from the first two working parties to employees.
4. What recommendations would you make for establishing a permanent system of employee participation at FCS? Justify your case.

■ References

1. David Wimpress, Personnel Director of ICL UK, and quoted in Williams, M. (1993), 'Network Support', *Personnel Today*, March.
2. Cell leader, Flowpak Engineering, and quoted by Bratton, J. (1992) *Japanization at Work*, London: Macmillan, p. 188.
3. Richard Johnston, personnel manager of Flowpak Engineering, and quoted in Bratton (1992), *Japanization at Work*, p. 188.
4. Quoted in ACAS (1987), *Working Together: The Way Forward*, Leeds: ACAS.
5. Interview with ACAS spokesperson, October 1987. See Bratton, J. and Sinclair, L. (1987), *New Patterns of Management*, Leeds: ACAS.
6. Katz, D. and Kahn, R. (1966), *The Social Psychology of Organizations*, New York: John Wiley & Sons, p. 428.
7. Johns, Gary (1992), *Organizational Behaviour* (3rd ed.), New York: Harper Collins, p. 374.
8. Comment made by a respondent and quoted in Bratton and Sinclair (1987), *New Patterns of Management*, p. 10.
9. Ibid., p. 12.
10. Ibid., p. 24.
11. ACAS, CBI, TUC (1987), *Working Together: The Way Ahead*, Leeds: ACAS, p. 8.
12. Interview with Nalgo representatives.
13. ACAS spokesperson, Leeds, October 1987 and quoted in Bratton and Sinclair (1987) *New Patterns of Management*, op. cit., p. 39.

CHAPTER 11

Industrial Relations

Change has narrowed the scope of collective bargaining, diminished the role of stewards, and brought the prospect of a much more unitarist approach to industrial relations . . . the pluralism at the heart of Donovan philosophy . . . is being discarded[1]

The workforce went down to 250. People began to think; 'I'm on my bike here if I'm not careful.' So the strength of the union went away.[2]

The management is definitely more aggressive . . . Since Christmas of 1986, they got rid of a lot of the older workforce which was the old stalwart union men.[3]

■ Chapter outline

Introduction
Trade unions
Industrial relations
Management and industrial relations
Collective bargaining
Collective agreement
Recent developments in collective bargaining

Chapter objectives

After studying this chapter, you should be able to:

1. Explain contemporary trends in UK industrial relations.
2. Explain the pattern of trade-union membership and union structure.
√3. Describe how trade unions affect the human resource management environment.
4. Explain the nature and importance of collective bargaining.
5. Understand the significance of economic and political changes to the process of collective bargaining.

■ Introduction

Analysis of recent empirical evidence reveals that British industrial relations has been substantially modified by a combination of economic, political and social factors. Indeed, 25 years after the Donovan Report was published, the change might be so substantial that the Donovanist industrial-relations model, and the very label 'industrial relations', is an anachronism in the 1990s (see, for example, Guest, 1991; Millward *et al.*, 1992; Dunn, 1993). In Chapter 1, we provided a glimpse of some of these economic and political developments and discussed the beginning of a process of change and adaptation by management and labour. Since the election of the Conservative government in 1979, many observers consider the 1980s, and in particular the years 1983–7, as a 'watershed' in British industrial relations. And, although the history of British industrial relations can cite a number of watersheds, what is not in doubt is that the 1980s have witnessed major contextual changes in industrial relations, including the rejection by the British Conservative government of compromise, the introduction of trade union legislation to curtail union activities, marking the end of the so-called 'voluntarist' tradition that dates back to 1871; mass unemployment and a diminution of trade-union membership, institutional protection, and bargaining power.

The experience of fundamental changes in the context, institutions and processes in the industrial relations system was not unique to the United Kingdom. In the rest of the European Community in the 1980s, the traditional pattern of industrial relations underwent profound modifications. In some respects, the pattern of European industrial-relations systems remains sharply diversified, as it was in the 1970s. But in other respects, comparative analysis identifies similarities between European member states, pointing to what writers refer to as a 'transnational convergence' (Baglioni and Crouch, 1991). Through-out Europe the drive for competitive advantage has been pursued consistently and universally, and employers and managers have demonstrated initiative and determination in remodelling their national industrial-relations system. For example, European employers have increasingly exercised their prerogative over key business decisions and enhanced management legitimacy, with government help, by popularizing the ideological argument for the veneration of the 'marketplace'. European trade unions have been weakened numerically and politically and have been forced, in general, to retreat. The trade unions' participation in the collective bargaining process has similarly been marked by retreat and action to defend living standards, working conditions and rules governing the use of human resources (Baglioni and Crouch, 1991, pp. 14–19).

In North America the global competition of the 1980s has resulted in changes in the United States that have prompted some writers to describe changes as the 'transformation of American industrial relations' (Kochan *et al.*, 1986). Although the transformation thesis might be an exaggeration of the perceived changes in that country and the thesis is not universally accepted in the United States, US companies have, with the election of President Reagan and government indulgence, persuaded or compelled a weakened trade-union movement to accept significant changes in collective agreements and working practices. Further, US companies have increasingly turned to a union-free environment, what is referred to as a 'union-replacement' strategy. This management response to trade unions includes either relocating the business to a rural region where unionization is less well developed (for example, southern states such as Kentucky), and/or using consultants to run employee programmes to induce the workforce to consider withdrawing from their union. In North America there are however perceptible differences in transnational organizations.

Overall there appears to be evidence that in the United Kingdom and the United States the pressures for change, which have accelerated under the Conservative governments of Margaret Thatcher, John Major and Ronald Reagan, are significantly modifying both the behaviour of the two key 'actors' in the industrial-relations system, management and unions, and that these changes seem more than transitory and will in some degree become the accepted terrain for HR managers to operate in for the foreseeable future.

■ Industrial relations

Industrial relations is frequently an emotionally charged subject: media coverage of the subject tends to capture moments of unruly pickets, frustrated commuters unable to travel home, school pupils locked out of school, and in the past industrial relations has been at the centre of general election campaigns. The popular view is that industrial relations is about trade unions and strikes. The dramatic images portrayed by the popular media do not capture the daily reality of industrial relations. At the core of industrial relations is work and the employment relationship. The academic study of industrial relations focuses on the social institutions, legislative controls and social mechanisms which regulate and control the employment relationship. Gospel and Palmer define the subject as concerned with:

> The processes of control over the employment relationship, the organization of work, and relations between employers and their employees. (1993, p. 3)

The employment relationship is a social, economic and political relationship in which an employee provides manual and mental labour in exchange for rewards allocated by the employer (Watson, 1986). In organizations where employees are represented by a trade union, the 'price' of the exchange – the pay level – is determined through the collective bargaining process. Thus, at the core of industrial relations is work, and managing the interactions between the representatives of trade unions and management is the most significant area of HRM.

■ Industrial relations and the HRM cycle

Trade unions organize employees in the organization with a common interest and seek to regulate terms and conditions of employment through negotiation and agreements. Trade unions seek to exert influence on each of the four key constituent elements of the HRM cycle. Traditionally, trade unions influence *rewards*: union representatives attempt to maximize the reward side of the wage-effort contract. In the area of *recruitment and selection*, in some industries, most notably printing and construction, trade unions might maintain considerable control over external recruiting because the company may employ union members only. Trade unions also take an active interest in *human resource development*. They try to ensure that training opportunities are distributed equitably and that the employer adheres to the principle of maintained or improved earnings during training. Perhaps most controversially, the whole area of *appraisal* poses challenges to unions and management alike. The central tenet of traditional trade unionism has been the collectivist culture, namely the insistence on rewards according to the same definite standard and its application in the organization. Such collectivist goals have resulted in many British trade unions strongly resisting all forms of performance appraisal based on individual merit. In a democratic society trade unions pose a considerable challenge for an organization pursuing an HRM strategy.

This chapter focuses on the union–management relationship and how this affects the HRM approach to managing employees. The purpose of this chapter is threefold. First, to provide essential information about British trade unions, including the subjects of union goals and philosophy, union membership and union structure. Second, to explain the role of management and government in the industrial relations system. Third, to describe the nature and purpose of collective bargaining and explain how it affects two important areas of human resource management – the grievance and the disciplinary processes.

■ Trade unions

In the 1970s, British trade unions were considered powerful social institutions which merited close study. One eminent scholar referred to trade unions as 'one of the most powerful forces shaping our society' (Clegg, 1976, p. 1). Between 1968 and 1979 trade union membership increased by 3.2 million to 13.2 million, with union density exceeding 55 per cent. The sheer scale of union increase represented a 'decade of exceptional union growth '(Bain and Price, 1983, p. 6). In contrast, since the election of the Conservative Party to government in 1979, the membership of British trade unions has fallen by over 4 million, standing at 9 million and union density around 38 per cent in 1992. This reduction has prompted commentators to call the 1980s the 'decade of non-unionism (Bassett, 1987). There is a growing belief that British trade unions remain isolated from the centres of company decision-making. This section seeks to explain what has happened to British union membership and why in the 1980s; it considers British union membership and density and goes on to examine trade union structure and workplace trade unionism.

■ Trade union membership

The significant decline in aggregate membership of British trade unions is shown in Table 11.1. In 1979 TUC-affiliated membership reached a peak of 12 175 000. Since then membership has fallen by 4 418 000, or 36 per cent, though this includes the loss of the electricians' union, the EETPU, which was expelled from the TUC in 1988. From the peak year of 1979, union density – that is, actual union membership as a proportion of potential union membership – fell from 54.2 per cent to 37 per cent. The decline in aggregate union membership exceeded the decline in employment largely because of the continuing contraction of the private manufacturing sector which is the unions' traditional area of recruitment. Despite these losses the TUC remains the second largest (after the German GAB) national trade union centre in Western Europe. Surveys of different sectors of the British economy reveal differential density figures.

In the 1980s, the proportion of workplaces with union members was 66 per cent; by 1990 this proportion had fallen to 53 per cent (Millward *et al.*, 1992). The same survey also seems to indicate that union density had fallen substantially, from 58 to 48 per cent, between 1984 and 1990. The decline was more marked for manual employees, down from 66 to 53 per cent. The fall in union density was

TABLE 11.1   **Aggregate union membership and density in the United Kingdom, 1979–91 (thousands and %)**

	TUC unions only	*All unions in UK*	*Density % *
1979	12 175	13 289	54.2
1980	11 601	12 947	52.8
1981	11 006	12 106	49.7
1982	10 510	11 593	47.9
1983	10 082	11 236	46.3
1984	9 855	10 994	44.5
1985	9 586	10 821	43.4
1986	9 243	10 539	42.2
1987	9 126	10 475	42.0
1988	8 652	10 308	41.4
1989	8 404	10 043	40.3
1990	8 193	9 810	39.3
1991	7 757	9 489	38.1
1992	7 301	9 015a	36.1a

* Density figure is calculated on figures for All UK unions and potential union membership (civilian employment plus unemployment).
(a) Author's estimates based on membership decline 1987–92.
Source: TUC figures: *TUC Congress Reports* and *TUC Bulletins*; UK figures from *Department of Employment Gazette*.

also substantial in private manufacturing and the public sector. A survey of 115 high-technology workplaces in south east England also found that 80 per cent of workplaces did not recognize trade unions (McLoughlin and Gourlay, 1992, p. 675). Millward *et al.* concluded that in 1990 the public sector still had the highest union density at almost 75 per cent, private manufacturing was second, below 50 per cent, and private services third with about 25 per cent. Overall, however, the pattern of the distribution of union density altered little over the period (1992, pp. 60–1).

In the European Community and North America trade union density in the 1980s has been highly variable. In three of the EC member states, Belgium, Denmark, and Ireland, trade union membership increased by 7, 12, and 2 per cent respectively, France and West Germany recorded no change, and Italy, the Netherlands and the UK recorded a 6 per cent decline between 1979 and 1985. In North America, trade union density increased by 1 per cent in Canada, but fell by 7 per cent in the United Sates over the same period (Kelly, 1988, p. 269).

■ Interpreting trade union decline

The aggregate membership of TUC affiliates fell by 4.3 million from 1979 to 1991. The two largest unions, the AEU and TGWU, lost members at a rate above the average, reflecting the growth in unemployment in their traditional industrial recruitment areas (see Table 11.2). Although the general pattern clearly indicates that membership and density have declined significantly and continually since 1979, there is debate about the precise scale of the trend, its cause and likely duration. Part of the problem is measurement. Estimates of the decline in union density between 1979 and 1986, for example, range from as little as 8.3 percentage points to as much as 12.1 percentage points. These strikingly different estimates occur because the key statistic of union density can be measured in nine different ways, depending on which of three different data series for potential membership, and trade union membership, are used (see Kelly and Bailey, 1989).

TABLE 11.2 Incidence of union representatives, by sector, 1990 (percentages)

	All establishments	Private manufacturing	Private services	Public sector
Representatives present for:				
Manual workers only	59	88	52	47
Non-manual only	56	72	46	58
Manual & non-manual workers	71	93	64	67

Source: Adapted from Millward *et al.*, 1992. Used with permission.

Union derecognition is spreading

ALMOST one in five companies employing over 1,000 people have partially or wholly withdrawn trade union recognition in the past five years, and a quarter of those did so at most or all their sites.

Moreover, of those companies opening at least one new site during the period, 59 per cent have not granted union recognition to the largest group within their workforce.

However, 24 per cent have granted recognition at all sites opened and, in the case of UK-owned companies, 47 per cent have recognised unions at some or all new sites.

The findings come from the second company-level industrial relations survey which was conducted in mid-1992 among a representative sample of 176 UK and over-seas owned companies.

Discussing them at this month's annual conference of the British Universities Industrial Relations Association (BUIRA), Warwick University's Paul Marginson pointed out that the picture was somewhat different in the case of acquired sites.

Of the 82 per cent of companies which reported taking over one or more operating sites as going concerns in the past five years, over 90 per cent had maintained union recognition.

Only eight companies (5 per cent) had withdrawn recognition, and this tended to be to conform with arrangements elsewhere in the company.

The most commonly cited factors leading to derecognition were falling union membership and privatisation.

The survey, funded by the ESRC and the Employment Department, and carried out by researchers at Warwick Templeton College, Oxford, and Sheffield University, also looked at the changing scope of collective bargaining, changes in pay bargaining and the nature of employer approaches in large firms that are displacing those based on collective recognition.

As far as pay determination is concerned, it found that payroll budget negotiations are dominated by the accounting and finance function (71 per cent); in only 7 per cent of cases were negotiations led by personnel/IR people.

However, when it comes to policing the budgets, the personnel function comes into its own. Only a small proportion of companies allow business unit managers to exceed payroll budgets, and personnel department authority is more than twice as likely to be needed to implement a pay award in excess of budgets than that of the finance function.

Detailed findings will published in September by Warwick University's Industrial Relations Research Unit.

Source: Personnel Management Plus, July 1992. Used with permission.

Kelly (1988), using one estimate of 50 per cent density, argues that British trade unions face 'big problems', but these are not sufficiently serious or novel to talk of a crisis or watershed: 'British trade union membership has held up reasonably well compared with previous recessions' (1988, p. 271). The estimate is calculated by counting only civilian employment as potential union membership. In contrast, an estimate of only 39.3 per cent union density, counting the working population (civilian, plus unemployed) minus the armed forces, leads Bassett (1988) to argue that: 'Non-unionism is now dominant in Britain . . . and the real role-model models for British industrial relations are now no longer the consensual, unionised examples of ICI and Ford, but the dynamic, entrepreneurial and non-union examples of McDonald's and IBM' (1988, p. 45–7). The different measurements of trade union density may be measuring different facets of trade unionism. To assess trade union influence on the government or wider society, for example, a broad measure of union density, including the unemployed as potential union members, is argued to be more appropriate. However, it is also argued that it is not appropriate to include the unemployed in a measure of union density if the object is to estimate bargaining power, because the long-term level of high unemployment has an insignificant impact on the bargaining process (Kelly and Bailey, 1989). Kelly's interpretation has an ideological purpose: refuting that British trade unions have 'lost their way'. Bassett's account is also written with a clear purpose – to demonstrate that the developments during the 1980s created an era of 'new industrial relations'.

One influential explanation of variations in rates of unionization over time, and differences at any one time between industries and occupation groups, categorizes the determinants under six headings: composition of potential union membership, the business cycle, employer policies and government action, personal and job-related characteristic, industrial structure, and union leadership (Bain and Price, 1983). However, although the Bain and Price approach is comprehensive, it is difficult to 'disentangle' the relative importance of each of the six determinants in interpreting aggregate union decline in the UK since 1979. The 1980–1 recession, the 'business cycle' determinant, accounted for much of the decline in union membership, with substantial contraction of employment amongst highly unionized manual workers in large manufacturing organizations. Within the 'business cycle' framework, Disney (1990) suggests the downturn in union density in the 1980s was caused by 'macroeconomic' factors. Trade unions' traditional difficulties in recruiting and gaining recognition in the private services sector, smaller establishments, foreign-owned plants, and newly established 'green-field' sites have intensified. As a recent TUC document acknowledged: 'Unions are finding it generally difficult to recruit and bargain in the fastest growing parts of the economy'.[4]

Following the election of a Conservative government in 1979, public policy towards trade unions shifted away from positive encouragement of trade-union recognition. The suggested determinant, government action, clearly can affect unionization. Public policies that create a favourable environment for union recognition will initiate a virtuous circle of recognition and membership increase. The circle can be put into reverse by adverse policies and government 'example-setting' or role model (Towers, 1989). Freeman and Pelletier (1990), using a quantitative analysis of changes in union density, estimate that the Thatcher government's industrial relations laws reduced British trade union density by 1 to 1.7 percentage points per year from 1980 to 1986. This type of analysis, however, is fraught with problems: it is very difficult to disentangle cause and effect in dealing with trade union law (Disney, 1990).

Views differ on the question of whether employers have in fact used the recession and trade union legislation to change radically the structure of workplace industrial relations. In 1983, one survey of large manufacturing plants compared the changes in British industrial relations since an earlier survey by the Warwick Unit in 1978. It found that there had been little decline in union density: 'the overall picture . . . is one of continuing high levels of membership' (Batstone, 1984, p. 210). There had been no significant change in non-recognition of unions in the establishments. As regards shop steward organization, Batstone writes that there has been 'no significant change' in either shop-steward density, the number of senior shop stewards or full-time convenors (1984, p. 217). The studies by Edwards (1985) and Batstone et al (1986) into workplace trade unionism reached similar conclusions. Batstone and his colleagues pointed out, for instance, that there has been no fall in union density in 50 organized plants covered by their survey. Making 'crude comparisons' with earlier surveys (Brown, 1981), they found that the number of members per steward has not fallen over the six years and may even have 'fractionally increased' (Batstone *et al.*, 1986, p. 77).

Explanations for this decline in union density have been offered by, for example, Beaumont (1987) and more recently Millward *et al.* (1992). Beaumont argues that union organization in the U.K. is being shaped by factors that transcend the current recession. His contention is that the structural changes are no more than particular manifestations of the consequences of capital's changing preferences for non-union labour. The study by Millward *et al.* (1992) comments on the main determinants of union membership changes between 1984 and 1990. The variation in union density was explained by structural characteristics, such as changes in establishment size and the age of the workplace: 'older workplaces have higher densities', argue Millward *et al.* (1992, p. 63). Workforce characteristics such as the proportion of employees on part-time contracts were also important in explaining union membership.

In 1986, Millward and Stevens argued that the basic fabric of workplace trade unionism, measured by the presence of a steward at the workplace, had survived the recession and the legal assault by the Thatcher Government. Despite the substantial decline in the number of manual stewards in private manufacturing between 1980 and 1984, the shop-steward system remains intact. The data seemed to suggest, however, that the majority of stewards in the UK economy were employed in the public sector. Therefore, 'the stereotype of the trade union representative as a manual shop steward in manufacturing industry evidently needs revision' (1986, p. 86). One of the most significant findings in 1990 has been the overall decline in the proportion of workplaces with recognized unions where at least one shop steward was reported. In the period between 1984 and 1990, the number fell from 82 per cent to 71 per cent, and the fall was particularly concentrated in smaller establishments. In the highest density establishments, with 90 per cent or more membership, Millward and his colleagues found 'little or no change' in the incidence of union representatives (1992, pp. 110–12). The pattern of representation across broad sectors is given in Table 11.2.

Trade unions recognized for representing both manual and non-manual employees were much more likely to have shop stewards in the workplace; this is particularly the case in private manufacturing. In the United Kingdom, unlike the United States or Canada, collective bargaining is less formalised and legalistic and employers do not face legal constraints on de-recognition. Bassett (1988) argues that de-recognition of unions is a small but growing trend in Britain. Of 21 known examples of de-recognition, two – the government's intelligence centre (GCHQ) and British Rail's senior managers – were in the public sector; the others ranged from chemicals to book publishing. A survey of British-based companies in the UK found 39 cases of either de-recognition, threat of de-recognition or an attempt to move to a single-union arrangement.[5]

The spate of examples of de-unionization has been associated with the growing adoption of the human resource management approach. Addressing the Institute of Personnel Management Conference in 1987, Mr John Monks, deputy general secretary of the TUC, said that while most companies used to be at least neutral, and often favourable, towards unions, recent labour relations practice and theory, originating from the United States or Japan, in the main attempted to persuade workers that trade unions now no longer served any useful purpose (*Financial Times*, 23 October 1987). The analysis of trade union decline in the 1980s emphasises the 1980–1 recession and the interplay between long-term economic developments, the shift towards the service sector, the increasing numbers of peripheral workers, and the adverse political and legal environments. Evidence that trade unions in the advanced industrialised economies are taking a more pragmatic approach and reorienting their political activities has come from a comparative study of the AFL–CIO in the United States, the TUC in Britain, and the DGB in West Germany. The study concludes that these union confederations in the 1980s have begun to move away from the 'high politics' of influencing government policy, and towards re-establishing their support among their membership (Taylor, 1989).

■ Trade union structure

The word 'structure' in relation to trade unions describes their external structure or job territories; an area of the labour market where the union aims to recruit. A union's internal structure, the relationship between its parts, is referred to as trade union government. The traditional discussion of British trade unions divides them into four types: craft, industrial, general and white-collar unions.

Historically, the craft union came first and typically based itself on the principle of recruiting skilled employees in distinct trades or occupations. A craft union, such as the Amalgamated Society of Engineers (ASE), restricted membership to those workers who had served a recognized apprenticeship. The advantages of this form of unionism were obvious: the union could regulate the

Single union at Nissan UK plant

By John Ardill,
Labour Correspondent

The Amalgamated Union of Engineering Workers has signed a single union agreement with the Japanese car company Nissan for its plants under construction at Washington, Tyne and Wear.

It won the deal in competition with the Transport and General Workers' Union and the General, Municipal and Boilermakers' Union.

Union and company stressed that the deal was not, as similar deals are usually described, a strike-free agreement. It outlaws industrial action while negotiations are taking place internally through a works council or are under conciliation at Acas, the advisory, conciliation and arbitration service.

But the final procedural stage of binding arbitration is not automatically triggered and the union can constitutionally reject arbitration and call a strike.

The first stage of the Washington plant will be completed by August next year. It will initially employ 470 workers to assemble 24,000 Stanza models a year from imported Japanese kits. About 50 staff have already been taken on. Mr Takashi Ishihara, president of Nissan, has said that a second stage is almost certain to go ahead by 1990. It would cost £300 million, employ 2,700, and produce 100,000 cars a year. This project will qualify for special assistance from the Department of Trade and Industry of up to £35 million. In recent advertisements Nissan has claimed that the British content in the Washington cars will eventually be over 70 per cent – higher than in the case of Ford or General Motors.

The plant will have only two grades of manual worker-manufacturing operators, who will be responsible for materials handling, cleaning up and first line maintenance and quality control, as well as assembly work; and technicians, who the company hope will eventually be multi-skilled craftsmen. Supervisors will be aided by team leaders who will be recruited soon.

Working practices will be similar to those in Nissan plants everywhere in the world, where there is little or no union involvement. The supervisor will be the pivotal figure, organising workplace meetings with groups of employees before the start of each shift.

They will discuss a variety of issues, particularly quality control, for several minutes and they may be encouraged to undertake pre-shift exercises alongside the assembly line. But they will be optional – and there will be no company song.

The personnel director, Mr Peter Wickens, told a London press conference yesterday that company and union were agreed "on the need to breakaway from the rigid strait-jacket of specifically defining every little task an employee is allowed to do." All employees will be paid annual salaries with progression through salary ranges dependent on individual performance.

He said the agreement was the same in all essential principles as that the company would have signed with the other unions with which it had discussions. The AUEW was chosen as the one to which workers in the North-east were most likely to want to belong.

The agreement, which covers blue and white collar staff, was denounced last night by the AUEW's white-collar section. TASS because it provides a 39-hour week for all – two hours more than is normally worked by white collar engineering staff.

Mr John Tuchfield, TASS's assistant general secretary, claimed that it was a hypocritical act on the part of a union committed to the shorter working week, undermining current negotiations on working time between the Confederation of Shipbuilding and Engineering Unions and the Engineering Employers' Federation.

Source: Guardian, 23 April 1985. © *The Guardian.* Used with permission.

supply of its type of labour and therefore influence the exchange for the labour. In contrast, industrial unions aimed to recruit all the workers within a given industry regardless of their occupation or level of skill. On this principle, all employees of the steel industry, whatever their actual job, should belong to a single inclusive union for steel workers. This structure has the advantage of eliminating the problem of multi-unionism and demarcation disputes; it also simplifies the collective bargaining between employee groups and management representatives. The general unions date from the 1880s with the growth of 'new unionism'. By definition, they recruit across both occupational and industrial boundaries, and in theory general unions recognize no restrictions on their potential membership. The advantages claimed for this type of union structure are numerous. It can adapt to shifting patterns in the labour market and by virtue of their size, such unions can provide extensive services – for example legal, welfare, research, education – to their membership. The fourth category, the white-collar unions, describes an identifiable and significant sector of the labour market which is organized into unions. An example of such a union would be the National Union of Journalists (NUJ).

Technological change has undermined the feasibility of craft unions as a type of organization. Reductions in public expenditure, privatization, corporate restructuring and falling employment levels have made industrial and general unions more vulnerable than some specialized unions. The membership of the NUR has shrunk from about 202 000 in 1979, to 150 000 in 1987, and the NUM has fallen from 284 000 to 133 000 during the same period (Waddington, 1992). The TGWU's membership has fallen from 2.8 million in 1979 to 1.1 million in 1991, a fall of 60 per cent, compared with the fall of 36 per cent in the TUC's remaining total affiliated membership (see Table 11.3).

The recruitment of non-manual occupations has also changed significantly over the last two decades. Again, technological change has created new occupations in computing and the service sector thus blurring the once clear distinction between manual and non-manual. Thus, the traditional classification of unions into craft, industry, general and white-collar is no longer applicable. In essence, the traditional classification confuses rather than clarifies; one distinguished observer of British industrial relations described the old classification of unions as 'slogans of dead ideological debate'.

In Britain a traditional response of the unions to falling membership and revenue has been mergers and amalgamation. Since 1979 the number of trades unions affiliated to the TUC has fallen from 109 to 52, almost entirely from mergers. A philosophy of 'big is best' seems to be emerging in the trade union movement. The process of merger and absorption is sometimes seen as a prelude to further 'natural growth', to mitigate the effects of membership decline. Mergers allow for extensions of existing recruitment bases as the post-merger union is in practice regarded as organizing from the recruitment bases of the pre-merger unions (Waddington, 1988). For example, following the merger of ASTMS and TASS to form the MSF, the new union now recruits engineers, clerical workers, insurance and banking staff, tobacco workers and sheetmetal

TABLE 11.3 Change in membership of the 10 largest TUC affiliated unions, 1979–1991 (thousands and %)

Union		1979	Affiliated Membership 1991	% Change 1979–91
1.	TGWU	2 862	1 126	−60.6
2.	GMB	967	862	−10.9
3.	NALGO	753	759	+0.8
4.	AEU (Engineering)	1 298	622	−52.0
5.	MSF*	691	604	−12.5
6.	NUPE	691	551	−20.3
7.	USDAW	470	341	−27.4
8.	GPMU	na	270	
9.	UCATT	347	202	−42.0
10.	COHSE	212	201	−5.2
Total TUC Membership		12 175	7 757	−36.3
Number TUC Unions		109	52	−52.2

(*) Formed from a merger with Technical, Administrative & Supervisory Staff (TASS) and Association of Scientific, Technical & Managerial Staff (ASTMS) in 1987.
Source: TUC figures *TUC Congress Reports* and *TUC Bulletins*.

workers. Recent mergers of some public-sector unions has created the 1.4 million UNISON union, representing workers in local government, health, higher education, electricity, gas and water.

The structure of British trade unions is recognized to be complex and diverse. The competitive scramble to seek membership anywhere has created trade-union structures which are even more bewildering and incomprehensible. The major structural characteristic of British trade unions in the 1990s is the predominance of horizontal organizations, that is, large individual unions having members distributed over a wide range of different industries. This contrasts sharply with the vertical organizations of industrial unions which exist in most other European countries. Further, the membership distribution among individual trade unions is skewed. At one extreme there is a relatively small number of trade unions with a disproportionate share of total union membership, whilst at the other extreme there is a large number of unions with very small memberships. As the data in Table 11.3 shows, the ten largest TUC affiliated unions have a total membership of over 5 million, 68 per cent of all TUC membership.

■ Union bargaining power

There has been considerable debate on the effects of the decline in union membership and density on unions' bargaining power. The contraction of employment in the unionized manufacturing sector is widely assumed to undermine union bargaining strength. Various indicators of union bargaining power, strikes and earnings, appear contradictory.

The most noticeable feature of Figure 11.1 is the fall in the number of stoppages during the 1980s. In the 1970s, with both Conservative and Labour governments, the number of stoppages each year never fell below 2000. Throughout the 1980s the figure has never gone *above* 2000. During that time, the figure for 1989 was 701, which compares with 781 in 1988, 1016 in 1987 and an annual average of 1271 over the period 1979–88. The 1989 figure of 701 stoppages was the lowest recorded figure for any year since 1935 (*Employment Gazette*, July 1990). The figures for 1991, supplied by the Central Statistical Office, give the number of working days lost through industrial action to be 800 000, the lowest figure since records began 100 years ago (see Figure 11.1). Although comparisons involving the number of strikes must be made with caution because of the exclusion of some of the smallest stoppages from the statistics, nonetheless the trend is unequivocally downward, and secondary industrial action has virtually disappeared as a union tactic. The number of working days lost through strikes also plummeted in the 1980s; the 1984 figure was a result of the miners' strike. The reasons may be numerous: draconian fines meted out to the print unions (Kelly, 1988), the failure of the miners' strike leading many workers to doubt whether going on strike would be successful, and the pre-strike ballot provisions of the Trade Union Act 1984 (Bassett, 1987). But all earlier evidence suggests that the strike pattern is strongly cyclical: propensity

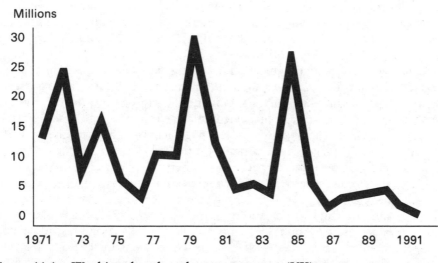

Figure 11.1   Working days lost due to stoppages (UK)

Source: *Personnel Today*, February 1993.

to strike rises during economic booms and falls during a recession. Further, the strike pattern in the 1980s cannot be used as an unambiguous index of trade union power, nor does it mean that strikes are a thing of the past (Kelly, 1988).

However, trade unions through collective bargaining have been able to achieve rises in rates of pay equal to or greater than the rate of inflation. Virtually throughout the 1980s the earnings curve remained above the price curve (Kelly, 1988). Evidence has also been provided on trade union influence in technological change at work which suggests that unions' influence on the process of technological change has been limited (Batstone *et al.*, 1987; Daniel, 1987; Bratton, 1992). Overall it is reasonable to conclude that the 1980–1 recession, high levels of unemployment, a Conservative government which embraced deregulation, the free market, and a government less than sympathetic to trade (British) unions, have all combined to restrict the ability of unions to influence the outcomes of collective bargaining.

■ Management and industrial relations

Management plays a predominant role in shaping industrial relations in the workplace and, usually, employees and their unions react to management initiatives. In the 1980s, British scholars have shown a much greater interest in the study of management. There is a large body of literature which examines the effects of 'Taylorism' (see Chapter 3) and technological change on the organization's control of its employees (see, for example, Knights and Willmott, 1986). There is also a number of studies that has examined how British managers have responded to the challenge of trade unions and how, since the Donovan Report, management has reorganized the conduct of workplace industrial relations (Nichols and Beynon, 1977; Purcell and Sisson, 1983; Millward and Stevens, 1986; Millward *et al.*, 1992).

The management of an organization involves choices and constraints. On the one hand, management may seek to maintain unilateral control of the organization by retaining or extending its managerial prerogative or the right to management. Alternatively, management may accept the legitimacy of trade unions in the decision-making process – management by agreement. In the 1970s, public policy and managers were strongly influenced by the recommendations of the Donovan Commission. In the 1980s, there is evidence to suggest that employers shifted more towards individualistic approaches to managing human resources (see Chapter 2). This trend finds expression in the changing terminology, for example, employee relations, rather than the traditional concept of industrial relations (see Marchington and Parker, 1990). Some researchers see management, in the British context, as the key element in the so-called 'new industrial relations'. In essence, the argument is that management has introduced new initiatives, found new confidence and changed the emphasis in its industrial relations policies. Not surprisingly, the new industrial relations thesis has been contested. To examine management's decisions and actions in industrial relations we need to focus on the concept of strategic choice, managerial styles, and industrial relations strategies.

■ Constraints and choices

The variations in organizational design and relations between managers and employees will be shaped by the strategic choices facing top management. John Child (1972) first used the concept of strategic choice to emphasize the role of managerial choice, rather than technology, in shaping organizations and work. The importance of the concept of strategic choice is that it highlights the question of who makes decisions in business organizations and why they are made. Moreover, the concept draws attention to the fact that decision-making is essentially a 'political process in which constraints and opportunities are functions of power exercised by decision-makers in the light of ideological values' (Child, 1972, p. 16). The constraints which affect organizational decision-makers include the government, technology, culture and domestic and global economic conditions. These environmental constraints affect all organizations eventually and 'tend to direct choices along particular channels while curtailing other modes of initiative' (Poole, 1980, p. 40). However, although strategic choices on such issues as organizational design and the management of human resources are taken by top management, they can be modified by other key players, particularly by trade unions (Child, 1972, pp. 13–14).

■ Managerial styles

Managerial style in industrial relations is related to the managerial variables between managerial prerogative at one end and management by agreement at the other. Fox (1966) first proposed two contrasting styles of management, the pluralist and the unitary, according to the degree of legitimacy afforded by management to the trade unions. In 1974, Fox developed four different styles of industrial-relations management: traditionalist, sophisticated paternalist, 'sophisticated moderns' and 'standard moderns'. The *traditionalist* approach is associated closely with authoritarian management which is hostile and refuses to recognize trade unions. The *sophisticated paternalistic* approach is also associated with a refusal to recognize trade unions, but it differs from the traditionalist style because management develops key elements of the human resource management cycle to ensure that individual employees are committed to organizational goals and their needs are mostly satisfied, and that trade union membership is inappropriate and unnecessary. Among large British businesses, this style might be found in such companies as Marks & Spencer and the American companies such as IBM, Mars and some of the Japanese companies located in Britain. The third type is the *sophisticated moderns*. This style of management accepts the growth of trade union power and the inevitability of collective bargaining as a social mechanism for establishing the terms and conditions of the employment relationship. Purcell and Sisson subdivided this group between constitutionalist and consultor (1983, pp. 115–16). The fourth type, the *standard modern*, is essentially pragmatic, with managers changing their approach to trade unions in response to internal and external changes and pressures.

The typologies of managerial styles were further developed by Purcell (1987), with an elaboration of two dimensions of style: *individualism* and *collectivism*. Individualism referred to 'the extent to which the firm gives credence to the feelings and sentiments of each employee and seeks to develop and encourage each employee's capacity and role at work' (1987, p. 536). Collectivism, on the other hand, referred to 'the extent to which the organization recognizes the right of employees to have a say in those aspects of management decision-making which concern them' (1987, p. 537).

Marchington and Parker (1990) had difficulty applying Purcell's model empirically in their study of employee relations at four organizations. In response to their concerns regarding the concepts of individualism and collectivism and the problem of application, they developed an alternative set of dimensions of managerial style: the *investment–orientation* approach depicts the extent to which managers are concerned with controlling labour costs or developing employees and the *partnership orientation* dimension, is 'management attitudes and behaviour towards the trade unions in the workplace' (1990, pp. 235–7). In a more recent article, McLoughlin and Gourlay (1992) stress the importance of allowing for the coexistence of individual and collective approaches in the management of the employment relationship. McLoughlin and Gourlay identify two dimensions of managerial style. The *individualism/collectivism* dimension refers 'to variations in the 'mix' of individual and collective approaches to regulating different substantive and procedural aspects of the employment relationship' (1992, p. 674). Here there is a spectrum which runs from high individualism to high collectivism: 'High levels of individualism or collectivism do not denote the exclusion of the other approach to job regulation, merely that the one is more predominant in the 'mix' than the other', state the authors. The *strategic integration* dimension represents the extent to which there is 'a tight coupling of strategic intention with workplace practice' (1992, p. 674). Again there is a spectrum from low, little formalization of policies or procedures to high strategic integration, see Figure 11.2.

These different managerial beliefs and styles can provide insight into the nature of management and the diffusion of HRM-type practices. For example, In a subsample of 30 workplaces, both unionized and non-unionized, McLoughlin and Gourlay identified distinctive managerial styles corresponding to their model: ' "Type I" (high strategic integration/high individualism) were found at a third of the workplaces' (1992, p. 678). McLoughlin and Gourlay's findings also provide evidence for 'the existence of HRM type approaches defined in terms of high degrees of strategic integration and a stress on individualized modes of job regulation' (1992, p. 685). It is, however, important to understand that management styles can change depending on the economic and political climate.

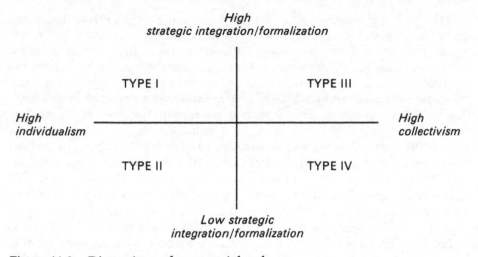

TYPE I   TYPE III

High   *High*
individualism   *collectivism*

TYPE II   TYPE IV

Low strategic
integration/formalization

Figure 11.2   Dimensions of managerial style

Source: McLoughlin and Gourlay, 1992, p. 675.

For instance, Marsh (1982) found that the organizations he surveyed thought they had become 'less autocratic and paternalistic and more participative and consultative . . . more "formal" and more "negotiating" in their approaches to employee relations' during the 1970s. Further, within a group of companies there can be differences of approach between establishments; there can also be differences between various levels in the hierarchy, and differences between divisions within the same organization. The presence of key personalities, the nature of the business, technology, and the uncertainty caused by the intensification of competition are just some of the factors used to explain the variety and the changes over time in the way managers approach the management of industrial relations (Purcell and Sisson, 1983).

■ Management strategies

A modern corporate strategy is a plan for interacting with the competitive environment to achieve organizational goals (Daft, 1992). Organizations also develop functional strategies, which are the plans and procedures developed by the various functional areas within the organization: manufacturing, finance, marketing, industrial relations and human resource management. All these functional strategies are developed to facilitate the implementation of the corporate strategy. It is important to stress that the human resource management and the industrial relations strategies – or to use the more generic term, the employment strategy – are formulated and developed as part of the corporate planning process. According to Gospel and Littler an employment strategy refers to: 'The plans and policies used by management to direct work tasks; to evaluate, discipline, and reward workers; and to deal with their trade unions' (1983, p. 10).

The concept of managerial strategy has given rise to fierce debate amongst academics (see Child, 1985; Hyman, 1987). The assumptions of rationality, the levels of formulation and the relation between strategy and outcomes are some of the questions addressed by scholars.[6] To implement strategy at corporate level, organizations must integrate the various functional strategies, as Figure 11.3 shows.

Since the early 1980s, the volatile economic and political environment, caused by the prospect of economic union in Europe and the free trade agreements in North America, has in turn caused companies to search for alternative industrial relations strategies. Within the context of industrial relations in Europe in the 1990s, the outcomes of the collective bargaining process will have a direct impact on senior management's ability to implement the business strategy. For instance, under the emerging monetary system, British managers will need to ensure that local pay and productivity movements correspond with those of other EC competitors. Therefore, it is much less likely in the 1990s than in the 1970s that the industrial relations manager will enter the negotiations with a 'do your best' mandate from top management. The following quote illustrates the likely pressures in the area of pay negotiations: 'Previously we would have a management meeting. I would then do the negotiating. If at the end of the day I had to go two or three per cent more than we intended, that would be it . . . Now, if I want to go outside the budget I have to get permission from head office.'[7]

In the United States and Britain three broad industrial-relations strategies can be identified: union recognition, union exclusion and union opposition.

The *union recognition* strategy is defined here as a decision by top managers to accept the legitimacy of the union role and, in turn, of collective bargaining as a process for regulating the employment relationship to support their corporate

Figure 11.3   **Functional strategies that support corporate-level strategy**

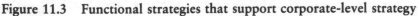

strategy. The reform and restructuring of workplace bargaining arrangements during the 1960s and 1970s, especially in some manufacturing sectors, have been characterized as an industrial-relations strategy designed to engender 'a degree of order, regulation and control' (Nichols and Beynon, 1977, p. 129). The strategy would also, 'strengthen rather than weaken their [management] control' (Purcell, 1979, p. 28) and, in Purcell and Sisson's terms, 'the overriding need was to gain control of industrial relations in the workplace' (Purcell and Sisson, 1983, p. 102). Recent research suggests that even in the inimical environment of the 1980s, a number of important Japanese companies choose a union-recognition strategy to achieve employment objectives. albeit in a modified form (Bassett, 1987, Wickens, 1987). In Britain, between 1984 and 1990, there was apparently a significant decline in the adoption of a union-recognition strategy. The proportion of workplaces adopting a union-recognition strategy was down, from 66 per cent to 53 per cent (Milward *et al.*, 1992, p. 70).

The *union exclusion* strategy means that top management have decided to achieve their strategic goals by curtailing the role of trade unions. The strategy involves business decisions by top management to, for example, introduce new technology, to relocate to another part of the UK or European Community, to sub-contract out work, or to adopt the more aggressive tactic of de-recognition of a union (Anderson, 1989). De-recognition refers to a decision by top management to withdraw from collective bargaining in favour of unilateral arrangements for the governance of employment relations. Douglas Smith, chair of ACAS, said in October 1987 in his address to the IPM Conference that 'across the spectrum there were now managements whose intention was increasingly to marginalise trade unions'. One study identified 50 cases of de-recognition and four unsuccessful attempts at derecognition in Britain (Claydon, 1989) and, in the provincial newspaper sector, Smith and Morton (1993) provide evidence of employers eliminating unions from the decision-making process. According to one observer of employers' strategies, however, the propensity of management to de-recognize a trade union and withdraw from collective bargaining 'remains small and heavily concentrated in newspaper publishing and coastal shipping' (Kelly, 1990, p. 51). In the USA there is evidence that a relatively large percentage of companies have adopted a union exclusion strategy and an increasing number of top management have decided to decertify (de-recognize) the existing union (Cappelli and Chalykoff, 1985). The employment relationship is dynamic and therefore, when management create a non-union environment, it is not necessarily permanent. Moreover, the successful implementation of a union exclusion strategy must always be followed by a union opposition strategy (Anderson, et al. 1989).

The *union opposition* strategy is defined here as a decision to maintain the status of a non-union company by pursuing a number of tactics such as employee participation, job redesign and paternalistic human-resource-management policies. Given that the majority of business organizations are not unionized, we can assume that union opposition is the most prevalent industrial relations strategy in the UK. Researchers argue that employee participation schemes increase employees' motivation and commitment to organizational goals and, therefore, reduce the need for a trade union (see Chapter 10). Innovative work structures, such as self-managed teams (see Chapter 3) generate a 'customer-driven' ethos within the organization, enable management to communicate directly with its subordinates, and encourage employees to identify with the co-workers in the team rather than with the craft or occupation; these job-design techniques are associated with the adoption of a union opposition strategy (Kochan *et al.*, 1986). Management have also used key elements of the HRM cycle and paternalistic HRM policies to avoid trade unions. The selection process can be used to screen out applicants likely to be prone to joining a union, and training can be used to build commitment to the organization. Further, an effective internal communication system is central to human resource programmes to avoid unionization, writes Anderson (1989). The retail giant Marks and Spencer exemplifies the union opposition strategy: the company's chairman and chief executive put it like this: 'Human relations in industry should cover the problems of the individual at work, his or her health, well-being and progress, the working environment and profit-sharing. Full and frank two-way communication and respect for the contribution people can make, given encouragement – these are the foundations of an effective policy and a major contribution to a successful operation . . .'[8]

The choice of an appropriate industrial relations strategy for a particular organization will depend upon the interrelationship between constraints and strategic choices and between managerial objectives – as delineated by the corporate strategy and alternative management styles. Whatever industrial relations strategy is selected, it must also be evaluated in order to identify where objectives have been achieved and where they have not. For example, comparative measures of industrial conflict, cooperation and grievance rates can be used evaluate an industrial relations strategy. Finally, it is also important to recognise that there is no single strategy adopted by employers and managers. Management can choose from a variety of strategies. As Gospel and Littler state: 'The combination of strategies has been highly complex, and employers have searched in a zig-zag backwards and forwards movement between them (1983, p. 12). The implications of the European Single Market and the growing globalization of corporate structures will further compel top management to make strategic choices about their manufacturing process, marketing and finance, and how they will arrange related aspects of human resource and industrial relations management (Gospel, 1992).

■ Collective bargaining

We have mentioned the term 'collective bargaining' on numerous occasions in this chapter. In this section we describe the purpose and importance of collective bargaining. We explain the structure of collective bargaining in Britain and outline the provisions found in most collective agreements. Finally, we discuss some recent developments in collective bargaining and, looking forward, the way in which collective bargaining is undergoing transition. Collective bargaining is a process of determining some of the rules affecting the employment relationship, rather than management acting unilaterally. Collective bargaining is:

> An institutional system of negotiation in which the making, interpretation and administration of rules, and the application of statutory controls affecting the employment relationship, are decided within union–management negotiating committees.

Several important points arise from this definition. First, collective bargaining is a process through which representatives of the union and management jointly determine some of the employment rules. Secondly, there are two types of rules: substantive and procedural. Substantive rules establish terms and conditions of employment: pay, hours and holidays. Procedural rules regulate the way in which substantive rules are made and interpreted, and indicate how conflicts are to be resolved. Thirdly, the parties which negotiate the collective agreement also enforce agreement. The British system of collective bargaining is perhaps most noted for its lack of legal regulation. Collective agreements, with a few exceptions, are not regarded as contracts of legal enforcement between the parties.[9]

Numerous writers have commented upon the importance of collective bargaining in British industrial relations. For instance: 'the joint regulation of employment . . . is central to British industrial relations . . . the process of industrial relations is essentially a process of collective bargaining' (Clegg, 1979, p. 5). In the early 1990s, we have seen significant changes in the pattern of bargaining, both in the public and private sectors. However, collective bargaining is still a major source of employment rules and the main method used to handle industrial conflict. Further, substantial elements of pay and benefits are determined directly or indirectly through collective bargaining for over two-thirds of all employees in Britain.

■ Collective bargaining structure

The structure of collective bargaining is viewed by the parties as a crucial factor shaping the process and outcomes of collective bargaining. Clegg (1979) believes that an understanding of the structure and working of collective bargaining is the key to understanding British industrial relations. The structure of collective bargaining is the framework within which negotiations take place and defines the scope of employers and employees covered by the collective agreement. In Britain, there is no single uniform structure of collective bargaining, and the major structural characteristic of the system is wide variety. This variety arises from differences in respect of three interrelated features of the collective bargaining structure: bargaining levels, bargaining units, and bargaining scope.

Collective bargaining is conducted at several levels. Collective bargaining may be multi-employer bargaining. This arrangement involves a number of employers reaching a central collective agreement on pay and conditions with recognised trade union(s); the collective agreement covers all those companies that are signatories to it. Collective bargaining can also be single-employer bargaining. This form of collective bargaining, particularly in large multi-plant organisations, can either be centralised or decentralised. Where a holding company covers a group of companies, one single collective agreement for the whole group may be negotiated between the parent company and the recognised unions. However, the level of single-employer bargaining can be conducted at the level of the subsidiary companies or below, at the divisional level or at the level of the individual plant. Some multi-plant companies have a single-company agreement applying to all their plants, while other similar companies have separate agreements at each plant.

In practice survey evidence shows that collective bargaining structures are closely linked with business structures. In firms which operate in a single industry, decision-making is more centralised and the pattern of union recognition and collective bargaining is more uniform than is the case in more conglomerate companies, where there is much more diversity. An interesting case which illustrates the complex pattern of collective bargaining is that of *Bond v. CAV Ltd [1983]*, IRLR 360. In this case the judge had to work out the terms of the contract for an employee and therefore had to examine the collective agreement. It was found that the collective agreement existed at three levels: Bond's basic wage was set by a national agreement between a confederation of trade unions and an employers' association. Additional payments to Bond were determined by a collective agreement between union and management representatives of CAV Ltd, at factory level. Finally, an individual bonus scheme was determined at departmental level within the factory, by an agreement between the shop steward and the departmental supervisor. Such complexity is extreme

TABLE 11.4   Basis for most recent pay increase in private manufacturing, 1984–1990 (percentages)

	Manual employees		Non-manual employees	
	1984	1990	1984	1990
Result of collective bargaining	79	70	59	50
Most important level:				
Multi-employer	24	19	8	6
Single-employer, multi-plant	19	15	19	17
Plant/establishment	35	34	31	24
Other answer	2	2	*	3
Not result of collective bargaining	21	30	41	50

Source: Millward *et al.*, 1992, p. 223. Used with permission.

but it is certainly not rare. The level at which pay is determined is given in Table 11.4. Between 1984 and 1990, fewer employees had their basic rates of pay primarily determined by industry or multi-employer agreements with trade unions (Millward *et al.*, 1992, p. 223). According to Millward *et al.*, the shift away from multi-employer negotiations was accompanied by an increase in bargaining structures at enterprise or company level (1992, p. 355). Bargaining units refers to the specific category of employees covered by an agreement or set of agreements. At each level of collective bargaining choices have to be made about which categories of employees should be included or excluded by the collective agreement. Management has to make decisions, for example, on whether to include non-manual employees in the collective agreement.

■ Collective agreement

The outcome of collective bargaining is a collective agreement. The collective agreement has been described as an 'industrial peace treaty' (Wedderburn, 1986, p. 270). The collective agreement is not legally enforceable and therefore there is no legal remedy if either party reneges on the deal, but both sides have an interest in keeping industrial peace. The absence of legal enforceability in the UK is one of the principal divergences in the output of the UK, US and Canadian industrial relations. Bargaining scope refers to the range of issues covered or the subject matter of collective agreements. The content of collective agreements varies widely. Generally, the greater the level of aggregation (national or industry-wide agreements), the fewer the subjects that can be covered in detail.

The following are some of the typical provisions found in collective agreements in Britain:

1. Union recognition clause
2. Wage rates and benefits
3. Hours of work and overtime
4. Working arrangements
5. Technological change
6. Disciplinary procedures
7. Grievance procedures
8. Arbitration clause
9. Status quo clause
10. Redundancy.

Of the ten items listed above, four require closer examination. All collective bargaining is dependent upon trade union recognition and the union recognition clause is one of the most fundamental clauses in the collective agreement. The essence of the employment relationship is the exchange of work effort for remuneration. Wage rates and benefits are, of course, at the heart of the collective agreement. Employers agree to pay wages and benefits, and in return they become entitled to control the work activities of employees during the time for which they are paid. The outcome of collective bargaining – the 'price' of the exchange – is decided by the balance of power between the two parties and the negotiating skill of the participants. The term 'working arrangements' refers to a range of different activities associated with the wage–effort exchange: allocation of work, work-teams, functional flexibility. In the absence of trade unions, management normally controls decisions affecting work organization and job design. For management, the criteria for decisions about the way work is designed and allocated are rooted in its concern to maximize productivity and quality and to minimize labour costs. The concept of functional flexibility, in which employees are moved from job to job, crossing traditional craft or job boundaries depending on their skill match and level, has enjoyed a great vogue in the 1990s. These issues look very different from the employees' standpoint. Employees and, in a unionized workplace, their unions are concerned that too much managerial discretion can result in the deskilling of jobs, lack of autonomy, intensification of work, and job insecurity. Thus, union representatives have sought to influence through the bargaining process arrangements that affect work organization, training, and job security.

In many workplaces in the 1980s, technological change became a central issue in collective bargaining. Differences between employers and employees over the introduction of new technology have been occurring since the Industrial Revolution. In the 1980s, trade unions throughout Western Europe have sought to confront the issue of technological change caused by developments in microelectronics. The British TUC's policy statement of 1979[10] indicated a desire to encourage microtechnology, while controlling any negative effects through collective bargaining. To date, few employers have been prepared to involve employees and their unions in the process of technological change, at least not through the use of new technology agreements. A number of authors have documented the influence of trade unions on the process of technological change. Daniel's (1987) survey showed that the negotiation of technological change was rare and a study by one of the authors also found that the influence of union representatives on technical change had been minimal (Bratton, 1992). A contrasting interpretation, however, based on evidence from twelve case studies, suggests that union workplace representatives may be able to exert more influence on the outcome of technological change than surveys suggest (Price, 1988). Similarly, Batstone *et al.* (1987) argued that in practice stewards' involvement could be subtle and significant. It seems that in the 1980s technological change was generally supported by employees and trade union representatives and, perhaps more significantly, shop stewards and full-time union officials were usually even more supportive (Daniel and Millward, 1993).

■ Strategic choice and collective bargaining

In terms of the structure of collective bargaining management might have to exercise strategic choice in at least two key areas: bargaining levels and bargaining units. In large multi-establishment companies management has to make a choice of level of collective bargaining – whether the bargaining is multi-employer (membership of employers' association), corporate bargaining or single-establishment bargaining. Purcell and Sisson (1983) highlight the fact that managements in similar circumstances, can have different approaches to levels of bargaining. After the 1979 national engineering strike, GEC and Philips withdrew from membership of the EEF. However, in choice of bargaining levels they moved in diametrically opposite directions. GEC decentralised bargaining around constituent profit centres, whereas Philips centralised bargaining at national level. Decentralized single employer bargaining often allows trade-union negotiators to 'leapfrog' over wage settlements reached by other negotiating committees in the industry or geographic region. However, there are several advantages associated with single-establishment collective bargaining. The collective agreement can be tailored to the specific needs of a company or plant rather than to the more general needs of an industry (for example, multi-employer agreements would be inappropriate when pay is largely determined by job evaluation work study). The company or plant collective agreement can also reflect more accurately the product market circumstances and the company's ability to pay. Thus, collective bargaining is at the level of the profit centre and this arrangement can exert more control over union representatives. For example, when BL and Ford shifted from plant- to company-level bargaining in the early 1980s, this undermined union solidarity. The militant plants such as Cowley (BL) and Halewood (Ford) were isolated and neutralised by being outvoted in pay and strike ballots (Purcell and Sisson, 1983). As the authors argue: 'The levels at which collective bargaining takes place both reflect the balance of power between managements and trade unions and are a major influence on it' (1983, p. 109).

■ Recent developments in collective bargaining

Since the early 1980s, British industrial relations has been an area of significant change, including major pieces of legislation and so-called 'new style' collective agreements. In the late 1960s, the Donovan commission preached the value of joint regulation of key elements of the employment relationship, the 'pluralist ethic'. In 1993, 25 years on, the buzzword is the 'de-collectivizing' of industrial relations, and the pace setters are entrepreneurs such as Anita Roddick of Body Shop and Alan Suger of Amstrad, not Lord Donovan.

As mentioned earlier, there has been much debate on whether the 1980s were the start of a new industrial relations era in Britain. In the 1990s, the debate has taken on a European flavour and the concept of convergence in employment systems is also attracting the attention of academics (Cressey and Jones, 1991). Debate on the question of change started in the mid-1980s, prompted by the turbulent economic and political situation in Britain, and generated a number of well-publicised discourses. On the one hand, there are those who argue that the

1980s were a watershed in industrial relations, a period of marked, profound and widespread changes (Bassett, 1986). On the other hand, there are those academic who argue that the most significant feature was the continuity of union–management relations. In 1985 Nissan UK signed a single union agreement and this created a fierce debate on so-called 'new style' collective agreements. In 1986 Lucas Industries discontinued national pay bargaining and two years later the Independent Television Authority announced its intention to discontinue national pay bargaining. Further, in the public sector, school teachers lost their collective bargaining rights in 1987. In this section we focus on some of the significant developments in collective bargaining since the late 1980s.

Survey evidence and cases have identified new initiatives in collective bargaining and collective agreements: decentralised bargaining levels, greater labour flexibility, long-term pay settlements, single-union agreements and no strike provisions in the agreement. Between 1984 and 1990, for instance, the aggregate coverage of collective bargaining fell from 71 per cent to 54 per cent in establishments of 25 or more employees. Drawing data from a variety of sources, Brown (1993) puts the 1990 results in a historical context, see Table 11.5. The data are not precise, but he argues the fall in the percentage of employees covered by collective agreements is incontrovertible. This finding is one of the most dramatic changes in the character of British industrial relations (Millward et al., 1992). The notion of 'new style' collective agreements has received widespread publicity. ACAS has referred to them as 'new style' agreements, the trade unions have referred to them as 'strike-free' agreements. The agreements caused a fierce debate within the trade-union movement – 'realistic' v 'sweet-heart agreement' – which eventually led to splits in the TUC. The electrical union, the EETPU, which was expelled from the TUC, argued that their new style agreements did not prevent employees striking because the collective agreement was not legally enforceable; workers could still withdraw their labour. There are elements in the so-called new style agreements that have been around for a long time and Lord McCarthy, a seasoned industrial-relations academic, sees their roots deep in long-standing practice.

TABLE 11.5   Employees covered by collective bargaining, 1968 and 1990

	1968	1973	1984	1990
Proportion of all employees covered	65	72	64	47

Source: Brown, 1993, p. 191.

The package of provisions contained in the new style agreement underpins Bassett's (1986) thesis of new industrial relations. The new style collective agreements not only had a single-union clause but also encouraged greater flexibility in the deployment of human resources. For example, Sanyo:

All employees are expected to work in any job which they are capable of doing. In-plant training is provided, and job rotation is practised throughout the company. There are no job descriptions, and all production, inspection and most clerical staff are paid the same job salary. (Bassett, 1986, p. 96)

In 1990 the Ford Motor Company's collective agreement required employees to be flexible by creating: 'Integrated manufacturing teams, equally split among skilled and semi-skilled operators, with jobs interchangeable'.[11] Another feature of the new style collective agreement is the inclusion of pendulum arbitration. Bassett (1986) argues that pendulum arbitration is at the heart of the new collective agreements. Its use as a strike substitute by the EETPU is at the centre of the charges of ceding the right to strike. This form of arbitration, also known as final-offer or 'flip-flop' arbitration, is defined in Toshiba's collective agreement as: 'The terms of reference of the arbitrator will be to find in favour of either the company or the trade union. A compromise solution shall not be recommended (Bassett, 1986, p. 109).

The prospect of a dispute going to pendulum arbitration, of one side wholly winning or wholly losing, feeds back into the negotiation process, making the negotiating committee 'more realistic, forcing each side to draw towards the other – so towards a settlement' (Bassett, 1986, p. 113). A substantial fall in the provision of third-party conciliation and arbitration was, however, reported by Millward et al. (1992).

Strike-free deals are far from free of problems, but those advocating such agreements argue that they are a good deal freer of difficulty than the collective-bargaining practices they are replacing. Recent data, however, seem to suggest that so-called new style agreements have not become part of 'mainstream' collective bargaining. Pendulum arbitration and no-stike agreements were an ephemeral fad; they applied to only a minute fraction of workplaces, according to Millward *et al.* (1992). As Kessler (1993) states: 'most employers with the balance of power so strongly in their favour had no need to resort to arbitration: they could adopt a 'take it or leave it' attitude towards the unions' (1993, p. 223). Moreover, new style collective agreements could simply have been a product of unemployment, insecurity and fear.

In the post-Maastricht period, with the development of economic and monetary union there will be pressures on collective bargaining structures and processes in an attempt to maintain national competitiveness. Management has to make strategic choices about degrees of centralized and decentralized configurations of collective bargaining and practices. Whatever collective bargaining arrangement is chosen, the negotiators will need to ensure that the outcomes are consistent with those being negotiated in other comparable companies in the EC. Moreover, the outcome of collective bargaining in the leading EC countries, such as Germany, will in the future have Europe-wide importance (Gospel, 1992). For their part, trade unions have to make decisions related to the development and strengthening of their transnational links and to supporting a more legally enforceable system of collective bargaining.

HRM IN PRACTICE 11.3

NHS trust gets close to 'no strike' deal

By Phil Hilton

A DEAL which makes it "pretty well impossible" for strike action to occur has been reached at a National Health Service Trust for the first time.

The Homewood Trust in Chertsey has signed an agreement which amounts to a virtual no-strike deal through the use of conciliation and binding pendulum attraction.

The trust has established single-table bargaining and a 'partnership' deal which, says director of human resources Chris Wilson, makes it "pretty well impossible for the unions to take industrial action".

Tim Carter, staff side secretary, was adamant the agreement was not a no-strike deal. "If we reach a failure to agree, we retain the right to ballot members if members want a ballot. Hopefully the need for strike action will be minimised."

The arrangement allows one side to opt for conciliation if there is no agreement in the course of conventional negotiations. During conciliation all industrial action is suspended.

If conciliation fails to bring the two sides together, then binding pendulum arbitration is an option. But both sides have to agree before it can be triggered.

The only opportunity for strike action within the agreement is if one side refuses to accept a failure of conciliation in order to move to arbitra-tion. Wilson said that in that case "the deal wouldn't be worth the paper it's written on."

Pendulum arbitration has previously been restricted to the private sector where, according to recent research, it can be established without an explicit no-strike clause.

The aim of the partnership is to reduce the possibility of disrupting service to patients and clients. The trust includes two mental health centres, a substance misuse team and a resource centre for people with learning disabilities.

The agreement was the product of 18 hours of negotiation over a number of weeks and includes single-table bargaining for all groups, including professional organisations such as the British Medical Association and the Royal College of Nursing.

Members of the eight bodies will have four representatives at the single table, elected to represent all staff. Carter said that they would have an equal say in negotiations and that no members-to-seats ratio would operate. "We are not into numbers games. All the staff side members will get equal representation."

Both sides have committed to work towards a single pay spine, to establish a minimum wage and local performance management and pay.

Source: Personnel Management Plus, April 1992. Used with permission.

■ Summary

British trade unions have lost 36 per cent of their membership since 1979. The decline in aggregate union membership has exceeded the decline in employment, largely because of the continuing contraction of the private manufacturing sector, which is the unions' traditional area of recruitment. However, despite the fact that British trade unions face big problems, these are not sufficiently serious or novel to talk of a crisis. A recurring theme in this chapter has been variety. Variety is a characteristic of trade union structure, management strategies and collective bargaining configurations. The process of recent trade union amalgamation and mergers has created an even more complex and diverse union structure. Management industrial-relations strategies are the result of constrained strategic choices, and have the object of maintaining managerial control and achieving corporate objectives. There is no single strategy adopted by management, and employers and managers can choose a variety of human resource and industrial relations strategies. The role of trade unions is being questioned, and management is playing a much more proactive role than ever before in determining the regulation of the employment relationship.

Collective bargaining is the process through which representatives of the union and management meet to negotiate the pay and conditions of work. The structure of collective bargaining is fragmented and diverse and is a key factor shaping both the process and the outcomes of the negotiations. All aspects of collective bargaining are in flux; pressures for change have come and will come from the growing globalization of corporate structures, the expansions of markets and free trade, the convergence of monetary and fiscal policies in Europe, and the shifting balance of power between management and unions.

■ Key concepts

- Industrial relations
- Trade union
- Shop steward
- Management style
- Collective bargaining

- Union density
- Union structure
- Managerial prerogative
- Management strategy
- Collective agreement

Discussion questions

1. What is meant by the term 'industrial relations'?
2. In what ways have economic and political developments over the last decade affected British industrial relations?
3. 'The growth and structure of British trade unions cannot be understood without reference to contextual factors.' Explain this statement.
4. 'Management industrial relations strategies are the result of strategic choices.' Discuss.
5. To what extent, and why, can Japanese management techniques be viewed as a union exclusion strategy?

6. Define collective bargaining structure and assess whether collective bargaining in Britain is too fragmented or too centralized to function effectively in enlarged European product and labour markets.

■ Further reading

Bridgford, J. and Stirling, J. (1991) 'Britain in a social Europe: industrial relations and 1992', *Industrial Relations Journal*, Vol. 22, No. 4, Winter.
Dunn, S. (1993), 'From Donovan to . . . Wherever', *British Journal of Industrial Relations*, Vol. 31, No. 2.
McLoughlin, I. and Gourlay, S. (1992), 'Enterprise without unions: the management of employee relations in non-union firms', *Journal of Management Studies*, Vol. 29, No. 5, September.
Labour Research (1992), 'Where are the super-unions?', *Labour Research*, Vol. 82, No. 9, September.
Towers, B. (ed.) (1989), *A Handbook of Industrial Relations Practice*, London: Kogan Page.

■ Chapter case study   East Yorkshire City Council

Rose Peller, the newly appointed Chief Executive of East Yorkshire City Council, had a mandate to restructure the City's local government. One of her first tasks was to set up a quality committee of senior managers to transform the Council's culture, employee attitudes and performance. Her objective: to introduce total quality management (TQM) throughout the Council's administration. Workshops on TQM started with the senior management team and department managers. Some of the workshops on leadership aimed to turn old-fashioned, local government managers into 'active leaders', trying to enthuse instead of dictate.

The proposed changes are physical and cultural. Part of the restructuring is to introduce open plan throughout the Council's buildings, both in terms of dismantling counters between staff and customers and getting managers out of their offices. It is envisaged that the manager's role will become one of facilitator and employees, after they become organized into quality teams, will have greater autonomy and no longer hand the problem-solving automatically to managers. In addition, Rose Peller, with support from the Conservative controlled council, is planning to introduce performance-related pay (PRP). PRP will be linked to personal goals rather than office targets. Together with TQM it is expected that PRP will contribute to the new culture in local government. At a planning meeting, Rose Peller expressed her views in a forceful manner: 'since the department managers will be working in teams, they should know more about the people they are working with, which should make the appraisal system fairer. The more people work together and get rid of these hierarchical barriers the better,' she said.

East Yorkshire City Council employs 620 manual and non-manual employees: 85 per cent of the Council's workforce are in UNISON, the recently created public sector union.

Source: Devised by J. Bratton.

Assignment

As an assistant HR officer at East Yorkshire City Council, you have been asked to produce a report for the planning committee on the industrial relations and negotiating issues associated with the introduction of TQM and PRP. Your report should include the anticipated reaction of the trade union, UNISON, and the union's objectives in future negotiations between senior management and the union.

■ References

1. Dunn, Stephen, (1993), 'From Donovan to . . . Wherever', *British Journal of Industrial Relations*, Vol. 31, No. 2, p. 182.
2. George Wyke, personnel manager, Servo Engineering, and quoted in Bratton, J. (1992), *Japanization at Work*, London: Macmillan, p. 128.
3. Andrew, machine operator, Servo Engineering, and quoted in Bratton, *Japanization at Work*, p. 109.
4. Trades Union Congress (1988), *Meeting the Challenge: First Report of the Special Review Body*, London: TUC, p. 5.
5. Labour Research Department (1988), 'New wave of union busting', *Labour Research*, Vol. 77, No. 4, London: Labour Resarch Dept.
6. For a review of the literature and the debate, see Littler, Craig, 'The Labour Process Debate: A Theoretical Review 1974–1988', in Knights, David and Willmott, Hugh (eds) (1990) *Labour Process Theory*, London: Macmillan.
7. Richard Johnston, personnel officer, Flowpak Engineering, quoted in Bratton, *Japanization at Work*, p. 162.
8. Lord Sieff (1981), chairman and chief executive of Marks & Spencer, and quoted by Purcell and Sisson (1983) 'Strategies and Practice in the Management of Industrial Relations', in G. Bain (ed.), *Industrial Relations in Britain*, Oxford: Blackwell, p. 114.
9. *Ford Motor Co.* v. *Amalgamated Union of Engineering and Foundry Workers* (1969). For a discussion of this important judgment see Davies, P. and Freedland, M. (1984) *Labour Law: Text and Materials*, London: Weidenfeld & Nicolson, p. 779.
10. Trades Union Congress (1979), *Employment and Technology*, London: TUC.
11. *Guardian*, 16 January 1990.

CHAPTER 12

Back to the Future

There can be very few organizations which would want to argue other than that the people they employ and the way that they are employed and managed is critical to success, yet it appears that many of them are still neglecting this knowledge.[1]

The UK's active deregulation policies in the eighties and the nineties are at odds with those in other EC countries.[2]

The 1992 struggle for survival of even large organizations and the major changes attendant on privatization, while discouraging a return to the past, were not necessarily conducive to the establishment of new institutions . . . The rhetoric of management discourse remains to be translated into the reality of management practice.[3]

■ Chapter outline

Introduction
HRM: continuity or transformation?
Contextual influences on HRM
HRM functions: the future
Summary

Chapter objectives

After studying this chapter, you should be able to:

1. Explain the evolving role of HRM in the 1990s.
2. Discuss the trends influencing business organizations and explain the effect these trends will have on the HRM function.

■ Introduction

This book started by examining the evolution of human resource management and examined some of the theoretical models used to study human resource management. It was acknowledged that all personnel or human resource management activity involves ambiguity. It was also emphasized that there are a range of situational or contextual factors that impact on human resource management activities within an organizational setting. The purpose of this chapter is to examine the future of HRM against the background trends in British and western capitalism. The complexities, interdependencies and particularities of national experiences and organizational needs make the task of predicting the future an heroic, some may say foolhardy, challenge. The evidence gathered in the preceding chapters, however, points to a number of developments during the 1980s and early 1990s that have affected the way managers manage the employment relationship and, in all likelihood, will continue to influence management practice towards the year 2000.

■ HRM: continuity or transformation?

In Chapter 1, we discussed the change from personnel to HRM. To some this change represents the use of a new label and emphasizes the limited and piecemeal diffusion of the HRM style, with only islands of innovation in HRM. The sustainability of the HRM paradigm was also questioned. One set of perspectives, therefore, emphasizes the superficial nature and continuities in managing the employment relationship. For others, the changes represent a transformation of human resource management. This set of perspectives has emphasized the differences between the stereotype personnel and human resources models. Whereas personnel management evokes images of 'welfare' professionals interfering and hindering the line manager, of reactive 'fire-fighting' management, and of submitting to militant shop stewards, HRM emphasized strategic integration and the human resource management profes-sional as a member of the senior corporate team, of proactive management, and activity opposed to trade unions. Some writers have asserted that in the absence of an adequate definition, HRM may be an 'ideological project masquerading for greater individualization and work intensification' (Sisson, 1993, p. 202). There might be some truth in this. We emphasized that defining HRM is problematic but, based on the review of the literature and our own research, we concluded that the changes are not just a change in name only. There are radical changes taking place in UK organizations in the way people work and are managed.

In his assessment of changes in human resource management in Britain, Guest (1991) argues that HRM now represents a new orthodoxy which has partly replaced the pluralist Donovan model. By new orthodoxy, Guest means what constitutes good practice and what the appropriate role model for employee relations should be. Guest has warned of the danger of rhetoric being well ahead of reality, of 'talking up' HRM; the evidence from the USA and UK reveals no general trend, and much of the innovation in HRM is 'piecemeal and lacking in the crucial ingredient of strategic integration' (Guest, 1990, p. 387). The Brewster and Smith (1990) survey that reported only 50 per cent of respondents claimed that the person responsible for human resources was involved in the formulation of corporate strategy. Hendry and Pettigrew (1990) also emphasize that there is no straightforward link from business strategy to HRM. Guest's (1991) conclusion for personnel management, of data presenting 'a depressing picture' of the amount of innovation in human resource policy, may well be valid. He also notes exceptions to this general picture. HRM innovations are to be found in foreign-owned companies and some major UK multinationals.

Rothwell's (1993) review also supports the view that as far as human resource policies are concerned little has changed, or it is 'business as before', as Legge (1988) puts it. Rothwell emphasizes that despite greater senior management recognition of the importance of HRM issues in increasing competitive advantage in the 1990s, 'the rapid pace of change imposed by external even more than internal pressures has not necessarily meant that they [personnel directors] have been more strategic and less reactive than under a previous employee relations tradition' (1993, p. 148).

Thus, we are left with a number of problems that must be addressed before predicting the future of HRM. First, the evidence suggests that perhaps the greatest challenge facing HRM professionals is an internal issue: convincing senior and middle management that human resource activities do contribute significantly to organizational goals. It is likely that the HRM 'thumb-print' will prove to be far less of a euphemism than such a predecessor as 'human relations' (Ulman, 1992). Survey data accords with this thinking that some of the concepts and practices associated with the HRM model appear to be implanted in a growing number of British workplaces (Millward *et al.*, 1992; Storey, 1992). In the mid-1990s the increasing influence of the EC Social Charter is likely to compel UK managers to reappraise their social ideals and focus less on US values and more towards European models. In other words, the gap between the rhetoric and the reality on the HRM paradigm needs to be closed.

Second, capitalist societies are characterized by constant innovation and change and, as noted in the introduction to this chapter, future human resource management activities and their role within the organization will be affected by external pressures. The major external pressures affecting British business include the globalization of markets, international competition, technological progress, national macroeconomic conditions, national public-policy changes such as employment legislation, and cultural changes. Each of these external pressures affect companies differently. As a result, the evolutionary process of change in the management of human resources will be different across sectors, and therefore give rise to different outcomes in the 1990s.

■ Contextual influences on HRM

■ Economic pressures

It has been argued elsewhere (see, for example, Leadbeater, 1991; Marquand, 1991) that the 1980s was indisputably a good decade for advocates of capitalism.

The global economy enjoyed eight years of sustained growth, with buoyant international trade and an investment boom. In 1989, with the collapse of East European communism, capitalism was further 're-energised' (Leadbeater, 1991). The political and economic upheavals have created a world economy which is becoming more homogeneous and more competitive as market capitalism is increasingly accepted as the universal organizing mechanism.

In the early 1990s, however, the euphoria linked to the new world order has been replaced by a mood of uncertainty. Britain endured its second major recession in a decade and the position of the UK economy relative to its main European competitors remained weak. The 1980–1 recession swept through British manufacturing in the Midlands and the north of England, Scotland and Wales. The 1990–2/3 recession, in contrast, cut a swathe across the service sector in the south of England, as well as manufacturing in the north; it also adversely affected people in white-collar jobs as well as manual jobs. Unemployment reached 3 million in early 1993. At the time of writing, the recession was apparently coming to an end and the 'green shoots of recovery' could be seen. While UK output and consumer expenditure is expected to rise, the public-sector borrowing requirement is also increasing as the tax base weakens. Many of Britain's economic problems were attributed to the high interest rates required to maintain sterling's exchange rate within the ERM (exchange rate mechanism). In September 1992 this monetary policy collapsed with Britain's 'temporary' withdrawal from the ERM and an effective devaluation of 14 per cent. The government, having lost one form of simplistic macroeconomic management, now seeks another based on continuous rounds of public spending cuts and implicit tax increases.

There is also uncertainty over developments in Europe: the Single European Market, European Monetary Union, and the rise of nationalism. Cressey and Jones (1991) identify a number of complex processes occurring in the European Community which will, if fully developed, affect HRM. First, an opting for the seemingly more successful institutional arrangements for employment regulation and labour market guidance amongst national EC governments. The British programme of National Vocational Qualifications, for example, can be seen as a partial replication of the German system with hopes of standardization of qualifications across the EC to encourage the free movement of labour. The second process is the political intervention of the EC in employment regulations. The Social Chapter, for example, resisted by the UK government, could have a significant effect in standardising 'social rights' for job security and training across the EC. According to Due et al. (1991) EC cooperation in the future indicates the creation of: 'common European legislation which will establish a framework for 'job regulation' in the individual member states, based on . . . the Roman–Germanic system' (1991, p. 99).

The negotiations at Maastricht produced the Treaty of European Union signed by the member states of the European Community on 7 February 1992. Two important outcomes of the Maastricht Treaty will affect HRM over the next decade. The implementation of EC employment law through collective bargaining is explicitly recognized; secondly, a role for the social stakeholders at EC level in formulating EC labour law is introduced. At the Maastricht Summit Article 118B was approved: 'The Commission shall have the task of promoting the consultation of management and labour at Community level and shall take any relevant measure to facilitate their dialogue by ensuring balanced support for the parties . . . ' (Bercusson, 1992, p. 184).

The third process is the 'internationalisation' of organizational business strategies and practices. For example, a new collective agreement between British unions and Ford of Europe to incorporate flexibility provisions effectively promotes 'intra-corporate convergence' of Ford's European operation. Cressey and Jones (1991), however, emphasize that

> a vulgar convergence thesis is no more applicable in contemporary Europe than it was in the 1960s . . . It would . . . be equally simplistic to assume that the forces for convergence are irrelevant. (1991, p. 494)

The UK government reached new heights in its notoriety as it resisted attacks from all sides in attempting to ratify the Maastricht Treaty. In negotiating an opt-out from the Social Chapter, it was attempting to continue its policy of providing an employment law framework that strengthened the hand of management and kept organized labour in its place. It was also attempting to sell the UK to foreign investors as *the* country in Europe that would not be hampered by cost-increasing provisions required by the Social Chapter. In other words, cheap UK labour could be used as a competitive weapon, thus reinforcing the forces that have maintained the low-skill base of the UK. The cycle of low skills and low quality identified by Finegold and Soskice (1988, p. 22) seems destined to continue.

■ Technological pressures

Technology has acted as a catalyst for change in organizations, and creates pressures on management, unions and employees by changing the quantity and quality of work. In the 1980s, two developments, microprocessor-based technology and Japanese-style manufacturing techniques, attracted considerable interest amongst managers, trade unions and academics. Bratton (1992) reported the increasing use of Japanese-style techniques in 'non-exceptional' establishments. In 1989, Dankbaar found evidence of convergent developments between European countries in terms of functional flexibility and teamwork arrangements because of competitive pressures. In the UK, Mueller (1992) also reported 'a far-reaching degree of convergence between countries. Functional flexibility . . . has become necessary on technical and productivity grounds (1992, p. 202). However, in clear contrast to Mueller's claim, Guest (1991) asserts that on functional flexibility there is 'little evidence that companies have embraced it with an enthusiasm' (1991, p. 156). These contrary interpretations of one form of technological change suggest that the evidence is partial and incomplete and will so remain until there are more detailed organization-level data that critically evaluate changes in the labour process. Looking towards the 'factory 2000', a new generation of integrated technologies will probably involve fundamental shifts in organizational design, and HR issues are likely to assume considerable strategic importance (Bessant, 1993). Moreover, it is argued that the benefits of advanced technology will only be fully realized if a strategic approach is adopted to the management of human resources (Clark, 1993). Certainly, technological change will continue to be another major challenge to the HRM specialist.

■ Political pressures

At a General Election in 1992, the Conservatives were elected for the fourth consecutive time. The Conservative government under the leadership of John Major has pursued two related economic policies in the form of privatization and deregulation. A major focus of its employment policy over the last decade has been the reduction of union power and union exclusion as representatives of labour interest. Smith and Morton argue that

> union exclusion policies constitute an integral, if subordinate, component of the contemporary restructuring of work organization and the employment relationship, the object of which is to consolidate the *de facto* redistribution of power to employers within new institutions for the management of employment relations in order thereby to counter any resurgence in labour's collective power. (1993, p. 108).

To put it another way, union exclusion is designed to keep or enhance managerial control if the labour market or government change.

Perhaps the most far-reaching changes in employment law in the 1990s will be in the area of equal opportunities. A recent study on gender pay equality revealed wide differences in the pay structures between EC member-states, the problem of convergence in labour standards, and the ineffectiveness of equal pay legislation in the absence of a more general regulatory mechanism (Rubery, 1992). She goes on to argue that:

> if the problems of women's pay inequality stem from the failure of the pay system to provide for labour standards, then a more general approach is required, indicating a greater rather than a weaker role for intervention from the Commission. (1992, p. 619).

Towards the year 2000, the countervailing power of the European Community might convince the UK government to revive its interest in and support for orderly collective bargaining.

In 1991, the launching of the 'Opportunity 2000' initiative by Business in the Community, with the endorsement of John Major, represented a breakthrough in attitudes towards the recognition that some form of positive action was needed to change patterns of occupational sex segregation. In 1992, the Department of

Employment took over responsibility for the UK's Equal Opportunities Commission (EOC) and the Women's National Commission (Rothwell, 1993). Also the provision of more after-school and holiday child-care facilities for working women with school-age children was the priority of a Women's Issues Working Group established in 1992. With these initiatives, the Social Chapter and European Directives, the political and legal context seems likely to be of continued importance to HRM departments in the coming years.

■ HRM functions: the future

We have discussed some key economic, technological and political pressures that will affect both work organizations generally, and HRM in particular. There are many possible directions in which organizations will manage their workforce in the next decade. Each of the pressures for change will not be equally strong in organizations. Every work organization faces different external and internal pressures and each HR strategy is likely to be unique to that company. With this in mind, what lies ahead in the years to 2000 for HRM? How are work organizations likely to respond to these pressures in terms of managing HR? Let us examine each of the four key constituent elements of the HRM cycle.

■ Selection

As we have suggested, the increased levels of global competition are creating long-term pressures for corporate restructuring. In much of British industry falls in profitability continued while layoffs accelerated. Major companies – British Airways, British Coal, Ford, Jaguar and Rolls-Royce, for example – announced record redundancies in 1992. The clearing banks also announced layoffs. Another trend expected to continue is the disappearance of many middle management jobs as new work structures offer opportunities to empower employees and flatten organizational hierarchies. A British Institute of Management survey found 80 per cent of managers expecting to make restructuring changes (Wheatley, 1992). The future trend in HRM organizations for selection will be towards screening for people with the ability and willingness to be flexible and display organizational commitment – the 'right' people. Thus, although academics find the flexible firm model wanting and report that flexibility practices in firms is opportunistic and tactical rather than strategic, HRM managers under the influence of cost-cutting pressures will have to develop accurate predictors for criteria such as flexibility, quality, commitment and team-player.

■ Appraisal

Productivity improvements will be of vital importance to HRM in the next five years. It is likely that appraisal systems will be used more frequently, primarily to identify competencies and key skills development. In other words, appraisal systems are likely to become more results-orientated, in that rewards will be closely tied to employee and/or team performance, and more development-focused where reciprocal flows of information are released and development opportunities identified. HRM specialists will have to train more managers to use appraisal and assessment methods as part of the creation of a learning-and-developing culture, but will the dual judgement/development purpose of appraisal be too much for them to accommodate?

■ Human resource development

Human resource development will take on added importance in the late 1990s as organizations respond to competitive and public-policy pressures. Chapter 9 argued that training and development is an investment. It is difficult to predict changing attitudes to HRD as investment. At a time when laying blame for national economic shortcomings has shifted from the traditional scapegoat 'the British strike problem' to 'the training problem', it is difficult to distinguish between good intentions and good practice (Rothwell, 1993). Increasingly, HRM specilaists will be required to implement a growing range of HRD programmes, from basic cross-cultural awareness, language and training to management competencies. Moreover, HRD will probably, at least in those organizations where investment in people is already given a high priority, shift towards a regular pattern of continuous updating of employee skills (Bessant, 1993). Women development training will become important, given that training is the only form of positive action permitted under the sex discrimination legislation. As more organizations implement total-quality-control (TQC) procedures, training in quality is also likely to be important for HRM departments. However, UK organizations remain slow to accept the importance of utilizing and developing the potential of their employees. The barriers are there to be broken down, both within the minds of employees and managers and in the structures, systems and practices of organizations. If HRM is to have any significance at the end of the century it will be in the way that employees uncover the potential that lies within them and the way organizations facilitate this process and reconcile employee needs with the needs of the organization.

■ Rewards management

The reward function will continue to present major challenges to HRM professionals. The Social Chapter is a framework for EC action on issues directly pertinent to the HRM department, including reward management. It is likely that the Community's intervention in the employment laws of member states will affect pay and benefits – for example, equal pay for work of equal value. However, in the area of benefits, there have also been significant European Court decisions allowing women to stay at work after the state retirement age (the Marshall case), and men to benefit earlier from company pension schemes (the Barber case). In the future, HRM departments face the challenge of seeking ways to control benefits costs, and simultaneously comply with the provisions of the Social Chapter (Stirling, 1991).

Changes in collective bargaining are expected to continue. The 1990 Workplace Industrial Relations Survey (WIRS) has shown a trend towards greater polarization of payment systems between the non-unionized private-sector establishments and the public (or recently privatized) and private unionized ones. Although a study by Gregg *et al.* (1993) found no important relationship between directors' pay and the performance of their companies, it is likely, in the non-unionized sector, that there will be continued interest in linking pay to individual performance. In the unionized sector, HRM specialists will continue to be involved in collective bargaining, although it is difficult to envisage a return to the sort of 1970s Donovan-style model. As Brown remarks,

> It is also unlikely that there will be a relaxation in the degree of control of whatever collective agreements continue to be concluded. Unionized employers are likely to cherish the controls they have built up over personnel matters in recent years. (1993, p. 198).

During the 1980s it became fashionable for writers to dismiss trade unions as either an anachronism or irrelevant in an organization following an HRM style (for example, Bramham, 1989). We do not share this view. European unions are likely to orientate towards 'business unionism with a European social conscience' and become possibly more homogeneous (Hyman, 1991), but they will not wither and die. The propensity for HRM specialists to convene informal meetings with union representatives is likely to continue (Poole and Mansfield, 1993). However, as Kelly (1990) insists, most employers will continue to behave pragmatically and opportunistically as far as union organization and collective bargaining are concerned. Chapter 11 discussed the need for companies to ensure that, given the emerging European monetary regime, domestic pay and productivity movements are synchronized with those in other EC states (Gospel, 1992). HR specialists will continue to offer expertise in the negotiating process.

■ Summary

The changing fortunes of management, employees and trade unions were briefly documented in Chapters 1, 2 and 11. In the foreseeable future it is likely that British management will remain in the ascendancy. Yet a look to the 1940s, 1960s and early 1970s should provide a constant reminder that the employment relationship is dynamic and ever-changing. There is a school of thought that sees union membership and collective bargaining changes as representative of a paradigm shift away from the old Donovan-type model. However, despite growing pressures on unions, technological change and the need for employers to acheive sustainable competitive advantage, in our view the 1990s could herald a period of collectivist optimism. There are at least three reasons for this: first, only trade unions provide a countervailing power to management, and as survey evidence seems to demonstrate, workers who do enjoy the protection of collective bargaining are, on average, more favoured than non-unionized workers (Brown, 1993); second, union representatives are committed to technological change (Daniel and Millward, 1993); and third, workplace union organization can provide an important basis for cooperation and help promote greater employee participation and involvement (Kessler, 1993).

Looking forward to 2000, then, it is reasonable to conclude that HRM will play a key role in meeting the challenges posed by external and internal pressures and enhancing organizational effectiveness.

■ Key concepts

- Globalization
- Single European Market
- European Monetary Union
- Convergence

- Social chapter
- External pressures
- Internal pressures
- European model of HRM

Study questions

1. Discuss the major external changes during the 1990s which will have the most impact on HRM practices in the future. Explain the impact.
2. To what extent will there be both convergence and divergence in the way European companies manage their human resources in the 1990s?
3. Would a more homogeneous and business orientated European trade union movement be a positive or negative development for Britain? What role, if any, should governments play in such developments?

■ Further reading

Bercusson, B. (1992), 'Maastricht: a fundamental change in European labour law', *Industrial Relations Journal*, Vol. 23, No. 3.

Due, J. *et al.* (1991) 'The Social Dimension: convergence or diversification of IR in the Single European Market?', *Industrial Relations Journal*, Vol. 22, No. 2.

Hyman, R. (1991), 'European Unions: Towards 2000', *Work, Employment and Society*, Vol. 5, No. 4.

Thurley, K. (1990), 'Towards a European Approach to Personnel Management', *Personnel Management,* September.

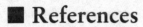 References

1. Brewster, C. and Smith, C. (1990), 'Corporate Strategy: A No-Go Area for Personnel', *Personnel Management*, July.
2. Towers, B. (1992), 'Two speed ahead: Social Europe and the UK after Maastricht', *Industrial Relations Journal*, Vol. 23, No. 2.
3. Rothwell, S. (1993), 'Annual Review Article 1992', *British Journal of Industrial Relations*, Vol. 31, No. 1.

Glossary

Assessment centre The combination of assessment techniques at a single event to make judgements about people for selection/promotion and/or to provide feedback to employees on areas for development.

Attraction Favourable interaction between potential applicants and images, values and information about an organization.

Autonomy The extent to which a job allows employees freedom and discretion to schedule their work and decide the procedures used to complete it.

Bargaining scope The range of issues covered by the subject matter of collective agreements.

Behaviourally Anchored Rating Scale (BARS) A performance appraisal technique with performance levels anchored by job-related behaviours.

Briefing groups Groups called together on a regular and consistent basis so that organization decisions and the reasons for them may be communicated. Group members may in turn meet with another briefing group so that information is systematically communicated down the management line.

Career management Activities and processes to match individual needs and aspirations with organization needs, set within an integrative framework.

'Careless worker' model Assumption that most accidents at work are due to an employee's failure to take safety seriously (or to protect him/herself).

Collective agreement The outcome of collective bargaining, an agreement between employers and trade unions respecting terms and conditions of employment. In the UK the agreement is not legally enforceable.

Collective bargaining An institutional system of negotiation in which the making, interpretation and administration of rules, and the application of the statutory controls affecting the employment relationship, are decided within union–management negotiating committees.

Competencies Underlying characteristics of a person which result in competent or effective performance taking into consideration the nature of the tasks and the organization context.

Communication The process by which information is exchanged between a sender and a receiver.

Competences The outcomes of work performance in an occupational area with specified performance criteria.

Core workforce Workers with organization-specific skills and high discretionary elements in their work.

Developmental approach (to appraisal) An attempt to harness the potential of employees through the discussion of the development needs of employees.

Diagnostic approach (to manpower planning) The use of manpower data to understand manpower problems so that appropriate action can be taken

Emergent learning Learning derived by interaction with evolving situations such as dealing with customers; used in the formation and formulation of strategy.

Employee involvement   Processes providing employees with the opportunity to influence decision-making on matters which affect them.

Face validity   How selection and assessment techniques appear to those subjected to them.

Fordism   The application of Taylorist principles of job design to work performed on specialised machines, usually based on flow-line production assembly work. First applied by Henry Ford.

Group technology   The grouping of machines and workers to form a logical 'whole task' which can be performed with minimum interference.

Human relations movement   A movement which grew out of the Hawthorn experiments conducted by Elton Mayo in the 1920s which emphasizes the psychological and social aspects of job design.

Human Resource Development (HRD)   A term used to indicate training and development as an organization's investment in the learning of its people as part an HRM approach.

Human Resource Management (HRM)   That part of the management process that specializes in the management of people in work organizations.

Human Resource Planning (HRP)   An HRM approach to planning set in the context of organization views of people as the source of competitive advantage.

Image projection   A loose model of the values, personality and attitudes of potential employees directed at appropriate labour markets.

Industrial relations   The processes of regulation and control over the employment relationship.

Japanization   A term used to encapsulate the adoption of Japanese-style management techniques such as team or cellular production, just-in-time and total quality control systems in western organizations.

Job analysis   The systematic process of collecting and evaluating information about the tasks, responsibilities and context of a specific job.

Job Characteristic Model   A job design model developed by Hackman and Oldham (1976) suggesting that five core job characteristics – skill variety, task identity, task significance, autonomy and feedback – result in positive work experience.

Job description   Descriptions of tasks and responsibilities that make up a job, usually derived from job analysis.

Job design   The process of combining task and responsibilities to form complete jobs, and the relationships of jobs in the organization.

Job enlargement   The horizontal expansion of tasks in a job.

Job enrichment   Processes that assign greater responsibility for scheduling, coordinating and planning work to the employees who actually produce the product.

Job evaluation   A systematic process designed to determine the relative worth of jobs within a single work organization.

Job rotation   The periodic shifting of a worker from one task to another to reduce monotony and/or increase skill variety.

Joint consultation   The involvement of employee representatives in discussion and consideration of matters which affect employees.

Labour market segmentation   A method of classifying the ways in which organizations seek to employ different kinds of worker.

Learning climate Physical and psycho-social variables in an organization which affect the efficiency of employees in realising learning potential.

Learning company A concept representing an ideal of whole organization learning by all employees and the use of learning to transform the organization.

Learning cycle A modern view of learning emphasing learning as a continuous process. Usually linked to the work of Kolb (1984).

Learning transfer Learning from HRD acitivities transferred to workplace behaviour and performance.

Line manager responsibility The acceptance by line managers of responsibility for the development of subordinates.

Low quality product-low skill equilibrium Finegold and Soskice's (1988) explanation of the UK's failure to educate and train its workforce to the same levels as its comeptitors.

Managerial prerogative A belief that managmement should have unilateral control within an organization.

Manpower planning Processes, techniques and activities to ensure the necessary supply of people is forthcoming to allow organization targets to be met.

Manpower planning techniques and modelling Application of statisitical techniques to models of manpower stocks and flow, allowing calculation of manpower decisions.

Organizational communication The systematic provision of information to employees concerning all aspects of their employment and the wider issues relating to the organization in which they work.

Organizational politics Those activities that are not required as part of a manager's formal role, but that influence the distribution of resources for the purpose of promoting personal objectives.

Paradigm A framework of thinking based on fundamental assumptions providing explicit and implicit views about the nature of reality.

Pay equity Pay relationships among jobs both within an organization (internal equity) and between comparative or competing organizations (external competitiveness).

Pendulum arbitration Form of arbitration which prohibits the arbitrator from recommending a compromise solution. The arbitrator must find in favour of either the employer or the income.

Performance appraisal Analysis of an employee's capabilities and potential drawn from assessment data of past and current work, behaviour, and performance, allowing decisions to be made in relation to purpose – e.g. HRD needs.

Performance control approach (to appraisal) Means by which employee performance can be measured, monitored and controlled.

Peripheral workforce Workers outside the core workforce (e.g. temporary or casual workers).

Personnel specification Profile of the requirements of a person to fill a job used as a framework to assess applicants. Requirements may be expressed as Essential and Desirable.

Pluralist perspective A view of workplace relations which assumes that management and employees have different goals but seeks a reconciliation of such differences.

Realistic job previews An opportunity for applicants to obtain a realistic picture of a job through job sampling, video, shadowing and case studies.

Recruitment   Processes to attract applicants within appropriate labour markets for vacant positions within an organization.

Reliability   A statistical measure of the extent to which a selection or assessment technique achieves consistency in what it is measuring over repeated use.

Reward   All forms of financial returns and tangible services and benefits employees receive as part of the employment relationship.

Scientific management   A process of determining the division of work into its smallest possible skill elements and how the process of completing each task can be standardized to achieve maximum efficiency. Also referred to as Taylorism.

Selection   Processes to establish the most suitable applicants for vacant positions within an organization from a number of applicants.

Shared responsibility model   A view that the best way to reduce levels of occupational accidents and disease and improve health and safety at work lies with co-operation between employers and employees.

Systematic training model   An approach to training encouraged by Industrial Training Boards in the 1960s, based on a four-stage process of Indentifying Training Needs and Specifying Objectives, Designing a Programme, Implementing Training and Evaluation.

Taylorism   A management control strategy named after F. W. Taylor. A systematic theory of management, its defining characteristic has been the identification and measurement of work tasks so that the completion of tasks can be standardized to achieve maximum efficiency (see also Scientific Management).

Time and motion study   The systematic observation, measurement and timing of movements in the completion of tasks to identify more efficient work behaviour.

Training champions   Senior managers who contribute to an organization's philosphy of support for training and development.

Transformation process   Behaviour by which an employee converts attributes, skills, knowledge and attitudes into work outcomes and results.

Union density   A measurement of current union membership expressed as a percentage of potential union membership.

Union recognition strategy   A management strategy to accept the legitimacy of a trade union role and of collective bargaining as a process for regulating the employment relationship. This contrasts with union exclusion, a strategy to curtail the role of trade unions, and union opposition, a strategy to maintain a non-union company.

Unitarist perspective   A view of workplace relations which assumes that management and employees share common goals.

Validity   A statistical measure of the extent to which a selection or assessment technique actually measures what it sets out to measure. Criterion Validity measures the results of technique against criteria such as present success of existing employees (Concurrent Validity) and future peformance of recruits (Predictive Validity).

Welfare management   The acceptance by employers of responsibility for the general welfare of their employees.

Work   Physical and mental activity that is carried out at a particular place and time, according to instructions, in return for money.

Working arrangements   Activities associated with the work-effort exchange: allocation of work, work-teams, functional flexibility.

Bibliography

Abercrombie, N. and Warde, A. (1988), *Contemporary British Society*, Cambridge: Polity Press.

Abernathy, W., Clark, K. and Kantrow, A. (1983), *Industrial Renaissance: Producing a Comparative Future for America*, New York: Basic Books.

ACAS (1988), *Labour Flexibility in Britain: The 1987 ACAS Survey*, London: ACAS.

Ackroyd, S. *et al.* (1988), 'The Japanisation of British Industry', *Industrial Relations Journal*, Vol. 19, No. 1.

Anderson, J. *et al.* (1989), *Union–Management Relations in Canada*, Ont: Addison-Wesley.

Allen, J. and Massey, D. (eds), (1988) *Restructuring Britain: The Economy in Question*, London/Milton Keyes: Sage/Open University.

Anthony, P. and Norton, L. A. (1991), 'Link HR to Corporate Strategy', *Personnel Journal*, April.

Armstrong, M. (1987), 'Human Resource Management: a case of the emperor's new clothes?' *Personnel Management*, August.

Arvey, R. D. and Campion, J. E. (1982), 'The Employment Interview: A Summary and Review of Recent Research', *Personnel Psychology*, Vol. 35, pp. 281–322.

Ashworth, P. D. and Saxton, J. (1990), 'On "Competence"', *Journal of Further and Higher Education*, Vol. 14, No. 2, pp. 3–25.

Atkinson, J. (1984), 'Manpower Strategies for Flexible Organizations', *Personnel Management*, August.

Atkinson, J, (1985), 'The Changing Corporation', in D. Clutterbuck, *New Patterns of Work*, Aldershot: Gower.

Atkinson, J. S. (1989), 'Four stages of adjustment to the demographic downturn', *Personnel Management*, August pp. 20–4.

Atkinson, J. S. and Meager, N. (1985), 'Introduction and summary of main findings' in *Changing Work Patterns*, Atkinson, J. S. and Meager, N. (eds), London: National Economic Development Office, pp. 2–11.

Baglioni, G. and Crouch, C. (1991), *European Industrial Relations: The Challenge of Flexibility*, London: Sage.

Bain, G. S. (ed.) (1983), *Industrial Relations in Britain*, Oxford: Blackwell.

Bain, G. S. and Price, R. (1983), 'Union Growth: Determinants, and Density, in G. S. Bain (ed.) *Industrial Relations in Britain*, Oxford: Blackwell.

Baldwin, T. T. and Ford, J. K. (1988, p. 65), 'Transfer of Training: A Review and Directions for Future Research', *Personnel Psychology*, Vol. 41, pp. 63–105.

Barlow, G. (1989), 'Deficiencies and the Perpetuation of Power: Latent Functions in Management Appraisal', *Journal of Management Studies*, Vol. 26, No. 5, pp. 499–517.

Bansler, J. (1989), 'Trade unions and alternative technology in Scandinavia', *New Technology, Work and Employment*, Vol. 4, No. 2.

Bassett, P. (1987), *Strike Free: New Industrial Relations in Britain*, London: Papermac.

Bassett, P. (1988), 'Non-unionism's growing ranks,' *Personnel Management*, March.

Bate, S. P. and Murphy, A. J. (1981), 'Can Joint Consultation become Employee Participation', *Journal of Management Studies*, Vol. 18, No. 4.

Batstone, E. (1984), *Working Order*, Oxford: Blackwell.

Batstone, E., Gourlay, S. *et al.* (1986), *Unions, Unemployment and Innovation*, Oxford: Blackwell.

Batstone, E. *et al.* (1987), *New Technology and the Process of Labour Regulation*, Oxford: Oxford University Press.

Beaumont, P. B. (1987), *The Decline of Trade Union Organization*, London: Croom Helm.

Bennision, M. (1980), *The IMS Approach to Manpower Planning*, Brighton: IMS.

Beer, M., Spector, B., Lawrence, P. R., Quin Mills, D. and Walton, R. E. (1984), *Managing Human Assets*, New York: Fress Press.

Bell, D. (1989), 'Why manpower planning is back in vogue', *Personnel Management*, July pp. 40–3.

Bengtsson, L. (1992), 'Work organization and occupational qualification in CIM: the case of Swedish NC machine shops', *New Technology, Work and Employment*, Vol. 7, No. 1.

Bercusson, B. (1992), 'Maastricht: a fundamental change in European labour law', *Industrial Relations Journal*, Vol. 23, No. 3.

Bessant, I. (1993), 'Towards Factory 2000: Designing Organizations for Computer-Integrated Technologies', in J. Clark (ed.).

Bevan, S. (1991), *Staff Retention – a manager's guide*, Report 203, Brighton: IMS.

BIM (1977), *Employee Participation: The Way Ahead*, quoted in M. Salamon (1987).

Blackaby, F. (ed.) (1979), *De-industrialisation*, London: Heinemann.

Bland, M. (1980), *Employee Communications in the 1980s: A Personnel Manager's Guide*, London: Kogan Page.

Bosquet, M. (1980), 'The Meaning of Job Enrichment', in T. Nichols (ed.) *Capital and Labour*, Glasgow: Fontana.

Boxall, P. F. (1992), 'Strategic Human Resource Management: Beginnings of a New Theoretical Sophistication?' *Human Resource Management Journal*, Vol. 2, No. 3.

Boydell, T. H. (1976), *Guide to the Identification of Training Needs* (2nd edn), London: BACIE.

Bramham, J. (1988), *Practical Manpower Planning*, London: IPM.

Bramham, J. (1989), *Human Resource Planning*, London: IPM.

Bramley, P. (1989), 'Effective Training', *Journal of European Industrial Training*, Vol. 13.

Brannen, P. *et al.* (1976) *The Worker Directors*, London: Hutchinson.

Bratton, J. (1991), 'Japanization at work: the case of engineering plants in Leeds', *Work, Employment and Society*, Vol. 5, No. 3.

Bratton, J. (1992), *Japanization at Work: Managerial Studies for the 1990s*, London: Macmillan.

Bratton, J. and Waddington, J. (1981), *New Technology and Employment*, London: WEA.

Bratton, J. and Sinclair, L. (1987), *New Patterns of Management: Communications and Employee Involvement in Local Government in Yorkshire and Humberside.* A report for Leeds City Council.

Braverman, H. (1974), *Labour and Monopoly Capital*, New York: Monthly Review Press.

Brewster, C. and Smith, C. (1990), 'Corporate Strategy: A No-Go Area for Personnel?', *Personnel Management*, July.

Brown, W. (ed.) (1981), *The Changing Contours of British Industrial Relations*, Oxford: Blackwell.

Brown, W. (1986), 'The Changing Role of Trade Unions in the Management of Labour', *British Journal of Industrial Relations*, Vol. XXIV, No. 2.

Brown, W. (1993), 'The Contraction of Collective Bargaining in Britain', *British Journal of Industrial Relations*, Vol. 31, No. 2.

Bullock, Lord (1977), *Report of the Committee of Inquiry on Industrial Democracy* (Cmnd. 6706) London: HMSO.

Burack, E. (1986), 'Corporate business and human resource planning practices: strategic issues and concerns', *Organizational Dynamics*, 15.

Burawoy, M. (1979) *Manufacturing Consent: Changes in the Labour Process under Monopoly Capitalism*, Chicago University Press.

Campbell, D. J. and Lee, C. (1988), 'Self-Appraisal in Performance Evaluation', *Academy of Management Review*, Vol. 13, No. 2, pp. 3–8.

Cappelli, P. and Chalykoff (1985), 'The Effects of Management Industrial Relations Strategy: Results of a Survey', quoted in Anderson *et al*. (1989).

CBI (1986), 'Checking on Employee Involvement: The CBI Communication Audit,' *Employment Gazette*, October.

Chapman, R. (1990), 'Personnel management in the 1990s' *Personnel Management*, January.

Charlton, J. H. (1983), 'Employee Participation in the Public Sector: A Review', *Journal of General Management*, Vol. 8, No. 3.

Child, J. (1985), 'Managerial Strategies, New Technology, and the Labour Process', in D. Knights, H. Willmott and D. Collinson (eds).

Child, J. (1972), 'Organizational structure, environment and performance: the role of strategic choice', *Sociology*, Vol. 6, No. 1.

Clark, J. (ed.) (1993), *Human Resource Management and Technical Change*, London: Sage.

Clarke, T, (1977), 'Industrial Democracy: The Institutional Suppression of Industrial Conflict' in T. Clarke and L. Clements *Trade Unions under Capitalism*, London: Fontana.

Clausen, C. and Lorentzen, B. (1993), 'Workplace Implications of FMS and CIM in Denmark and Sweden', *New Technology, Work and Employment*, Vol. 8, No. 1.

Claydon, T. (1989), 'Union de-recognition in Britain in the 1980s', *British Journal of Industrial Relations*, Vol. XXVII, No. 2.

Clegg, H. (1976), *Trade Unionism under Collective Bargaining*, Oxford: Blackwell.

Clegg, H. (1979), *The Changing System of Industrial Relations in Great Britain*, Oxford: Blackwell.

Clegg, S. and Dunkerley, D. (1980), *Organization, Class and Control*, London: RKP.

Clutterbuck, D. (ed.) (1985), *New Patterns of Work*, Aldershot: Gower.

Coates, D. (1975), *The Labour Party and the Struggle for Socialism*, Cambridge: Polity.

Coates, D. and Hillard, J. (1986), *The Economic Decline of Modern Britain: The Debate Between Left and Right*, Brighton: Wheatsheaf Books.

Coates, K. and Topham, T. (1980), *Trade Unions in Britain*, Nottingham: Spokesman.

Codrington, C. and Henley, J. S. (1981), 'The industrial relations of injury and death: safety representatives in the construction industry', *British Journal of Industrial Relations*, Vol. XIX, No. 3.

Conway, H. E. (1987), *Equal Pay for Work of Equal Value Legislation in Canada: An Analysis*, Ottawa: Studies in Social Policy.

Cooke, R. and Armstrong, M. (1990), 'The Search for Strategic HRM', *Personnel Management*, December.

Coriat, B. (1980), 'The Restructuring of the Assembly Line: A New Economy of Time and Control', *Capital and Class*, No. 11.

Cowling, A. and Walters, M. (1990) 'Manpower Planning – where are we today?', *Personnel Review*, Vol. 19, No. 3, pp. 3–8.

Craig, M. (1981), *Office Workers' Survival Handbook*, London: BSSR.

Cressey, P. and Jones, B. (1991), 'A new convergence? Introduction to Special Issues of Work, Employment and European Society', *Work, Employment and Society*, Vol. 5, No. 4.

Crouch, C. (1982), *The Politics of Industrial Relations* (2nd edn), London: Fontana.

Curnow, B. (1989) 'Recruit, retrain, retain: personnel management and the three Rs', Personnel Management, November pp. 40–7.

Daft, R. (1992), *Organization Theory and Design*, St Paul: West.

Daniel, W. W. (1987), *Workplace Industrial Relations and Technical Change*, London: Frances Pinter.

Daniel, W. W. and Millward, N. (1983), *Workplace Industrial Relations in Britain*, London: Heinemann.

Daniel, W. W. and Millward, N. (1993), 'Findings from the Workplace Industrial Relations Surveys', in J. Clark (ed.).

Dawson, C. (1989), 'The Moving Frontier of Personnel Management: Human Resource Management or Human Resource Accounting?', *Personnel Review*, Vol. 18, No. 3.

Denham, D. (1990) 'Unfair dismissal law and the legitimation of managerial control', *Capital and Class*, No. 41.

Department of Employment (1974) *Company Manpower Planning*, Manpower Papers, No. 1.

Dermer, J. (ed.) (1992), *The New World Economic Order: Opportunities and Threats*, New York, Ont.: Captus Press.

Devanna, M. A., Fombrun, C. J. and Tichy, N. M. (1984), 'A framework for strategic human resource management', in C. J. Fombrun *et al.*, *Strategic Human Resource Management*, Chichester: John Wiley.

Dex, S. (1988), 'Gender and the Labour Market' in D. Gallie (ed.) *Employment in Britain*, Oxford: Blackwell.

Dickens, P. and Savage, M. (1988), 'The Japanisation of British Industry? Instances from a high growth area', *Industrial Relations Journal*, Vol. 19, No. 1.

Disney, R. (1990), 'Explanations of the decline in trade union density in Britain: an appraisal', *British Journal of Industrial Relations*, Vol. 28, No. 2.

Donnelly, E. (1987), 'The Training Model: Time for A Change', *Industrial and Commercial Training*, May/June, pp. 3–6.

Donovan, Lord (1968), *Royal Commission on Trade Unions and Employers' Association,Report*, Cmnd, 3623, London: HMSO.

Dore, R. (1973), *British Factory, Japanese Factory*, London: Allen & Unwin.

Dore, R. P. and Sako, M. (1989), *How the Japanese Learn to Work*, London: Routledge.

Due, J., Madsen, J. S. and Stroby-Jensen, C. (1991), 'The Social Dimension: convergence or diversification of IR in the Single European Market', *Industrial Relations Journal*, Vol. 22, No. 2.

Duncan, W. J. (1989), 'Organizational Culture: Getting a Fix on an Elusive Concept,' *Academy of Management Executive*, 3.

Dunn, S. (1993), 'From Donovan to . . . Wherever', *British Journal of Industrial Relations*, Vol. 31, No. 2.

Dyer, P. (1984), 'Studying Human Resource Strategy: An Approach and an Agenda', *Industrial Relations*, Vol. 23, No. 2.

Edwards, P. K. (1985), *Managing Labour Relations Through the Recession*, University of Warwick, IRRU.

Edwards, M. R. and Sproull, J. R. (1985), 'Making Performance Appraisals Perform: The Use of Team Evaluation', *Personnel*, March pp. 28–32.

Eva, D. and Oswald, R. (1981), *Health and Safety at Work*, London: Pan Original.

Evans, A. L. and Lorange, P. (1989) 'The Two Logics Behind Human Resource Management', in P. Evans, Y. Doz and A. Laurent, *Human Resource Management in International Firms*, London: Macmillan.

Farnham, D. (1990), *Personnel in Context*, London: IPM.

Feltham, R. (1992), 'Using Competencies in Selection and Recruitment', in *Designing and Achieving Competency*, Boam, R. and Sparrow, P. (eds), Maidenhead: McGraw-Hill.

Fine, B. and Harris, L. (1985), *The Peculiarities of the British Economy*, London: Lawrence and Wishart.

Finegold, D. and Soskice, D. (1988), 'The Failure of Training in Britain: Analysis and Prescription', *Oxford Review of Economic Policy*, Vol. 4, No. 3, pp. 21–53.

Fonda, N. and Hayes, C. (1986), 'Is More Training Really Necessary?', *Personnel Management*, May, pp. 64–9.

Foulkes, F. (1980), *Personnel Policies in Large Non-Union Companies*, Englewood Cliffs, NJ: Prentice-Hall.

Fox, A. (1985), *Man Mismanagement* (2nd edn), London: Hutchinson.

Freedman, A. (1985), *Changes in Managing Employee Relations*, New York: The Conference Board.

Freeman, R. and Pelletier, J. (1990), 'The Impact of Industrial Relations Legislation on British Union Density', *British Journal of Industrial Relations*, Vol. 28, No. 2.

Friedman, A. (1977), *Industry and Labour: Class Struggle at Work and Monopoly Capitalism*, London: Macmillan.

Friedman, A. (1986), 'Developing the managerial strategies approach to the labour process', *Capital and Class*, No. 30.

Garnett, J. (1983), *The Manager's Responsibility for Communication* (8th revised edn), London: Industrial Society.

Garrahan, P. (1986), 'Nissan in the north east of England', *Capital and Class*, No. 27.

Georgiades, N. (1990), 'A strategic future for personnel?', *Personnel Management*, February.

Gospel, H. F. (1992), 'The Single European Market and Industrial Relations: An Introduction', *British Journal of Industrial Relations*, Vol. 30, No. 4.

Gospel, H. and Littler, C. R. (eds) (1983), *Managerial Strategies and Industrial Relations*, London: Heinemann.

Gospel, H. F. and Palmer, G. (1993), *British Industrial Relations* (2nd edn), London: Routledge.

Graham, I. (1988), 'Japanisation as mythology', *Industrial Relations Journal*, Vol. 19, No. 1.

Green, F. (ed.) (1989), *The Restructuring of the UK Economy*, London: Harvester Wheatsheaf.

Gregg, P. (1973), *A Social and Economic History of Britain, 1760–1972* (7th edn) London: Harrap.

Gregg, P., Machin, S. and Szymanski, S. (1993), 'The Disappearing Relationship Between Directors' Pay and Corporate Performance', *British Journal of Industrial Relations*, Vol. 31, No. 1.

Griffiths, A. and Wall, S.(1989), *Applied Economics* (3rd edn), London: Longman.

Guest, D. E. (1986) 'Worker Participation and Personnel Policy in the UK: Some Case Studies', *International Labour Review*, Vol. 125, No. 6.

Guest, D. E. (1987), 'Human resource management and industrial relations', *Journal of Management Studies*, Vol. 24, No. 5.

Guest, D. (1989a) 'Personnel and HRM: can you tell the difference?', *Personnel Management*, January.

Guest, D. (1989b), 'HRM: Implications for Industrial Relations' in J. Storey, *New Perspectives on Human Resource Management*, London: Routledge.

Guest, D. (1990) 'Human Resource Management and the American Dream', *Journal of Management Studies*, Vol. 27, No. 4.

Guest, D. (1991), 'Personnel Management: The End of Orthodoxy?', *British Journal of Industrial Relations*, Vol. 29, No. 2.

Hackman, J. R. and Oldham, G. (1980), *Work Redesign*, Reading, Mass.: Addison-Wesley.

Hakim, C. (1987), 'Trends in the flexible workforce', *Employment Gazette*, November.

Hakim, C. (1990), 'Core and periphery in employers' workforce strategies: evidence from the 1987 ELUS survey', *Work, Employment and Society*, Vol. 4, No. 2, pp. 157–88.

Hall, D. T. (1986), 'Dilemmas in Linking Succession Planning to Individual Executive Learning', *Human Resource Management*, Vol. 25, No. 2, pp. 235–65.

Hammarström, O. and Lansbury, R. (1991), 'The art of building a car: the Swedish experience re-examined', *New Technology, Work and Employment*, Vol. 6, No. 2.

Hampden-Turner, C. (1990), *Charting the Corporate Mind*, Blackwell: Oxford.

Harper, S. C. (1983), 'A Developmental Approach to Performance Appraisal', *Business Horizons*, September/October, pp .68–74.

Harris, L. (1988), 'The UK economy at a crossroads', in *The Economy in Question*, J. Allen and D. Massey (eds), London: Sage.

Harris, M. M. (1989), 'Reconsidering the Employment Interview: A Review of Recent Literature and Suggestions for Future Research', *Personnel Psychology*, Vol. 42, pp. 691–726.

Hendry, C., Pettigrew, A. and Sparrow, P. (1988), 'Changing patterns of human resource management', *Personnel Management*, November, pp. 31–41.

Herriot, P. (1989), *Recruitment in the 1990s*, London: IPM.

Herriot, P. and Fletcher, C. (1990), 'Candidate-Friendly, Selection for the 1990s', *Personnel Management*, February, pp. 32–5.

Hertzberg, F. (1966), *Work and the Nature of Man*, Chicago, Ill.: World Publishing Co.

Herzberg, F., Mausner, B. and Snyderman, B. (1959), *The Motivation to Work*, New York: John Wiley.

Hirsh, W. (1990), *Succession Planning: Current Practice and Future Issues*, IMS Report No. 184, Brighton: IMS.

Hobsbawm, E. J. (1968), *Industry and Empire*, London: Weidenfeld and Nicolson.

Hogarth, T. (1993), 'Worker Support for Organizational Change and Technical Change', *Work, Employment and Society*, Vol. 7, No. 2.

Honey, P., (1991), 'The Learning Organisation Simplified', *Training and Development*, July, pp. 30–3.

Huczynski, A. and Buchanan, D. (1991), *Organizational Behaviour* (2nd edn), London: Prentice-Hall.

Hyman, R. (1987), 'Trade Unions and the Law: Papering over the Cracks?', *Capital and Class*, No. 31.

Hyman, R. (1988), 'Flexible Specialization: Miracle or Myth?', in R. Hyman and W. Streeck (eds).

Hyman, R. (1989), *Strikes* (4th edn) London: Macmillan.

Hyman, R. (1991), 'European Unions: Towards 2000', *Work, Employment and Society*, Vol. 5, No. 4.

Hyman, R. and Streeck, W. (eds) (1988), *New Technology and Industrial Relations*, Oxford: Blackwell.

IDS (1988), *Flexibility Working*, Study 407, London: Incomes Data Services.

IDS (1990), *Flexibility in the 1990s*, Study 454, London: Incomes Data Services.

IRRR (1989a), 'Decentralised Bargaining in Practice', No. 440, 23 May.

IRRR (1989b), 'Decentralised Bargaining in Practice', No. 454, 19 December.

Jackson, M. P. (1987), *Strikes*, Brighton: Wheatsheaf Books.

Jacobs, R. (1989), 'Getting the measure of managerial competence', *Personnel Management*, June.

Jenkins, C. and Sherman, B. (1979), *The Collapse of Work*, London: Eyre Methuen.

Johnson, C. (1988), *Measuring the Economy*, London: Penguin.

Jurgens, U. (1989), 'The transfer of Japanese management concepts in the international automobile industry', in S. Wood (ed.) (1989), *The Transformation of Work?* London: Unwin Hyman.

Karasek, R. A. (1979) 'Job demands, job decision latitude, and mental strain: implications for job redesign', *Administrative Science Quarterly*, Vol. 24, No. 2.

Keenoy, T. (1990), 'Human Resource Management: Rhetoric, Reality and Contradiction', *International Journal of Human Resource Management*, Vol. 1, No. 3.

Keep, E. (1989), 'Corporate Training Policies: The Vital Component', in J. Storey (ed.) *New Perspectives in Human Resource Management*, Routledge: London, pp. 109–25.

Kelly, J. (1985), 'Management's Redesign of Work: Labour Process, Labour Markets and Product Markets', in D.Knights *et al.* (eds).

Kelly, J. (1988), *Trade Unions and Socialist Politics*, London: Verso.

Kelly, J. (1990), 'British Trade Unionism 1979–1989: Change, Continuity and Contradiction', *Work, Employment and Society*, Special Issue, May.

Kelly, J. and Bailey, R. (1989), 'Research note: British trade union membership, density and decline in the 1980s', *Industrial Relations Journal*, Vol. 20, No. 1, Spring.

Kenney, J. and Reid, M. (1986), *Training Interventions*, IPM: London.

Kessler, S. (1993a), 'Procedure and Third Parties', *British Journal of Industrial Relations*, Vol. 31, No. 2.

Kessler, S. (1993b) 'Is there still a future for the unions?', *Personnel Management*, July.

Knights, D. and Willmott, H. (eds) (1986), *Managing the Labour Process*, Aldershot: Gower.

Knights, D., Willmott, H. and Collinson, D. (eds) (1985), *Job Redesign: Critical Perpectives on the Labour Process*, Aldershot: Gower.

Kochan, T. A. *et al.* (1986), *The Transformation of American Industrial Relations*, New York: Basic Books.

Kolb, D. A. (1982), 'Problem management: learning from experience', in S. Srivastva *et al.* (eds), San Francisco: Jossey Bass, pp. 109–43.

Kolb, D. A. (1984), *Experiential Learning*, Prentice Hall: Englewood Cliffs.

Lash, S. and Urry, J. (1987), *The End of Organized Capitalism*, Cambridge: Polity Press.

Latham, G. P., Saari, L. M., Pursell, E. D. and Campion, M. A. (1980), 'The Situational Interview', *Journal of Applied Psychology*, Vol. 65, pp. 422–7.

Lawler, E. (1986), *High Involvement Management*, San Francisco: Jossey-Bass.

Leadbeater, C. (1991), 'Marketing the World', *Marxism Today*, January.

Legge, K. (1989), 'Human resource management: a critical analysis' in J. Storey (ed.) *New Perspectives on Human Resource Management*, London: Routledge.

Leicester, C. (1989), 'The Key Role of the Line Manager in Employee Development', *Personnel Management*, March, pp. 53–7.

Levinson, H. (1970), 'Management by Whose Objectives?', *Harvard Business Review*, July/Aug. pp. 125–34.

Lewis, R. (ed.) (1986), *Labour Law in Britain*, Oxford: Basil Blackwell.

Littler, C. R. (1982), *The Development of the Labour Process in Capitalist Societies*, London: Heinemann.

Littler, C. R. and Salaman, G. (1984), *Class at Work: The Design, Allocation and Control of Jobs*, London: Batsford.

Long, P. (1986), *Performance Appraisal Revisited*, London: Institute of Personnel Management.

Loveridge, R. (1983), 'Labour market segmentation and the firm', in *Manpower Planning: Strategy and Techniques in an Organisational Context*, Edwards, J. *et al.* (eds), Chichester: John Wiley, pp. 155–75.

Lowstedt, J. (1988), 'Prejudices and wishful thinking about computer aided design', *New Technology, Work and Employment*, Vol. 3, No. 1.

Lunn, T. (1987), 'A Scientific Approach to Successful Selection', *Personnel Management*, December, pp. 43–5.

Mabey, C. and Iles, P. (1991), 'HRM From the Other Side of the Fence', *Personnel Management*, February, pp. 50–3.

MacInnes, J. (1987), *Thatcherism at Work: Industrial Relations and Economic Change*, Milton Keynes: Open University.

Maloney, P. (1983), 'The Business of Communicating and the Communication Business', *Personnel Management*, December.

Marchington, M. (1987), 'A Review and Critique of Research on Developments in Joint Consultation', *British Journal of Industrial Relations*, Vol. XXV, No. 3.

Marchington, M. (1989), 'Problems with team briefings in practice', *Employee Relations*, Vol. 11, No. 4.

Marchington, M. and Parker, P. (1990), *Changing Patterns of Employee Relations*, London: Harvester Wheatsheaf.

Marchington, M. and Wilding, P. (1983), 'Employee Involvement Inaction?', *Personnel Management*, December.

Marsick, V. J. (1987), *Learning in the Workplace*, London: Croom Helm.

Maslow, A. (1954), *Motivation and Personality*, New York: Harper & Row.

Massey, D. (1988), 'What's happening to UK manufacturing?', in J. Allen and D. Massey (eds), (1988).

Mathias, P. (1969), *The First Industrial Nation*, London: Methuen.

Mayo, A. (1991), *Managing Careers*, London: IPM.

McGregor, D. (1957), 'An Uneasy Look at Performance Apprasisal', *Harvard Business Review*, Vol. 35, No. 3, pp. 89–94.

McGregor, D. (1960), *The Human Side of Enterprise*, New York: McGraw-Hill.

McIlroy, J. (1988), *Trade Unions in Britain Today*, Manchester: Manchester University Press.

McKendrick, E. (1988), 'The rights of trade union members: Part I of the Employment Act 1980', *Industrial Law Journal*, Vol. 17, No. 3.

McLoughlin, I. and Clark, J. (1988), *Technological Change at Work*, Milton Keyes: Open University Press.

McLoughlin, I. and Gourlay, S. (1992), 'Enterprise without unions: managing employment relations in non-union firms', *Journal of Management Studies*, Vol. 29, No. 5.

McShane, S. L. (1992), *Canadian Organizational Behaviour*, Boston: Irwin.

Meyer, H. H., Kay, E. and French, J. R. P. (1965), 'Split Roles in Performance Appraisal', *Harvard Business Review*, Vol. 43, pp. 123–9.

Milkovitch, G. T. and Newman, J. M (1990), *Compensation* (3rd edn), Boston: Irwin.

Miller, P. (1987), 'Strategic Industrial Relations and Human Resource Management – Distinction, Definition and Recognition', *Journal of Management Studies*, Vol. 24, No. 4.

Miller, P. (1989), 'Strategic HRM: what it is and what it isn't', *Personnel Management*, February.

Millward, N. and Stevens, M. (1986), *British Workplace Industrial Relations 1980–1984*, Aldershot: Gower.

Millward, N., Stevens, M., Smart, D. and Hawes, W. (1992), *Workplace Industrial Relations in Transition*, Aldershot: Dartmouth Press.

Mintzberg, H. (1976), 'Planning on the left side and managing of the right side', *Harvard Business Review*, July/August pp. 49–58.

Mintzberg, H. (1978), 'Patterns in Strategy Formation', *Management Science*, Vol. 24, No. 9, May, pp. 934–48.

Mintzberg, H. (1983), *Power In and Around Organizations*, Englewoods Cliffs, NJ: Prentice-Hall.

Mintzberg, H. (1987), 'Crafting Strategy', *Harvard Business Review*, July/August, pp. 66–75.

Mintzberg, H. (1989), *Mintzberg on Management*, New York: Collier/Hamilton.

Mintzberg, H. (1990), 'The Design School: reconsidering the basic premises of strategic management', *Strategic Management Journal*, Vol. 11, pp. 171–95.

Morgan, G. (1980), 'Paradigms, Metaphors, and Puzzle Solving in Organization Theory', *Administrative Science Quarterly*, Vol. 25, pp. 605–22.

Morgan, G. (1986), *Images of Organization*, London: Sage.

Mottaz, C. (1988), 'Determinants of Organizational Commitment', *Human Relations*, Vol. 41, No. 6, pp. 467–82.

Mueller, B. (1992), 'Flexible working practices in engine plants – evidence from the European automobile industry', *Industrial Relations Journal*, Vol. 23, No. 3.

Munro-Fraser, J. (1971), *Psychology: General, Industrial, Social*, London: Pitman.

Nichols, T. and Beynon, H. (1977), *Living with Capitalism: Class Relations and the Modern Factory*, London: Routledge and Kegan Paul.

Nkomo, S. M. (1988), 'Strategic planning for human resources – let's get started', *Long Range Planning*, Vol. 21, No. 1, pp. 66–72.

Northcott, J. and Rogers, P. (1984), *Microelectronics in British Industry: The Pattern of Change*, London: Policy Studies Institute.

O'Higgins, P. (1986), 'International Standards and British Labour Law', in R. Lewis (ed.). (1986).

Oliver, N. and Wilkinson, B. (1988), *The Japanization of British Industry*, Oxford: Blackwell.

O'Reilly, J. (1992), 'Subcontracting in banking: some evidence from Britain and France', *New Technology, Work and Employment*, Vol. 7, No. 2.

Ouchi, W. (1979), 'A Conceptual Framework for the Design of Organizational Control Mechanisms', *Management Science*, Vol. 25, No. 9, pp. 833–48.

Paddison, L. (1990), 'The Targeted Approach to Recruitment', *Personnel Management*, November, pp. 54–8.

Pahl, R. E. (ed.) (1988), *On Work: Historical, Comparative and Theoretical Approaches*, Oxford: Blackwell.

Pappas, J. L. and Hirschey, M. (1990), *Managerial Economics* (6th edn), Montreal: Dryden Press.

Pearson, R. (1991), *The Human Resource*, Maidenhead: McGraw-Hill.

Pedler M., Boydell, T. and Burgoyne, J. (1988), *The Learning Company Project Report*, Employment Department.

Pedler, M., Burgoyne, J. and Boydell, T. (1991), *The Learning Company: A Strategy for Sustainable Development*, Maidenhead: McGraw-Hill.

Penn, R., Lilja, K. and Scattergood, H. (1992), 'Flexibility and employment patterns in the paper industry: an analysis of mills in Britain and Finland', *Industrial Relations Journal*, Vol. 23, No. 3.

Perkins, G. (1986), *Employee Communications in the Public Sector*, London: IPM.

Peters, T. and Waterman, R. (1982), *In Search of Excellence*, New York: Harper & Row.

Pettigrew, A., Sparrow, P. and Hendry, C. (1988), 'The Forces that Trigger Training', *Personnel Management*, December, pp. 28–32.

Piore, M. and Sabel, C. (1984), *The Second Industrial Divide*, New York: Basic Books.

Pitfield, M. (1984), 'Studying to be a Personnel Manager', *Personnel Management*, November.

Plachy, R. J. (1987), 'Writing Job Descriptions that Get Results', *Personnel*, October, pp. 56–63.

Pollard, S. (1965), *The Genesis of Modern Management*, London: Arnold.

Pollard, S. (1969) *The Development of the British Economy, 1914–1967* (2nd edn), London: Arnold.

Pollert, A. (1988a), 'Dismantling flexibility', *Capital and Class*, No. 34.

Pollert, A. (1988b), 'The flexible firm: fixation or fact?', *Work, Employment and Society*, Vol. 2, No. 3, pp. 281–316.

Poole, M. (1980), 'Management strategies amd industrial relations', in R. Mansfield (ed.) *Managerial Roles in Industrial Relations*, Aldershot: Gower.

Premack, S. L. and Wanous, J. P. (1985), 'A Meta-Analysis of Realistic Job Preview Experiments', *Journal of Applied Psychology*, Vol. 70, No. 4, pp. 706–19.

Price, R. (1988), 'Information, consultation and the control of new technology' in Hyman and Streeck (eds).

Pryce, V. and Nicholson, C. (1988), 'The problems and performance of employee ownership firms', *Employment Gazette*, Vol. 96, No. 6.

Purcell, J. (1987), 'Mapping Management Styles in Employee Relations', *Journal of Management Studies*, Vol. 24, No. 5.

Purcell, J. and Sisson, K. (1983), 'Strategies and Practice in the Management of Industrial Relations', in G. Bain (ed.).

Quin Mills, D. and Balbaky, M. (1985) 'Planning for Morale and Culture', in R. Walton, and P. Lawrence (eds), *Human Resource Management: Trends and Challenges*, Boston, Mass.: Harvard Business School Press.

Randell, G. (1989), 'Employee Appraisal', in K. Sisson (ed.) *Personnel Management in Britain*, Oxford: Blackwell.

Rarick, C. A. and Baxter, G. (1986), 'Behaviourally Anchored Rating Scales (Bars): An Effective Performance Appraisal Approach', *SAM Advanced Management Journal*, Winter, pp. 36–9.

Robbins, S. P. (1989), *Organizational Behavior* (4th edn) London: Prentice-Hall.

Robens, Lord (1972), *Safety and Health at Work*, Cmnd 5034, London: HMSO.

Rodger, A. (1970), *The Seven Point Plan* (3rd edn), London: NFER.

Rolfe, H. (1986), 'Skill, deskilling and new technology in the non-manual labour process', *New Technology, Work and Employment*, Vol. 1, No. 1.

Rose, M. (1988), *Industrial Behaviour*, London: Penguin.

Rothwell, S. (1993), 'Annual Review Article, 1992', *British Journal of Industrial Relations*, Vol. 31, No. 1.

Rubery, J. (1992), 'Pay Gender, and the Social Dimension to Europe', *British Journal of Industrial Relations*, Vol. 30, No. 4.

Salaman, G. (1981), *Class and the Corporation*, Glasgow: Fontana.

Salamon, M. (1987), *Industrial Relations: Theory and Practice*, London: Prentice-Hall.

Sass, R. (1982), 'Safey and Self-Respect', *Policy Options*, July-August.

Schein, E. (1978), *Career Dynamics: Matching Individual and Organizational Needs*, Reading, MA: Addison-Wesley.

Schneider, B. (1987), 'The People Make the Place', *Personnel Psychology*, Vol. 40, pp. 437–53.

Schonberger, R. (1982), *Japanese Manufacturing Techniques: Nine Hidden Lessons in Simplicity*, London: Collier Macmillan.

Schuler, R. S. (1989), 'Strategic Human Resource Management and Industrial Relations', *Human Relations*, Vol. 42, No. 2.

Simpson, B. (1986), 'Trade Union Immunities', in R. Lewis (ed.) (1986).

Sisson, K. (ed.) (1989), *Personnel Management in Britain*, Oxford: Basil Blackwell.

Sisson, K.(1993), 'In Search of HRM', *British Journal of Industrial Relations*, Vol. 31, No. 2.

Smith, A. R. (1980), *Corporate Manpower Planning*, London: Gower Press.

Smith, P. and Morton, G. (1993), 'Union Exclusion and the Decollectivization of Industrial Relations in Contemporary Britain', *British Journal of Industrial Relations*, Vol. 31, No. 1.

Sparrow, P. R. and Pettigrew, A. M. (1988), 'Strategic Human Resource Management in the UK Computer Supplier Industry', *Journal of Occupational Psychology*, Vol. 61, No. 1.

Spencer, B. (1989), *Remaking the Working Class? An Examination of Shop Stewards' Experiences*, Nottingham: Spokesman.

Stirling, J. (1991), 'This great Europe of ours: trade unions and 1992', *Capital and Class*, No. 45.

Stone, T. H. and Meltz, N. M. (1988), *Human Resource Management in Canada* (2nd edn) Toronto: HRW.

Storey, J. (1988), 'The people–management dimension in current programmes of organizational change', *Employee Relations*, Vol. 10, No. 6.

Storey, J. (ed.) (1989), *New Perspectives on Human Resource Management*, London: Routledge.

Storey, J. (1992), *Developments in the Management of Human Resources*, Oxford: Basil Blackwell.

Szyszczak, E. (1986), 'Employment protection and social security', in R. Lewis (ed.) (1986), *Labour Law in Britain*, Oxford: Blackwell.

Taylor, A. (1989), *Trade Unions and Politics*, London: Macmillan.

Taylor, H. (1991), 'The Systematic Training Model: Corn Circles in Search of a Spaceship?', *Management Education and Development*, Vol. 22, Part 4, pp. 258–78.

Temporal, P. (1978), 'The Nature of Non-Contrived Learning and its Implications for Management Development', *Management Education and Development*, Vol. 9, pp. 20–3.

Thompson, P. (1989), *The Nature of Work* (2nd edn), London: Macmillan (1st edn 1983).

Thurley, K. (1990), 'Towards a European Approach to Personnel Management', *Personnel Management*, September.

Tomaney, J. (1990), 'The Reality of Workplace Flexibility', *Capital and Class*, 40.

Torrington, D. and Hall, L. (1987), *Personnel Management: A New Approach*, London: Prentice Hall.

Towers, B. (1989), 'Running the Gauntlet: British Trade Unions under Thatcher, 1979–1988', *Industrial and Labor Relations Review*, Vol. 42, No. 2.

Towers, B. (1992), 'Two speed ahead: Social Europe and the UK after Maastricht', *Industrial Relations Journal*, Vol. 23, No. 2.

Townley, B. (1989), 'Employee Communication Programmes', in K. Sisson (ed.).

TUC (1979), *Employment and Technology*, London: TUC.

Turnbull, P. (1986), 'The Japanisation of British industrial relations at Lucas', *Industrial Relations Journal*, Vol. 17, No. 3.

Tyson, S. and Fell, A. (1986), *Evaluating the Personnel Function*, London: Hutchinson.

Ulman, L. (1992), 'Why Should Human Resource Managers Pay High Wages?', *British Journal of Industrial Relations*, Vol. 30, No. 2.

Verlander, E. G. (1985), 'The system's the thing', *Training and Development*, April, pp. 20–3.

Vroom , V. H. (1964), *Work and Motivation*, New York: John Wiley.

Waddington, J. (1988), 'Business Unionism and Fragmentation within the TUC', *Capital and Class*, No. 36.

Waddington, J. (1992), 'Trade union membership in Britain, 1980–1987: unemployment and restructuring', *British Journal of Industrial Relations*, Vol. 30, No. 2.

Wagner, R. F. (1949), 'The Employment Interview: A Critical Summary', *Personnel Psychology*, Vol. 2, pp. 17–46.

Walter, D. (1987), 'Health and safety and trade union workplace organization: a case study in the printing industry', *Industrial Relations Journal*, Vol. 18, No. 1.

Walton, R. (1985), 'From Control to Commitment in the Workplace', *Harvard Business Review*, March/April, pp. 77–84.

Watson, T. (1986), *Management,Organization and Employment Strategy*, London: Routledge and Kegan Paul.

Watson, T. J. (1977), *The Personnel Managers*, London: Routledge.

Watson, T. (1989), 'Recruitment and Selection', in *Personnel Management in Britain*, Sissons, K. (ed.), Oxford: Basil Blackwell.

Weick, K. E. (1982), 'Managerial thought in the context of action', in *The Executive Mind*, Srivastva, S. *et al.* (eds), San Francisco: Jossey-Bass, pp. 221–41.

Wedderburn, Lord (1986), *The Worker and the Law* (3rd edn), London: Penguin.

Wheatley, M. (1992), *The Future of Middle Management*, Corby: BIM.

Wickens, P. (1987), *The Road to Nissan*, London: Macmillan.

Wilkinson, A., Allen, P. and Snape, E. (1991), 'TQM and the Management of Labour', *Employee Relations*, Vol. 13, No. 1, pp. 24–31.

Wilkinson, B. and Oliver, N. (1989), 'Obstacles to Japanisation: The Case of Ford UK', *Employee Relations*, Vol. 12, No. 1.

Willman, P.(1986), *Technological Change, Collective Bargaining and Industrial Efficiency*, Oxford: Clarenden Press.

Wood, S. (ed.) (1983), *The Degradation of Work? Skill, Deskilling and the Labour Process*, London: Hutchinson.

Wood, S. (ed.) (1989), *The Transformation of Work*, London: Unwin Hyman.

Wood, S. (1991), 'Japanization and/or Toyotaism', *Work, Employement and Society*, Vol. 5, No. 4.

Woodruffe, C. (1992), 'What is meant by a competency?' in *Designing and Achieving Competency*, Boam, R. and Sparrow, P. (eds), Maidenhead: McGraw-Hill, pp. 16–30.

Index